MW00784049

Adolph Rupp and the Rise
of Kentucky Basketball

Adolph Rupp
and the Rise of
Kentucky Basketball

James Duane Bolin

UNIVERSITY PRESS OF KENTUCKY

Copyright © 2019 James Duane Bolin

Published by The University Press of Kentucky,
scholarly publisher for the Commonwealth,
serving Bellarmine University, Berea College, Centre
College of Kentucky, Eastern Kentucky University,
The Filson Historical Society, Georgetown College,
Kentucky Historical Society, Kentucky State University,
Morehead State University, Murray State University,
Northern Kentucky University, Transylvania University,
University of Kentucky, University of Louisville,
and Western Kentucky University.
All rights reserved.

Editorial and Sales Offices: The University Press of Kentucky
663 South Limestone Street, Lexington, Kentucky 40508-4008
www.kentuckypress.com

Unless otherwise noted, photographs are from the author's collection.

Cataloging-in-Publication data is available from the Library of Congress.

ISBN 978-0-8131-7720-5 (hardcover : alk. paper)
ISBN 978-0-8131-7724-3 (epub)
ISBN 978-0-8131-7723-6 (pdf)

This book is printed on acid-free paper meeting
the requirements of the American National Standard
for Permanence in Paper for Printed Library Materials.

Manufactured in the United States of America.

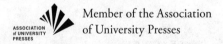

Member of the Association
of University Presses

For Dr. Humbert S. Nelli

And

For Evelyn Seaton Bolin, Wesley Seaton Bolin, and Cammie Jo Bolin

Contents

Illustrations follow page 200

Prologue

Adolph Rupp stormed into the locker room, threw off his brown suit coat and flung the silver belt buckle—a consolation prize—against the far wall. The coach's outburst stunned the reigning national champions of college basketball. It was December 30, 1948, and the University of Kentucky Wildcats had just lost to St. Louis 42–40 in the final game of the prestigious Sugar Bowl Tournament in New Orleans.

The Wildcats did not lose many basketball games. Even before Rupp's arrival in 1930, his predecessor, John Mauer, had a 40–14 record over three seasons before leaving to become coach at Miami University of Ohio. Along came Adolph Frederick Rupp, a brash young all-purpose Midwestern high school coach with no college coaching experience. He built on Mauer's success and turned Kentucky into a dynasty, winning four NCAA championships in an 11-year span starting in 1948. Going into that game in New Orleans, the Wildcats were 362–71 during Rupp's tenure, and the team that lost that night to St. Louis would finish 32–2 and win a second straight national title, with a starting five of Alex Groza, Ralph Beard, Wallace "Wah Wah" Jones, Cliff Barker, and Dale Barnstable.

Kentucky held a commanding 27–18 halftime lead against the Billikens, but in the waning minutes of the game, unheralded Louis Lehman scored seven crucial points to give St. Louis the victory, and the Wildcats had to settle for those silver belt buckles as the runner-up prize. Then came Rupp's locker-room tirade, which probably even shocked players long accustomed to such outbursts. "I wouldn't give that to my nigger on the farm," Rupp blurted out.[1]

One of Rupp's more legendary dressing room explosions had occurred at halftime of a game on January 8, 1945. The Wildcats led an overmatched Arkansas State team 34–4, and one player had scored all four of the Indians' points. When Rupp walked into the home locker room in Alumni Gymnasium, he demanded, "Who is guarding No. 12?" Kentucky's All-American Jack Parkinson looked up meekly and said, "Coach, I am." Rupp barked, "Well, get on him, because he is running absolutely wild!"[2]

But Rupp's venomous "nigger on the farm" outburst was an entirely different matter, and it provides another insight into an individual who played a leading role in the development of big-time college sports in America during the twentieth century. To many Americans, Adolph Rupp remains an icon of racism, a lingering reminder of the Southeastern Conference's role in the segregated South. Within the Bluegrass State, however, he continues to be held in reverence by most of the Big Blue faithful. In a 2001 *Lexington Herald-Leader* series framed around the question, "What is the Legacy of Adolph Rupp?" almost every contribution from the newspaper's readers contained some defense of the coach's stand on the race issue.[3]

Rupp's defenders see a very different "Man in the Brown Suit" than the caricature presented by his critics. They suggest that the critical image of Rupp is exaggerated, if not misplaced. When George Will referred to Rupp as "a great coach and a bad man" in a 1991 newspaper column, Rupp's son wondered how Will could be "that ignorant and dumb." A granddaughter remembered a kind man who took his family to Pralltown—an African American section of Lexington—each summer to "distribute Shrine Circus tickets to all the black children in the neighborhood."[4] Others recall the Rupp who once told a radio interviewer that black players owed their quickness to the fact that "the lions and tigers caught all the slow ones."[5]

And then there was the "testimony" of Marie Jackson, the widow of Dr. V. A. Jackson, the Wildcats' team physician from 1965 until 1972, the year the university forced Rupp to retire. Mrs. Jackson remembered a different Rupp from the gruff, public image he presented to the press, although she agreed that the coach had always been genuinely concerned about the almighty dollar. By the end of his coaching career, Mrs. Jackson believed that "Coach was a very wealthy man; he kept his money. He wasn't very giving at that time."[6]

In a 2010 interview at her comfortable home in Paducah, Mrs. Jackson said, "Now, remember honey, I told you that he never likes a yes person; be honest with him, what you believe in."[7] Perhaps, that is why the Jacksons got along so well with Rupp: they were honest with him. Dr. Jackson's honesty did not allow him to tell Rupp that a player could play when he really was not able to play. For Marie Jackson, a devoted Baptist, honesty usually centered on matters of faith. So when the world-renowned evangelist, Billy Graham, held a spectacular crusade in 1971 on the grounds of Stoll Field directly across Euclid Avenue from Memorial Coliseum, complete with big screens set up in the coliseum for the overflow crowds, Rupp was at first stunned and more than a little agitated.

When the Jacksons visited the Rupps soon after the crusade, she knew what to expect. "So when we walked to the door," Mrs. Jackson recalled,

> they always met us at the front door and Coach would give me a hug, and Mrs. Rupp would hug [Dr. Jackson], and then [Coach] just stepped back real fast, and you know he had a little chubby tummy, so he stepped back and put his hands down and said "Marie, I want you to tell me something." "What's that coach?" "Why in the world did you Baptists bring this man in here and fill Memorial Coliseum and set up screens. This man just swept the town. But I couldn't believe that Stoll Field and Memorial Coliseum were both packed. You never did anything like that for Uncle Adolph."[8]

Now Marie was stunned. "I looked at him and he said to me [again]," she recalled, "Did you hear me, Marie? You all never did anything like this for Uncle Adolph." What Uncle Adolph liked best about Marie Jackson was her beauty and her quick wit. "Coach," she told him, "all I can say is it looks like Billy Graham had something better to sell than you do."[9]

Marie Jackson believed that it was from that point that Rupp "really started talking about heaven." Mrs. Jackson had always thought that underneath the gruff Rupp was "a good person," but as a good Baptist, she also believed that "there are a lot of good people who aren't Christians." "He went to a church," she said, "but there are a lot of people who go to church who really aren't [Christians]." Mrs. Jackson believed that despite all of the hullabaloo, Rupp "was always fearful." So in her witnessing campaign to the self-proclaimed "greatest coach on earth," Marie Jackson remembered that "we just started out like that, and I know he was a man who could not be pushed, but he said that he watched me, he watched my lifestyle, and he always said I was different."[10]

Mrs. Jackson continued,

> I go to bed at 9 o'clock every night, so he would call the house when Billy Graham would be on television then, and say "Doc, I know Marie's already in bed, but tell her she'd better wake up; that Graham man is on." It kept being on his mind. I just kept talking to him as we were together, and I was doing mission work in Haiti at that time, from [1971–1993], summer missions in Haiti, so we started talking and I just gave him the plan of salvation, and he was ready to give his life totally to Christ, and it was at that time he gave me some money because we were opening a clinic in Haiti, and he gave me money to take to Haiti to put in on the clinic there. You know, sometimes when we give our life to Christ, you know I hope it was for real. I think I told you before the day when he was dying, I went to see him because I wanted to give him a hug, and I went in to see him and I reached out and held his hand, and he said "I know why you're here. I'll see you in heaven."[11]

Very few people ever knew of Adolph Rupp's deathbed confession of faith. "I didn't talk about it, because he was a man of celebrity," Mrs. Jackson said, "and his family, we didn't talk about it much. His wife knew, but I don't know if Herky knew. A lot of people I've been able to tell because a lot of people loved him and hoped he'd made things right. Because they saw this gruff person on television, and he really wasn't that gruff person. And there weren't many days that Dr. Jackson and I . . . didn't thank God for the privilege of knowing Adolph Rupp the man; not only the basketball coach, but Adolph Rupp the man, and that was such a privilege."[12]

So, who was the real Adolph Rupp, the coach and the man? What is his legacy? What should it have been? How much was he a product of his times? How much did he do? How much more could he have done? How much did he leave undone? Like so much surrounding the "Baron" of basketball, the reality often lies obscured beneath many layers of legend. Certainly, Rupp's attitudes and actions—or inactions—on the issue of race are significant if we are to understand the role that sports played in

America in the twentieth century. Race is not the issue that defines Rupp's role, however. This complex man contributed significantly to the rise of college sports as a big business in the twentieth century. Of course, Rupp was off the scene before realizing the huge profits brought on by television to college sports. In 1980, three years after Rupp's death, NBC paid $8.8 million for the rights to broadcast the men's NCAA basketball tournament. In 2016, when a consortium of CBS and Turner Sports made the most recent eight-year deal to carry the NCAA tournament the price tag had sky-rocketed to $8.8 billion. Adolph Rupp could never have fathomed that.

That is not to say that Rupp was not a savvy businessman. He used his success on the hardwood to venture into other lucrative business concerns. He dabbled in insurance, banking, tobacco warehouses, and bourbon distilleries. He played the stock market. As a Shriner he was also involved in philanthropic ventures—in 1950 he was chosen as one of the ten outstanding Shriners in America.[13] Yet all of these interests paled in comparison with farming. Rupp raised award-winning American Hereford cattle on his Bourbon County farm and served as president of the Kentucky Hereford Association. And, of course, he made Kentucky basketball into a big business.[14]

The story of Adolph Rupp adds another dimension to the ongoing discussion of the role of sports in American society. It is a story that begs for the telling.

Introduction

"Had you ever heard of this little place, Lexington, Kentucky, before you came out here from California?" A piano tuner assigned to set up a concert grand piano for the Lawrence Welk Orchestra at the 1976 opening ceremonies for the new Rupp Arena in downtown Lexington asked the question in a conversation with a sound-man from Welk's entourage. "Had you ever heard of this little place?" he asked the technician. "Lexington, Kentucky! Lord, yes!" the soundman bellowed. "I used to hear it about 19 times every day. All day long, from the time I got up to the time I went to bed. Rupp, Wildcats. Rupp, Wildcats. That was our grace at the table. Rupp, Wildcats, Lexington, Kentucky—we lived with those names. That was all we heard." Only at the end of the conversation did the piano tuner find out that the California soundman had played on John Wooden's basketball team at UCLA.[1]

Adolph Rupp made University of Kentucky basketball famous—and infamous—from New York City to Los Angeles. But who was this man, this basketball coach? How did he succeed so spectacularly? And how, in a way, did he fail so miserably?

Rupp was at once an exceptional character and an ordinary individual. He concerned himself primarily with the bottom line, winning college basketball games, and making a life centered around a rectangular hardwood court. Other coaches have mirrored his self-centeredness and gargantuan ego—if on a smaller scale—again and again in a cut-throat environment where such attitudes of superiority seem to be necessary for success. Rupp's private life, his devotion to family and philanthropy—as

6

well as to making money—also seem characteristic of many other coaches. Lesser masters of the publicity game have copied the persona that he cultivated for the press, though usually not as successfully. Former players recall that in postgame interviews, Rupp always *won* the games, but his players *lost* them.[2]

The Baron yearned for, even demanded, positive attention from the press, but he didn't always get it. In 1958 *Sports Illustrated* referred to him as "America's most controversial basketball coach."[3] Rupp often quoted an excerpt from Pakenham Beatty's poem "Self Reliance," lines that he felt "contained a good philosophy for every coach":

> By your own soul learn to live,
> And if men thwart you, take no heed,
> If men hate you, have no care;
> Sing your song, dream your dream,
> hope your hope and pray your prayer.[4]

But the dreams, hopes, and prayers of any coach ultimately depend on the skills and determination of young athletes. A coach's ability or inability to relate to players can translate into wins and losses. Rupp had his own way. Bill Spivey, a seven-foot All-American at UK in the early 1950s, said Rupp "was unique. He wanted everybody to hate him—and he succeeded. He called us names some of us had never heard before."[5]

Other coaches and business leaders alike admired Rupp's determination to be the best in his business—even at the expense of popularity with his players—and the fact that he achieved that goal. Rotary Club members would smile and nod knowingly when he quoted the lines of Grantland Rice: "When the Great Scorer comes to mark against your name, He writes not that you won or lost, but how you played the game." But Rupp quickly countered, "I do not believe that the author of these words ever meant them to apply to basketball, football or baseball. If he did, why do they keep score in these contests?"[6] Rupp penned the line for an article he was invited to write for *Sports Illustrated* in 1958, but he usually told it in more colorful and forceful language: "Well, everyone just loved [the Grantland Rice poem] and quoted it all over. See, they even got me to re-memberin' it. But it's a joke. The hell with how you played the game. They still keep score, don't they?"[7]

Rupp's unique take on such aphorisms became a significant part of the mystique of "the Man in the Brown Suit." It might be a cliché to say that Adolph Rupp was larger than life, but he was. Prominent national sportswriter Dave Kindred recalls that he "was a kid reporter" for the *Louisville Courier-Journal* when he first encountered Rupp in person. The coach was standing outside his office in Memorial Coliseum, and Kindred remembered thinking, "Good, he's tall. A legend should be tall."[8]

At his forced retirement in 1972, Rupp was the winningest coach in college basketball history with 876 victories and only 190 losses. "He was the man by whom all other coaches were measured," as former UK All-American Frank Ramsey put it.[9]

Although his relationship with Rupp remained strained to the end because of his own involvement in a 1951 point-shaving scandal, Alex Groza, a member of the Wildcats' 1948 and 1949 National Collegiate Athletic Association (NCAA) championship teams and a three-time All-American, said Rupp "probably forgot more basketball than most coaches know." Groza marveled at the coach's "sixth sense" in practice. "I can see Ralph Beard going in for a crip shot [*sic*], and [Rupp] says, 'Uh-oh, hold it up. Wah Wah [Jones], you were out of position.' How the guy detected it I'll never know. So you ran it again and again to satisfy the man. You ran it to perfection."[10]

Beard noted that Rupp "won big with little players, big players and middle-sized players. He won with talented players and untalented players—all kinds." Beard, a ball-handling whiz whom Rupp once called his best player ever, concluded: "All that I was in basketball, I owe to him."[11]

Stan Key, a cocaptain of Rupp's final team in the 1971–1972 season, contended that the debt goes far beyond individuals. "Without somebody of his character and his ability," Key said, "I'm not sure college basketball would be what it is today."[12]

But while his mark has not been erased, it has faded. Even before Rupp's retirement, UCLA's John Wooden had shattered the Baron's record of four NCAA championships and went on to win ten. Kentucky's total number of victories, most of them under Rupp, is still higher than any other collegiate team, but Dean Smith, Bob Knight, and now Mike Krzyzewski have since exceeded Rupp's personal total. Pat Summitt, in women's basketball, surpassed them all.

Yet Rupp remains particularly significant for Kentucky. He forged an identity that united a backward state separated within by complex political, social, economic, and geographic divisions. At least in the commonwealth, this shared identity is perhaps Rupp's most enduring legacy. Another cliché: Folks from Pikeville to Paducah still follow the Wildcats religiously, paying homage season after season to the program built and sustained for 42 years by Adolph Rupp.

But along with the Baron's many accomplishments came devastating failures. Although the coach himself was never implicated, the 1951 point-shaving scandal involving members of his 1948 Fabulous Five revealed a culture of wrongdoing that continued to plague UK's basketball and football programs into a new millennium. Rupp's boast that the gamblers "couldn't touch my boys with a ten-foot pole" provided ample fodder for gleeful critics eager to bring down "the bumptious baron," as a *True* magazine article was titled. Rupp's close ties to bookie Ed Curd, who ran a $50,000-a-day gambling business from his perch above Lexington's Mayfair Bar on East Main Street, made the coach particularly suspect when the scandal broke. The full extent of Rupp's friendship with Curd may never be revealed, but the bookmaker sometimes traveled with the team to New York for games at Madison Square Garden.[13] The gambling connection was too obvious to ignore, too real to dismiss out of hand, and too important to treat lightly. Rupp made it all too easy for Groza, Beard, and Dale Barnstable to fall into the trap.

Even more devastating was the possibility that Rupp's on-court success bred a growing emphasis on sports in the commonwealth's high schools and colleges at the expense of any serious regard for education. In 2005 Kentucky ranked last among the 50 states in per-pupil spending, according to one survey.[14]

Rupp wrote in 1958 that "some college professors complain about the fact that students exhibit more taste for athletics than for intellectual studies. I must admit I find that true to a large extent." Instead of lessening an emphasis on athletics, however, he argued, "We should rather bring back to the classroom the liberal spirit which once inspired it and still inspires athletics. Unfortunately, the teachings which we have in the classroom have come from a few great minds and they have been passed on from generation to generation until they have become dull."[15]

Though it's too much to blame a state's educational woes on a basketball coach with a master's degree from Columbia University, the very success and statewide pride Rupp brought to Kentucky athletics provided a convenient excuse for ignoring more daunting problems of literacy, graduation rates, and abysmally poor test scores.

And with Rupp, the question of race always hovered like an ugly cloud over the UK program until his successor, Joe B. Hall, fully integrated the team. When Orlando "Tubby" Smith, an African American, became the Wildcats' coach in 1997, some fans, black and white, snickered and wondered how the Baron would have taken the news. Loyal sportswriters like Dave Kindred, Earl Cox, and Billy Reed dismissed the spotlight glare on Rupp and the race issue as an example of "presentism," maintaining that prevailing attitudes of the times and the southern environment in which he lived and worked kept him bound in his racial views. Kindred argued that Rupp actually "disliked all people equally, whatever their color, if they happened to stand in the way of his team winning a game."[16]

In April 1991, *Sports Illustrated* published what Kindred called "its Rupp as racist number," calling the coach a "charming p.r. rogue" whose politics "leaned toward the KKK."[17] In December of that year—the hundredth anniversary of basketball's founding—conservative columnist George Will devoted an article to Rupp's failures on the race issue. After he repeated the same accusations that he had read in the *Sports Illustrated* piece, Will's devastating conclusion was that Rupp was "a great coach and a bad man."[18]

Kindred, a former sports columnist at the *Courier-Journal* in Louisville who didn't consider Rupp a friend, said he never heard a racist word in the dozen years he knew him. "Not that hearing racist talk would have been a shock," Kindred wrote in 1991. "Unless we have achieved racial harmony in the past few minutes, racist talk is everywhere." He gave a specific example from the Baron himself. In a 1974 interview Rupp told Kindred he had been less than impressed with Lexington when he came by train from Freeport, Illinois, to interview for the UK job in 1930. "Bear in mind that where Memorial Coliseum now stands, there were 55 little nigger one- and two-room shacks back then," Rupp recalled. "Bear in mind that I got a cab from the Southern Depot to Alumni Gym, and we went through an awful area of town. They took me to eat at the university cafeteria and out the third-floor window I could see all those little nigger shacks. I wasn't used to anything like that."[19] Noting also that his guest room at the Lexington YMCA "wasn't fit for a cat," Rupp thundered, "Good gawd almighty, what kind of place is this Kentucky?"[20]

Kindred excused Rupp for his use of such language: "That's what they were called in 1930. Nigger shacks. He said it matter-of-factly." But Rupp uttered that 1930 description in 1974, and Kindred failed to make that point. He suggested flatly that "Coaches talk racist trash because they are human. They also are right-wing political creatures who revel in their roles as authoritarian figures. They want to create victory, nothing else. Society, be damned."[21]

Rupp's family also has attempted to salvage his legacy. Following the Will article, Rupp's son, Adolph II ("Herky"), asked, "How can George Will be that ignorant and dumb?"[22] Herky Rupp repeatedly argued that denigrations of his father came from individuals who never knew him. He emphasized the softer side of his famous father: "Naturally, my father expected me to act in a certain way, but he wasn't harsh or unreasonable about it. He made no excessive demands of me." Writing in the *Lexington Herald-Leader*, D. G. FitzMaurice suggested that "unlike W. C. Fields, who when asked how he liked children, reportedly replied, 'fried, madam, fried,' Rupp cherished children."[23]

As a child, Herky served as a UK ball boy, attended team meetings and practices, and was allowed into the locker room, which is where one oft-quoted story about Rupp arose. Longtime Kentucky sportswriter Earl Cox, who probably remembered more Rupp anecdotes than any other man before his death in 2016, related that "at halftime of one game, the players were silently waiting to hear from their coach, but all they heard from the bathroom was the following: 'Herky, move over. Herky, move over. Herky, dammit, you're peeing all over my leg!'"[24]

Herky was quick to point out that his father "did a lot of things for people that we don't talk about," such as providing free circus tickets to children at the local Shriners hospital. Rupp's granddaughter, Carlyle Farren Rupp, contended that his largesse was especially extended to African American children. In an article written in response to George Will's piece, she revealed that every summer the family would go to the poor black section of Lexington known as Pralltown—those "nigger shacks"—and distribute Shrine Circus tickets to all of the children.[25]

"I've gotten a lot of publicity for being a mean man, but it's not true,"

Rupp once said. "The fact is I've got an invitation to coach both basketball teams when I go through the pearly gates."[26]

Rupp's last years at UK coincided with the development of my own intense interest in basketball. Having moved back to Kentucky from Texas and Tennessee in 1967, I was immediately introduced in the summer before my sixth-grade year to the state's religious devotion to basketball. For me and others, however, the Baron's glamour already had faded. Our family still lived in Tennessee in March 1966, so the significance of Kentucky's NCAA championship loss to Texas Western (with its all-black starting five) did not register on a 10-year-old boy more interested in baseball. But in the larger sphere of a nation enmeshed in an increasingly unpopular war in Vietnam and reeling from the assassination of President Kennedy in 1963 and Martin Luther King Jr. and Robert Kennedy in 1968, the 1960s marked a turning point in the civil rights movement. The profound meaning of Texas Western's victory over Rupp's lily-white Wildcats was not lost on more perceptive students of American culture.

For this adolescent boy, loyalty to UK basketball brought acceptance and identity in a tiny western Kentucky county-seat town where one polio-stricken seventh-grade history teacher made a point of commenting on the level of basketball he observed during recess. Another west Kentuckian, Stan Key, who lived out his dream of playing for Rupp, remembered mimicking such UK greats as Louie Dampier and Pat Riley in playground games in the 1960s.[27] In my town the courthouse crowd regularly ambled across the street to my father's drugstore to discuss the previous night's game—which the Wildcats probably had won—and similar discussions preceded the Sunday school lesson at church.

For me, however, Rupp's last teams lacked the excitement and exotic appeal of other college teams in the late 1960s and early 1970s, though I believe it was his insistence on a fast-paced style that made all of the rest possible. I could certainly admire the play of Dan Issel, Mike Pratt, and Larry Steele, but after they were gone, Rupp's teams were not as glitzy or as successful. His first black scholarship player, Tom Payne, showed promise but played only one season before being drafted as a hardship case by the Atlanta Hawks. Lefthander Tom Parker was a fine shooter, but his steady play simply didn't elicit the same excitement as other Southeastern Conference (SEC) and Big Ten players. Jim Andrews was at once solid and dependable. Only Stan Key merited my praise, however, and that was primarily because he hailed from Calloway County in my end of the state. Instead, on the outdoor court behind my grade school, I tried to emulate LSU's "Pistol" Pete Maravich and Purdue's Rick Mount (I carried a picture of "Rick the Rocket" in my wallet throughout high school).

By 1970 other teams and players had eclipsed the old man still wearing that old brown suit and propping his ulcerated foot on a pillow at courtside, but we all rooted for his Wildcats just the same. When my high school basketball coach dropped off a 45-rpm record, a terrible tune repeating the awful refrain, "Remarkable Rupp, Remarkable Rupp, the Basketball Whiz," I played the thing over and over again on our living-room stereo.

When the university's mandatory retirement age of 70 forced Rupp out in 1972, high schoolers in my circle were convinced it was time for the old man to go, even while our parents hoped the board of trustees would grant an exemption. Rupp went out fighting, refusing to resign on his own, even though his longtime assistant, Harry Lancaster, admitted that he "didn't coach the last fifteen years he was here. He was out of it as soon as the game started." Lancaster concluded that Rupp "was a sick man," and Rupp himself suggested in a last-ditch effort to keep his job that "if they force me to retire, then they might as well take me out to the Lexington Cemetery."[28]

He was wrong, but only by about five years. He dabbled in professional basketball with the Memphis Tams and Kentucky Colonels, flirted with an offer to coach Duke University, and battled diabetes and cancer. He lived to see the dedication of a new downtown arena named in his honor. His death in 1977 marked the end for a man who changed a sport and a state.

Today a visitor to Lexington Cemetery might wind around tree-lined lanes past the impressive monument to Kentucky statesman Henry Clay, the marker for Confederate general John Hunt Morgan, and the graves of the Breckinridges before finally reaching Adolph Rupp's burial site. Made of white granite with a basketball sculpted near the top beneath the name "RUPP" inscribed in large letters, the monument is striking in that the word "Kentucky" does not appear in the inscription. Instead, Rupp wanted to be remembered in this way:

U.S. Basketball Coach 42 years
Olympic Coach 1948
Four NCAA Championships
National Basketball Hall of Fame

Herky Rupp said his father chose the spot because of the "big shady oak tree" growing there.[29] Harry Lancaster is buried nearby. When Lancaster became UK's athletic director, in effect becoming the boss of his former boss, their relationship soured. The oak tree no longer stands near the graves of Rupp and Lancaster. A storm blew it down, much like the friendship that couldn't survive a whirlwind of change and power and ego.

Each year in March, around the time of the Sweet Sixteen, the Kentucky high school boys' basketball tournament in Rupp Arena, a steady stream of pilgrims finds their way to the cemetery. "They always ask directions to Rupp's grave," said Mark Durbin, a cemetery official. "You see fathers bringing their sons here. Old fans, young fans. Adolph Rupp will never be forgotten, not in Kentucky."[30]

But Chip Alexander of *The News & Observer* in North Carolina, who has written eloquently of the annual pilgrimage to the gravesite, noted that "many memories of Rupp's career have faded," and that "many of Rupp's deeds were accomplished so long ago, sandwiched around World War II, when the South and Lexington and the university and basketball were all so different."[31]

Surely, as L. P. Hartley began his 1953 novel *The Go-Between*, "The past is a foreign country; they do things differently there." According to historian David Lowenthal, the conjured-up past is "largely an artifact of the present. However faithfully we preserve, however authentically we restore, however deeply we immerse ourselves in bygone times, life back then was based on ways of being and believing incommensurable with our own." Lowenthal believed that "the past's difference is, indeed, one of its charms: no one would yearn for it if it merely replicated the present. But we cannot help but view and celebrate it through present-day lenses."[32]

Ed Smith, a communications professor at Kentucky's Georgetown College, was convinced that the "charms" of the past would be of interest to University of Kentucky and Adolph Rupp fans. So in 2000, in character as Rupp, Smith auditioned for the Kentucky Humanities Council's Chautauqua Series, in which actors portray characters from Kentucky's past—

people such as Daniel Boone, Simon Kenton, Henry Clay, and York, the slave companion of Lewis and Clark.[33]

At first hesitant to take on the portrayal, Smith eventually decided that Rupp "had so much to do not just with Kentucky basketball but with Kentucky, because it's more than just the game. The way we think about Kentucky basketball and sport in general goes back to him." The Humanities Council agreed, and Smith, a Lexington native with only vague memories of the coach, listened to hours of Rupp interviews and pieced together a convincing portrayal with a script based largely on verbatim quotes.[34]

But then, Adolph Rupp pretty much painted his own portrait over the years. In 1960 Pulitzer Prize–winning writer Jimmy Breslin described Rupp's voice as "a nasal, bottled-in-dear-old Kaintucky twang which he made sure to acquire when he came to the school from the Midwest." Breslin went on: "'So you're going to write a story?' Rupp will say to a sportswriter he knows. 'Why, that's just fine. We'll sit down together and make this a great story. I'll tell you how we'll do it. Let's brag on me and my team. Write up something real good about us. People will love it. . . . Now don't you say I said this,' Rupp will say. 'You say it yourself. It'll look a bit better than if you have me boosting myself.'"[35]

The Rupp that emerged in Smith's 40-minute performance was "likeable, but with a caustic streak." At one point the character stated, "I'd rather be the most hated winning coach in the country than the most popular losing one."[36] Smith also portrayed the Baron's pain and feelings of betrayal brought on by the point-shaving scandal. One topic Smith refused to tackle, however, was Rupp's views on race. He argued that the setting of the program, at the end of a day in 1972, wasn't a time when Rupp would have discussed the issue. Smith prepared himself to deal with the issue in the question-and-answer sessions following each performance, but the subject came up only "maybe nine times" in more than 30 presentations in 2001 and early 2002. No one raised it at all after a performance at a largely African American cultural festival in Danville. When it did come up, according to Smith, "the question is usually posed by someone in the audience when there's a lull in the Q & A. I get the sense . . . that it's sometimes posed as a straw to stir the drink. I've never met with open hostility."[37]

Perhaps the response would be different outside Kentucky. The absence of controversy surrounding Rupp was certainly not the norm during his illustrious career. Still, we must proceed cautiously to try to understand a figure who came to dominate college basketball in the middle decades of the twentieth century, a figure who changed a state, a sport, and the culture of higher education. Basketball is not a complicated game, but its rise to its lofty place in the milieu of American culture is more difficult to trace and understand. The career of Adolph Rupp gives us a structure to understand the transformation that did take place.

So, is this the story of a complex individual in a simple sport, or is it the story of a simple, driven man who came to dominate and transform his sport? What could be more straightforward than the rise of the son of immigrant parents from humble roots on the plains of Kansas to the pinnacle of his profession? Rupp's journey took him to Lawrence, Kansas; to Marshalltown, Iowa; to Freeport, Illinois; to Lexington, Kentucky; to London and other cities in Europe and Asia; to hamlets in the rolling hills of western Kentucky and the mountain hollows of eastern Kentucky; to college towns in the Deep South; and to Madison Square Garden in the Big Apple. It eventually took him to the National Basketball Hall of Fame in Springfield, Massachusetts, where basketball began in 1891, invented by James A. Naismith, one of Rupp's mentors at the University of Kansas.

The journey began, however, at the dawn of the twentieth century among his neighbors and his own German Mennonite family in the little farming community of Halstead, Kansas.

1

The Halstead Years, 1901–1919

"This is Adolph Rupp. I was born in Halstead, Kansas, on September the second, nineteen hundred and one. Kansas at that time, of course, was almost in two different parts."[1]

Thus one of college basketball's most enigmatic figures began a series of remarkable ramblings. Successful, colorful, crusty, and controversial, Rupp waxed on and on with little prompting from his interviewer, Russell Rice, the retired sports information director and assistant athletic director at the University of Kentucky. Rice retired from the athletic department in 1989, but from 1969 until just before Rupp's death in 1977, he conducted a series of interviews with the basketball legend.

It is clear from the interviews that an aging Adolph Rupp remembered his childhood in Halstead, Kansas, as at once comfortable and demanding, if not idyllic. Rupp grew up in relative comfort in that he was surrounded by family and friends and, despite his father's early death, comparative stability. Yet, his early years were also demanding. His family and friends expected him to play a useful role in the closed society into which he was born and reared. Rupp's rural upbringing in a Mennonite, German-speaking family in the wheat fields of the American plains certainly did not presage his later career as a record-breaking coach in a sport whose origins were purely American and urban.

Rupp's father and mother had followed other European immigrants to central Kansas in the latter years of the nineteenth century. His father came from Einsiedel, Austria, and his mother from Greenstadt, Germany. By the late 1880s the central Kansas frontier—what would become the counties of Harvey, McPherson, and Reno—attracted hundreds of European immigrants very much like Heinrich Rupp and Anna Lichti. Many of them belonged to the Mennonite Church, a Protestant pacifist sect whose members came to America for two reasons, according to Rice: "to escape compulsory military service and to farm the land."[2]

The foreign immigration department of the Santa Fe Railroad actively promoted settlement in this area as the rail lines pushed west after the Civil War. In 1860, a year before statehood, the population of Kansas numbered 100,000, and the territory had only 5 miles of railroad tracks. By the time the first Rupps arrived in the 1880s, the state of Kansas had almost a million residents and more than 3,000 miles of track.[3]

In Harvey County, Russian Mennonite immigrants founded the farming community of Halstead in 1877, naming it after noted journalist Murat Halstead. Today it bills itself as "the biggest little city in Kansas," pointing to medical facilities, an active chamber of commerce, and flourishing commercial and industrial sectors. From the beginning, however, the Mennonites came to farm. Bringing with them a strain of hard winter wheat known as "Turkey Red," they built a mill at the confluence of the Little Arkansas River and Black Kettle Creek, where Kit Carson and Chief Black Kettle held a famous "Pow Wow" some years before.[4]

Adolph Rupp's parents came to Halstead only a few years after the founding of the town, Heinrich Rupp in 1882 and Anna Lichti in 1891. Heinrich moved with his mother, two brothers, and two sisters, and Anna with her father and a younger brother. An elderly Adolph Rupp remembered very little about his family's European roots. "My father came from Galicia; that was the royal crown colony of Austria," Rupp recalled. "He came to this country and, of course, had very little knowledge of anything. He did not have a lot of education."[5]

Heinrich, called Henry in his new American home, worked as a mill hand at the Warkentin Mill for a decade before meeting Anna. They married in 1893 and moved to a small farm south of town, where Heinrich bought tools on credit and started farming. He eventually made enough money to buy a spread located seven miles north of Halstead (Adolph recalled that farm was 120 acres, but his sister Elizabeth remembered it as 160). The couple planted wheat, corn, sorghum, and oats, and maintained a large garden that included an acre of potatoes.[6]

Out of necessity, farming on the central Kansas plains was a family affair, and Heinrich and Anna had six children—five sons and a daughter—to rear and love: Otto, Theodore, Henry, Adolph, Elizabeth, and Albert, in that order. All were born in the small frame farmhouse. Even at 86, Theodore remembered a "chill in the air" on September 2, 1901, when the family summoned Dr. Arthur E. Hertzler to the Rupp farm. Theodore sat in the living room of the old house in 1983 and reminisced about the birth of his younger brother. "This is where Adolph Rupp was born," he recalled. "Right here in this room. We didn't have any maternity wards like we have in town today. Right over there around that stove is where Dr. Hertzler warmed his hands when he got here." At the time Otto was 7, Theodore 5, and Henry 2½. The family hoped that the fourth child would be a girl, but it would be another two years before Elizabeth was born. Albert came along in 1906.[7]

In 1910, at only 48 years old, Heinrich Rupp died of cancer. Adolph was only 9, but his father had a lasting influence on all of the children. "When Daddy said something, that was the law," Rupp said many decades later. "There was no one ever talked back to him. We did exactly what we was supposed to do. In fact, that's typical of the Mennonite faith, that the father is head of the household."[8] Rupp was to follow his father's patriarchal example less with his own children than with his surrogate family, the boys on his basketball teams.

With Heinrich's death, work responsibilities shifted, and the family made adjustments to survive. Elizabeth could not imagine how her mother coped with the loss. Adolph admired his mother's tenacity: "As I recall, we had two or three consecutive crop failures there and times were really rough. Mother kept us all together, and we did the best we could. Each one was assigned a definite task, what we had to do, and we were expected to do it. And my oldest brother took a little authority on himself and felt that he had the right also." Otto quit school at 16 to take charge of the farm. The fourth son's chief assignment was to feed the hogs. The communal nature of farm life also meant that young Adolph assisted neighbors in times of need. "They always called on me because I think I turned in an honest day's work and they liked to have a boy that would do that kind of work," he said.[9]

For Kansas homesteaders, the prosperous years that followed the Civil War had ended by the 1880s, when droughts, falling commodity prices, and the end of the long cattle drives left the state's economy in shambles.

The decline continued into the twentieth century. For the widow Rupp and her six children, hard times began long before the Great Depression of the 1930s. "As I get older," Elizabeth reminisced almost 80 years later, "I just don't know how she managed, really."[10]

The Rupp children grew up bilingual, although Adolph spoke strictly German until he was six years old. "You can imagine what happened," Elizabeth said. "My oldest brother probably knew no English when he started school, but the second brother, you see, learned some from him, and then by the time the third brother came along he had learned a little more from the first two, and so by the time I came along and my youngest brother came along, of course, we knew a good deal of the English, because many of our friends, our closest neighbors . . . didn't speak German at home."[11]

The Mennonite ministers conducted services in German before eventually transitioning to English, and for six weeks each summer the Rupp children attended "German school," where every class was conducted in German.[12] Adolph's later "Baron" nickname was one he cultivated not only for its dictatorial overtones, but also because of his cherished family heritage.

Rupp entered his first year at Halstead High School with the world at war, though the United States didn't enter the conflict until 1917. In 1915 two full columns of the weekly *Halstead Independent* newspaper continued to be printed in German.[13] In the November 4, 1915, issue, a photograph with the caption "Pay Day in the German Army" showed German paymasters in Galicia (native home of Heinrich Rupp) stationed in front of a castle to divvy out soldiers' monthly pay. A writer suggested that "statistics show the Kaiser's men send back home from the front every month between sixty and seventy million marks."[14]

By 1918 a weekly serial titled "Outwitting the Hun," and articles with headlines such as "Allies Give the Germans No Rest," "Hun Grip on France Broken," and finally "Huns Sign Truce Which Ends War" had replaced these sympathetic pieces. Any semblance of a less than patriotic response to the allied cause by Halstead's German Mennonite population soon vanished. As early as 1915, the Halstead High senior class presented the school with two large statues of Washington and Lincoln, and regular meetings of the Halstead Loyalty League and the Vigilance Committee supervised a proper response to the war. In September 1918 the Loyalty League asked the town's four churches to stop using the German language in services, and all pastors, priests, and congregations complied. The Vigilance Committee called for similar action in the town as a whole, and signs reading "Don't Speak German in Halstead" soon popped up throughout the community. Although Halstead's population was only 1,166 in 1919, sales of victory bonds reached $100,000, $20,000 over the town's quota.[15]

Still, the extreme suppression of anything German—sauerkraut became "liberty cabbage"—did not go unquestioned by a people proud of its rich heritage. Rupp remembered when German was replaced as the required "foreign" language at Halstead High School: "Along came World War I, and some of the old cranks in the neighborhood thought that German was a bad thing to be teaching in high school. And so a few of those old cranks stormed up and demanded that German should be ousted from the teaching in the high school and that French and Spanish should be substituted." With characteristic sarcasm, he added: "Well, of course, that's a wonderful thing; there were no Frenchmen out there in the neighborhood that I could see and never heard of any, in fact."[16]

Adolph barely missed the draft—he did not turn 18 until after the armistice had been signed—but his brother Henry was listed among the 92 Harvey County men "called into the army" in 1918.[17] Anna and the children, still reeling from the death of the patriarch, adjusted to a wartime economy by working even harder on the farm.[18] "The work had to be done, and the work was done," Adolph Rupp recalled. "I remember life was rugged, very difficult, and there wasn't a great variety." They cured their own hams, smoked their own sausages, and canned "all the vegetables, all the berries, all the plums and everything else that we could get that grew wild out in the sand hill region" a few miles away, he added.[19]

In the summers Rupp worked from sunup until sundown on a threshing crew, and he recalled thinking at the time that the hard labor "would develop us and make us into a much better basketball player."[20] Basketball season began once school started in the fall. A weight-training and running regimen was, of course, unheard of in those early years only a generation after James A. Naismith had invented the game in Springfield, Massachusetts, in 1891.[21] By the second decade of the twentieth century, however, the game already had become a welcome diversion, if not a serious business, for Rupp and his brothers and friends.

It should not be surprising that the sport found a home in Kansas. After all, Naismith was the first basketball coach at the University of Kansas from 1898 to 1907, and interest soon spread to rural areas across the state.[22] When Adolph was eight or nine, about the time of his father's death, he played basketball with his brothers at home and at school during recess and at noon. "I think it would have been in the seventh and eighth grade when he did a good deal of practicing at home," his sister Elizabeth remembered. "I suppose that all of the boys played basketball because there were so few of us in that school that I think as soon as they, perhaps from third or fourth grade on, they would all play together."[23] Rupp recalled that his first basketball was "made of a gunnysack. It was round and filled with rags and hay. Mother stitched it together. The nice thing about that basketball was that you couldn't dribble it, so there was no such thing as individual play. You couldn't have had an Oscar Robertson in those days. You had to pass or shoot."[24]

Later on, he and his classmates sold box suppers to earn enough money to buy a new ball each year. "They wore out pretty fast on the dirt," explained Glenn Lehmann, Adolph's friend and teammate. "We played at recess, and we'd wolf down our lunches and go outside to play basketball. Except when the slough froze over; then we'd skate."[25]

The Rupps bought their first automobile sometime around 1915, but they still depended on a horse and buggy for the trip to the high school, seven miles away in town. During Adolph's junior and senior years, the children avoided the daily buggy ride by renting rooms in town during the school year. Elizabeth remembered that Henry got a job in a meat market and Adolph worked long hours in the grocery store to earn the rent money. All of the children went home on the weekends to help on the farm. During the harvest, farm work took precedence over school work. Superintendent William Thompson postponed the start of the 1918–1919 school year, Adolph's senior year, until September 9 because of "the demand for labor."[26]

Adolph Rupp entered Halstead High as one of 27 freshmen, but only 16 remained in his senior class. His high school career coincided with the World War I years, and the war changed school life along with everything else. School officials kept a closer watch on the physical health of students. They monitored students' tobacco use, especially among the boys. A local newspaper writer believed that boys using tobacco "can easily be picked out, their school work shows the result of their dissipation." Teachers and coaches expressed concern especially for basketball players, as "the basket ball season will soon be on and any boy who belongs to the Athletic Association and is known to use tobacco will be denied the privilege of playing or practicing."[27]

The school held chapel services each Friday, and speakers provided the usual advice for upright living. In November 1915, the Reverend Robertson, a popular chapel speaker, "very pleasantly entertained with reminiscences of former school days and school conditions when the birch rod was the chief piece of apparatus which the school possessed."[28] The young sport of basketball fit very neatly into the plan of teachers and administrators to maintain strict discipline in a nurturing, healthful environment.

That was exactly how James Naismith had envisioned it. A "preoccupation with health" for the urban masses, coupled with a desire to glorify God in everything—at first referred to as "muscular Christianity"—encouraged Naismith, an ordained minister, to invent a game designed to promote fitness and discipline. Naismith also believed the new sport would provide a proper American indoor alternative to football during long, cold New England winters.[29]

It served the same purpose in rural Kansas, where front-page columns in the *Halstead Independent* demonstrated the importance of the sport for students and town folk alike. The Halstead High Dragons had already garnered considerable basketball success before Adolph Rupp's freshman year, winning two state championships. In those early years tournaments were organized much more loosely than today. Rupp remembered that "at the end of the year anyone that had a basketball team and wanted to enter it into a tournament went to Lawrence, Kansas, where they played on cross courts in old Robinson Gymnasium two games at a time and eliminated the teams in that way. Sometimes 30 or more teams would enter that tournament." The players "had to pay their own expenses, they stayed at fraternity houses and whoever would put them up."[30]

Halstead won the first state tournament, played in 1909. "Of course, that set Halstead afire," said Rupp, who was only eight at the time. "You can imagine a little town out there out on the plains with about twelve hundred people being the state champions in basketball." With most of its players back, Halstead repeated in 1910.[31] "The state championship ignited a spark in our community," Rupp recalled. "Everybody talked basketball. We finally got the school board to get two posts, build backboards, and put baskets up in the yard at District 33 (the one-room school for grades

1–8). I don't remember if we had any nets. I don't think so, but the board did give us a basketball. It cost four dollars. It had a bladder and a little tube. We'd blow up the bladder, tie the tube, lace her up, and away we'd go."[32]

Rupp didn't play for the varsity as a freshman in 1915–1916, and it was just as well. The Dragons lost the season opener at Moundridge 62–17, and then, with Theodore "Tate" Rupp at center, dropped its home opener to Winfield 38–14, "an inglorious defeat," according to the local paper. Although a newspaper writer hoped "that the boys have learned some new stunts and how to handle the ball and hit the basket and will give a good report of themselves," no "new stunts" were forthcoming after the Christmas break.[33] Tate Rupp eventually left the team, other players were held out because of poor grades, and Halstead continued to lose. The *Halstead Independent* reported that "the Halstead Highs, or more properly speaking, the Halstead Lows, tightened their grip on the bottom of the percentage column . . . losing the game to Newton by the cruel score of 85 to 11." The writer did not mince words in pointing to one unnamed culprit: "There is one good basket ball player in the High School who does not take enough interest in his school work to keep his grades up to passing, hence he is not allowed to play. The team needs him and he likes to play but not bad enough to dig on his lessons."[34] The Dragons ended a disastrous 1–16 season with a 110–13 loss to Newton that still stands as the most lopsided victory in Newton's history.[35]

Adolph Rupp played only sparingly during his sophomore year, when Halstead bounced back to earn an invitation to the state tournament as an independent after dropping out of the Arkansas Valley League and having to piece together a schedule from week to week. The team even defeated Newton, which went on to win the state title.[36]

After a two-year apprenticeship, Adolph became the Dragons' leading player during his final two seasons. The starting center at a bit over six feet tall, he scored a career-high 37 points in a 79–19 rout of Burrton during his junior year. He also became the team's de facto coach; the school principal was the coach in name only, and the players were accompanied only by a chaperone on road trips. "Adolph was the field general," teammate Glenn Lehmann recounted. "I remember once I had a nosebleed and the coach was going to put in a sub. Dolph wouldn't let him."[37]

Rival Newton, meanwhile, was coached by Frank Lindley, who compiled a 570–109 record and won eight state championships from 1914 to

1945. Rupp regarded Lindley as "the finest coach in high school in the early days. He would have to be ranked as the number one coach in the world because he studied the game." Rupp remembered one game against Newton when Halstead built a quick 16–2 lead and Lindley called a timeout. "Of course, we never had a coach, so we just stood around," Rupp said. "And he, of course, told them to start using the screens and their plays which they were saving for Wichita." Newton came back to tie the score by halftime, "so the coaching of this man Lindley really showed up."[38]

The playing conditions were as primitive as the coaching in those days. At neighboring Sedgwick the court was housed in a dilapidated store building with a pot-bellied stove near the sideline. Rupp recalled that "one night one of the boys went in for a crip, hit the door and went outside. Since there were no steps, he had to run around the front of the store to get back in."[39]

At Burrton games were played on a cement floor in a garage. "On game nights," Rupp remembered, "they moved out the cars, swept the floors, and went to it." Moundridge used an old church building with no marked sidelines or baselines. Halstead held its games in City Hall, where, according to Lehmann, "the ceiling was about two feet above the backboards." "You couldn't arch the ball much," Rupp noted. Lighting came from gas lamps covered with wire wastepaper baskets, and a hot air register sat directly in the middle of the court. Lehmann's older cousin, Ward Lehmann, fell through the register during a game.[40]

Undoubtedly, Rupp learned more basketball from Frank Lindley than from any of his own chaperone-coaches. Already James Naismith's old ideal of basketball as a players' game, with coaches playing minimal roles, had become obsolete. One scholar of the game wrote that "Naismith was especially out of touch in his persistent belief that his creation should be played for fun, exercise, and the building of character." Naismith himself holds the distinction of being the only losing basketball coach in the history of the University of Kansas.[41]

Television and corporate sponsorships were still far in the future, but less than three decades after the invention of basketball, Adolph Rupp was already well aware of the importance of winning and of the role that coaches could play in directing the outcome of a game.

Back in the Arkansas Valley League, Halstead secured the league championship during the season. In March 1918, the local newspaper announced plans for the Dragons to enter a Class C tournament in Wichita for schools enrolling fewer than 50 boys. Halstead qualified with 43, but Rupp and his teammates apparently were unsuccessful in the tournament, or perhaps the influenza epidemic resulted in the event's cancellation. For whatever reason, the Halstead paper failed to write up the tournament's results. In fact, it reported only one more game in that 1917–1918 season, a 33–32 victory over Valley Central on March 18.[42] By 1918 teams had to be invited to the state tournament and tiny Halstead, despite winning the Arkansas Valley League, was passed over. Unable to advance to the state tournament, Halstead ended the season with a one-point victory over a larger consolidated district, the other wins over a string of tiny schools.

Raging on and on and peaking in central Kansas in the autumn of 1918, the influenza epidemic disrupted Halstead's 1918–1919 school year and basketball season. School officials dismissed classes, and Rupp and his teammates could not practice until after Christmas. An abbreviated season began with a 28–21 victory at Burrton on January 10, though the Halstead newspaper observed that "the influenza epidemic and lack of practice showed in the work of both teams, neither playing steady consistent basketball." Rupp, the captain, scored 16 points.[43]

Halstead finished 9–3 that season, all of the losses to Reno County. The action became more physical as the season went on. In a victory over Burrton in which Rupp scored 27 points, a spectator observed that "for roughness the game has not been equaled on the Halstead court for many years. The first half of the game was little more than a roughing match with a goal thrown now and then for variety."[44] In a game against Florence, Roland Mitchell committed 21 fouls. Players weren't disqualified on their fifth back then.[45] The *Halstead Independent* reported each of the Dragons' games in some detail, and home basketball games became one of the most popular social activities of the town for both students and adults.

That so much attention centered on a team playing a game that had been invented only a few decades earlier certainly made an impression on young Adolph Rupp. "We always packed the old city hall," an elderly Rupp recalled. "We had all that hoopla, rah, rah, rah. And at the end of the year we held a big banquet," which "consisted of roasting wieners and marshmallows over a bonfire in Chappie Master's pasture at the edge of the town. We sang a few songs, and that was our banquet. We had our fun. We learned some fundamentals in life that perhaps the boys and girls aren't learning today."[46]

Basketball wasn't his only extracurricular activity. As a freshman Rupp joined Der Deutsche Verein, one of the school's several literary societies. With its motto "Ubung Macht den Meister" ("practice makes the master"), Rupp learned that the discipline required to maintain a successful farm, stock a grocery store, or fashion a winning basketball team also could be applied to training the mind. He became Halstead High's leading debater and starred in the senior play.[47] His role in "The New Co-Ed" wasn't a stretch. He played Richard Bradley, "an all-around athlete and a big shot" who fell in love with a girl. Rupp remembered that he was supposed to hold his hand over his heart when proposing to her. Instead, he "accidentally just put it down over my stomach, and everybody in the entire audience laughed and I never lived that down for weeks around there."[48]

After another summer of hard work on the farm, Rupp left Halstead by train for Lawrence to attend the University of Kansas. There he would meet and learn from one of the early basketball coaching giants—and from the man who invented the game.

2

The University of Kansas and the Jayhawk Café, 1919–1923

A dolph Rupp had starred on the basketball team during his final two years at Halstead High School, and he wasn't bashful about saying it. "Now I think the records will show," he later boasted, "that in the first game of basketball that I ever played . . . I got ten field goals and we beat Sedgwick 67–17 and we won the championship that year and, of course, we won the championship the following year also." He was referring to championships in a small mid-Kansas conference made up of tiny rural schools. He never played in a state tournament game, but he excelled against those little schools. "The records will also show . . . that I averaged nineteen points a game in the two years that I played on the high school basketball team at Halstead."[1]

The records will also show that during four years at the University of Kansas, one on the freshman team and three on the varsity, Rupp failed to score a single varsity basket. Not lettering until his senior year, he played only a minor role in the Jayhawks' great success as one of the nation's premier early basketball teams. Still, the lessons he learned about basketball and life from Forrest "Phog" Allen, the Kansas coach, and from James A. Naismith, the inventor of the game who was then a professor at the university, along with four years of steady work at the Jayhawk Café, served him well and provided a solid foundation for his future success.

Rupp did not have his college and professional life mapped out when he walked across the stage in Halstead's civic auditorium to receive his high school diploma. He had not taken college entrance examinations or applied for academic scholarships. Nor had college coaches, eager for him to display his skills and work ethic on their campuses, courted him. The current hullabaloo associated with recruiting student-athletes was unheard of between the two world wars of the first half of the twentieth century. Rupp simply began to ponder what he would do next. Surrounded by family and friends in a close-knit farming community that provided a nurturing, well-rounded environment, he nonetheless yearned for a life away from the demands of the farm and the scrutiny of small-town life.

"Most of the boys and girls decided to go to the smaller colleges in the area," Rupp recalled, and "a great number of them went to Emporia College and Emporia State Teachers College." His friend Roy Lehmann—from a family other than that of Rupp's high school teammate, Glenn Lehmann—made up his mind to go to the university in Lawrence to study geology. Rupp had not decided on a major yet, but his friendship with Lehmann convinced him to consider the state university, too. "We all got on this train, must have been about eight or ten of us, and we all stopped in Emporia," he recalled. The tiny Emporia College campus did not impress him. They went across town to the teachers' college, which Glenn Lehmann eventually attended, but Roy "kept pecking away at me all the time," Rupp remembered. "Adolph," he would say, "go to the best. If you are going to amount to something, go to a big school. . . . Take your bags, and you go with me." By five o'clock that evening they were on their way to the depot in Emporia to catch a train for Lawrence, about 100 miles down the line.[2]

Rupp instructed the conductor to let them off at the university, but when they got off the train on campus, no one was there. Except for one women's dormitory, all of the Kansas students lived downtown. Rupp and Lehmann "shelled out another nickel" and headed for town on a streetcar, which deposited them in the heart of the student district at about Fourteenth Street. As Rupp later remembered it: "There we stood with our suitcases, and I said to one of the boys walking past . . . where would be a chance to find a room?" The boy replied, "All you have to do is just go up and down the street here. They've got signs up if they've got any rooms available, and go in, take a look at 'em, and if it suits you, fine. If not, go to the next place. There's plenty of rooms around here." Rupp and Lehmann did as they were told and soon found a "Rooms for Rent" sign. "We went in there and everything was fine," Rupp recalled. Or so he thought. The landlady charged them seven dollars apiece before they could bring their bags inside, and when Rupp immediately asked about a bathroom so he could freshen up, he was told, "We don't have a bathroom here." Even with his rural upbringing, he was caught off guard. "You don't have a bathroom?" he asked incredulously. "No," a boy answered, "but we got a little outhouse back here . . . and they got a wash basin in there, and you'll have to get your water and wash that way." "Great day!" Rupp said. "No wonder this room was vacant. I'm not gonna like this at all." But finding nothing better to rent in the student district, he resignedly decided, "We'll do just fine."[3]

The next day, a Monday, the two farm boys went up the hill to enroll for classes at the University of Kansas. Rupp remembered the scene: "Everybody rushing around, shaking hands and embracing each other." And "poor little Roy and myself, we just kind of played it by ear, and finally we went through the lines and then we found half of the classes were closed and they pushed us into these other classes." Rupp wound up with trigonometry, English, literature, and other subjects. "It was a good load anyway," he said. "I tell you I had all I could handle." At the end of the registration line "came that awful thing where they extracted our tuition: $45." Rupp tried to argue, "I thought it was a state school, that everybody got to come there," but to no avail. "So immediately I parted with $45, and with the $7 I had spent the night before on my room, it left me a little short."[4]

In 1919 basketball scholarships were nonexistent, as were federal or state student loans. Rupp had worked in the fields the previous summer to earn money for college, but he ended up taking that money out of the bank for an appendix operation in August. No one recruited in those days. Rupp remembered that "the president of Emporia State Normal School came to visit me one time while I was working in the grocery store and said that they would like to have me come to his school, and that was the only contact I had."[5]

At Kansas, all first-year students received freshman caps that they were required to wear during the fall semester. Rupp later declared: "Woe be it to any freshman that passed Green Hall—that was the law school building, the first building on the campus—if he was a green little ol' freshman and he didn't have that freshman cap. Those law students all had paddles, and they'd just simply take you and put you down along that sidewalk and they'd wallop the daylights out of you. And I'll tell ya,' there's only one exit off of that campus, and that was by that law school. And you wouldn't forget that freshman cap. They had a way of inflicting punishment on these freshmen that showed absolutely no mercy at all."[6]

Rupp participated as a freshman in the class "Olympics," which consisted of a sack race, a tug-of-war, a relay race, a push ball, an obstacle course, and a "tug ring," an odd battle that involved pulling an automobile tire from the 50-yard line of the football field (a game also concocted by James Naismith). The competition pitted the freshman class against the sophomores, and it taught Rupp a lesson in the art of winning. As he explained it, "the freshmen always won these 'Olympics' because the freshmen really put their heart and soul into the thing, and the sophomores, of course, being fat cats, they didn't show up" with as much enthusiasm. Why were the freshmen so motivated? Because if they won, they got to throw away those despised caps at the Thanksgiving Day football game against Missouri. "As soon as the game was over," Rupp remembered, "all the freshmen sailed their caps up into the air, and that was the end of paddling and everything else."[7]

Rupp needed a job to make ends meet, and he was surprised to learn that work wasn't nearly as easy to find in Lawrence as it had been in Halstead. "All the jobs were taken," he said. "[I] just finally got to the place where I'm getting desperate. For weeks and weeks and weeks, I just didn't know what to do." Roy Lehmann had finally found employment at the Jayhawk Café, a popular little eatery near campus, and Rupp told him to be on the lookout for any positions that might come open there. In the meantime, he earned a little spending money doing the kinds of chores he knew back in Halstead. After class he would "go out into the country and help fill silos," and on weekends he picked pears and apples in the orchards of the area.[8]

With no cafeteria on campus, Rupp would buy a loaf of bread and cold cuts for lunch—and often breakfast, too—and in the evening he would go out for as reasonably priced a dinner as he could find. A far cry from the fruits and vegetables, and country ham and eggs that he enjoyed back on the farm, but he was determined not to go back home. His older brothers had both stayed on the farm, and his younger brother worked at various businesses—a meat market, a clothing store, as an insurance salesman, and finally as an oil broker. Adolph had been the only one of the boys to go to college. "Oh, I don't think he ever considered not going," recalled sister Elizabeth, herself a University of Kansas graduate. "Adolph didn't want to be a farmer, and I think he always expected to go to college."[9]

It is perhaps ironic that he returned to farming in Kentucky in middle age after earning renown as a basketball coach. Of course, his life as a gentleman farmer—owner of the Four Leaf Clover Farm in Bourbon County outside of Lexington, with hired workers raising tobacco and caring for his Hereford cattle—was a far cry from the hard life in Halstead. That early experience persuaded him to seek a college education to prepare him for another line of work. "I was determined I wasn't going home," Rupp recalled. "I was going to stay there if I didn't get anything to eat. I was going to stick around there."[10]

Finally, somebody at the Jayhawk Café quit. Lehmann found out and told Rupp. He later recalled, "I got up there as fast as I could, and sure enough I landed the job." Diligent and determined, Rupp held it until his last day of college. Thinned down from a summer of sweat in the threshing fields and a diet of bread and cold cuts, Rupp now started to gain some weight, although it is difficult to imagine when he had time to eat. "To work in my basketball, and to work in my studies, and to work at the Jayhawk turned out to be quite a chore," he said. After he worked various hours at the café as a freshman, the owners allowed him to take the 8 p.m. to midnight shift during the week and 8 p.m. to 1 a.m. on weekends beginning in his sophomore year.[11] Rupp described a typical day in the life of this Kansas student-athlete in the early 1920s:

> I'd get up in the morning and go to the Jayhawk and get breakfast. Then I'd go up on the campus, and I'd stay in the library all day and study. [I] wouldn't come down for lunch or anything; I just stayed there and studied. I'd go to class whenever I was supposed to be in class. I'd do all of my outside reading—and they assigned a lot of outside reading in those days—and I got that all out of the way and made good grades. And then about a quarter to eight, I'd show up at the Jayhawk because they didn't want us to eat on their time. They wanted us to eat on our time. So I'd get something to eat, and then put on an apron at eight o'clock when the night crew showed up. We were ready to go. That's how I worked my way through school.[12]

"If it hadn't been for the Jayhawk Cafe, I wouldn't have had a college education," he concluded, looking back. "I was always grateful to them for that because it shows that if a man is willing, if a man is determined, he can always get along."[13]

Finally settled into college life in fall 1919, Rupp went to his first basketball practice. With no recruiting then and no formal tryouts, "it was just a general invitation that was extended through the student newspaper that everybody that wanted to try out for the team [should] come out."[14] And with three football players on the varsity basketball squad, Coach Karl Schlademan decided to wait until after the football season to begin practice.

Schlademan had recently been named as the fourth head coach of the Jayhawks, taking over from W. O. Hamilton, whose decade-long tenure had produced a record of 125–59. The first coach, of course, was Naismith, who was hired in 1898 not as a basketball coach—the school had no team—but to lead the physical education program and to serve as the institution's religious director. The university apparently already had some interest in the new sport even before its creator's arrival. The *Lawrence Journal* reported on December 2, 1896, that "there is talk of organizing a basketball team at Kansas University and challenging teams in Kansas City and other places where the game has become popular. A great many of the members of the faculty and students of the University are playing the game now and it promises to become even more popular."[15]

Amos Alonzo Stagg, the University of Chicago football coach, recommended Naismith for the job. Stagg's wire to Kansas officials lauded Naismith as "inventor of basket-ball, medical doctor, Presbyterian minister, tee-totaler, all-around athlete, non-smoker, and owner of vocabulary without cuss words." When he accepted the position at a salary of $1,300 per year, Naismith's contract made no mention of basketball, but because interest already was high in Lawrence, he soon organized a team. That fledgling squad played its first game in Kansas City on February 3, 1899, losing 16–5 to the Kansas City YMCA team. In its first home game one week later, however, Kansas routed the Topeka YMCA 31–6 for the school's first victory. Fifty curious spectators attended that game. The *Kansas Weekly* reported that "after two minutes of play [a Kansas player] threw a goal and the first applause was heard. This gingered the Varsity boys and they played so fast that the visitors could offer little interference."[16] Except for games against Haskell Institute, Independence College, and William

Jewell College, the Jayhawks competed against various YMCA teams and athletic clubs in that first season to produce a 7–4 record.

Although Naismith downplayed the importance of winning, he tried to upgrade the program by scheduling—without success—road games against Yale and Chicago. Still, as a growing list of colleges added basketball as a team sport, he was able to schedule games with several other schools by his final season in 1907. Early that season Naismith's boys lost to the Baker University Wildcats 39–24. Baker's coach was Forrest C. "Phog" Allen, one of Naismith's former players. When Allen had sought counsel from his coach about a future career in coaching for himself, Naismith tried to discourage him: "You can't coach basketball, Forrest. You play it." Allen ignored his mentor's advice, and when Naismith stepped down as coach in 1907 to return to the classroom and the pulpit, the school named Allen to succeed him. Naismith completed his nine seasons at Kansas from 1898–1907 with a losing record of 55–60, a winning percentage of .478.[17]

Allen was born in 1885 in Jamestown, Missouri. Athletic from the first, he and his five brothers played football, basketball, and baseball around Independence, where they grew up. W. T. Allen admonished his sons to concentrate on more important things than games and sports: "You're wasting your time. You're just fooling your time away playing ball and that kind of stuff. You'll never amount to anything that way." Young Forrest didn't heed that advice, either. After graduating from Independence High School in 1905, he played for Naismith at Kansas for two seasons (1905–1906 and 1906–1907) before leaving school to continue as the Baker University coach in nearby Baldwin City. In 1903 Allen also had joined the Kansas City Athletic Club (KCAC), where he played for the new basketball team and was named its manager, or coach, in 1904.[18]

Still a teenager, Allen showed the leadership skills at the KCAC that would serve him well for the rest of his career. In 1905 he staged "one of the greatest basketball series in the history of the game," according to the *Jayhawker Magazine and Yearbook.* The Buffalo Germans had won the Pan-American Championship in Buffalo in 1903, and when they won the tournament at the St. Louis World's Fair in 1904, they were recognized as world champions. Allen set up a championship series between the Germans and his own team. When KCAC officials, afraid that the venture would be a financial failure, balked at the plan, he agreed to underwrite it himself. Kansas City defeated the Germans two games to one, with Allen making 17 free throws in the final game. More important for the athletic club, the series paid off handsomely and KCAC membership grew from 400 to more than 1,000 in about a year.[19]

Allen enrolled at the University of Kansas in 1905, played for Naismith and coached Baker University during his second year before leaving school to coach full time. He came back to complete class work for his degree and also became at age 22, in 1907, the head coach at what would become his alma mater when he graduated in 1909. In fact, in the 1908–1909 season the tireless young man coached three teams at once—Kansas, Baker, and Haskell Institute (on an Indian reservation)—compiling a 74–10 record altogether.

Under Allen, the Jayhawks moved into the new $100,000 Robinson Gymnasium, erected after several years of urging by Naismith and designed after the YMCA building in Springfield, Massachusetts, where he had invented the game. The gymnasium's inaugural game against Ottawa University on December 13, 1907, resulted in a lopsided 66–22 victory in which the Jayhawks jumped out to a 31–0 lead and finished with the most points in the history of the program to that point. The boy coach experienced immediate success. He upgraded the schedule, playing nearly twice as many games as his predecessor by his second season. Naismith's last Kansas team had finished 7–8 against other colleges, YMCAs, and even a military company team. Allen's first team capped an 18–6 season with a 28–25 victory over Nebraska for Kansas's first Missouri Valley Conference championship. Even though the Jayhawks repeated as conference champs the next year and went 25–3, Allen dropped out of the business for a few years to study osteopathic medicine. He returned to coaching in 1912 at Warrensburg Teachers College (later to become Central Missouri State University), where he handled all sports. He finally came back to his alma mater in 1919 as director of athletics.[20]

In the decade that Allen was away from Lawrence, W. O. Hamilton coached the Jayhawks to five conference championships, but his last four years had seen a decline. His teams went 6–12, 12–8, 10–8, and 7–9 in those seasons before he resigned with a solid overall record of 125–59. Karl Schlademan took over before the 1919–1920 season, Adolph Rupp's freshman year.

After his first game, a 37–22 home victory over Emporia State on

January 6, 1920, Schlademan resigned abruptly to concentrate on his other duties as coach of the track team. The individual who took his place was no stranger to Jayhawker basketball, but now it was *Dr.* Forrest C. Allen, osteopathic physician. When he became athletic director, Allen had planned to coach the freshman basketball team as well, but with Schlademan's sudden resignation the athletic board asked him to step up to the varsity. Schlademan was persuaded to take the less rigorous position of freshman basketball coach in addition to his track job.

Naismith remained at the university as a professor of physical education after resigning as coach, and some of Adolph Rupp's most vivid and cherished memories of his four years in Lawrence involved his encounters with the game's founder. "He was not a difficult man to find because he was always in the gymnasium early and late," Rupp recalled. "He was a hard worker. He was interested in developing the youth of the land." With so many young men enrolling at Kansas after World War I, Rupp believed that Naismith "was chiefly concerned in seeing that these boys would maintain a good physical condition and not get out of shape, because he believed that that was harmful and that everyone should be required to take some form of physical education."[21]

Rupp's personal instruction from Naismith, however, came not on the basketball court but in the classroom and in drop-in meetings in the professor's office. "I remember the first class I ever had under Dr. Naismith was a class in hygiene," he said in an interview in the 1970s. "He was a very interesting teacher. He taught largely from his huge knowledge; he seldom had any notes. He lectured very interestingly and he talked very plainly. He didn't hesitate to call a spade a spade." According to Rupp, Naismith "was mainly concerned to see that the boys conducted themselves the way gentlemen ought to that attend a state university." He said Naismith himself never cursed or lost his temper, two traits that clearly didn't rub off on his young admirer. Naismith maintained an interest in basketball, often attending Allen's practices, but he told Rupp "many, many times that he never believed that the game of basketball would ever be a game that would draw national attention, and he never believed that it would grow to a point where admission would be charged to see the game played." In fact, Naismith even thought at first that the "tug ring" game he'd invented with those tires on a football field might have more staying power.[22]

Naismith had an open-door policy. "I'd often go into the office and just sit down and shoot the breeze with him," Rupp remembered. "He always had time to talk, he always was interesting. He had a little Canadian accent and he had a moustache, and he always had that twinkle in his eye. You could always tell he was glad to see you." The two remained friends after Rupp came to Kentucky, and when the International Olympic Committee decided to add basketball as an Olympic sport in 1936, it was Rupp who kept Naismith out of the room while the committee was voting to send him to Berlin. Rupp was finally summoned "to bring the doctor in," and "when they told him that they had decided to send he and his wife to the Olympic Games, the doctor choked and was really deeply impressed with the fact that now the game had really and truly become an international sport where teams from all over the world were competing, and it made him so happy to think that the game was being played in the Olympics."[23]

Naismith made a lasting impression on Rupp. "I learned a lot from this man," he said. "I learned a lot of his philosophy, his philosophy of life, the way he felt about things. And then, of course, he passed a lot of this on to Dr. Allen. From the two of them I got the philosophy of basketball that I now embrace."[24]

In reality, of course, Naismith regarded basketball merely as a healthy pastime, a convenient way for young people to stay physically fit through the long, cold months of winter. The game never should interfere with, but only complement, a student's quest for a well-rounded education. And to Naismith, coaches were merely peripheral figures. One of the great ironies of sports history is that Naismith's insistence on the highest ideals of amateurism was dismantled by the changes that would come at the hands of the enthusiastic young man who shadowed his office door in between classes and shifts at the Jayhawk Café.

So too did Rupp eventually throw over another of the progressive beliefs of his mentor. Naismith's biographer, Bob Rains, wrote that basketball's inventor developed "strong feelings against segregation" during his World War I service in France and along the Mexican-American border. Naismith worked for slow progress for African Americans during his years at Kansas. He was never able to integrate the university's basketball teams, but he did work to admit blacks to the university's swimming pool. Kansas had a requirement that all students pass a swimming test and for years African American students had been given automatic passes for the requirement so that they did not enter the pool reserved for whites only. Naismith changed all that at Kansas.[25]

Along with Rupp, Naismith also mentored John McLendon, who would go on to become the first African American head coach in professional basketball when George Steinbrenner hired him to coach the Cleveland Pipers in 1961. Earlier in 1944, as coach of the North Carolina College for Negroes (now North Carolina Central University), McLendon led his all-black team to victory in a "secret game" against the Duke Medical School team, behind closed doors, in an empty gym, and in defiance of North Carolina's segregation laws. McLendon said that Naismith "didn't know anything about color or nationality," adding that, "Everything I ever did when I was coaching, I can trace back to him."[26]

Although Rupp coached William Moseley, an African American at Freeport High School, before his first year in Lexington, Kentucky, and then worked with Don Barksdale, a six-foot-six-inch forward on the 1948 United States Olympic basketball team, as the national team's assistant coach, Rupp never successfully recruited an African American player to the University of Kentucky until 1969, at the end of his basketball career. Rupp never adopted Naismith's strong stand against segregation; at least there was no evidence of that once he came to the Bluegrass after 1930.

One of Adolph Rupp's passions incubated in the Kansas wheat fields and coming into full flower in Bluegrass pastures was simply his quest for wealth. Again, in contrast to Rupp, James Naismith cared little for the acquisition of great wealth. Historian Michael Beschloss wrote that, if Naismith cared for mammon, he "might conceivably have patented his basketball invention and become a very rich man, but he had no passion for financial gain." Beschloss believed that basketball's inventor would be "astounded by the big-money world of today's game," citing as an example the December 2010 Sotheby's sale of Naismith's own 13 basketball rules, handwritten on yellowed pages back in 1891 and sold at auction for $4.3 million, "the largest price ever for a piece of sports history." Beschloss wrote about Naismith and his views on race and money on May 2, 2014, the same day that a groundbreaking was held on the campus of the University of Kansas for a new sports complex which would cost $18 million.[27] One wonders what Naismith would think.

In light of Naismith's views on race, his lack of concern for money, and his belief that basketball should be a game for players and not for coaches, it is really not accurate to describe him as Adolph Rupp's mentor. Rupp repeated over and over, "I learned a lot from this man. I learned a lot of his philosophy of life, the way he felt about things." If he learned it, he soon forgot it, or came to ignore it completely.[28]

If Rupp retained little of the philosophy of James Naismith, he also would stray from many of the tenets of Phog Allen, whom he characterized as "a great man." Both Allen and Rupp were strict disciplinarians, but Allen applied that to his personal life as well. Rupp remembered him as "a health addict." "He believed in jogging," Rupp later recalled. Never one to pay much attention to his own physical fitness and someone who suffered from various debilitating illnesses throughout his life, an elderly Rupp made light of the Kansas coach's preoccupation with health and wellness, stating cryptically that Allen "took such good care of himself that I believe that it was possibly one of the causes maybe of his downfall." Allen would rise early for a regimen of fingertip push-ups, and he required his players to do them the same way at the beginning of each practice. "That was supposed to strengthen your fingers to such an extent that when you shot that basketball, your fingers had a lot of snap and strength to them and you wouldn't sprain your fingers," Rupp said. "Well, I had a sprained finger every year I was there, so it didn't help me a great deal."[29]

Allen demanded respect. In later years Rupp usually referred to him as Dr. Allen, but when telling Allen stories he sometimes lapsed into calling him Phog. At Kansas the players addressed their coach as Dr. Allen or Doc—at least they did after Allen collared the team captain and told him it sounded "a little undignified for us to call him Phog" and instructed him to hold a team meeting on the matter. "I think most of us called him Doc from there on," Rupp remembered. And according to Rupp, Allen "took great pride in his personal appearance. He had to just look the best. And whenever a photograph of the team . . . was made, everybody had to absolutely have a nice haircut and everything had to be just so. He believed in perfect dress in every respect. He wouldn't put up with any of this sloppy business at all. And that was the kind of a life that he lived."[30]

Freshmen could not play on the varsity back then, and the Allen-Schlademan job switch made the 1919–1920 season "kind of a jumbled-up affair" for Rupp and his fellow first-year players. Allen "had us out for basketball as freshmen and then turned us over to Schlademan, and Schlademan didn't care much about basketball, and I don't know if we got any coaching at all or not," an elderly Rupp said. About all he could remember from that season was that the freshmen were "mainly cannon fodder for the varsity, because the varsity was very streamlined at that time and they'd kick us around pretty good."[31]

Though vague in many of his college basketball recollections, Rupp had other memories of his freshman year. "You remember that first year because it makes a great deal of impression on you," he said. The pep rallies, in particular, stood out in his mind: "We used to get together and meet up on the campus, and we had men cheerleaders. We didn't have any pompom girls or any girl cheerleaders; they were all men. We used to really give the 'Rock Chalk, Jayhawk, KU' some rip-roaring sound that you could hear all over that town. . . . I remember Robinson Gymnasium seated about fifteen hundred downstairs. We had bleachers that we put up. We could crowd three thousand in there because we also had a track upstairs and we put chairs up there."[32]

Rupp also remembered the lingering effects of the influenza epidemic during his freshman year. University officials canceled all parties, dances, and other campus activities, and only the players' families were allowed into some of the basketball games. The university lifted restrictions with the end of the flu scare later in the semester, and the students made up for lost time. Rupp served on the Varsity Dance Committee of the student council and helped organize a dance every Saturday night. "We had a big hall that we rented downtown," he recalled, "and it was always packed to capacity." Looking back from the 1970s, he said, "I believe we were organized a little better in those days than we are now. . . . Our automobiles are taking a lot of our people away from our organized affairs now. We didn't have cars in those days. I don't know of ten students that had automobiles on our campus. They were absolutely unknown."[33]

According to Rupp, alcohol was another scarce commodity, although it certainly wasn't unknown. Those were the early years of Prohibition, and the state of Kansas led out in the temperance movement. "Not only did they have a federal law against it, but a state law, a city law, and every other kind of a law," Rupp said, adding that "the more laws you pass, the more people try to violate them." This was true for Rupp and his friends.

"The students used to always get together at these fraternity houses where they'd go to these varsity dances, and they'd have a couple of nips before they'd show up," he remembered, "although it was strictly understood that anyone that would be caught with liquor on their breath would be automatically suspended from school." Rupp couldn't recall anyone ever being suspended, and that was no accident. The dean of men and the dean of women supervised the dances, but Rupp and other students "kept them off in a corner where they didn't get around too well."[34]

The state also banned cigarette sales, with about as much success. "We sold cigarettes at the Jayhawk Café," Rupp said. "One day the agents swooped down on us. I guess it was the city cops; we had failed to give them a complimentary meal or something, so they thought they'd make it a little rough on us. They came in there and they caught us with three or four cartons of cigarettes." "Ducky" Ingalls, one of the proprietors, appeared in court and argued that the cigarettes were for his own use. "It was pretty hard to convince the police judge that you need three or four different brands of cigarettes for your personal use, but he got by with it [and] got his cigarettes back," Rupp recalled. "We put 'em back under the stove, and whenever anyone came in and we didn't see anyone snoopin' around, if anyone wanted cigarettes they were sold just like they were every other place in the state of Kansas at that particular time."[35]

Rupp played on the varsity team as a sophomore, but he rarely appeared in games and continued to serve as "cannon fodder" in practices. The *Jayhawker* yearbook identified the young fellow from Halstead as "Udolph Rupp," a center who "played his first season for Kansas." The *Jayhawker* identified Rupp as "a hard worker, and by his early showing will be there next season." But in spite of the hours the players devoted to conditioning under Allen, Rupp's yearbook photograph showed a melancholy, frowning young man with kneepads, slumped shoulders, and already the hint of a paunch.[36]

Although he failed to earn a letter again in his junior season, the 1922 basketball photograph showed a slimmer Rupp appearing more fit and confident, with hands on hips and shoulders squared. A writer described him as "another one of Dr. Allen's dependable substitutes. While not being a regular, Rupp showed up exceptionally good in tight places in the games he did play in. Rupp has been on the Varsity squad two years, has made all of the basket ball trips and can be depended upon to be back next season."

The writer praised his versatility "in that he is both a guard and a forward, holding down either position equally as well as the other." Listed as a center in his sophomore year, Rupp was the classic practice player and undoubtedly mimicked opposing players as Kansas prepared for opposing teams.[37]

Rupp finally earned a letter as a senior. He was listed as "Adolph Fred Rupp" in the yearbook, which stated that he "has been a strong guard on the team for three years. He showed up mighty good in twelve games."[38] Although Rupp's presence on the court was never crucial to the Jayhawks' success, from the sidelines and in practices he learned the rudiments of basketball from one of the early giants of the game.

Basketball had changed since he began playing on the dirt farm court outside of Halstead. The "standing guard," deemed a necessity throughout his high school career, had been eliminated. Instead, college teams used a five-man offense, with one guard getting back with each shot to prevent a long pass for a layup at the other end. At Kansas, rather than devoting practice time to developing new offensive and defensive sets, Allen concentrated on the basics. Rupp did not think the Jayhawks "ever had a definite set of plays" on offense while he was with them, but Allen deployed a new zone defense to counteract the screening, picking offense that University of Missouri coach Walter Meanwell installed. "We couldn't stop it," Rupp remembered, so "Phog put in a zone defense with two men back" close to the basket to control the boards.[39]

Innovations did not interest Allen very much. He made a few adjustments to deal with the new twists created by Meanwell and others, but in his long and tedious practice sessions, Allen continued to emphasize the basic drills that he had used from the outset of his career. In fact, Rupp believed that his mentor "spent entirely too much time on fundamentals," an odd criticism from a coach who became famous for machine-like practice drills in an atmosphere of military precision and discipline. Rupp explained that during Allen's practices "we used sometimes ten or fifteen minutes throwing hook passes." "Why, we didn't use any hook passes in a game," an elderly Rupp remembered. He said the Jayhawks practiced "a lot of those things in those days in our fundamental drills that did not pertain to the game." In his own coaching career, Rupp made constant adjustments to the ever-changing nature of basketball, especially in his early years at the University of Kentucky. But as for repetitious drilling for the sake of fundamentals, he later stated, "We don't do that anymore. We only use things today to develop fundamentals that will be used in our team play."[40]

Rupp recalled that under Allen, "the first day of practice always was about as brutal as anything that you could get. He would practice and practice and practice, pivoting and pivoting and pivoting, all those things, until the blisters would be on your feet the size of a dollar. But he'd keep you out there." Rupp later claimed that at UK he would limit his practices to one hour during the first week. "I tell our boys that as soon as your feet begin to burn, drop out," Rupp also explained. "Or we used to have some ice water and the boys would go over and put their feet in the ice water for a while to take the heat off and then dry their feet and come back out, and they always said that worked out very nicely." Allen "didn't believe in any of that stuff. . . . He never worked three times a day, but he would work twice a day, especially during the holidays or on days we were not in school."[41] According to Rupp, "Phog had no idea of time; time didn't mean a thing to him. He'd start at 2 o'clock in the afternoon, if he felt like it, and practice till 6:30, and then sometimes get us back in the evening and practice some more."[42]

At the same time, Rupp credited Allen as "a great developer of ideas . . . and whether it worked or didn't work, he stayed with it and worked with it and worked it."[43] One of those cherished ideas was that long Christmas layoffs were a bad thing, and he presaged modern coaches by requiring his players to practice throughout the winter break. "One year he took us up to Minneapolis," Rupp recalled, "and after practicing up there for about four or five days or longer, we played the University of Minnesota." In Rupp's senior year, Allen let the players go home for Christmas Day but called them back on December 26 and took them to Omaha to work out for several days before playing Creighton. The players were roused from bed each morning at 5 and practiced twice a day. They stayed three or four to a room at the Blackstone Hotel and played cards until midnight despite Allen's lights-out edict at 10 or 10:30.[44]

Allen's nutritional philosophy was equally stringent. "Everything was light," Rupp recalled. "I don't know if it was due to the fact that we didn't have any money or due to the fact that Phog actually believed that. He was a great crank on eating." Rupp remembered that during his four years at Kansas, "We had one steak, and that was a mistake because the hotel didn't have a piece of roast beef." Breakfast might be half a canned peach, although Allen told the players to "put a lot of sugar in it because that gives you a lot of energy."[45] That wouldn't do for Rupp, who eventually started skipping Allen's meager pregame meals. "I could go down to the Jayhawk Café and eat anything I wanted to, and I knew that to walk up on the campus and eat half of a peach scarcely furnished me with enough energy to get back off of the campus." He would tell his coach that he didn't believe he ought to eat before a game. "It made me nervous," he claimed to avoid scrutiny, "and it upset my stomach."

Although Rupp rebelled against the regimen at the time, he eventually came to believe that Allen had the right idea. "I think today the modern athletes eat too much," he asserted in his later years. "I believe that. I sincerely do. And I think we spoil these kids, and I think we overfeed them, and I think as Phog always said, 'a hungry tiger fights the fiercest.'"[46]

So the Jayhawks feasted on their opponents. Each of those holiday trips led up to the season opener; they served as intense training camps. The trip north during Rupp's junior year resulted in a 32–11 victory over Minnesota, and the Omaha trip the next year produced a 29–7 rout of Creighton in which Kansas led 15–1 at halftime. "I remember just as distinctly as if it were today," an elderly Rupp said, although his renditions of the story sometimes varied. "We held them without a field goal until the last minute of the ballgame, when one of their boys threw one in about twenty-five feet," he recounted in one interview. In another retelling, he said that "one of their Irish boys took a desperation shot from thirty or thirty-five feet out and hit it. That was the only field goal that they got all night." The Jayhawks already looked forward to challenging Missouri for the Missouri Valley Conference championship and, as it turned out, the national title. After the Creighton game, Rupp and his teammates celebrated with a prophetic cheer: "Now, what'll we do, what'll we do; here we go to beat Mizzou!"[47]

An even more memorable trip came at the end of that season. Summoned from class to meet Allen at the gym, the players caught the 10 a.m. interurban train for Kansas City, where they had a long, strenuous workout at the Kansas City Athletic Club before boarding another train for the next leg of the journey to Columbia. The players hadn't eaten anything since breakfast and, failing in his effort to get any food put on the train in Sedalia, Allen wired ahead for 60 cheese sandwiches. "Just a piece of bread with a piece of cheese in it," Rupp remembered. "Oh, it was the driest thing." When they stopped for the night before reaching Columbia, Allen decided it would be "bad for the stomach" to eat that late, so he gave the players only a wafer and a cup of hot chocolate. They "kind of looked at each other as if to say, 'Well, when are we gonna eat,'" Rupp recalled. "We hadn't had anything to eat since morning except for that old dry cheese sandwich, but to bed we went, [and] got up early in the morning" to continue on their way. At Cowan, Missouri, they waited for another train from Columbia to pick them up, but it "ran a shoe off" the driving wheel. Allen called for a bus, and the players lounged around "two or three Negro cabins," as Rupp put it.[48]

Allen remembered the story a little differently in *My Basket-ball Bible*, published in 1924, the year after the trip. He wrote that the team was stranded at McBain, just nine miles from Columbia. And his rendition is eerily reminiscent of a scene that Rupp himself would describe upon his arrival by train in Lexington to interview for the Kentucky job in 1930. According to Allen, "McBain, aside from the station and a typical Missouri negro eating shack, does not exist. True to the traditions of the South, these negroes who ran the eating shack served only their own color. But on this morning, they were asked to serve eleven hungry white men who had eaten only dry sandwiches for dinner the evening before. So the colored population moved out of the shack and our basket-ball team moved in. We sat on soap boxes for chairs and ate from dry goods boxes for tables. The menu was 'Ole Missouri sow-belly and eggs,' some half-cooked oatmeal with milk—all washed down with bitter coffee." In his 1937 book, *Better Basketball: Technique, Tactics, and Tales*, Allen revised the tale a tad: "All was either washed down with bitter coffee or left to stick in our throats. We looked upon the drinking water with suspicion."[49]

In Rupp's telling of the tale, Allen talked one of the women into cooking breakfast, but there were only four or five eggs in the shack. So "the first four or five guys that sat down got an egg apiece and a piece of bread, and she cooked a little coffee and the rest of us didn't get anything."[50]

Instead of a bus, what Allen called a "picnic truck," basically a moving van with seats in it and canvas curtains on the sides to keep out the weather, picked up the team. About a mile and a half down the road, a fan belt broke. The driver repaired it with a piece of barbed wire cut from a farmer's fence, and they were on the road again, singing as they went. Allen started it with the Kansas alma mater and followed with "I'm a Jay-Jay-Jay-Hawk." "It was imperative that we keep up the team morale," the coach wrote, "for the big battle was to be staged in less than eight hours." The Jayhawks finally made it to Columbia around noon to ready themselves for the game that evening.[51]

Road-weary and grimy, the players nonetheless were put through a brief workout before showering and going to a hotel at 1 p.m. for a long-awaited meal, which turned out to be the solitary steak dinner of Rupp's college career. They followed that welcome feast with a short walk, a two-hour nap, and a two-mile hike "to overcome grogginess." Then came a snack of weak tea, toast, and sliced peaches at 5 p.m. before they finally had a 30-minute team meeting to discuss Missouri's style of play. That's how the Kansas basketball team got ready for a game that would decide the national championship of 1923.[52]

Each team made only one field goal in the first half, and the score stood at 6–6 at the break. In an era before managers and trainers, Rupp and the others who hadn't seen action busied themselves getting water and towels for the weary starters during the short halftime intermission. Allen described the scene: "In the Kansas dressing room, five substitutes worked feverishly over five panting men. It was serious business. Not a word was spoken. A bigger battle loomed ahead. For four minutes, the regulars rested, relaxed, eyes closed and cold packs on their heads." Piling on the melodrama, he wrote: "Sensitive ears all over the state of Kansas were waiting for news of victory. We were in the hands of the enemy, half through and scores even, and even scores did not win games. More power was needed." According to Allen, that power came from the taunts of Missouri fans: "Down the stairs came the sounds of that familiar battle cry, 'Eat that Rock-Chalk Jay-Hawk up! Eat that Rock-Chalk Jay-Hawk up! Yea, Missouri!' This was the cement that bound. In the minds of these boys, the game took on a new meaning. Before, it meant two universities; now, it meant two states. The Kansans went on the court again with jaws set, souls on fire."[53]

So much for James Naismith's ideal of a wholesome team game to promote physical fitness. Allen had transformed basketball into a gargantuan battle between two states—the righteous, beleaguered Jayhawkers from Kansas against the border ruffians from Missouri.

Kansas went on to win 23–20 to complete a 16–0 season in the Missouri Valley Conference, and the Helms Foundation named the "ever victorious" Jayhawks the 1923 national champions. As with most Jayhawk games during his varsity career, Adolph Rupp had watched the whole thing from the bench. Allen did not make a single substitution. Afterward, Rupp and the other substitutes helped the exhausted, cramping star, Paul Endacott, to the basement dressing room, where Allen "worked on him twenty minutes" before they could get him comfortable. To the coach, "this picture of these men who had given their all, bent over their team mate who had given part of his superhuman self, lasts."[54] That solemn rendering of the event indicated a tendency as early as the 1920s to make basketball more than a game. At stake was nothing less than honor—for the individual, the team, the university, the state, and for the game itself.

Certainly, Rupp reveled, albeit somewhat vicariously, in the joy of victory and the satisfaction of success at such a high level of collegiate sports.[55] He also soaked up the attitudes of Phog Allen and his Jayhawker teammates. Lawrence, like Halstead, was almost devoid of African Americans. The Halstead High School senior play in which Rupp had starred had presented a stereotypical, comic portrayal of a black porter. During the early 1920s in Lawrence, contemporaries remembered only one elderly free black man in town. Rupp's attitude toward African Americans developed around the telling and retelling by teammates and classmates of stories and jokes full of racial stereotypes and degradations. He told the story again and again of the "negro shacks" and the inadequate breakfast provided by the black women during the momentous trip to Missouri for the 1923 championship game. Phog Allen, Rupp's mentor, revealed his own prejudices in his books.

Allen had an impact on Rupp in other ways. Even though Rupp often joked about his coach's quirky rituals, he built his own career on idiosyncratic superstitions. Rupp's own legendary eccentricities, "the Baron of the Bluegrass" and "the Man in the Brown Suit" monikers, his widely known superstitions, did not materialize out of thin air. He learned these from a mentor, perfected them as a diligent student, and then calculated to create a larger-than-life character.

So too would the discipline and machine-like precision with which Allen coached the Jayhawks become a hallmark of Rupp's teams at Kentucky. That might also have been a product of the times. Even a farm boy like Rupp would have read about the deadly efficiency of the new weapons of World War I, and the roaring twenties were a decade of consumption, an age that glorified efficiency in business and industry. Even in a rural state like Kansas, sportswriters used industrial terminology. At the end of Rupp's sophomore year, the *Jayhawker* predicted that "the inexperienced team of this season will be a scientific, well-oiled machine by next year and should give somebody a hard race for the Valley title." The 1922 *Jayhawker* suggested that by season's end "the Kansas five worked up a scoring machine." Then in 1923, Rupp's senior season, one writer stated that "no other school in the Valley had a quintet with as machine-like floor work and basket shooting and with its integral parts so perfectly co-ordinated."[56]

It would be a stretch to suggest that Adolph Rupp was an integral cog in that machine. In 1923 the *Jayhawker* listed him as one of eight "old stand-bys" who "turned out in addition to good secondary material when Coach Allen issued the call for basketball candidates."[57] Phog Allen himself stated, "If I said [Rupp] was a great player, I'd only be indulging a professional courtesy." But Paul Endacott, the Jayhawks' star guard, wryly noted, "Rupp was forced to sit there [on the bench] and listen for three or four seasons. He had to pick up something."[58] Clearly, he did.

Rupp graduated in 1923 with a degree in economics. In addition to basketball and his job at the Jayhawk Café, he served on the Professional Pan-Hellenic Council as a representative from Delta Sigma Pi, the professional commerce fraternity; was on the men's student council; chaired the institution's Olympics committee; and was an enthusiastic member of the K Club. He took advantage of all that the state university had to offer.[59]

Rupp remembered his graduation on a hot June day in a big tent where "some important fellow"—the commencement speaker—"tried to save not only the country, he tried to save the world that day; a long-winded old guy." After Rupp walked across the platform to receive his diploma "came that awful realization that you had to find a job." Unable to find lucrative employment, he stayed in Lawrence to begin graduate school in economics.[60] Several stops in three states would follow before he came to the place that would define him for the rest of his days.

3

Before Big Blue, 1923–1930

After graduating from the University of Kansas, Adolph Rupp tried to land a banking or business job in Topeka or Wichita but found nothing. "I went to the biggest bank in Topeka," he remembered. "One of the officers told me the only way you're going to get anywhere in the banking business is to marry into the family. I told him I wasn't sure I wanted to get in it that much. That closed the door on my banking career." So he tied on his apron at the Jayhawk Café again and entered graduate school as a teaching assistant in the economics department. He helped Phog Allen with the basketball team as an "unofficial coaching assistant," and he supervised economics classes and graded papers in the mornings. Though he described it as "a thankless job," it did have its benefits.[1]

"Whenever these cute little ol' girls found out who was grading the papers, you don't realize how popular you get all at once," Rupp recalled as an old man. Characteristically chauvinistic, he said that "girls didn't like to study any more in those days than they do now, especially economics." Even though the jazz age was a decade in which new educational and career opportunities opened up for women in many cities and towns, Kansas coeds seemed slow to take advantage, at least in Rupp's opinion. "They didn't care about that a great deal," Rupp said. "I don't know if you should teach girls economics. Maybe you ought to just hand them a little money every morning, and when they get that all spent that's the end of the economics for them."[2]

But anxious female students would search out the young graduate assistant at the café. "They'd ask me a lot of questions, you know, but

49

[then] I'd get those papers back and find just blank, blank, blank pages that they hadn't answered," Rupp recalled. "And then [there was] that true and false thing, and that sure was a mess." He said,

> Those little ol' things would come in there and want to know what their grades were, and I'd tell them, "Well, I just don't remember what your grades were. You'll have to go up and get that from the professor." Then the professor would tell them, "Well, you got an F," or something like that. Then they'd come down cryin' and want to know if I couldn't do something about it, that they were going to get kicked out of their sorority if they don't get a good grade. Of course, that wasn't my fault. My fault was that I had to grade those papers and just give them the grade that they earned.[3]

Rupp admitted that he eventually became a little more lenient, especially with "the essay-type questions. I knew the professors weren't going to check two hundred papers and see if I wasn't a little lenient with some of these little angels, so I helped some of those little girls a little bit."[4]

In December he learned of a midyear opening at a tiny high school in Burr Oak, a town in north-central Kansas near the Nebraska line. Principal Ira Brammell received a strong letter of recommendation from Phog Allen, and the school hired the 23-year-old Rupp to teach history and coach football and basketball.[5] He weighed an opportunity to go to Arkansas City at the same salary, but reluctant to return to his old stomping grounds and work for a Halstead rival, he decided on Burr Oak, where he wound up coaching "all of it": football, basketball, baseball, and track. "I don't know why I ever took that job," he said later.[6]

He soon learned that the challenges of coaching and teaching in a small school in rural Kansas did not match the idealistic memories of his own high school days, when he was the de facto basketball coach. Upon his arrival at Burr Oak, he discovered that the basketball team had no gymnasium and the football team had no uniforms. "Imagine my surprise when the football players showed up in overalls, saying there was no equipment at the school," he said. Principal Brammell and his young coach met with the superintendent and school board and got the go-ahead to order uniforms, but permission came with strict instructions: "Order as little of it as you can get by on." Rupp and Brammell paid the bill themselves, and when both left the school for other positions a year later, they threatened to take the uniforms with them until the school board finally agreed to reimburse them.[7]

Undoubtedly missing the college-town excitement of Lawrence, Rupp wrote to a friend back in Halstead on October 2, 1924: "Things around here are pretty dry. We could use a little rain. The wheat is fast getting into the ground and people are getting ready for the winter. I understand it gets as low as 22° below zero here. If that's the case, I am going to order me some galvanized underpants to keep from freezing." As for the prospects for his first team, he assured his friend that "I am going to have a pretty good football team here. My line will weigh about 160 and backfield about 153. They are pretty fast also and have some dandy plays." With no gymnasium, the basketball team practiced and played at the town's lumberyard in a ramshackle barn that doubled as a skating rink. "Whenever they didn't skate, we could play basketball in there," Rupp recalled, "and that was a mess." "You can imagine skating in there," he said, "and getting the floor all slick and everything else and then having basketball practice." After a year and a semester, he concluded, "I had all I wanted. I didn't want any more of that."[8]

We know nothing about Rupp's teaching in Burr Oak's history classroom, but he did like to read history in later years. With a degree in economics and one semester of graduate work in that subject, he taught out of his field, but that was not unusual in the early twentieth century, when some schools still hired teachers without degrees at lower salaries. We do know that he made an impression on his students on the football field, the basketball court, and the track. Wilbur Naylor played quarterback in football and guard in basketball on Rupp's first teams. A 96-year-old Naylor remembered him as "pretty strict" but also "a very personable individual." Practices lasted only an hour, but Rupp would have held them even on Sundays if the school board hadn't denied him permission. Rural Kansas was not yet willing to disrupt a day of rest and worship to accommodate an eager young coach.[9]

Naylor remembered Rupp's football team as only "average," but basketball was a different matter. The *Burr Oak Herald* reported on January 22, 1925, that Rupp coached the "best Burr Oak boys' team that ever fought for the orange and black."[10] With immediate success at tiny Burr Oak, Rupp soon looked for a bigger stage. Back home to visit his family at

Thanksgiving in 1924, Rupp met fellow Halstead native Bryan R. Miller, who recently had graduated from Kansas State Teachers College in Pittsburg and had just been hired as principal of Marshalltown High School in central Iowa, one of the state's largest schools. Miller asked Rupp if he would "like to go with him and teach basketball to central Iowa boys." Rupp immediately responded, "You bet I would!" With words that he would later echo at another job interview, he added: "Take away Coach Allen and there's no one in the state of Kansas who knows basketball like I do. And I'll bet there's no one in Iowa who knows basketball like I do either." So in the summer of 1925, the two Kansans loaded their bags into Miller's touring car "and headed north by northeast to a place neither had even heard of a year or so earlier."[11]

Rupp was impressed with Marshalltown, where the school board already had decided to build a new high school to be completed the next year. He moved into the YMCA, "where all the young men stayed," and he and his new friends would "all go swimming in the evening, and play cards and have a good time." But he soon got a jolt. When classes started in September, the board had yet to make an official decision on the head basketball coaching position that Miller had promised to Rupp.[12] Russell E. Dickinson, a young assistant coach already at the school, wanted the job. Dickinson's brother, Warren, also taught and coached in the district, and both brothers were described as "popular and well-known men about town." With the support of the faculty and despite pleas from Miller and Rupp—in what would become a familiar refrain, Rupp bragged to the board that he "was the best basketball coach in the entire Midwest"—Russell got the job. As a consolation prize, Rupp was offered positions as coach of the wrestling team and line coach of the football team. "I didn't know anything about wrestling," he said many years later. "I'd never seen a wrestling match in my life."[13]

With no other prospects, he accepted the assignment and tried to make the best of it. He checked out a book on wrestling from the public library, then walked to a small house on South First Street to talk with one of the town's best-known residents. Allie Morrison, a high school senior only four years younger than Rupp, had made a name for himself by winning an Iowa Amateur Athletic Union (AAU) wrestling championship as a junior. Morrison, described by Rupp as "a clever little rascal," was too old to compete in high school during the second semester of his senior year, so

Rupp asked him to serve as his assistant coach. It was agreed that Morrison "would handle the technical aspects of coaching, while Rupp would still be the authority figure and prime motivator."[14]

"I didn't know one hold from the other," Rupp admitted. "All I knew is that you take a guy and throw him on his back and try to pin him; that's all I knew about it." He claimed he would "sneak" into practices and try to learn all he could, and he concluded that "Allie was doing a fine job."[15] Rupp would repeat this coaching pattern to some extent later in his career as basketball coach at Kentucky. He turned over responsibility for devising and teaching specific defensive sets and offensive plays to assistants such as Paul McBrayer, Elmer "Baldy" Gilb, and Harry Lancaster, while Rupp remained the primary motivator. He would perfect the art of motivation not so much through inspiration, but through intimidation and fear. And just as he soaked up, spongelike, the wrestling rules and training tips from Morrison during that one-year stint in Marshalltown, he would one day absorb basketball strategy from his knowledgeable assistants during long evening sessions and automobile trips to high school games in central Kentucky.

Even as a novice wrestling coach, Rupp applied ideas about proper training that he had learned from Phog Allen. One writer suggested that he "watched over the eating habits of his charges like an old mother hen" and "regularly checked the homes of his Bobcat wrestlers for curfew violations at night." The Bobcats responded to the teaching of Morrison and the motivation of Rupp by going undefeated through the regular season and entering the Iowa High School Athletic Association's new state tournament in 1926 as the odds-on favorites. When Marshalltown's superintendent refused to allow the ineligible Morrison to accompany the team to Ames, Rupp—who later referred to himself as simply "a faculty sponsor" (much like those "chaperones" back at Halstead High)—had to go it alone, relying on what he had learned of proper maneuvers from his young assistant.[16]

The team stayed in a fraternity house in Ames, and the night before the tournament, Marshalltown's 80-pound wrestler fell from a top bunk and severely injured a shoulder. Rupp remembered that the young man "cried all night long" and said he would have to disqualify himself.[17] Rupp wouldn't hear of it. "You've got to wrestle," he remembered telling him, noting that with only four competitors in the division, Marshalltown would earn a point just for starting the match. "If you don't win anything, we'll at least get one point out of the deal." In another conversation he admitted he had not realized that a point would be gained simply for participating. Instead, he argued that the wrestler must compete for another reason: "I don't care if he's pinned in a second, every Bobcat will take the mat. No one will ever quit!"[18] For whatever reason, Rupp forced the 80-pounder to take the mat. He was pinned immediately, but that single point was the margin of victory in the meet. "By Jove," Rupp said, "That was the point that we won the state wrestling championship with."[19]

"You can imagine how I felt walking up there and getting the trophy for having coached the state championship team," Rupp said. "Oh, they had a big crowd. They turned out crowds there and at Oklahoma State bigger than they do for basketball. . . . Man, that place was jammed."[20]

It was a considerably more sheepish Rupp who presented the trophy to Principal Miller at the Marshalltown winter sports banquet that year. "I never felt as bad in my life as I did that day," he said, "when I knew I was presenting something to a high school and didn't have a thing to do with it except that I was just the chaperone of the team. Allie Morrison should have had the credit for it, and of course we gave him all the credit for it. He was just a tremendous help, and if it hadn't been for Allie, I don't think we'd have had a wrestling team that year, because I sure didn't know anything about it." One witness recalled Rupp's specific words that evening: "Yes, I was the coach of this team, but I'm not the man responsible for our state championship. That man is sitting right over there."[21]

In an interview in the 1990s, Morrison's daughter said her father "always spoke so highly of Coach Rupp, and he never forgot that banquet when Rupp was presented with the Iowa wrestling trophy after the team had won the state meet. He always talked about how Rupp stood before that crowd and told everyone that it was Allie Morrison who really deserved to be up there accepting the trophy."[22] One writer noted that Russell Dickinson, "whose Bobcat cagers had suffered through another mediocre season, shooting two-hundred set shots, under-handed free throws and running the offense at a crawl," was also in the audience that night.[23]

Rupp had a close relationship with Morrison, who wound up following him to Illinois, at Rupp's urging, to attend the University of Illinois in Champaign rather than the University of Iowa. While at Illinois, Morrison remained unbeaten in AAU competition—that was before the debut of the NCAA tournament—and won the 135-pound division at the 1928 Olympics in Amsterdam, the first Iowan to earn an Olympic gold medal in any sport. An injury ended his wrestling career soon after that, but he graduated from Illinois in 1930 with a degree in English and physical education, and he taught and coached in high school for many years.[24]

"Dad always said that Coach Rupp was the greatest influence on him during his final year in Marshalltown, and he did his best to steer Dad away from Iowa and to Illinois," Morrison's daughter said. Her father once told her that Rupp felt he "would be much better off away from the glare of the publicity that the star wrestler was receiving in Iowa. You have to realize that he was still undefeated in high school and AAU. His fame had become more regional and even national, but Rupp thought that a college career based in Illinois, where Allie wasn't as well-known, would allow Allie to concentrate on wrestling without having to handle all of the build-up and publicity."[25]

Rupp had cultivated several Illinois contacts of his own through James Naismith and Phog Allen. The one that was to prove particularly important was Craig Ruby, the head basketball coach at the University of Illinois. He had played for Walter Meanwell at Missouri, and Meanwell, Ruby, Allen, Naismith, and Rupp had a mutual respect for each other.

At the same time Rupp was steering Morrison toward Illinois, he was looking in that direction himself after a single year at Marshalltown. Ruby recommended Rupp for a high school coaching position in Illinois. "I got a letter one day from Freeport, Illinois, wanting to know if I would be interested in their job," he recalled. "Well, there would be no harm in going over there and looking at this thing." He hopped a train to Freeport, booked a room at the YMCA, and went to meet the principal the next morning. He was immediately taken with L. A. Fulwider. He "should have been the principal of every high school in the United States," Rupp claimed, adding that Fulwider was a man "that you just don't run across very often in the school system. This fellow was just as loyal as he could be." Rupp, who also was impressed with the brand-new school building and gymnasium, was promised the reins of an already successful basketball program and a job as the line coach in football, at a $300 raise over his salary at Marshalltown. It was an easy decision.[26]

"Well, of course, I hated to leave there," he said. "I didn't know anyone at Freeport, and I was just going into another strange situation. You can move too many times, but I knew this was a good opportunity. I wanted to coach basketball anyway. I didn't want to fool with this wrestling anymore. And I wanted a job of my own. And I was getting $300 more going into a beautiful school system, and the people I met there all looked honest to me. They tried to talk me out of it there at Marshalltown, but I stayed hitched."[27]

He did heed the advice of Principal Miller and the Marshalltown school superintendent, however. "Those men insisted that I go on and get my master's degree," Rupp recalled. "They said if you're going to get any-where in the school business, you've got to have an advanced degree." So he and another young teacher took a train to Columbia University's Teach-ers College in New York and enrolled in summer classes. He did that for four straight summers before earning his master's and a principal's diplo-ma. "I was going in the school-teaching business," Rupp said.[28]

Although he knew no one in Freeport upon his arrival, he found himself in somewhat familiar surroundings. Rupp described the northern Illinois town as "just a small, little, German-Dutch community in an ag-ricultural area," and the preponderance of students with German names such as Ruthe, Becker, Rinehart, Goetz, and Schlegal made him feel at home. In fact, the Freeport of 1926 must have appeared to be a larger, more prosperous version of Halstead, Kansas. Just as Rupp had done in his youth, many rural Freeport High students took rooms in town from Mon-day morning until Friday afternoon, and many students earned spending money through after-school jobs.[29]

"The farmers there were very, very thrifty," Rupp said approvingly. "They had very fine homes; they had very fine farms. The barns were nice; the outbuildings were all nice." The corn, cattle, and hog farming, cou-pled with several factories, made for a stable economy. "It was said at the time that Freeport did not have a depression," he noted, and that "Free-port, along with Hershey, Pennsylvania, did not miss a payroll during the big Depression." Another benefit, as one writer suggested, was that with Chicago nearby, a winning basketball coach "could get plenty of metro ink."[30]

But despite the familiar feel, everything in the community was new to Rupp. He taught in a new building, coached in a new gymnasium, and lived in a new YMCA, which had 70 sparse but comfortable rooms for young teachers, salesmen, and others with nowhere else to stay. At that time the YMCA also served as a social center. "We had a bowling alley, we had a pool room, we had swimming pools, and we just enjoyed staying there," Rupp recalled. A restaurant opened in the building later on, and he took most of his meals there.[31]

Rupp lived in a room adjoining that of a young man named Elmer Hoffman, who became his scorekeeper and best friend. The two soon developed an evening routine, walking to Tinsley's Cigar Store to buy a Chicago newspaper that arrived on the Hawkeye Limited at around 8:30, then checking it for sports scores and stock-market numbers. Like so many others during the bull market of the 1920s, Rupp and Hoffman bought some stocks, although they certainly weren't major investors. "We had one or two men there in town that gave us some very fine tips on some stocks that made us some good money, and we thought this thing had been going on pretty good," Rupp remembered. "It beat teaching school, and we thought, by George, this was an easy way to make some money, only to find out that in 1929, in one afternoon, we lost about everything that we had and then some."[32]

Freeport High was situated on a 25-acre tract of land, and the 1,500-seat gym, dedicated the year before Rupp's arrival, was described in one newspaper report as "such a spacious hall [that] many of the fans [were] really wondering whether they were in Freeport or in some foreign college city seated in a regular college gymnasium." For Rupp, this was promising indeed.[33]

He taught history and found himself coaching track in addition to basketball and football. As would be the case at the University of Kentucky four years later, he took over a basketball squad that already knew great success. The Freeport Pretzels—sometimes called the "Holmesmen" in tribute to star player Glenn "Pat" Holmes—had won the state championship in 1915. They did it again in 1926, the year before Rupp arrived, this time with Holmes as the head coach. Holmes also won a national championship in high school football in December 1925, when Freeport traveled to Pittsburgh as "the champions of the Middle West" and defeated East champion Ellwood City, Pennsylvania, 13–7.[34]

Holmes's phenomenal success actually created the opening for Rupp.[35] The popular Holmes had received several offers at higher pay in 1925 but, realizing that Freeport had excellent prospects in both football and basketball in the coming year, he wisely postponed a move. He eventually became the freshman basketball coach at the University of Wisconsin, where he worked under Rupp's old nemesis Walter Meanwell.

Holmes's success had been due in part to his practice of surrounding himself with able assistants. Jimmy Laude, a former University of Iowa star, taught defense and went on to become head coach of archrival Rockford High, where he gave Rupp fits during his brief tenure at Freeport. Then there was Paul "Spats" Moon, who stuck around awhile under Rupp before becoming head coach at Davenport High in Iowa, where he would amass a 541–111 record and win seven state titles in 26 seasons. Rupp's later attitude toward his players seemed to mimic Moon, who distanced himself from them. Ken Buckles, who played for Moon in Davenport, recalled, "Losing was unthinkable. You didn't get the kick you were supposed to out of victories, because you were so relieved you didn't lose." Even after lopsided victories, "he never said, 'Nice game.' He just walked through the locker room and went on out the back of the gym." Nor did Moon mind the heckling of opposing fans. "When you're as good as we are, you've got to expect things like that," Moon said.[36]

But Rupp took something else from Moon: his trademark fast-break offense. "We averaged more points a game than teams do now because we ran up and down the floor," Buckles said in 2002.[37]

Rather than a true assistant, Moon coached the "lightweight" team at Freeport. Holmes had garnered his fame with the "heavies," the varsity. Illinois's unique system of high school athletics at the time provided for two divisions, heavyweight ("regulars") and lightweight ("ponies"), in both basketball and football. Boys weighing less than 135 pounds played in the lightweight division in basketball. In football the cutoff was 140. It was designed to increase participation and level out competition, but Rupp said there was one drawback: the overzealous lightweight coach who "got these kids that weighed about 140–145 pounds and had them train down and lose weight to take them off of the heavyweight squad so that he'd have a good lightweight team."[38]

That had been an issue at Freeport, and as the new heavyweight coach, Rupp made an early appointment with Principal Fulwider to discuss it. "I told the principal I didn't think much of that," he remembered. "I thought that the heavyweight team was the team that represented the school and that anybody that I wanted I ought to have." Fulwider listened patiently and, "after fussing around a little bit," agreed with Rupp. So the new coach "got a nice bunch of boys out and we went to work."[39]

In the four years that Rupp coached at Freeport, he established patterns that he would take with him to Kentucky. He followed a very successful coach, stuck to a particular style of play, and relied heavily on dependable assistants for offensive and defensive strategy while he served primarily as the motivator, pushing the players to work harder and produce more. He also carefully cultivated the press, often planting stories with local reporters that cast him as the demanding mentor, never satisfied with his team's performance. In this regard, Freeport proved to be a perfect place for Rupp. Tiny, isolated Burr Oak, Kansas, did not have access to media outlets necessary to satisfy his craving for attention. Freeport was close enough to Chicago to get some of that "metro ink."[40]

Rupp inherited a team that had won the state championship the year before, but the only returning player was a strong, versatile guard named Ralph Ruthe, who was captain of both the basketball and football teams. The rest of the boys—50 tried out—had never played "lightweight ball or anything." So Rupp "had to go to work fundamentally, right from the very beginning." As early as October 1926 he began to conduct daily basketball classes "for the benefit of the boys not out for basketball" so he could prepare them to play the following year.[41]

With each week, he learned more and more about the prospects for the approaching season. With a weak front line, he shifted Ruthe from his back-guard position to center. "The local forwards and centers have been doing very well at goal throwing," a writer concluded in what was to become a weekly account of the team's progress. "But Rupp is not entirely satisfied, feeling that they need plenty of practice at that end of the game," he explained further. "Both Rupp and (assistant George) Zuelke appear to know the game very well, and the manner in which they go about their work indicates they will have a team that Freeport will not have to be ashamed of. Both men believe in driving their players to the limit, which appears to be a good theory with high school athletes."[42]

The Pretzels had several preseason scrimmages against smaller schools in the area, which were eager to play in Freeport's spacious new gymnasium. Rupp went home to Halstead during the Christmas break and missed the first "exhibition," an 18–14 double-overtime loss to the Illinois School of the Deaf, coached by former Freeport student Robey Burns. "It was during the Christmas holidays, and the principal said that it didn't make any difference whether I stayed there or not," Rupp said, but he admitted it was a mistake to miss even an exhibition game.[43]

The Pretzels lost another warm-up game in December, 32–25, to an alumni team of players from the 1926 state champions, but they won their regular-season opener 21–16 against Dubuque, Iowa, in January. One reporter said the Pretzels showed flashes of good basketball—undoubtedly the "result of the hard drills given them by the local mentor last week"— and could be "at least an average team by the end of the season."[44] Rupp would not be satisfied with average. After the game he talked with a local reporter and planted the following story:

> If the heavies do not come through in proper shape this season, the blame is due to the fact that there are too many blind girls in Freeport High School.
>
> Every time there is a call for classes at the school each day, most major basketball players lead fair co-eds through the halls of the building and up to their classrooms. The broad-shouldered athletes invariably have one or two of the co-eds hanging on well-muscled arms.
>
> Coach Rupp has come to the conclusion that the fair damsels must be blind or they could find their way to the classroom without the aid of the gallant cage warriors. He added that the interference of the maids upset his well-laid plans to make his athletes think basketball as well as play it.
>
> Of course, he also wants them to think of their studies, but he feels that the athletes cannot devote a certain portion of their minds to the co-eds, another portion to their studies and still have another portion left for basketball.[45]

Not the first or last coach to blame poor play on a preoccupation with girls, Rupp imposed a 10 p.m. curfew and discouraged his players from attending evening social functions. Russell Rice believed that Rupp "was particularly nervous about the effect of females on his boys' rest and on their powers of concentration." He once banned two players from practice for a week after catching them parking with girls in an isolated cemetery. "Love affairs have wrecked many a good ballclub," Rupp later told a civic group. "I consider them along with the player's physical development and proper basketball instruction."[46]

Freeport beat West Aurora 25–22 in its first Big Seven Conference game, then lost three in a row to Belvidere, East Aurora, and Streator. A newspaper report said the team was "lacking in coordination," with the offense and defense both "very weak." One writer already was wondering if Rupp had lost control of things: "Some of the fellows of the team have not been keeping very rigid training," even though "Coach Rupp has put the men on their honor in regard to this. The men should realize that their conditioning means a great deal to the game they play, and any player who is out late, night after night, will be dead on his feet in a game."[47]

Perhaps a Rupp-planted story. In any event, he apparently "dished up an entirely new line of offensive attacks for his boys," and the result was a 20–19 victory over Elgin. "Rupp changed the style of attack of his team, gave them new plays and brushed up their defense as well as offense during the week," the *Freeport Journal-Standard* reported. "The improvement was such that many of the fans marveled at the exhibition, giving Rupp and Zuelke full credit."[48]

Another win over Belvidere was followed by a 36–24 defeat to New Trier, the Chicago Suburban League champion. Next up was a 9–0 Joliet team, and Rupp apparently used the motivational style he came to be known for at Kentucky. A reporter wrote that the coach "has cussed and discussed the play of the heavies for some time and is now in hopes of getting them in the mood where they will make themselves overcome all obstacles and set out to win or die in the attempt." Rupp and Zuelke "were doing their utmost to flail their charges into shape, and from all reports the boys seem to be responding." For a boost of confidence before the big game, Rupp pitted his starters against the subs—the "Lost Battalion," a nickname he used again at UK—and the regulars ran up the score.[49]

It all paid off in a 19–17 victory, and the press was enthralled. One reporter gushed that "Coach Rupp and his charges could have had the whole town had they but asked for it." Comparisons with the previous year's championship team were suddenly forgotten.[50] Now reports of the Pretzels' season turned rosy. Even when Streator thrashed Freeport, 38–12, the day after the upset of Joliet, the local paper downplayed the loss because it wasn't a conference game and because Rupp had used his younger reserves most of the way to get an idea what he would have the next year. Already he had mastered the art of playing the media.[51]

Freeport followed the Streator debacle with a 32–15 win over DeKalb. But with a chance to tie Joliet for the league title, the Pretzels were thrashed by Rockford, 29–13, in the regular-season finale after leading 11–7 at halftime. "The Freeport aggregation went down fighting and has no alibis to offer for the defeat," the local paper reported.[52] Rupp's rivalry with Rockford coach Jim Laude would intensify, but they also became friends. Each summer they both attended the Columbia University Teachers College, where they took classes together, had dinner together, and compared notes on basketball strategy.[53]

With two weeks to prepare for the district tournament in March, Rupp scheduled scrimmages with Laude's Rockford team. The preparation apparently helped, because Freeport beat Warren, 28–11, in the first round, although the *Freeport Standard-Journal* reported that "Raggedy Ann never looked more ragged" than the Pretzels. They rolled past Rockton, 44–11, and South Beloit, 35–11, the next two nights before losing the final to Rockford, 33–15. Rupp's first Freeport team finished 10–7, a far cry from the 17–3 and 19–2 records of Pat Holmes's last two teams, but at the awards banquet Rupp opined that his team "had developed much better than anyone had expected."[54]

Rupp singled out one letterman for special recognition: junior William Moseley, one of only six African Americans at Freeport High and the only one on the athletic teams (Moseley apparently tried out for everything). Although he rarely saw action in basketball that season, Rupp lauded his determination to participate. Moseley had "been out for every branch of athletics for the past three years," but the letter Rupp awarded him was his first. Rupp "praised the stick-to-itiveness of Moseley and offered it as an example to the other boys of the school."[55] Moseley, a husky 5-foot-10-inch junior, rode the bench throughout the season, but contributed to the team nonetheless.

The way had been paved for a black athlete such as Moseley to participate in Freeport sports a decade earlier by George Dewey Lipscomb, who became in 1917 the first African American graduate of Freeport High School. By all accounts Lipscomb had been a remarkable student. A brilliant orator, Lipscomb went on to earn a degree from Northwestern University and then taught at Wiley College, Virginia State, and Howard University as a professor of English and speech. Not an athlete, at Freeport

Lipscomb played in the band and competed on the debate team. He won an Illinois state championship in oratory.

Chosen to deliver the class valedictory address at his 1917 graduation, Lipscomb thanked those at Freeport who "have taken me into their friendship and have treated me as a brother in this great family." Lipscomb also thanked the Freeport faculty for "laboring with us during the past four years in a most zealous manner." Freeport's first African American graduate reserved special praise for Principal Fulwider, the administrator who had hired Rupp and who Rupp believed "should have been principal of every high school in the United States." "I can say for myself," Lipscomb said, "that it is [Principal Fulwider] who has been, to a great extent, the incentive causing me to dream dreams of success and to make these dreams a reality. Our association with him and others of this faculty will greatly aid us in the future to see our tasks clearly and execute them in a creditable manner." With the world at war, Lipscomb concluded his valedictory address by stating that "the greatest enemies to peace and harmony are narrow-mindedness and selfishness. Against these evils must be waged our greatest war for the advancement of civilization."[56]

Rupp surely heard older Freeport faculty members recall Dewey Lipscomb's achievements as the first black graduate of Freeport High School. Rupp himself had had little contact with African Americans at Halstead or the University of Kansas, or at either of his first two teaching and coaching jobs. Indeed, in Kansas, Rupp had only encountered black caricatures and stereotypes in a senior class play or at a roadside shack on a Jayhawk road trip. At Freeport, however, he found an environment that at least gave African Americans an opportunity to participate and even excel. Concerned with his image and determined to be successful and to be recognized for his success, Rupp followed the lead of the respected principal, W. A. Fulwider, a leader who had facilitated the integration of Freeport High School over a decade before Adolph Rupp's arrival. During the basketball banquet at the end of his first season as the head coach of the Freeport Pretzels, Adolph Rupp went out of his way to praise the contributions of a little-used African American substitute named William Moseley.

After another summer at Columbia, Rupp assisted new football coach Robert H. Wiecke in the 1927 season.[57] One of the newcomers on the squad was William Moseley, who wound up starting several games at half-back. The Freeport newspaper referred to him as "Moseley, the colored boy" in almost every account of his play.[58]

Although football season was not yet over, Rupp began basketball practice early in November. To unearth hidden talent in the student body, he organized an impromptu intra-school league in which physical education classes would play each other, with no returning basketball lettermen allowed to participate.[59] He encouraged these novice players with a range of competitions, giving out trophies to the winners of free-throw contests and "21" games as well as to the best all-around athlete.[60]

With only four lettermen back on the heavyweight squad, Rupp would have to rely on six lightweight players moving up, plus any prospects he might spot in those gym matches.[61] He also organized the "Lost Battalion," composed of freshmen and sophomores "not good enough to make the regular squad."[62]

Arthur Steffen, captain of Freeport's lightweight squad the previous season, emerged as a team leader, and Rupp named him captain of the heavyweights. William Moseley and some of the other football players arrived after that season ended.[63] Originally penciled in as a reserve, Moseley stepped into the lineup when Steffen suffered a knee injury in the opening game.[64] The problem was that Moseley graduated when the winter term ended in mid-January. He went out in fine fashion in a 32–15 rout of East Aurora. As a reporter put it, Freeport's "colored guard . . . sang his swan song last night. Bill dribbled down the floor in lightning fashion to cage a pair of goals and barely missed two others."[65]

The newspaper gave unbridled praise to Moseley, calling him "a clever player whenever he took the ball down the court. . . . The fans always expected Mose to pull some new trick and it was very seldom that they were disappointed. . . . Bill has been out for football, basketball and track, but never has he had a chance to show his stuff like he has in the present basketball season. . . . The school regrets the loss of Moseley and wishes him his just desserts."[66] The newspaper reporter presented Moseley as a trickster, sort of a Harlem Globetrotters clown, juking and jiving down the court. The reporter referred to Moseley as "Bill" and "Mose," while using only the last names of Freeport's white players. Even as Rupp played William Moseley on his integrated high school team, a reporter resorted to black stereotypes to describe the "antics" of an African American athlete in northern Illinois in the late 1920s.

A tireless Rupp did everything he could to gain an advantage over his rivals. With an open date on February 10, he took his players to watch Joliet play Rockford, the Pretzels' next two opponents. It was also the season that he established a trademark of his coaching career. Rupp told the tale himself: "It was during my second year at Freeport that I bought me a fine-looking new blue suit to replace that old brown thing I had been wearing all the time I had been there. When we lost the game that night with me wearing that new suit, I said, 'Hey, this blue won't get it done.' From then on I wore nothing but brown to my teams' games."[67] The coach who became "The Man in the Brown Suit" started the superstitious practice in Freeport, Illinois, in 1928.

The scouting trip went for naught. Freeport lost to Joliet 24–23 and to Rockford 33–29.[68] A flu-ridden Rupp missed the latter, and the local newspaper played on that melodramatically: "With the coach, A. F. Rupp, sick in bed, voiceless, and unable to appear at the most important game of the year, the Freeport High School heavyweight wrecking crew applied the air brakes to the so-called Laude super-special, but the special did not stop, and Freeport was handed the most glorious and heartbreaking defeat which has ever been suffered." Assistant George Zuelke coached the team in Rupp's absence, and the writer suggested that "too much praise cannot be given him considering the circumstances that existed." Another reporter criticized the players: "They appeared to be dead on their feet. The offense of the locals was far off color; while the guarding of the locals would at times have failed to stop a grade school team."[69]

The Pretzels reached the district tournament final before losing to Rockford again, 28–21, to finish an 11–5 season. In the off-season, Rupp and several alumni organized a Lettermen's Club to increase school spirit before he was off to Columbia for his third summer of classes.[70] Rupp returned in the fall of 1928 to discover that Paul Moon, the highly successful coach of the lightweights, had taken a coaching job in Davenport, Iowa. When the school named George Kloos from Muscatine, Iowa, as Moon's replacement, Rupp engineered a change in operation of the basketball program. Now the lightweights would practice with the heavyweights. Both teams would receive instruction from both coaches, with Rupp concentrating on the offense and Kloos the defense, although Kloos later said that his "main job was sitting on the bench and holding Rupp down."[71]

The new format gave Rupp total control of Freeport basketball at a time when the football team was enduring a winless season. He opened practice on the earliest date yet, October 1, and 70 boys reported. They immediately started working on fundamentals. Longtime University of Kentucky sports information director, Russell Rice believed that those Freeport players knew instantly that Rupp would not settle for anything less than their best. George Schmelzle, the Pretzels' center from 1928–1930, said: "Rupp wouldn't let you waste time. You automatically played to win basketball games."[72]

Remarkably, the local paper devoted more space to preseason drills in 1928 than it had given to regular-season games during the 1926 state championship season. "Coach Rupp is taking charge and drilling the men in everything which pertains to basketball," a reporter wrote on October 6, going into minute detail. "Mr. Rupp gave a demonstration of how to make a perfect pivot and had the squad going through each position in the pivot slowly and then working up to swift action. There was some dribbling the ball across the gymnasium floor and back again." After each drill, Rupp delivered a 10-minute speech to point out mistakes.[73]

Rupp benefited from the growing popularity of basketball in Illinois in the 1920s. Despite the gridiron heroics of Red Grange at the University of Illinois, on the high school level basketball enjoyed more popularity than football, baseball, or any other sport. In 1928, 520 of the state's 550 high schools had basketball teams, compared with 456 track programs, 253 football teams, and 215 baseball squads. Schools with football teams had an average of only 25 boys in uniform, whereas basketball averaged 50 boys on both lightweight and heavyweight teams.[74] At Freeport the precipitous decline of the football program after the national championship of 1925 made basketball even more popular during Adolph Rupp's years there. In 1928 the football "heavies" went 0–5–1; the lightweights 0–5.

So many boys had come out for basketball that Rupp announced that only a "select few lettermen from last year" would be issued shoes and uniforms. All others would have to provide their own. Addressing the lettermen, Rupp said there would be "strict enforcement of all rules, such as no eating between meals, no smoking or dissipation of any sort."[75]

Freeport finished the regular season 11–5, the signature victory being a 20–18 squeaker over Chicago city champion Crane Tech.[76] Two of the losses were in overtime to Jim Laude's Rockford squad. But the Pretzels lost their last two games, and with a string of injuries to key players, their tournament prospects seemed bleak. Instead, they turned that 1928–1929 campaign into Rupp's greatest at Freeport.

The Pretzels blew through the district, demolishing South Beloit, 41–16, and New Milford, 50–8, to set up a rematch with hated Rockford in the final. Rupp and Freeport finally got a measure of revenge by winning, 27–23, in "one of the most bitterly contested games staged here in recent years," according to a *Journal-Standard* reporter. "Coach Rupp deserves the congratulations and praise that were heaped upon him following his notable victory. . . . Rupp outsmarted the Rockford bunch at every turn of the game and demonstrated that he knows what to do in a pinch regardless of what the situation might be."[77]

The Pretzels headed for the sectional against Moline in the Plowboys' new 4,500-seat field house and won, 27–24; then took the sectional crown with a come-from-behind 27–21 victory over Orion. As with many of Freeport's "heart attack" wins throughout the season, "the Ruppmen's victory was another one of those slashing final period attacks that swept the opposition before them."[78] From there it was on to the state tournament on the University of Illinois campus in Champaign.

By now Rupp had established himself as a popular speaker, honing his delivery at every opportunity. A few days before he and his team left for Champaign, he spoke at Stockton High School's basketball banquet, where he emphasized his belief that "athletics makes school more interesting and sometimes draws boys to high school who never would have attended."[79]

A contingent of Freeport fans took the interurban or piled into cars for the trip to Champaign. Those who stayed home hovered around living-room radios to listen to the Pretzels' 30–28 first-round victory over Wheaton. Hopes for the school's third state title ended, however, with a 40–24 loss to Champaign in the semifinals.[80] "Although they battled hard from beginning to end, their efforts were all in vain," a student reporter wrote. Appreciative Freeport fans "gave their team a rousing cheer as they left the floor, and all are still proud of the great record made here by Coach

Rupp and his Freeport warriors." Freeport beat Peoria, 27–15, in the consolation game to finish 18–6, and Johnson City defeated Champaign for the championship.[81]

The student reporter gushed, "It can be truly said that Freeport has never had a more successful season than that of 1929, despite the fact that they previously won two championships. Coaches and critics agree that Rupp's machine was one of the best coached aggregations in the meet, and that means a lot."[82]

The 1929–1930 season, Rupp's last at Freeport, proved to be little more than a footnote to the previous campaign even though the Pretzels finished with a sterling 20–4 record. They hosted and won the 14-team district tournament but were eliminated in the sectional. Rupp, who earned his master's degree and professional diploma from Columbia in December, had become the "foxy local mentor" in the eyes of reporters, one of whom singled out a 25–15 victory over Joliet in which Freeport trailed 14–9 at halftime: "What happened in the locals' dressing room during intermission will no doubt never be known by the public, but it surely must have been inspirational, for before the third stanza was long underway, the Freeport five were well on their way to victory, holding a commanding lead."[83]

Rupp basked in the spotlight while at the same time making sure his players didn't grab too much of it for individual achievements. When captain Don Brewer was leading the conference in scoring, Rupp made it a point to "issue instructions to his entire squad to ignore all individual play, and anyone violating this injunction will be immediately yanked from the floor by the local tutor." Brewer's scoring average fell during the second half of the season.

Rupp's four-year record at Freeport stood at 59–22, not quite as good as the 65–19 mark of Pat Holmes, his unassuming predecessor.[84] The brash young Kansan had become a popular figure in town. He had joined the Elks Club, the City Club, and the exclusive Germania Society, whose members sometimes conversed in German. He played golf and handball with his scorekeeper buddy, Elmer Hoffman. In fact, during one golf outing, Rupp—ever the coach—suggested that Hoffman stop playing right-handed. Hoffman eventually became one of the best left-handed golfers in Illinois, winning tournaments into the 1970s.[85]

Rupp also stayed in close contact with area high school and college coaches throughout his tenure at Freeport. When he had free evenings during the basketball season, he often traveled to Madison to watch Walter Meanwell's University of Wisconsin teams in action. Meanwell, who was the Missouri coach when Rupp was playing for Kansas, "was kind enough to let me sit up in the press box with his team," Rupp remembered. The Badgers' bench was above the floor, and substitutes had to climb down a ladder to check into the game. From his press-box perch Rupp learned Meanwell's screening offense and game tactics, and he observed Meanwell's own brand of motivating players. "He would be up there hollering at his boys," Rupp recalled, "and I was amazed at some of the things he said. I got some of my vocabulary from him."[86]

Rupp also remained close to University of Illinois coach Craig Ruby, who had witnessed Freeport's third-place finish in the 1929 state tournament in Champaign. Rupp invited him to be the guest speaker at the Pretzels' 1930 postseason banquet, and it was Ruby who told him about a college coaching vacancy down in Kentucky.

4

Building a Tradition, 1930–1941

While Adolph Rupp maintained an already high-quality program at Freeport High School—and worked hard to build up his reputation with the press—the basketball fortunes of his future employer went from the depths of the school's worst season to one of its best. From 1926–1927 through the 1929–1930 campaign, the University of Kentucky Wildcats produced records of 3–13, 12–6, 12–5, and 16–3.

On the afternoon of February 6, 1903, the school's very first men's basketball game did nothing to indicate this would one day be the nation's winningest college program. What was then Kentucky State lost to nearby Georgetown College 15–6. The Cadets—the team's nickname taken from the institution's strong Reserve Officers' Training Corps (ROTC) program—played two other home games that year, losing to Lexington's Kentucky University, which would become part of Transylvania, and beating the local YMCA team. After the school's first 10 seasons of basketball, its won-lost record stood at an unimpressive 38–49.[1]

Not until 1909 did the team even have a coach; before then a manager "made the schedule, printed the tickets, collected money, paid the bills, was in charge of the team on the road and sometimes swept the floor." In 1909, the administration gave football coach E. R. Sweetland basketball coaching duties as well. The same year, Philip Corbusier, commandant and professor of military science and tactics, spoke before a chapel gathering of students and faculty about Kentucky's inspirational 6–2 football victory over Illinois on October 3. He remarked that the players had "fought like wildcats," and the press immediately began to refer to the university's athletic teams by that nickname. As Bert Nelli noted in *The Winning Tradition: A History of Kentucky Wildcat Basketball,* "one of the university's oldest traditions was born."[2]

With the hiring of a coach, the fortunes of the infant basketball program began to improve. In 1911–1912 Sweetland's basketball Wildcats went 9–0. The campus newspaper, the *Kentucky Kernel,* proclaimed the season "one glorious march from start to finish. Not only were we undefeated, but during the entire season not once was an opposing team even in the lead." A series of coaches continued to win, if not as spectacularly. With a master's degree in English from Vanderbilt University in hand, Stanley A. Boles came to UK in 1916 to help teach physical education. He coached football in 1917 and basketball in the 1917–1918 season. In basketball against Kentucky Wesleyan in Winchester, Boles's undergraduate alma mater, the outcome went on the books as a 21–21 tie because of a scorer's error not discovered until after the Wildcats had left town. Boles completed his head basketball coaching career at UK after one season with a record of 9–2–1.[3]

In 1918 Boles also helped organize the state high school boys' basketball tournament, and he directed it as the tournament manager for the 18 years it was held on the UK campus.[4] Known later as "Daddy" Boles because of the paternal role he played toward athletes, this influential leader served as UK's director of physical education until 1929, athletic director until 1934, ticket manager until 1946, and manager of veterans' housing until his retirement in 1955. In his role as athletic director, it was Boles who hired Adolph Rupp as head basketball coach in 1930.[5] Whether Boles ever used his Vanderbilt education in English in any of his official capacities at Kentucky is unclear, but Adolph Rupp's love of poetry would surely give the two something to talk about beyond basketball.

Beginning in 1919, Rupp's freshman year at the University of Kansas, UK hired a series of University of Illinois alumni to head the basketball program: George C. Buchheit (1919–1924), C. O. Applegran (1924–1925), Ray Eklund (1925–1926), and John Mauer (1927–1930). The lone exception was Basil Hayden, a Paris, Kentucky, native and captain of the 1920–1921 Wildcats. The university hired Hayden to coach the team in 1926–1927, when Eklund resigned abruptly at the beginning of the season.

Buchheit, a two-sport college star, had just graduated from Illinois when he came to UK to coach football and basketball.[6] His first team finished 5–7 in 1919–1920, but the following year, with Hayden and fellow Paris High School product Bobby Lavin leading the way, the Wildcats went 13–1, losing only to in-state rival Centre College 29–27. They defeated Georgia 20–19 in the Southern Intercollegiate Athletic Association (SIAA) tournament final in Atlanta to become "Champions of the South." In the estimation of team member Sam Ridgeway, this was "UK's first great success." Back home in Lexington, fans followed the tournament action at the Phoenix Hotel, where, according to the *Lexington Herald*, they "whooped and 'hollered' in glee," as the telegraph reports "were megaphoned from the mezzanine floor, and when the final wire came in and news was shouted 'Final score, Kentucky 20, Georgia 19,' the lid flew off with a bang and bedlam ruled."[7]

Buchheit brought with him the style of play he had learned in Illinois. Bert Nelli concluded in *The Winning Tradition* that it simply mirrored the style common in the Big Ten at the time. Wisconsin coach Walter Meanwell developed the system after 1912, and Illinois's Craig Ruby and other Big Ten coaches picked it up. Significantly, while at Freeport High and as a spectator at many Wisconsin games, Adolph Rupp learned the style as well. Under the "Illinois System," Buchheit kept one player under each goal, allowing the other three to roam the court. On defense, he demanded tough man-to-man coverage.

Although no one graduated from UK's "Wonder Team" of 1920–1921, Basil Hayden suffered a serious knee injury while competing in track, and defensive stalwart Sam Ridgeway fought a yearlong battle with diphtheria and never returned to the court. Buchheit's Wildcats went 10–6 in 1921–1922, losing to Mercer in the SIAA tournament. With a completely new lineup, they slumped to 3–10 the following year but rebounded to 13–3 in 1923–1924, Buchheit's final season. Although UK officials wanted him to stay, he left to take a job at Trinity College, a North Carolina institution that would become Duke University.

On December 13, 1924, C. O. Applegran, another former University of Illinois athlete, led the Wildcats into a new era with a 28–23 victory over Cincinnati in the first game played at Alumni Gym. Going 13–8, Applegran left after only one year. Ray Eklund, yet another Illinois alumnus, coached the Wildcats to a 15–3 mark in 1925–1926 but left abruptly at the beginning of the fall semester in 1926. Desperate for a last-minute replacement, the university persuaded Hayden to take over a week before the first scheduled game. With little returning talent, he suffered through a 3–13 season, the worst in UK basketball history. When Hayden decided he just "wasn't suited for coaching," university officials looked to Illinois again and found Johnny Mauer, who had been an All-American in basketball under Craig Ruby and a running back alongside Red Grange on Bob Zuppke's football team. Like other Illini alumni who came to UK, he was hired to coach both sports.[8]

Mauer used the "Illinois System" to take Kentucky basketball to a new level, posting records of 12–6, 12–5, and 16–3. Carey Spicer, one of his best players, remembered that Mauer employed the same Big Ten passing offense that Ruby used at Illinois. It emphasized low, short bounce passes in a structured offense. This so-called "submarine attack" also required a series of screens—"we called it blocking in those days," said Spicer—to free players for open shots. According to Paul McBrayer, who starred on all three of Mauer's UK teams, the coach "introduced the first outside screen ever seen in the South." Mauer taught players to screen for a dribbler and then roll to the basket or step back for an open shot. "I want to tell you it was a joy to play when the other team didn't know about those things," McBrayer said.[9]

Mauer's passing offense required players to be fundamentally sound. He demanded that they shoot, pass, and pivot correctly. More than one player, having learned to shoot incorrectly in high school, practiced it the Mauer way: two-handed from just above the waist, feet spread and one slightly behind the other, with eyes fastened on the goal. "Mauer would die if you ever shot a one-handed shot," Spicer recalled. He also said Mauer's teams took advantage of a fast-break opportunity, if it was there, but preferred a deliberate attack. Long rebounds sometimes provided a chance for the forwards to break quickly for the offensive end, but until the mid-1930s, the center jump after every field goal eliminated fast breaks after made baskets.[10]

In the later development of the game, guards covered guards on defense, but in the 1930s and into the 1940s, the guards—a team's best defensive players—covered the other team's forwards, the best offensive players. Because of their defensive positions under or near the basket, guards hauled down many defensive rebounds. With no 10-second rule, guards often did not cross midcourt, instead passing the ball ahead to the

73

forwards or center. Only rarely did guards take long two-handed set shots from beyond the foul line if the forwards or center were not free closer to the basket. (With no 3-second violation, centers could camp out under the basket, but there were few players taller than six feet five inches back then.) On defense, Mauer drilled his players on proper footwork—they were not allowed to cross their feet—and devoted hours of practice to stopping an opponent's attack.

Mauer's former players remembered him as a sound teacher of the game. "We would have gone and hid in our cells from the sight of the public if we had gone out and played and committed 20 errors in a ball-game like these teams do consistently day after day when I watch them play today," Paul McBrayer said in a 1980 interview. Coming out of Kentucky high schools with part-time coaches, players like McBrayer responded to Mauer's intense, disciplined practices. "We were all so happy to get the kind of coaching that John Mauer provided," he said.[11]

McBrayer, who coached in high school himself, was Adolph Rupp's assistant from 1934–1943, and after World War II he became a successful head coach at Eastern Kentucky State Teachers College (now Eastern Kentucky University). "I feel that John Mauer was responsible for the good basketball in the state of Kentucky that was to follow," he said. "He was a fine teacher of fundamental basketball, the fundamental basketball that I used throughout my coaching career." Paul Jenkins, the captain of Mauer's first UK team, established impressive records as a high school coach at Ashland and later at Louisville Male, where he coached Ralph Beard, arguably the greatest guard ever to play for Rupp. Lawrence "Big" McGinnis, another Mauer player, had a distinguished career at Owensboro High, where he coached Cliff Hagan, an All-American for Rupp at UK. Mauer also influenced high school coaches John Heber in Lexington and Tiny Jones in Mount Sterling, and McBrayer sent Ralph Carlisle to UK after coaching him at Kavanaugh High in Lawrenceburg.[12]

McBrayer remembered the first practice Mauer held with his new team in 1927: "He started that practice as though the players had never seen a basketball or a basketball game in their lives. He gave us a long speech in which he told us in detail what he wanted." McBrayer said that when he became a coach, "I started every season as if the team had never seen a basketball or a game in their lives. That's how well he sold me."[13]

While Mauer's players came to admire—and later as coaches themselves emulate—his disciplined approach to the game, players, fans, and newspaper reporters sometimes questioned his rigid system. Carey Spicer recalled, "I had a great peg shot where I could fake my guard out of the way and go in for a score, but Mauer preferred that I go through the set-up plays and not use my own natural ability. That was the only fault that I could ever find with Johnny." An All-American under both Mauer and Rupp, Spicer stated that Rupp let him use his pet move. "So I scored more and better," he proclaimed. Spicer's average jumped from 6.5 points per game during his junior year under Mauer to a team-leading 10.6 the next season under Rupp.[14]

McBrayer said he considered Mauer "a much better coach than Rupp," but Spicer wouldn't go quite that far. "Not better, but as good," he said. "He didn't have the personality to go with it." He noted that Mauer "didn't have much humor." "I think he lived and ate basketball," Spicer surmised. "That was his life." Spicer also said that Rupp "let us use our own natural ability along with our set offense. We could use more variations, which made [for] a better, higher-scoring [team]."[15]

Though Mauer related well to his players, he seemed unable to motivate them for big games. A *Kentuckian* writer pointed out in 1929 that southern sportswriters such as Morgan Blake and Ed Danforth agreed that even though the Wildcats were "the class of the South," they were "incapable of rising to great heights in tournament play. The Wildcat team plays orthodox basketball, and previous tournaments have proven the fact that an unconscious flip and run game fits best in the excitement and strain of a long tournament." Spicer said the ability to inspire is "something that some people have and some don't." "I think it's a gift, really. Mauer didn't have it," he further explained. "Rupp, because he gave you more latitude, you wanted to play for him. . . . Not that I didn't play hard for Mauer, but there was something about [Rupp] that just made you want to, and it wasn't his coaching. That wasn't it. It was the man."[16]

Rupp also displayed another ability that Mauer sorely lacked. Mauer never established a friendly relationship with the Lexington press. Louis "Little" McGinnis, the younger of two brothers who played for both coaches at UK, said Mauer "spent more time coaching than in public relations, which probably hurt him, in contrast to Rupp, who did things the other way." According to McBrayer, "Mauer was a man that wanted facts and wanted truth, and sportswriters invariably have wanted to write stories that would interest people. It had to be some controversy or something . . . that would attract attention. The actual fact of the thing does not appeal to them."[17]

Mauer didn't mind sportswriters criticizing his game strategy, but when they went after his players, that was another thing. McBrayer remembered that when a writer criticized Cecil Combs and the player's "daddy got real mad—you didn't talk about a man's son then"—Mauer stuck up for Combs and persuaded him to stay on the team.[18]

Mauer's problems with the Lexington press corps went beyond personality, revealing a darker side of southern sports in the 1920s. His Catholic faith proved to be problematic for some writers and some UK alumni. Lexington exhibited the same xenophobic, nativist tendencies of other larger American cities of that period, even though William Frederick "Billy" Klair, the city's political boss for much of the first 35 years of the century, had used his German and Irish Catholic connections to rise to power in Democratic politics. Residents of immigrant heritage made up a dwindling percentage of the city's population, however, and Klair's power illustrated more his own political acumen and willingness to play ball with the Bluegrass bluebloods. Even he felt the stigma of his German roots during the World War I years.[19]

As an Irish Catholic, John Mauer received intense criticism from sportswriters, not just because of his disciplined set offense, but also because he started the Catholic McGinnis boys ahead of Protestant players. According to Paul McBrayer, prominent Lexington sportswriter Neville Dunn especially disliked Mauer's lineup choices. It was one thing for a Catholic politician to wield power and influence, but apparently it was something else for an Irish Catholic basketball coach to play Irish Catholic boys while capable Protestants languished on the bench.[20]

"He had two of them [Catholics] playing on the first team," Louis McGinnis recalled. "There's criticism on every team. You know, the fellow on the bench . . . thinks he should be playing, [and] the other one that is playing thinks he should be." Dunn picked up on any discontent with Mauer in his columns in the *Lexington Herald*. "Evidently in what he was writing he didn't like [Mauer]," McGinnis recalled. "I know there wasn't any reason for it, but I don't know whether some of the players were talking; you know, they thought they ought to be playing." McGinnis admitted that he "really didn't know anything about it. I was just a kid down in the South . . . that happened to be playing and wasn't entered into politics or those sorts of things." McBrayer believed that criticism from Dunn and others and the obvious nativist sentiments of the town eventually drove Mauer from Lexington.[21] He moved on to Miami of Ohio and eventually to Army, Tennessee, and Florida. At the latter two stops he got the chance to go head-to-head with the man who succeeded him at Kentucky. As it turned out, UK replaced an Irish Catholic with a German Mennonite.

UK's long-established Illinois connection worked in Rupp's favor. University of Illinois coach Craig Ruby wrote a strong letter of recommendation for the young coach, according to the *Courier-Journal* of Louisville. Ruby knew Rupp, and he knew UK. Mauer had played for Ruby at Illinois, and Ruby came to Lexington for a coaching clinic in 1927. During that clinic he called UK freshman Carey Spicer onto the floor to help demonstrate the "guard-around offense." Ruby had a guard pass to a forward and, following a fake to the inside by the forward, he was to hand off to the guard cutting around the outside. Determined to demonstrate the impossibility of defending the maneuver, Ruby asked Spicer to try to break up the play. "All right," said Spicer, who promptly stepped in and deflected the first pass. A frustrated Ruby said, "Now you're not supposed to do that." Spicer responded, "You told me to break it up." "That's right," said Ruby, "[but] you play inside the forward there." Spicer took his position, and when the guard came around, he again broke up the play. Turning to Mauer, Ruby shouted, "Get that man off the floor. He'll never make your ballclub." Spicer later became an All-American.[22]

While Rupp coached at Freeport, he kept in close contact with Ruby. And when Rupp invited the Illinois coach to speak at his basketball banquet in 1930, Ruby told him about the opening at Kentucky. Rupp numbered among the 72 applicants for the position, and despite his lack of experience at the collegiate level, the UK athletic committee granted him an interview.

When Rupp came to Lexington in the middle of May, he admitted, "I wasn't too much impressed with the job down here." He hailed a cab at the Lexington depot to take him to the campus, and on the way he looked out the window to behold, as he described it in an interview with Russell Rice in the 1970s, "53 or 55 little shanties that were standing here where the coliseum now stands across from the stadium." Rupp used even stronger language in a 1974 interview with Louisville sportswriter Dave Kindred: "Bear in mind that where Memorial Coliseum now stands, there were 55 little nigger one- and two-room shacks back then. Bear in mind that I got a cab from the Southern Depot to Alumni Gym, and we went through an awful area of town. They took me to eat at the university cafeteria, and out the third-floor window I could see all those little nigger shacks. I wasn't used to anything like that."[23]

The "nigger shacks," along with his room at the Lexington YMCA "that wasn't fit for a cat," were almost more than the young coach could take. "Good gawd almighty," he thundered, "what kind of place is this Kentucky?"[24] He didn't even think Alumni Gym, though only six years old, measured up to the gym back at Freeport High.

Rupp met with the athletic council, chaired by Dr. William D. Funkhouser, dean of the graduate school. Other members included athletic director Daddy Boles, faculty representatives Enoch Grehan and E. A. Bureau, alumni representatives Louis Hillenmeyer and the formidable John Stoll—for whom the football field was named—and student representative Ellis Johnson. Only a freshman, Johnson had been a high school All-American in both football and basketball in Ashland, Kentucky. It was unusual for a freshman to gain a spot on the athletic council, but as Tev Laudeman of the *Courier-Journal* wrote, Johnson "was not an ordinary freshman." Laudeman believed him to be "the greatest athlete UK had ever landed."[25] Johnson took an active part in the council's interview with Rupp and the deliberations afterward.

The group took Rupp to the third floor of McVey Hall for lunch. Not only did he have to look out the window at the "nigger shacks" while he ate, but, as Rupp put it, "we got there late, and they didn't have anything at all left there." "I got one piece of fish and a stick of cornbread and a cup of coffee, and I didn't think that the people down in Kentucky were eating too well." As for the whole situation, "I just couldn't get steamed up about this thing too well."[26] Despite his apparent ambivalence, he impressed his interviewers. They had gone into the meeting realizing they faced a difficult task. Some fans felt the council should have matched Miami's offer that lured Mauer away.

But Rupp impressed the athletic council with his "manner and his refreshing approach to basketball." He must have emphasized his contrast in style with Mauer's system, because the *Kentucky Kernel* later reported that "Rupp is an advocate of the fast break system, which is the most popular system used in basketball at present." The *Kernel* promised that the "delayed offensive system of play" would no longer be employed by the Wildcats. Rupp took the train back to Freeport and waited 10 days before he received a telegram with the job offer.[27]

"A lot of things were going through my mind," Rupp recalled. With school still in session in Freeport, he was in the middle of track season, coaching the dash events. He had met a young woman named Esther Schmidt. "We were kind of getting interested in each other," he admitted. "I wasn't kind of too hot to leave [her]." Several members of the school board told him he would be foolish to leave a "lifetime job" at Freeport. Principal L. A. Fulwider assured him he could stay as long as he wanted, noting that Rupp's 67–16 record "is as good as we ever expect anyone to have." Fulwider told Rupp to take a day off and go downtown to talk with some townspeople about his decision.[28]

Rupp was convinced that his principal friend had plotted to have the Freeport businessmen dissuade him from taking the UK offer. "You shouldn't go down to a school like that," he recalled them telling him. "Why, who ever heard of Kentucky doing anything? They're not doing anything in football or basketball or anything else." Besides, Kentucky was "hillbilly country." Their spiel gave Rupp pause. "I got to thinkin' of those shacks that I passed on the way over from the depot to the gymnasium, and then the little shanties that I saw across from the stadium," he recalled. "I got to studyin' about it."[29]

But he visited one more businessman, who Rupp recalled was "up on a ladder hanging a sign" when he dropped by. The fellow climbed down and said: "Adolph, I'll tell you one thing. You take that job. You can always go to a better job from there than you can from here. You'll never get another chance to coach at another university, and while you've got the chance, you'd better take it." If it doesn't work out, "you've got enough degrees and you've got enough savvy, and the fact that you've coached at the University of Kentucky on a two-year contract will take care of it."[30]

When Daddy Boles phoned him on May 21, Rupp knew he had to make up his mind. Shortly after that conversation, he wired UK to accept the job. Fulwider called him into his office the next day and told him he'd made a terrible mistake. "He talked to me most of the morning," Rupp remembered. Fulwider advised him to give the decision some more thought, but Rupp replied, "I gave those people my word that I'm coming down there." He said the principal refused to accept his resignation "until the second-to-last day" before he left there.[31]

In later years, Rupp placed the emphasis on his personal struggle in making the decision. The real story, however, is not why a high school coach would accept a college job, but why any college would even extend an offer to a high school coach with no collegiate experience. The answer could be that in 1930 college athletics—especially basketball, which had been around for only a generation or so—had not had time to develop many coaches with years of successful experience. The list of 72 candidates for the UK job is no longer available, but despite Mauer's success, it is safe to assume that "name" college coaches in the North, East, and Mideast did not covet a position in a region where basketball continued to be a step-child to football. The Great Depression surely made any job appealing, so the UK list probably consisted of college assistant coaches, a few failed head coaches, and many high school coaches seeking to move up.

Certainly, Rupp's ties to the Kansas program of Phog Allen and James Naismith and his impeccable high school record were enough to make the search committee take a closer look. When the members sat down face to face with the confident 29-year-old, he impressed them with his savvy for the game and his promise of a new, more exciting style of play. Even though his Illinois connection with Craig Ruby helped secure an interview, Rupp distanced himself from Ruby's system, which Mauer had copied. In favoring a more popular fast-breaking style, he set himself apart from his predecessor and other aspirants for the job.

In the end, however, a classic Rupp story retold by Russell Rice has the ring of truth. When Pat Harmon, sports editor of the *Cincinnati Post* and *Times-Star*, asked a member of the athletic council why they hired the Freeport coach, the man replied simply, "Because he told us he was the best damned basketball coach in the United States, and he convinced us he was."[32]

Rupp's new boss, UK president Frank L. McVey, had more pressing interests than athletics. He wanted to build the state university into a first-rate academic institution. McVey became the university's third president in 1917—he would serve until 1940—and his strong stand for academic freedom endeared him to the faculty and improved the reputation of the university. He would serve as president of the Southern Association of Colleges and Secondary Schools, the National Association of Land-Grant Colleges and Universities, and the National Association of State Universities. In 1926, a year after the Scopes Trial in Dayton, Tennessee, McVey teamed with E. Y. Mullins of Louisville's Southern Baptist Theological Seminary to oppose two anti-evolution bills in the Kentucky legislature.[33] One vote in the Kentucky legislature kept from passing a similar anti-evolution statute for Kentucky's public schools as had passed in Tennessee.

President McVey later became president of the Southeastern Conference, an ironic position for a man who had displayed an ambivalence to intercollegiate sports from the outset of his academic career. In a 1925 letter to University of Alabama president George H. Denny, McVey asserted that "colleges ought to develop athletics for the entire student body instead of confining it to a few teams in given sports." "I do not mean by this that the purpose would be one of weakening the collegiate sports," he explained, "but of increasing the opportunities of students for inter-athletic games."[34] McVey also was concerned about the fanatical support for high school sports. After watching the Kentucky state high school basketball championship game in Alumni Gym in 1932, an event his own athletic director Daddy Boles helped inaugurate in 1918, McVey recorded in his diary that "a great crowd was there, much noise and confusion." "I wonder if such affairs are really a good thing for the schools," he wrote.[35]

But UK alumni and supporters wanted the school's intercollegiate sports programs strengthened, and McVey yielded to the pressure. In addition to building new men's and women's dormitories, a new chemistry building, McVey and Memorial Halls, a new dairy building for the UK farm, a new art center, and a new education building, he built Alumni Gymnasium, and completed additions to the football stadium all before Rupp's arrival.[36]

Rupp recalled in a 1971 interview that McVey was viewed as "very cold" by some people, but at a pep rally the president "would get up there and possibly have a little joke of some kind—not jokes the way they are today, nothing suggestive—but he'd have something." Also, he "usually would say that he hoped we would win half of the games because he didn't want to disappoint the other schools, because they also ought to win half of 'em." Winning half the games might satisfy McVey, but it would not please the alumni, and it certainly would not be acceptable for Adolph Rupp.[37]

McVey relied on William D. Funkhouser and Daddy Boles to handle all athletic matters. A popular zoology teacher, Funkhouser became dean of the graduate school in 1925 and eventually served as secretary of the SEC. "There was a great man," the coach said with typical Rupp hyperbole. "I mean a learned man, an educated man, a man that simply astonished the people around here by his knowledge." As SEC secretary, Funkhouser served as the de facto commissioner and, according to Rupp, "always tried to find a way for a boy to be eligible," no small concern to a coach.[38]

The university hired Rupp as "instructor in Physical Education, to have charge of varsity basketball and to assist in other sports." He claimed he received exactly the same salary as he did at Freeport: his two-year contract paid him $2,800 in 1930–1931 and $3,000 in 1931–1932. Those meager depression-era figures still far surpassed the pay of most UK professors, whose salaries ranged from $1,500 to $1,700 per year. Rupp's pay increased to $4,250 by 1935.[39]

After signing his contract, Rupp wrote to Daddy Boles to ask if there was any reason for him to come to Lexington that summer. Assured that he wouldn't be needed until school started September 1, he decided to stay in Freeport to attend to business—he had some securities to sell—and to court Esther Schmidt. It wasn't until the end of August that he stuffed most of his belongings into a trunk, put it on a train, and then drove to Kentucky. He later remembered, "I got in my car and drove down here, all the time wondering, 'Well, did you make a mistake or didn't you.'"[40]

When Rupp crossed the Ohio River into Kentucky, he saw the effects of the growing economic depression in a rural state, made even worse by a terrible drought. Though he'd known some harsh times growing up on the farm back in Kansas, he "had never seen it look any worse out there than it did here." But, he said to himself, "I'm used to this, so I'm right at home."[41]

Boles, head football coach Harry Gamage, and line coach Bernie Shively met him upon his arrival, and Gamage said he should report to the football field the next day. There Rupp was assigned to help Birkett Pribble with the freshman team, known as the Kittens.[42]

Rupp set up residence only two blocks from Stoll Field. His office in the gymnasium consisted of "a place in the hallway that had a beaver board thing put around it." There was no reason to lock the door, because anyone could just crawl over the top of the board to get in. "It was quite an office, I'll tell you one thing," Rupp laughed in a 1971 interview. "How I could recruit anybody in those days was a mystery to me. . . . We recruited Kentucky boys because they wanted to come to the state university."[43]

Rupp remembered the enthusiasm on campus for football in those days, with thousands turning out for pep rallies and bonfires the evening before home games. He found himself right in the middle of it. "Somehow it fell to my lot early to inherit the job of master of ceremonies," he recalled. "It was my duty, of course, to keep the thing going." He introduced President McVey and other speakers, including the coach of the visiting team, who inevitably spoke graciously of Kentucky hospitality and then listed the deficiencies of his own team. "They'd get up and usually tell about how their team was crippled and everything, and it would be a miracle if their team would win," Rupp recalled. "The usual line that most coaches put out."[44]

Curious about his new Kentucky home and eager to start making contacts in the area, Rupp ventured out to high school football games that first fall. Lyman Ginger, who later became his assistant and close friend, coached football at Winchester High School. In 1930 Ginger took his team down the road to face a Paris squad coached by Blanton Collier, who later became head coach at UK. When only two game officials showed up before the kickoff, Ginger spied the new UK basketball coach in the crowd and, figuring on his strong sports background and the fact that he un-doubtedly would be a neutral judge, asked if he would fill in. Rupp responded that he knew little about football rules and didn't really wish to do it, but if both coaches agreed, he would give it a try. Collier assigned him to be the head linesman, and Ginger explained the duties: "If you can see that line right across the football, stand so you can see straight across, and if anybody moves from either team across the line before the ball is snapped, why, you just throw your flag." Collier gave him a red flag and told him to "call off sides, and then . . . you mark the spot where [a ball carrier] goes out of bounds." Rupp supposed he could do that.[45]

At game's end, he approached Ginger and asked if he had made any mistakes. Ginger said he had done a satisfactory job, and the two continued to chat. Ginger mentioned that he also coached basketball, and he asked Rupp to come watch his team. "Tell me what we're doing wrong and make some suggestions," Ginger supplicated. Rupp thought a moment, then shrewdly responded: "Well, I doubt if I come. I don't want to get people mad at me and think that I'm taking sides, and if I came over and made suggestions with you, somebody else would get mad. I don't want to do that." Instead, he invited Ginger to attend his "coaching school" the following summer.[46] Rupp began those clinics in the first summer after his first season at UK, and they attracted area high school coaches eager to learn from a college mentor. Rupp remembered the interest that Wisconsin's Walter Meanwell and Illinois's Craig Ruby had shown in a promising Illinois high school coach. Now he was in a position to do the teaching.

Rupp's carefully crafted reputation accompanied him to Lexington. The *Kentucky Kernel* pointed to his "national recognition as a basketball player" on the "Ever Victorious" 1923 team at Kansas. The student writer pointed out that at six feet, Rupp "was the shortest man on the Jaywalker quintet." Not only did the writer misname the Kansas mascot, but he also failed to mention that Rupp did not start, saw little game action, and never scored a varsity point. He also noted that the new UK coach "declined to make any predictions for the coming season as he has never seen any of his material in action, nor does he know how they will perform under the new system."[47]

Perhaps the change in styles from Mauer's deliberate, "submarine" short-passing system to Rupp's free-wheeling, fast-breaking attack had been overstated—at Rupp's behest—from the outset. Two men who played for both coaches at UK certainly downplayed the extent of the change. Louis "Little" McGinnis said "there was no reason for Rupp to make a lot of changes. Don't forget that we were very successful the previous year and that Mauer was an excellent teacher and we were strong in the fundamentals." Indeed, the Wildcats had gone 16–3 under Mauer in 1929–1930. Carey Spicer, an All-American under both coaches, said Rupp allowed the players to "use our own natural ability along with the set offense we learned under Mauer. We could use more variations, which made for higher scores, but we used practically the same offense we had under Mauer."[48]

Spicer served as team captain under both coaches. As captain, Mauer entrusted Spicer with his complicated playbook. "I had the playbook with all the plays and all the variations," Spicer recalled. "So when Adolph came—and this was before the football season began—he called me to his office and sort of picked my brain about the type offense we had used." Rupp remembered it differently: "I told him what my plans were. Carey, of course, was very much impressed right away with what I said, and said that they were glad to have the opportunity to fast break and get an opportunity to score and have an opportunity to shoot and not be restrained the way they were before." According to Rupp, Spicer "got the word around to the other boys." "I think the other boys got a little confidence," Rupp said, "that maybe the coach was going to give them a better opportunity than they had before."[49]

Apparently, Rupp had forgotten that the Wildcats had gone 16–3 the year before. Spicer said that when he told Rupp he had Mauer's old playbook, the new coach asked, "Would you mind if I look at it?" When Spicer reported to his first basketball practice in November, after football season, he discovered, "We were using all the same plays and, in fact, all the same numbers as we had under Mauer."[50] Rupp simply added variations and allowed players more freedom. Making no mention of Mauer's Illinois offense, Rupp maintained, "We used about five or six standard plays based on outside screening, and they were very kind to us because the South still did not catch on to the screens."[51]

Spicer wasn't the only football player on the basketball team, so Rupp decided to conduct limited drills three times a week with the other players. The *Kentucky Kernel* reported that "Records Fall When Coach Rupp Summons Varsity Candidates" on October 15. In rhetoric reminiscent of the Kentucky frontier, the student writer stated that when Rupp "sounded the tocsin," 46 "aspiring and perspiring candidates" made up "the largest squad ever to report for the first practice of the year at the university." A later article upped the total to 57, a number that Rupp cut to 25 before the football players joined in after Thanksgiving.[52] Rupp continued a practice he had used with success at Freeport: getting large numbers of athletes to try out for his teams.

Rupp depended on the post-Thanksgiving infusion of six football players—Spicer, Ellis Johnson, George Yates, Darrell Darby, Bud Cavana, and Jake Bronston—because only Spicer and Louis McGinnis returned from Mauer's last team. Still, the cupboard was far from bare. Spicer, an All-American, and McGinnis were proven players. Sophomores Johnson and Darby had played on the Ashland High School team that won the national championship in 1928. Johnson had been a scholastic All-American in 1927 and 1928, the only player ever to earn the honor twice.[53]

In 1971 Rupp recalled that the local writers didn't give him "a chance to win scarcely any of the games." He wondered if he "had made a smart move to come down here or not." The *Kentucky Kernel* proclaimed that the "Basketeers are Team of One Big Question Mark." The article stated: "If Coach Rupp does come through with a winning team, he will be hailed as a miracle man, and he might do that very thing. His schedule, however, paints a gloomy picture for him."[54] Rupp's grooming of the press followed the pattern he had perfected at Freeport, where newspaper accounts of his first season made no mention of the fact that the school had won the state championship the previous year. At Kentucky the foundation laid by Mauer was all but forgotten in 1930. Rupp would be "a miracle man" if all went well.

Rupp called his players together and told them he wanted an aggressive style of basketball. "I want to go back to the pioneer spirit of our forefathers," he recalled telling them. "I said that the Pilgrims who landed on Plymouth Rock didn't look for security. I said, 'What security did Daniel Boone ask for when he penetrated the wilderness? What security did our pioneer mothers and fathers have when they carved their homes out of the western plains? All they wanted was an opportunity.' And I said, 'That's all I can offer you folks. Now, boys, let's not look for security. Let's look for opportunity. If we keep that philosophy in mind the rest of our lives, in whatever we do, you'll all become great someday.'"[55]

That opening monologue presented something new to a UK team used to the taciturn Mauer. And there was more. Likening the Wildcats to a well-trained army, Rupp told them: "I want a perfect harmony. I want a perfect execution of play. And I want perfect attention to details. If I can get that, we'll have a great team."[56] Only after that oration did Rupp begin his first practice session as coach of the Kentucky Wildcats.

With football season finally over, Rupp had his full team together for only a few weeks before its first game, a 67–19 shellacking of Georgetown College on December 18, 1930. According to the *Kentucky Kernel*, the Wildcats "introduced their new fast-break offense to the Lexington basketball fans in a convincing manner." Rupp used 17 players in what was "little more than a practice session for the superior Kentucky team." Although the writer reported that Rupp used Mauer's "guard offense," he also emphasized that Rupp's "new type of play is a great deal more interesting to watch than the system used last year by Coach Mauer." Aggie Sale scored 19 points and Louie McGinnis 16 to lead the Wildcats. For the hapless Tigers from Georgetown, Harry Lancaster "collected 10 points and otherwise played a wonderful game."[57] Lancaster became Rupp's assistant after World War II.

Kentucky next played Marshall in a benefit game for Lexington unemployment relief. The game drew only 800 spectators at $1 a head, and after the West Virginia school was paid $165 for traveling expenses, the remainder went to the unemployment fund. But when Coach Bobby Dodd and his Tennessee Volunteers came to town for Kentucky's fifth game, a crowd of 5,000 crammed into Alumni Gym to watch the unbeaten Wildcats win 31–23. Rupp remembered seeing 50- to 60-year-old men wearing freshman caps in order to get into the building.[58]

It was the seventh game of the season before the Wildcats left Lexington for a January 21 game at Vanderbilt. The players gathered at the Southern Depot, and when Rupp arrived he found most of them dressed in knickers and sweatshirts. "Boys, what in the name of the Lord are you guys showing up here for in clothes like that?" he exploded. "I'm taking around a bunch of university students, not a bunch of bums. I'm not packing around a bunch of bums. I'm packing around the finest boys from a fine university." He sent them back to their rooms to change into coats and ties before the train arrived. "You get out of these knickers and that darn fool stuff and let's get some class to this organization," he told them. "We get off of that train, I want you to look like something. This sloppy business is not going to get by as long as I'm coaching this team."[59] "We didn't have any more trouble after that," Rupp remembered. "The boys learned right quickly."[60]

Actually, the boys didn't learn about proper deportment on the road quite as quickly as he would have liked. After a trip to Atlanta, where the team stayed at the Georgian Terrace Hotel, Daddy Boles presented Rupp with a bill for $400. Hotel management complained of missing towels, lamps, blankets, and even silverware from the diner. Rupp immediately called a team meeting and presented the players with a list of the missing items. "I want all of that stuff brought to my office tomorrow," he said, "and if it isn't brought to my office tomorrow, then don't show up for practice." When he arrived at his makeshift office the next day, whoever on the team had been responsible had returned everything. "Sure enough, every single item showed up," Rupp said. "We boxed it up and sent it back to the hotel, and from then on we didn't have that problem." Rupp later proclaimed that he kept letters from hotel managers. He proudly stated,

"We conduct ourselves in a more gentlemanly fashion than any team in the Southeastern Conference, and I certainly am proud of that, and I'd rather have that said about us than the fact that we won a basketball game."[61]

They won plenty of those, starting off 10–0 before losing 25–16 at Georgia on February 13, 1931. "I'll never forget that game. If it were played yesterday, I'd remember it just as plainly as I do today," Rupp said. He always maintained that the Georgia coach got two sporting-goods salesmen to referee and refused to sign the order forms for their merchandise until after the game.[62]

The Wildcats followed that with a 29–26 loss at Clemson, which made for an interesting train trip to Atlanta for a game against Georgia Tech two days later. "We get on this cold sleeper and I have the lower berth, [and] Rupp has the lower berth across from me," Carey Spicer recalled in 1983. "I knew he was real unhappy that we lost this game that we shouldn't have lost. . . . He made us all get right to bed because it was cold and we wouldn't be getting any heat until we got hooked up, you know, to this other train line that was picking us up." Spicer and his teammates wrapped up in blankets and nestled into the Pullman berths.

After a few minutes Rupp reached across, parted the curtains, and said, "Spicer." "Yes, sir?" the team captain answered. "Come over and get in bed with me. I want to talk to you about this game." Spicer dutifully crawled across the aisle and into the coach's berth. "We talked there for about 10 minutes," he remembered. "The pros and cons of the game and what happened and why, what I thought about it and what he thought about it." Finally, Rupp snarled, "Spicer." "Yes sir?" Spicer answered. "Get the hell out of my berth," Rupp commanded. "You got it warm. Now get to bed." "That's the kind of guy he was," Spicer said five decades later. "He builds you up, you know, then he keeps you in your place."[63]

The Wildcats beat Georgia Tech and Vanderbilt to finish the regular season 12–2, then traveled back to Atlanta for the Southern Conference tournament, where they got past North Carolina State, Duke, and Florida to reach the final against Maryland. In that game they couldn't overcome what one sportswriter called "the greatest single exploit the 11 years of the Southern Conference basketball tournament has produced."[64]

Kentucky fell far behind early and trailed most of the way before taking a 27–25 lead on McGinnis's shot from near the sideline with a minute to play. After Maryland's Lewis Berger tied it with a basket, the referee brought the ball back to midcourt for the center jump, still required after every goal. The Terrapins won the tip, but Berger missed a "cripple" under the basket. According to Ralph McGill of the *Atlanta Constitution*, after Kentucky missed a shot, Maryland rebounded and Berger "dashed out as one of his mates passed him the ball past mid-floor. He turned, shot the ball forward. It arched but a little, going almost on a line, hit the back of the basket and dropped through the mesh with a swish. The swish of the ball was the blade that cut down Kentucky. The pistol sounded two seconds later." Berger's midcourt heave gave Maryland a 29–27 victory for the conference championship.[65]

McGill wrote that in a 1971 interview, a still bitter Rupp blamed the defeat on poor timekeeping, especially after Maryland tied the score at 27: "I'll always to this day, always to this day, not as an alibi, not as a cheap sport, question the time of that, because the time continued to run. From the time that the ball . . . went through the basket until you walked back to the center jump, the clock was not stopped but continued to run, and I remember we took a lot of time walking back there."[66] Rupp thought there were about 16 seconds left when Berger hit the tying shot. Ironically, Kentucky had lost to a team employing a slow-down offense strikingly similar to the Wildcats' old "submarine" attack under Johnny Mauer.

Although Rupp had made sure he announced to the press that the Wildcats' train would arrive in Lexington at eight o'clock the next night, he told Daddy Boles en route that no one would be there to greet a losing team. "You'll be surprised," Boles replied, and Rupp went back to shave for the first time all day.[67]

A huge crowd greeted the Wildcats as conquering heroes. "From the tone of the boisterous welcome given the returning basketeers, a stranger would have believed that the athletes had won a national championship instead of having been defeated," the *Courier-Journal* reported, "for there were hundreds of students and townspeople and the university band on hand roaring their cheers into the cold night air as Coach Adolph Rupp and his valiant warriors stepped off the train."[68] The team was paraded through town and finally taken to Alumni Gym for a celebration that included an address by President McVey. According to Rupp, McVey expressed his pride in the players and concluded that "it was the best they had been able to do in a long time."[69]

It probably didn't hurt that Rupp, according to Russell Rice, had wired the *Lexington Herald* with his take on the game: "Getting away to a bad start and fighting an uphill battle all the way, then forging to the front only to be denied by a long shot from mid-court with ten seconds to go, was a little too much for the Wildcats tonight. . . . The boys from old Kentucky staged the greatest comeback of the tournament, and their loss to Maryland is no disgrace. I only wish that the people at home could have seen the battle, for the fight they put up in the last half will live in my memory forever."[70]

The *Courier-Journal* reported that for the first time, UK put three players on the all-tournament first team. Then it turned its attention to the new coach, who "came in for his share of praise when he arrived here tonight. Coming to Kentucky last fall, unheralded and unsung, from a high school in Freeport, Illinois, Adolph Rupp took a crew of last year's castoffs and green material, with only one man who could be called a regular from the 1930 team, and coached that outfit almost to a championship his first year."[71] Rupp signed a new two-year contract, not as a member of the athletic department but as an instructor in the physical education department.

He never forgot that first UK team. In a 1971 interview he ticked off the names of the players and proudly noted the accomplishments of many of them after graduation. They were "all a bunch of fine students, all a bunch of good kids, all a bunch of conscientious workers, all a great bunch of boys to have around, and boys that even to this day call me their friend and I call them my friend."[72]

The rules in 1931 allowed basketball teams to conduct spring practices, and Rupp lost no time in preparing for his second season. In April he announced teasingly that he would use the spring sessions to teach his players "a revolutionary new shot," a half hook or "flip" close to the basket that had been perfected by "Frenchy" DeMoisey at Walton High School, where he had once scored 50 points in a game. Rupp tried without success to teach it to his other inside players.[73]

He had far better luck in his personal life. Esther Schmidt, whom he had courted back in Freeport, took a bus to Lexington during the summer after his first season at UK. She saw the campus and the town and met Rupp's new friends and colleagues, including Daddy Boles, Ruth and Bernie Shively, and Stella and Elmer "Baldy" Gilb (Shively and Gilb were assistant football coaches). "She was so pretty," Stella Gilb remembered. At the gymnasium, Rupp drew the group aside and asked: "Well, what do you think? Do you think I ought to go ahead and marry her?" Stella Gilb kept a vivid memory of the scene into her 90s: "I can't tell you what Ruth Shively said to him, but she called him 'you so and so and so and so; you'd be so lucky if you could get [her].' That was our answer; and of course, some months after that they got married."[74]

Russell Rice quoted Ruth Shively more precisely. "Anybody would be good enough for *you*," she told Rupp. According to Rice, she considered Rupp "the most self-centered person she had ever met. At age 90, she still couldn't find a good word to say about him." Ruth Shively told Rice that "there are many people who let a little power go to their head. He got a reputation, and he thought he was the most important person in the world."[75]

Nevertheless, Esther said yes.

Rupp returned to Freeport for the wedding on August 29, 1931. "I sneaked in there and swiped my wife away from her family," he joked. "We had a nice wedding and everything worked out nicely." After their honeymoon they set up housekeeping in a small apartment on Forest Park in Lexington.[76] Without exception, friends and acquaintances remembered Esther Rupp as a "delightful person," quietly supportive and loyal to her husband. She provided the stability at home so important for a successful coach in the public eye.[77]

And Rupp made sure he stayed in the public eye. *Lexington Herald* sports editor Neville Dunn, Johnny Mauer's old critic, found the new coach to be better copy. "Rupp is a person with a gloriously developed sense of humor," Dunn wrote, "a droll, witty man who knows basketball, makes a friend out of every new acquaintance, and is, in all the popular meaning of the phrase, 'a good sport.'"[78]

Rupp continued to use much of Mauer's rigid system while giving the players more freedom to use their talents, skills, and, as Baldy Gilb put it, "a lot of their own intuition. Adolph just let them play the way they had been playing. He wasn't going to change any offense or anything, but he let the kids do it their own way. Of course, Adolph [had] a few drills, and he'd run it and run it till it became muscle memory with them." In 1987 Gilb contended that Rupp "would still run the same drills when he quit coaching as he did when he started coaching. [He] did very little different from when he ended from when he started." Gilb agreed with that strategy because, after all, "there is not that much to basketball, to be very frank."[79]

While Rupp ran practices with precision and repetition, Gilb said that in games he cared more about the final score than perfect execution. "Adolph didn't care," he said. "All you have to do, just score for me. Go on. Put it in the basket. It doesn't matter how you do it." Just win, baby. And from the very beginning, he knew how to motivate his players to do just that. "Adolph was one of those kind that he could get 100 percent out of everybody that played for him," Gilb said. "They may not like him, they may have cussed him behind his back and all that, but they played for him. He got it out of them. Johnny [Mauer] couldn't get out of them what was in them. Adolph could."[80]

Gilb also remembered that as Rupp became more successful, he became more domineering: "You either did it Adolph's way or you didn't do it. You had to. [He] was one of the kind, you are either for him or you're against him. There wasn't any in between with him."[81]

In addition to the outside screens and "guard-around" offense left over from Mauer, the Kentucky coaches developed an inside screen that, according to Rupp, he stumbled upon in the mid-1930s. In the middle of a spring scrimmage he yelled: "Wait a minute! Wait a minute, boys. Stop! Run that thing over just exactly the way you ran it before." The players retraced the steps of the previous impromptu play, and Rupp hollered out, "I think we've got something here." After they ran the play yet again, he huddled them up to talk about the footwork for setting an inside screen. Perfection of the new maneuver helped the Wildcats dominate the Southeastern Conference because "the teams in the South did not know what we were doing." According to Rupp, the inside screen was his greatest contribution to basketball.[82]

Others remembered the origins of the inside screen differently. Kentucky players such as Bernie Opper believed that any innovations in the *X*s and *O*s came from assistant coach Paul McBrayer, not Rupp. McBrayer himself, not one to seek fame for himself, remembered that he had come up with the innovation of the inside screen during a UK practice session. In a 1984 interview with Humbert Nelli, Nelli asked McBrayer, "The inside screen came from where?" After a pause and a chuckle, McBrayer said, "I feel like that's one of my contributions to the team."[83]

Rupp brought McBrayer on as his assistant coach in 1934 and the players soon looked to the bright assistant for help with specific plays.

McBrayer also started keeping statistics not just in games, but in practices as well. "We started [that], in contrary to other publicity," McBrayer said in a 1984 interview. "We're probably the first team to ever start keeping detailed statistics not only on ballgames but on every practice. We had people that came that were taught how to do that; [they] came every day that we were going to have practice and kept them for me. There were files in my office and any time a boy came to my office to find how he was getting along we got that out. I didn't guess about [it]. Now I'm not saying that statistics is the whole answer," McBrayer said, but the assistant coach's innovation undoubtedly gave the Wildcats yet another advantage over SEC teams.[84]

In addition to practice statistics and the inside screen, McBrayer also added the second guard around, another play for which Rupp is usually given credit. Originally practiced by Blanton Collier at Paris High School, the play made good use of the superior guards that Kentucky always seemed to have on the team.[85]

One contribution Rupp undoubtedly made was of a sartorial nature. "As we kept winning and winning," Rupp recalled, "the press was very delighted with my brown suit. They thought that was a pretty good superstition, and they kept talking about it, and all the time we kept going along pretty good."[86] Neville Dunn took to calling him "The Man in the Brown Suit," writing after his first two losses as the UK coach that "maybe it was because Rupp's brown socks were in the laundry, or because he left his brown suit and brown tie at home, or because he had broken his rhapsody in brown by using it during a freshman game, or because the game was played on Friday the Thirteenth."[87]

After a particularly galling first half against Vanderbilt in just the seventh game of his tenure, Rupp asked guard Jake Bronston, "What were you thinking of when you were going bad out there?" Bronston replied, "I was wondering if you had on brown socks." Rupp pulled up his pants legs to prove that he did, and the Wildcats went on to win 42–37.[88] Rupp's Kansas mentor, Phog Allen, had his quirks, but Rupp carefully cultivated his various superstitions—finding bobby pins, spying a black cat—knowing that such silliness gave newspapermen something to write about.

Rupp also could be very entertaining. McBrayer remembered, "Rupp was a lot of fun to be with. He's got a great sense of humor. He was actually a real funny guy. And, ah, I think everybody appreciated that and the fact that he was winning all his games, why he was very popular." "There's no question about that," McBrayer said.[89]

In Rupp's second year, UK won its first 14 games before losing at home to Vanderbilt 32–31 to end the regular season. In the last Southern Conference tournament before the formation of the Southeastern Conference, the Wildcats went to Atlanta and defeated Tulane 50–30 on February 26, 1932, before facing North Carolina the next evening. Rupp recalled a front-page story in the *Atlanta Constitution* declaring that "the University of Kentucky would have to conform to all the rules and regulations of the Southern Conference and that [officials] would call Kentucky according to the rules the way they were called in the South, not the way we were accustomed to having them called up North."[90]

Seventy years after the Civil War, sectionalism remained an issue in America, in the context of the larger culture of race, of course, but also in the context of sport. One damn Yankee—Johnny Mauer from Illinois—had already befuddled southern coaches with the outside screen, which he had introduced in the late 1920s. Now coaches in the deep South had become all too familiar with Rupp's inside screen introduced by another damn Yankee coach from Illinois, who had again infiltrated the conference and in only his second year was already dominating the league with new-fangled ideas. No telling what he would do in the years to come if he were not curtailed early on. Word on the street was that he had even coached a black player on his teams at Freeport High School. "Of course, I knew we were going to get beat," Rupp remembered. He was right. North Carolina won 43–42.[91]

The Southeastern Conference was formed in 1932, and although Rupp did not play a role in its founding, he recognized that it would give him an even better chance to dominate. Georgia, Georgia Tech, Alabama, Alabama Polytechnic (later Auburn), Mississippi, Mississippi State, Louisiana State, Tulane, Tennessee, Sewanee, Vanderbilt, and Florida joined Kentucky as charter members. With the exception of Kentucky, those schools were more noted for football. Meanwhile, strong basketball schools Maryland, North Carolina, Duke, and North Carolina State, all members of the old Southern Conference, did not join the SEC. Kentucky's new league opponents often depended on assistant football coaches to direct the basketball teams. Rupp quickly shed his football duties to concentrate on basketball, and other SEC teams suffered for it.[92]

Jim Host, who received one of the first two baseball scholarships at the University of Kentucky in 1955, the same year he met Coach Rupp, described how inferior SEC coaches continued to plague other SEC schools long after Rupp arrived at UK. Harry Lancaster, the head baseball coach and Rupp's assistant, took Host down to the basement of Memorial Coliseum where the coaches' offices were located then to meet Rupp. In 1956, his sophomore year, Host became the color analyst for the university radio station WBKY, working with Ernie Coyle, who did play-by-play. The next two years, Host moved over to do play-by-play for basketball and football while playing baseball in the spring. So Host traveled with Rupp and the team on away games and got to know Rupp well. He saw especially how Rupp operated with opposing coaches, a method that he had polished since his early years to keep opposing SEC basketball sidelines filled with assistant football coaches who had little talent or real interest in the game.[93]

It was not unusual, for example, for Rupp to heap praise on an opposing coach after thrashing him by 30 or 40 points. "By gawd," Rupp would tell sportswriters following a game, "Coach [insert losing coach's name here] is one of the great coaches in the history of the game." He said, "Did you see the defense he tried to run against us? We had a helluva time with that the first few minutes of the game. Why our boys were having trouble with his defense." Of course, the next morning's headline read, "Coach Rupp Calls Coach [insert coach's name here] One of Greatest Coaches of the Game." Host said that Rupp was sure to play out that routine at every single town and city in the SEC to make sure the schools would keep the coach for another year, another year to insure another easy Kentucky victory.[94]

Rupp took some ideas from his brief career in football, including an emphasis on statistics. Henry Chadwick had introduced the use of statistics in the early years of baseball, but Rupp applied them to basketball as a way to correct weaknesses in his team. As an assistant football coach during his first semester at UK, he sat in the press box on game day and charted "how many yards had been made through the line over every position." He gave the charts to head coach Harry Gamage at halftime and after the game so Gamage could determine whether the linemen had done their jobs.[95]

During UK's first SEC basketball season, Rupp developed a detailed set of charts to gauge shots attempted and made, errant passes, intercepted passes, and fouls. Russell Rice considered these the forerunner of the extensive statistics kept today. If nothing else, Rupp's use of statistics indicated how the game changed. Tev Laudeman, who later wrote a compendium of Rupp's 42 seasons at UK, grew up in Lexington and often sneaked into Alumni Gym to watch the Wildcats practice. On Monday Rupp would gather the players around him and critique their performances in Saturday's game. He might tell a player: "You hit only two shots. That's not good enough. We have to hit 20 percent to win." Laudeman noted that by the 1960s, 40 to 45 percent shooting would be necessary.[96]

For the record, Rupp's teams went 15–3, 15–2, 21–3, 16–1, 19–2, 15–6, 17–5, 13–5, 16–4, and 15–6 (162–37 altogether) during his first decade at UK, winning one Southern Conference championship, four SEC titles, a regular-season cochampionship, and a Sugar Bowl crown. The Wildcats "slumped" to 17–8 in 1940–1941 before winning another SEC championship with a 19–6 record in 1941–1942. That was followed by a solid 17–6 campaign in 1942–1943. Rupp not only built his record on his domination of a weak conference but also on his innovative approach to the game, which earned him a reputation outside the region.[97]

Even though no scholarships were awarded for basketball when Rupp arrived at UK, from the very beginning he worked hard to find talented players. In a 1975 interview he told Russell Rice that "nowadays coaches subscribe to possibly 10 or 15 papers from Detroit, Pittsburgh, Indiana, St. Louis, Kansas City, and places like that." But in the early 1930s and throughout most of his career, he managed to win with Kentucky boys. After all, Rupp once said, "When a Kentucky baby is born, the mother naturally wants him to be president, like another Kentuckian, Abraham Lincoln. If not president, she wants him to play basketball for the University of Kentucky."[98]

With no budget for recruiting and little travel money, "we found about what we wanted in the *Courier-Journal* and the Lexington papers," Rupp said. "We did not go out and recruit where we stayed overnight. If we went somewhere, we went on our own. My assistant coach would look over some boys, naturally, and we'd see the boys play in the state tournament, which was held in Lexington."[99]

Before Rupp, recruiting had been haphazard. Forrest Sale, a star center at Kavanaugh High in Anderson County, had little contact with Johnny Mauer before deciding to come to UK in 1929. "Daddy Boles was the one who recruited me," Sale said in 1982. "I was just a country kid from Lawrenceburg out on the farm. . . . I wasn't the tallest player on the team, but I could always jump like a kangaroo." In one game he outscored the whole Versailles team. Still, Mauer never saw him play in high school, and Ohio State was the only college to recruit him. He picked UK because it was close to home and had an agriculture program.[100]

At UK Sale starred on an undefeated freshman team coached by Lynn Miller, and he acquired a nickname. He was in the shower after practice one day when teammate Morris Jackson asked, "Hey, where's the country boy. . . . Aggie?" The name stuck, and Aggie Sale flourished under Rupp, leading the team in scoring his final two years. As a junior he blocked five shots in the final minutes of a 29–28 victory at Tennessee that kept alive what became a 14-game winning streak. Rupp once called Sale "one of my five all-time greats. He was the most versatile of all my big men. He would play center with the best of them and forward equally as well. He was one of the smartest players I ever coached." The feeling was mutual. "My first impression of Rupp was his intelligence," Sale recalled. "Damn, he was smart."[101]

Rupp inherited Aggie Sale, but he found John "Frenchy" DeMoisey himself. The 6-foot-5-inch Walton High School center scored 50 points against Louisville Butler and 45 against Paris in the regional tournament, which "got me interested," Rupp deadpanned. His recruitment of DeMoisey presented a startling contrast to the high-intensity, cutthroat competition for players today. "I visited him and he was working on a road gang," Rupp recalled. "We sat in the shade on a creek bank, and I asked if he would like to attend UK. He told me he was making plans to attend Trinity College [which became Duke] because he was a minister's son and entitled to free tuition there. They had also promised him a job." Rupp later told DeMoisey that if he came to Kentucky, "tuition for the first semester was $31.50." Rupp added that he "would try to find someone to pay for the second semester or find some way he would work it out." DeMoisey enrolled at UK, and according to Rupp, "When he came out for the varsity as a sophomore in 1931, he told me he had paid tuition, room, and board through Christmas and would make the team or go home."[102] DeMoisey started for the Wildcats for three years and was an All-American in 1934. DeMoisey would later make a life in taking care of others, particularly

Rupp's friend, Kentucky governor A. B. "Happy" Chandler. After DeMoisey completed his playing career, he traveled with the governor and moseyed through the crowd when Chandler spoke. The 300-pound former All-American had a way of discouraging hecklers, and the governor always felt safe under DeMoisey's protection.[103]

Rupp told another recruiting tale about Dave Lawrence, whom he and assistant Birkett Pribble tracked down in Corinth, Kentucky. "He was working on putting a ditch in the road under a railroad track," Rupp remembered. "He was down in the mud digging around, and we talked to him and asked him to come to UK. There were some fences on the campus that needed painting, and that sounded better to him than fooling around with that dynamite, which gave him headaches, and digging in the mud." Rupp had never seen Lawrence play, learning of him by word of mouth and through the papers. This lone interview lasted just 15 minutes. "We just watched him work there," Rupp said. "That's all the contact there was. . . . That was the only time I ever saw the boy until he came here the first day of school."[104]

Rupp did not hesitate to use alumni as recruiters. Joe "Red" Hagan, a football and basketball star in Louisville—at both Male and St. Xavier high schools—had attended a football camp at Xavier in Cincinnati and planned to enroll there. Then UK alumnus Reed Miller stopped by his Louisville home and commanded: "Get in the car. We're going for a ride." "Where are we going?" a curious, but submissive Hagan asked. "Up the road a piece," Miller answered. They ended up on the UK campus, where the young athlete eventually accepted a football scholarship. After the 1935 football season, Hagan tried out for basketball without an invitation from Rupp and went on to earn three varsity letters, captain the 1937–1938 team, and hit probably the most spectacular shot in school history.[105]

Much to the consternation of James Naismith, the inventor of basketball and Rupp's old mentor, the 1937–1938 season began under a rule change that revolutionized the game. The rules committee eliminated the center jump after each made field goal. Naismith argued that the new rule would turn basketball "into a game of racehorse." If only Naismith knew.[106]

Toward the end of the season on February 14, 1938, Kentucky played Marquette, considered a vastly superior team with wins over Notre Dame, which had already defeated the Wildcats, and other fine squads. With only 12 seconds left in the contest before 4,000 fans at Alumni Gym, however,

UK had the ball with the score tied. The Wildcats inbounded the ball and made a couple of passes before getting it into the hands of Hagan. As the clock ticked down, Hagan heaved a two-handed shot behind the mid-court stripe. When the ball swished cleanly through the net giving the Wildcats a 35–33 victory over Marquette, the home crowd erupted and carried Hagan off the court. Governor A. B. Chandler bounded out of the stands, called for a hammer and a nail to mark the spot on the court from which was launched the longest shot in the history of University of Kentucky basketball up to that time. The distance measured 48 feet, 2¼ inches. And Red Hagan marked his spot in UK basketball lore. Hagan always thought that Rupp didn't care whether he came out for basketball or not.[107]

While Rupp had little trouble persuading Kentucky boys to attend the state university, he also had success luring players from other states. In 1935 he landed New York City schoolboy star Bernie Opper, who had seen the Wildcats play New York University (NYU) in Madison Square Garden early that year. Impressed in particular with UK's flamboyant center, LeRoy Edwards, Opper wrote a letter to Rupp, who invited him to "come on down."[108]

Opper's father advised him not to go, warning him, "It's going to be rough, you know, the prejudice and all that stuff." Indeed, in an era long before coast-to-coast and even international recruiting, Kentucky seemed like an exotic destination to an eastern, Jewish, city kid. "Take a New York boy out of New York and go down South, you know, it's a little different than it is today," said Opper in a 1980 interview. He thought, at first, he would attend NYU, but Rupp did his best to make the New Yorker feel right at home. Esther even accompanied her husband to meet him at the train station, and Rupp found him a room for the first semester. "I had a very enjoyable four years," Opper said. "Adolph was always a little rough sometimes, but you learned how to tolerate it. I guess he wasn't as rough in those years as he became later on, you know."[109]

Opper noticed a difference in style of play from what he had grown up with. In the East, "the block was illegal." "In other words, you had to make a pick and get out of there," Opper said. In the South, "if you established your place on the floor, you could use a body block." In a 1943 article in *Esquire*, writer Jimmy Jones saw it another way: "Rupp was one of the first college coaches to use the screening block in which there is no actual contact." He remembered Kentucky's loss to Long Island University in the 1938–1939 season at Madison Square Garden, where officials repeatedly called the Wildcats for illegal screens. "That is the custom in the East," Jones concluded, "to call a foul even when there is no contact on the play." By 1943, however, Kentucky's inside screening, initially so controversial in the South as well as the East, had been picked up by the eastern teams.[110]

Big Apple basketball also allowed more freedom in various styles of shooting. Opper said that in those early days Rupp insisted on two-handed shots. "And if you took a one-handed shot," he explained, "you'd be sitting on the bench talking to the coach." The only exceptions were layups and, for the pivot men, hook shots. A westerner at Stanford and a Kentuckian at Murray State University revolutionized shooting, however. According to *The Modern Encyclopedia of Basketball*, Hank Luisetti's "stunning one-handed shots"—the first jump shots ever seen in the East—helped Stanford defeat Long Island 45–31 in Madison Square Garden in 1936.[111]

Joe Fulks was born in the tiny town of Birmingham along the Tennessee River in western Kentucky in 1921. Birmingham is no more, submerged beneath the waters of Kentucky Lake with the building of Kentucky Dam, but as Fulks grew up there in the 1920s and early 1930s, he practiced jump shots using a ruined basketball filled with sawdust. With Congress's establishment of the New Deal's Tennessee Valley Authority in May 1933, federal authorities forced Birmingham residents from their homes and Fulks and his family moved from Marshall County to nearby Kuttawa in Lyon County. There, Fulks grew to six feet five inches, starred for Kuttawa High School, became known as "the Kuttawa Clipper," dominated the local competition, and perfected his newfangled jump shot. In his senior year in 1940, Fulks led the Kuttawa Lyons to the Kentucky state tournament, and even though the Lyons lost the first game of the tourney, Adolph Rupp knew enough to offer "the Clipper" a scholarship. Rupp was not the only big college coach to court the western Kentucky player, who many began to refer to as "Jumpin'" Joe Fulks.

Fulks turned down Rupp and played two years close to home at Murray State before entering the military where he played on various camp teams. After his military service his jump shot lifted him from Kentucky obscurity to world fame as a high-scoring Philadelphia Warrior in the late 1940s. He held the National Basketball Association's (NBA's) single-game scoring record of 63 points for a decade before Elgin Baylor broke it with a 73-point night, and then Wilt Chamberlain produced his 100-point miracle. The so-called "Babe Ruth of Basketball," Fulks was haunted all his adult life by alcoholism, which led to his murder in Kentucky in 1976. Because of the difficulties of his life and his tragic death, he is the most forgotten sports legend of our time.

In a sense, college basketball entered the modern era late in 1934, a decade before Luisetti and Fulks, when four teams played the first regularly scheduled doubleheader in Madison Square Garden. On December 29, 16,188 fans watched NYU defeat Notre Dame 25–18 and Westminster down St. John's 37–33. According to *The Modern Encyclopedia of Basketball*, "From that night on, the Garden became the showplace of college basketball," as "spectators in unprecedented numbers came to watch New York's strongest teams take on the best from around the nation."[112]

Ned Irish, a 29-year-old sportswriter for the *New York World-Telegram*, came up with the idea for "Garden basketball" after becoming frustrated trying to squeeze into cracker-box gyms to cover local college games; he even tore his pants climbing through a window to get into Manhattan's packed house. Irish quit his newspaper job and went on a one-man crusade as the "boy promoter" to secure the Garden for college doubleheaders. In 1934–1935 eight doubleheaders drew almost 100,000 fans. That helped college basketball financially, made it available to a wider audience, and spurred intersectional matchups. New York City became "the basketball capital of the nation," and performing in the Garden became every player's dream.[113]

Adolph Rupp made this dream a reality for his Kentucky players. In only the second college doubleheader held at the Garden, 16,539 fans—"the largest crowd in Eastern court history," according to the *New York Times*—saw the Wildcats lose to NYU 23–22. The game made UK center LeRoy Edwards a national star even though he was held in check by the Violet defense and, more to the point, the strict officiating on UK's screens. Notre Dame coach George Keogan had telegraphed Rupp to tell him about his own team's 25–18 loss to NYU a week earlier. Keogan blamed the defeat on the officiating and warned Rupp that, unless he took a "Midwest" official with him to New York, "you won't have a chance."[114]

NYU's Irving "Slim" Terjesen and Irwin "King Kong" Klein kept Edwards away from the basket, or, as Tev Laudeman put it, "All-American center LeRoy Edwards had a wrestling match in New York." Ralph John-son of the *Lexington Herald* stated it another way: "New York University's Cave men silenced 'Baby Leroy' Edwards, Kentucky's big scoring gun . . . to defeat the heretofore unbeaten Wildcats." Johnson wrote: "Big Ed Ed-wards was the center of attraction for the crowd when the Kentuckians romped out on the floor, and likewise drew considerable attention from the officials and his opponents once the battle was under way."[115]

Edwards fouled Sidney Gross late in the game, and the NYU guard sank a free throw to break a 22–22 tie. It was Edwards's fourth foul, which meant disqualification in those days, and that proved crucial on the ensu-ing jump ball, where his height had been decisive all night. This time NYU got the tip and ran out the clock.[116]

Writing for the *New York Times*, Arthur Daley called the game "a grand show that was put on for the amazing crowd . . . a struggle between teams that exemplified two entirely distinct types of basketball." His de-scription flies in the face of what Rupp had been promoting from the be-ginning of his tenure at UK. "The Violet displayed a brand of play that is indigenous to the East," Daley wrote. "It was one of the fast-break, the quick-cut for the basket and a short flick in. Kentucky, on the other hand, demonstrated something quite new to metropolitan court circles. The Southerners, with a background of twenty-nine victories out of their last thirty games and of seventy-six out of their last eighty-five, employ a slow, deliberate style of offense that is built around thirteen set plays. It was so sharp a contrast that the spectators, used to the swift-moving panorama of metropolitan basketball, were inclined to be impatient with the other type. But it was highly effective."[117] The NYU players were no shrinking violets; they had used their fast-paced style to win 22 in a row over two years.

Was Kentucky's play against NYU an anomaly? The final tally in the low 20s seems unusually low even in an era when a center jump followed every score. Kentucky had beaten Chicago 42–16 in the previous game, and after the loss to NYU, the Wildcats won a string of home games—66–19 against Chattanooga, 63–22 and 55–12 in back-to-back games against Tulane, and 48–21 over Tennessee—before a 33–26 victory at Alabama. They scored more than 50 points 10 times in the 1934–1935 season, in-cluding an 81–12 rout of Oglethorpe. Still, two late-season victo-ries—25–16 over Alabama and 24–13 over Creighton—indicated that they sometimes failed to execute a fast-paced style.

UK's scoring output did not increase significantly for several years even after the center jump was abolished in 1937. In the 1937–1938 season the Wildcats lost to Detroit 34–26, beat Alabama 27–21, and edged Tennessee 29–26. They played games in the 20s as late as 1941, usually against Johnny Mauer's Tennessee teams. In his 1943 *Esquire* article, Jimmy Jones concluded that Rupp's teams "alternate a fast and slow break, depending on the defensive setup and which man gets the ball." Georgia coach Elmer Lampe said, "They'll slow-break on a few plays, and then when your defense moves up leisurely to meet them, they'll fast-break you dizzy."[118]

Rupp blamed the 23–22 loss to NYU in 1935 on the referees, who repeatedly whistled the Wildcats for moving screens while letting the Violet players rough up LeRoy Edwards under the basket. "I can't understand why it's a foul when one of my boys moves toward the basket on a screening play and it isn't a foul when a New York boy drapes himself over the back of one of my country kids and hugs him around the arms," he fumed. Even the *New York Post* noted the uneven officiating: "The score says that NYU is the best college basketball team in the country and that the East still is supreme. But if Frank Lane, the ref from the Midwest, had worked the game, it's safe to assume big LeRoy Edwards would have been given a fantastic number of foul shots. Minor mayhem was committed on the person of Edwards by Terjesen and Klein. Something will have to be done or the game will become entirely too rough."[119]

Tev Laudeman of the *Courier-Journal* contended that the UK-NYU game eventually led to the three-second rule limiting the time an offensive player could stay in the foul lane. That rule change actually worked against dominant inside players like Edwards.[120]

Back home a reporter asked Rupp about the questionable officiating in the NYU game. His oft-quoted response, crafted around a biblical reference and perhaps fabricated later by the coach himself, became part of his arsenal of homespun rhetoric: "I really don't know. Riding back, I turned on the radio, and a broadcast from one of the churches in New York was on. The minister was speaking on the scripture, 'He was a stranger and they took him in.' That's all I know about what happened."[121] The New York trip gave Rupp a forum to float the idea of a postseason tournament to determine a national champion. "At the end of each season," he argued, "four or five teams throughout the country lay claim to a mythical national title. If the leading teams of each section would agree to play a round-rob-in tournament in some centrally located city, like Chicago, a sort of Rose Bowl champion in basketball would be crowned each year." Such an event would "tend to further interest in this sport throughout the country," and it would insure that "a more uniform code of rules interpretation, which is sorely needed, would soon be accepted."[122]

The idea of a national tournament was a natural outgrowth of Ned Irish's Madison Square Garden doubleheaders. Eventually organizers set up two tournaments. A group of New York sportswriters organized the first National Invitational Tournament at Madison Square Garden in 1938, and in 1939 the National Collegiate Athletic Association held its own tournament, "along the lines suggested by Rupp," according to Laudeman.[123]

Rupp's contributions to the game were undeniable, but back home in Kentucky, the head coach owed much to his assistant, Paul McBrayer. McBrayer became Rupp's assistant in 1934 and remained until he was inducted into the navy in 1943 during World War II. In *The Winning Tradition: A History of Kentucky Wildcat Basketball*, Humbert S. Nelli made clear how influential Paul McBrayer had been as Rupp's assistant from 1934 to 1943.

Player after player attested to McBrayer's contributions to the program. Bernie Opper said that McBrayer "was very, very influential. He was an excellent teacher of defensive and offensive basketball and rebounding." "Mac was a strong believer in defense and he put us through the paces," Opper explained. In the 1930s when Opper played, defense was all important. When he made All-American in 1939, Opper only averaged four or five points a game. Opper said that "LIU was being advertised as a point a minute team." But that meant that LIU only scored forty points a game.[124]

McBrayer carried what he had learned from Johnny Mauer over to his own coaching. Ken Rollins remembered that McBrayer drilled the players "on all of the basic fundamentals of basketball." "You would have thought that we had never been taught anything before," Rollins said, "but that was good." Even Rupp soaked in what McBrayer had to say. "Coach Rupp listened an awful lot to what Coach McBrayer was saying and suggesting," Rollins said.[125]

Red Hagan said that while he played (from 1936 to 1938) "at least two-thirds of the team looked to Mac for everything they did. I know I did and I think the others did too. Mac didn't want it that way but it just was because just about everyone on the team felt Adolph was not very knowledgeable about basketball." According to Hagan, it was only later "when Adolph became more successful that his word became law on the team." "I guess even on the campus," he said. Ed Lander, who played at UK during the early 1940s but watched practices as a teenager in the 1930s, remembered, "Mac did all the teaching and he was superb at teaching the mechanics of the game. He really made us better players than our talents warranted." "Any time something needed to be explained or corrected or something new was put in, he did it," Lander said. "Before and during the games Rupp said the inspirational things and Mac explained what we were supposed to do."[126]

In 1943 *Esquire*'s Jimmy Jones concluded that Rupp was "happy to be the most hated basketball coach in Dixie." Jones described a taxicab ride Rupp shared with Rear Admiral John Downes, coach of the Great Lakes Naval Station basketball team, en route to the Louisville Armory for a game in March 1942. The Baron turned to the sailor and remarked, "My boys are just a lot of pore li'l mountain boys, Admiral, and I just hope your boys won't treat 'em too rough, or they might get rough, too." Jones suggested that the conversation illustrated "Rupp's knack for making a combat out of basketball, and of grating up a profitable feud with his adversaries." He added that since Rupp's arrival at UK in 1930, he had "won a large and enthusiastic following of enemies who call him 'The Human Loud Speaker.'"[127]

From the 1930 to the 1943 seasons, Rupp's "pore li'l mountain boys" had claimed six SEC titles and built a 215–57 record against what the writer for *Esquire* called "the best competition available from all over the country." He failed to mention that the majority of those wins came in a football conference against schools that still did not take basketball seriously. Nonetheless, Rupp's Wildcats were the first team from the South to play in Madison Square Garden, and they represented the region three times in North/South matchups in the Sugar Bowl in New Orleans. In 1942 Kentucky won the NCAA Eastern playoffs against Big Ten champion Illinois before falling to Dartmouth.[128]

Jones asserted that Rupp had long since "buried the hatchet" with football coaches in his effort to raise interest in southern basketball, even promoting an all-star football game to benefit Lexington's crippled children's hospital. "Tough as he is in combat," Jones wrote, "the man's brusque and polemical exterior covers soft spots."[129]

Rupp also displayed personal toughness. In 1941 he came down with the flu the night before a game against Coach Clem Crowe's Xavier Musketeers in Cincinnati. With a fever of 104, Rupp checked into the hospital on the team physician's orders. But on game day, when he read Crowe's prediction of victory in a Cincinnati newspaper, he sat up in his hospital bed and bellowed to a nurse: "Where's my pants? I'm getting outta here!" That night, slumped and shivering on the bench, he directed the Wildcats to a 48–43 victory before returning to the hospital with pneumonia.[130]

Rupp had established a powerful court presence, which he earned with his own personality and through the meticulous preparation of his players in grueling practices. Jimmy Jones wrote: "Take good material, good competent coaching and good conditioning, and add the psychology and gab of a natural-born showman, and you have old 'Rupp and Ready' and the secret of basketball's rise to glory at the University of Kentucky."[131]

Rupp's success on the court and his imperious bearing made him a hated figure in gyms throughout the South. And that's just the way he wanted it. "He is willing to take the barbs since it stimulates enthusiasm for his game," Jones explained. "To the basketball fans of the South, Rupp is a sort of active human volcano going around spouting irritating verbiage, and naturally they simply have to leave their firesides on cold winter nights to go out and boo him."[132]

In little more than a decade as a college head coach, Rupp had transformed basketball, not so much in game strategies and style, but in the way the sport was emphasized by the media and perceived by fans. Before him, college basketball games were perfunctory affairs, covered briefly by the newspapers. Coaches met at midcourt before tipoff to exchange pleasantries, then met again afterward to offer polite congratulations. "The man in the brown suit changed all that," Jones wrote. "Now when The Baron brings his boys to town, there is no mistaking that something prodigious is in the offing. The papers for weeks have been writing about him, and the fans and village urchins have been thinking up choice invectives to hurl."[133]

It's notable that the emphasis was on the coach, not his players, just as it had been at Marshalltown, Iowa, and especially at Freeport, Illinois. Rupp also used the newspapers to drum up rivalries and feuds of his own concoction. Because of the state's reputation as the "seedbed of basketball,"

Indiana proved to be a natural target. "Tomorrow," he once remarked sarcastically, "the Philistines cross the River Jordan (the Ohio) and pass into the Holy Land." Early on, he developed a "promising little mountain feud" with West Virginia by claiming that during a game in Morgantown, the gymnasium lights dimmed when the Wildcats had the ball in their end of the court, but when the Mountaineers gained possession and headed up court, the lights "came on as bright as a saloon on Saturday night." Rupp held a special grudge against Georgia Tech coach Roy Mundorff, who had been on the national rules committee for years and frequently differed with the UK coach over rule interpretations. The two often squabbled at courtside and in pregame discussions, but when Kentucky went to Atlanta for the inaugural game in the Yellow Jackets' new arena, Rupp "got himself locked up in one of those new-fangled automatic johnnies" and didn't appear on the bench until nearly halftime.[134]

That feud paled in comparison with the battles against Tennessee, however. This natural rivalry intensified in 1938 when General Robert Neyland, Tennessee's legendary football coach and athletic director, hired Johnny Mauer, Rupp's predecessor at UK. Tired of Rupp's "aspersions at the expense of the Vols," Neyland gave his new coach "*carte blanche* to go out and get himself a basketball team." With money for scholarships— Tennessee previously had manned the basketball team with football players—Mauer did just that. He coached the Volunteers from 1938 to 1947 and had the highest winning percentage of any Tennessee coach. In 1941 the Vols defeated the Wildcats 36–33 to win the SEC tournament. Rupp chafed at the loss but knew that it would boost interest in basketball in the South. In the early 1930s a Kentucky-Tennessee game might draw 1,500 fans. A decade later it would pack gyms to the rafters in either Lexington or Knoxville, prompting UK to begin plans for a bigger arena to replace Alumni Gym.[135]

Esquire's Jimmy Jones concluded: "The Baron has proved by demonstration that a man himself and his game can flower and thrive on controversy."[136] In fact Rupp and the Wildcats continued to thrive despite America's entry into World War II after Pearl Harbor. The Wildcats went 19–6 in 1941–1942, winning the SEC tournament. Going 17–6 in 1942–1943, the Wildcats made it to the finals of the conference tournament but lost to Tennessee 33–30. During both seasons Rupp played a postseason game against a Great Lakes navy team to benefit the Navy Relief Fund.[137]

Rupp was forty years old when America entered the war in December 1941. His bad back kept him out of the war. Russell Rice said that the legend that Rupp sat out the war to raise a victory garden and search out talent in "the back roads of Kentucky" made a good story but "was only half true." Rupp's friend Bob Sparks told Rupp that he should preserve food for the war effort. As Rice tells it, Sparks "bought a bushel of peaches and suggested that they take them to the cannery of Lafayette High School." Rupp waited until after midnight to call Sparks to tell him "that he had made the greatest deal of his life. On the way home from the cannery, he had stopped at the A & P grocery just out of curiosity. In Aisle 5, he found a can whose label showed a girl holding a peach. The can cost thirty-nine cents." When Rupp figured the cost of the home-canned peaches—the sugar, the cans, and the peaches—he figured it at 42 cents a can. "I've called H. J. Heinz and made a deal with him," Rupp told Sparks. "He is not going to coach basketball, and I am not going to can any more peaches."[138]

Despite a continuing string of winning records from 1936 to 1941, Tev Laudeman wrote that, during those years, "hard times came to Adolph Rupp."[139] Still, Laudeman's assertion is relative. During that period, Kentucky posted records of 15–6, 17–5, 13–5, 16–4, 15–6, and 17–8. The Wildcats won the league championship three times. By Rupp's standards, however, this was not good enough. Despite the war's depletion of his players and a valuable assistant coach, "A Golden Era of Kentucky Basketball" dawned in the middle of World War II.

5

World War II and the Games March On, 1941–1945

On December 6, 1941, the evening before the Pearl Harbor attack, Kentucky whipped Miami of Ohio 35–21 in Alumni Gym. It was the first game of the season. After the events of the morning of the next day, that fateful Sunday, the world would never be the same. While some UK students prepared to volunteer for one of the branches of the armed forces immediately after final examinations, practices and the season continued on for the basketball Wildcats.

A week after December 7, the Wildcats lost a close one at Ohio State 43–41 but then won five, before losing the first conference game to Tennessee in Knoxville 46–40. After four wins, Kentucky lost back-to-back games to Alabama in Tuscaloosa and to Notre Dame in South Bend, before finishing off the regular season with four straight wins, and then making short work of the other SEC teams to win the conference tournament in Louisville.

Kentucky lost a post-season game in Louisville on March 14, against a Great Lakes navy team, then beat Illinois in the NCAA Tournament 46–44 in New Orleans, before losing to Dartmouth 47–28 to finish out the season 19–6. Rupp had no stars on the 1941–1942 team. The five leading scorers—Marvin Akers (7.6), Mel Brewer (7.0), Milt Ticco (5.8), Ermal Allen (4.9), and Ken England (4.9)—indicated a balanced attack, a hallmark of Rupp's teams since LeRoy Edwards averaged 16.3 in the 1934–1935 season.

Sportswriter Earl Cox remembered Ermal Allen, a senior forward on that 1941–1942 team, as one of the greatest all-around athletes in UK athletic history. A native of Morristown, Tennessee, and turned down by UT for being too small for SEC football, Allen was determined to show Gen. Bob Neyland, the famous Tennessee coach, that he had made a mistake. Rupp signed Allen on a combination scholarship and the 5-foot-11-inch, 165-pound forward played basketball for Rupp and football for both Ab Kirwan and Bear Bryant. He started at tailback for three seasons in football and made All-SEC for Rupp in basketball. As a golfer, Allen won Kentucky State Amateur Championship matches against Bobby Nichols and Frank Beard. He later became Tom Landry's top aide with the Dallas Cowboys before retiring in 1984.[1]

As a player for two UK coaching legends, Allen had a unique perspective. "I've seen [Bear Bryant] pull every recruiting trick in the book," Allen said. Bryant would say, "Ermal, you talk to the boy and daddy. I'll court the mama." Allen concluded that with Bryant, "the greatest thing he had going for him was leadership." Allen believed that Rupp was "the most egotistical of them all. He was good and he knew it, and he'd let everyone else know it. But he could get the job done. He could have been a success in football or anything. He believed he could do it." According to Allen, the greatest of Rupp's skills was the ability to bring 50 boys on the court, and "from that crowd, he could absolutely single out the guy who would be great." "It might not be one of the hotshots," Allen said. "He had a great knack for picking the right people."[2]

Despite his ability and accomplishments in three sports, Ermal Allen was not a basketball star. Adolph Rupp remained, by his own design, the star of the University of Kentucky Wildcats. For his teams to have balanced scoring year after year was just the way the Baron liked it. Tenacious defense and a machine-like offense translated into accolades for the Kentucky coach, rather than any individual player.

In the 1942–1943 season, Kentucky went 17–6, failed to win the SEC tournament—losing to Tennessee and Johnny Mauer 33–30 in the tournament final—and did not make the NCAA tournament. With his roster depleted by the war, Adolph Rupp and Athletic Director Bernie Shively had serious discussions about whether UK should attempt to field a team in the 1943–1944 campaign.[3] The future looked bleak for the Kentucky Wildcats. The University of Kentucky football team canceled its season in 1943, but the basketball team soldiered on in 1943–1944.

"Of course this is a freshman team," Rupp stated in a makeshift student basketball publication. "It will be the first time since the last war that freshmen will represent the University. This is a great responsibility for the boys to live up to, especially with the schedule they have to face. But with a little experience under their belts, they'll come around." The entire eighteen-man roster was indeed made up of freshmen, except for three sophomores—Tom Moseley, Bob Stamper, and Wilbur Schu. Both Moseley and Schu had 4-F classifications, which kept them out of the army. And even though Stamper was a sophomore, he was only 17 years old, still too young to go to war. Out of the fifteen freshmen of the squad, eleven were either seventeen years old or classified as 4-F.[4]

With that roster Rupp's team went 19–2, losing only on the road to Illinois 43–41 in the regular season. After sweeping through the SEC tournament, Rupp chose to go to the NIT rather than the NCAA, a common practice in those days, because there was more money to be made in New York City. After winning the first game 46–38 against Utah, Kentucky lost to St. John's 48–45. The Wildcats finished out the season with a convincing 45–29 victory over Henry Iba's Oklahoma A & M team in the consolation game. Freshman Bob Brannum was named All-American, and fellow freshmen Jack Tingle and Jack Parkinson had stellar seasons.

Brannum, Tingle, and Parkinson made the All-SEC first team and Wilbur Schu made the SEC second team. The team became known as Rupp's "Beardless Wonders." Schu, the elder statesman on the team, would go on to play for three more years, playing each year with his knees heavily bandaged. Ralph Beard remembered that Schu "didn't have that much ability, but he played on heart and guts." "He was one of those who sacrificed for the rest of the team," Beard said. "Every time that we'd go into Madison Square Garden, the organist would play 'Shoo Shoo Baby,'" he recalled. A natural leader, Schu sometimes talked too much. "He was always talking in the huddles," Beard said. "Adolph would say 'Schu, shut up so I can say something.'"[5]

Ralph Looney of the *Lexington Leader* wrote that Adolph Rupp was "the man who can always be depended upon to produce stories as entertaining as his basketball teams are successful." According to Looney, on the banquet circuit Rupp's "nasal voice always has a serious ring during a speaking engagement and he can also keep an earnest, poker-face while telling very funny yarns." One popular anecdote concerned the 1943 season when

"Rupp's net hopes were at a low ebb" because "the Army had taken all his former stars and there seemed to be no possibility of scraping up enough material for any kind of a team." UK's president, Herman L. Donovan, called in the coach and asked, "Coach, can we have a basketball team?"

"Why I don't know, Dr. Donovan," Rupp replied, "but I think we can have a team even if we have to play girls." Rupp explained in an aside, "I'd always secretly wanted to coach a girls' team anyway, and, by golly, I wasn't going to miss such an opportunity." Rupp continued. "When a notice that we were going to play girls appeared in the papers, the boys started rolling out of the hills—the idea seemed to appeal to them, too. After they came, I wasn't going to disappoint them, so I called the girls out. Strangely enough, all they wanted to do was scrimmage against the girls." (Rupp made a dramatic pause for laughter.) "We didn't have much of an offensive team, though. But what a defensive club! That was the only time I ever could assign a man to guard his opponent when he would really come through. Those girls were well guarded."[6]

Whether the 1943–1944 Wildcats practiced against girls or not, Rupp's team, led by Jack Tingle, Jack Parkinson, and All-American Bob Brannum, went 19–2. During a road game to Buffalo, New York, to play patsy Carnegie Tech, Rupp thought it would be good to show his players the sights. "We got into Buffalo just after the biggest snowfall of the year," Rupp recalled. "It was 20 inches deep. I got to thinking that maybe the boys would like to see Niagara Falls, so I asked [Bernie] Shively about it—he's the man who handles the money. Shively didn't think we ought to do it, but I told him how these boys were all just kids and just waiting to go to the Army, so we went."[7]

With the freezing temperatures, a huge mountain of ice had built up just below the falls. "It was a beautiful sight," Rupp remembered, but "thirty seconds after we got there I was standing with Shively, admiring the falls, and I noticed some men down the ice, attempting to climb up that great mountain." Rupp turned to the athletic director and said, "Anybody who would do a thing like that is crazy. Why, they might be killed. There certainly are a lot of crazy people in this world." According to Rupp, "Shive peered down at the sight over the rims of his spectacles and muttered: 'Well, Adolph. They're your boys!'"[8]

And so they were, according to Rupp's yarn. Rupp also added that he "followed them down on the ice." "Somewhat like Simon Legree and the hounds following Eliza in *Uncle Tom's Cabin*, he got 'em."[9] Rupp got 'em in time to beat Carnegie Tech 61–14.

Still, at times during the war years Rupp's plans for his teams were interrupted by the needs of Uncle Sam. "You'd start to build a team, and the first thing you know a boy would be drafted," Rupp said. "It got so I felt as if I was running a kindergarten." Despite Rupp's complaints he continued to win with his "kindergarten kids."[10]

In the five seasons between 1941 and 1945, Rupp won and won and won. His teams went 19–6, 17–6, 19–2, 22–4, and 28–2. He won SEC championships in four of the five seasons; indeed, he only lost one SEC game, a 35–34 loss at Tennessee in 1945, during one phenomenal stretch. Rupp won the NIT championship in 1946. This began the golden era in the Wildcats' storied program and the coach himself seemed to glitter and shine. As Mark Twain and Charles Dudley Warner would have it, though, this was also a Gilded Age for the program and for the coach, for beneath the glitter and glory would soon be buried the stench of corruption and scandal.

After going 8–1, with a lone loss to Illinois, early in the 1943–1944 season, Rupp enjoyed the full support of the relatively new president of the university, Herman L. Donovan. In a January 12, 1944, letter to Rupp, Donovan wrote, "My dear Coach Rupp. I do not know how to convey to you the pride we have in you and your boys who have covered themselves with glory on the basketball court. Everybody around the University, the alumni all over the state and the world, and the many friends of the University are immensely pleased with the great success you have had in the development of a new team under the most difficult circumstances." "What you have done again proves that you are a genius in your field," Donovan gushed. "I wish you continued success for the rest of the season and I feel sure that you will have it. Mrs. Donovan and I want you to bring the boys to Maxwell Place for a little supper when the battles are over."[11]

Rupp appreciated the glowing praise from his boss. "I wish to thank you for the nice letter you sent to me in regard to the basketball team this year," Rupp replied. "We have worked hard with these boys, and they have responded nicely to what we have requested them to do. I only hope that we may continue to hold most of these boys until the close of the season."[12]

Rupp had enjoyed the support of Frank L. McVey, the president who hired him. At first, McVey showed only a passing interest in sports. According to Rupp, the president's "attitude toward athletics was not as over powerful as some of the other presidents in the Southeastern Conference at the time." "If we won half of the games, he was happy," he said. As Rupp's success grew, however, McVey learned the positive role that sports could play in the life of the university. Rupp remembered McVey as "brilliant." "He was brilliant in the field of education and was regarded that way by the entire educational profession," Rupp recalled. McVey kept Rupp on his toes. "He had a vast knowledge of things," Rupp said, "and whenever you sat down and talked with him, you'd better have your information well in hand, because if you didn't, he'd soon get you down the pipe, and he'd lose you somewhere along the way." "Here was a man that didn't exert a great influence over athletics," he continued, "because his great overpowering thing was to make the University of Kentucky an educational institution and do the best he could in the field of education. And I would say that athletics were secondary as far as schoolwork was concerned here at the university." Under McVey, who presided over the university from 1917 to 1940, the institution grew in academic stature.[13]

Things changed when Donovan became president in 1941. It was during Donovan's tenure—1941–1956—that sports, at least football and basketball—became a big business at UK. And Rupp recognized the role that the president played. "Now, Dr. Donovan was more interested in athletics, possibly than . . . anyone else that we have ever had." "I don't think there's any question about that," Rupp asserted.[14]

Donovan came to the university from the presidency of Eastern Kentucky State Teachers' College with the support of Kentucky's governor Keen Johnson. According to Carl B. Cone, a member of the history faculty who wrote a history of UK, "Unlike his predecessor, Donovan lacked national stature either in his professional field, education, or as president of one of four teachers colleges in an educationally backward state." Cone wrote that "the circumstances of the appointment and reasonable suspicions of political influence behind it dimmed whatever luster he might have brought to the presidency." Just before Donovan's appointment, the board of trustees had abolished the Faculty Senate, but after two years of persuasion, Donovan convinced the board to reinstate the faculty body. Donovan believed this "hard-won success" to be "one of the outstanding accomplishments of my years as President of the University." According to Cone, the president's victory "reveals Donovan at his fighting best." Donovan earned the respect of the faculty and restored "the faculty's self-respect."[15]

Donovan's emphasis on athletics certainly earned the respect of Adolph Rupp, even though at times it seemed the president's primary concern was to field a winning football team. Along with appeasing the faculty, Donovan moved to gain the support of the Kentucky legislature in Frankfort. According to Rupp, "When he came here, he went before the state legislature, and he addressed them about two hours, and told them about the educational needs of the commonwealth as he saw it." "It was a great, great day," Rupp concluded. "And he felt that he had put over a very fine selling job to the state legislature." After his address, however, one of the legislators rose on the floor and asked the university president, "What are you going to do about getting us a football team?" "Well that set him on fire," Rupp said, "and he got up and talked about an hour more." After his experience before the legislature, Donovan "felt that he immediately could read the pulse of the people. And that pulse was that in order to have good public relations, and to do the things that he wanted done in the field of education, he would use athletics to build this good public relations image."[16] With his steadfast support of athletics, Donovan set a precedent that later UK presidents followed almost without exception.

Rupp believed that Donovan "was very thoughtful about this thing. He had a building program in mind. And many, many, many of the buildings on the campus today—[Rupp said this in September 1971]—are the result of this man's thinking." Rupp marveled, "I don't see how he accomplished everything that he did during the time that he served." Chief among his accomplishments, in Rupp's opinion, was the creation of an athletics association. "There was grumbling and growling," Rupp remembered, "so he called a meeting of all these sore heads, as he called them." "Now fellas," Donovan said, "I've heard about all of this I want to hear. Now let's put your money where your mouth is, or let's forget about the thing, and let me handle the athletics around here." He called for $100,000 to form an athletics association, an organization that would "pay a football coach what they ought to be paid, because [the university could not] pay anyone . . . more than $5,000, which was the constitutional limit at that time on salaries in the state." Donovan assured the "sore heads": "You're not going to get a top flight coach until you do." Rupp remembered that

"that kind of shook some of these bold fellows downtown, but they got busy and they formed some committees and they raised $100,000." "That's why today we have the University of Kentucky athletics association," he said, "a separate organization from the University of Kentucky." Under the new setup, taxpayers' dollars did not support athletics. Rather, gate receipts went to the association. "Now, in order to do that," Rupp said, "to keep this thing going, this $100,000 was merely a cushion that he wanted to use to fall back on in case we had bad years, and of course those bad years were sure to come, as they do in the lifetime of every school."[17]

Ironically, the new athletics association for which Donovan had fought so hard could now pay the football and basketball coaches more than the university president, indeed, more than the governor. By 1951, Rupp's annual salary was $8,500, with an additional $1,500 for expenses. Former president McVey recorded in his diary that he visited Donovan on February 2, 1945. "President Donovan evidently can have the headship of Peabody College at $12000 a year if he wants it," McVey wrote. "The thing that discourages him is the $5000 limit on salaries not so much on his own account but because it reduces the University to a low salary schedule when new appointments are made." McVey wrote that "some of our young men are going elsewhere because they have prospects of professorships from $6000 to $8000." McVey believed that "the situation is serious. The only hope appears to be a new constitution and that is a long process." The 1891 state constitution had imposed the $5,000 salary limitation, a measure that had been affirmed by a 1942 Court of Appeals decision. Carl Cone wrote that "the shackles that bound university personnel to the $5,000 salary limitation for state officials . . . were finally broken by a test case in 1947 and just in time: the restriction was beginning to pinch hard and threaten the very existence of the university." Former UK president Frank McVey wrote in his diary that it was "very good news for the University when the Court of Appeals handed down its opinion that the constitutional provisions limiting salaries to $5000 did not apply to employees but officers." "A university professor was an employee of the state and not an officer," McVey explained. "This opinion settles the salary question for schools and colleges and will permit them to get and hold better men than they can do now. There is great rejoicing on the campus but there are also a number of bridges to be crossed such as a legislature which will appropriate funds to meet the additions to salaries. Perhaps every professor looks to the President for an addition to his pay thinking he is as good as the next man. The President no doubt will advance perhaps fifty men to higher pay in the professorial rank."[18]

The academic side of the university now at least had a chance of keeping up with other comparable universities. On the athletic side, lean times for football came during World War II, when football was abolished for the 1943 season. Even after the football schedule was resumed in 1944, the program struggled for a time. The retired McVey wrote in his diary on October 13, 1945, that "the Wildcats . . . were defeated by the Georgian team by the score of 48–6." "I did not go for I feared that the score would be very one sided," he said. "Why does the Kentucky team march in the rear? The answer is poor personnel, unsatisfactory coaching and none too good generalship. Some say it is a matter of money. If that is the case we are in a bad way because our sources of money are not equal to those possessed by our opponents." After a 60–19 loss to Alabama in 1945, the former president wrote that at the end of the season "the noise of disgruntled alumni will be heard in no uncertain terms." "What will the University do?" McVey asked. "The answer is that the University will trail along after other southern teams and endeavor to get money to pay a coach a higher salary and give players support enough to keep Kentucky lads from going to the University's competitors." "Undoubtedly there will be some improvement," McVey asserted, "but I doubt that it will be enough to lift the Kentucky team to the top; but half way is better than the cellar where the team has resided thru many seasons."[19]

After the 1945 season, registrar Leo Chamberlain, who would become a vice president in 1947, said that President Donovan "had given hours to the matter of football for the past six weeks." McVey wrote that his successor as president at UK had taken up time with "the consideration of what should be a comparatively minor matter. Now the [University] proposes to go in on a big time basis to see if its football team cannot be brought to the front in athletic contests. The Alumni are pressing for results forcing the President to do something about the football situation." McVey predicted that "some betterment will result and the University's team may get up into the upper half but prospects of doing more than that are rather remote."[20]

By December 1945, President Donovan was defending the drive for a big-time football program, one that would match the success of Adolph

Rupp in basketball. Donovan's defense indicated the historic force of football in the Southeastern Conference. Even while Rupp won season after season, UK alumni clamored for football victories. Donovan spoke to the Lexington Rotary Club on December 6, 1945, about the necessity of improving the football program. Former president McVey attended the meeting and that evening wrote in his diary that Donovan "was quite happy in an ex tempore speech that carried conviction in the audience." Donovan laid out his proposal to raise $75,000 more for the athletics association "to get a big time football coach and thereby encourage boys in Kentucky to come to the University." McVey wrote that three Lexington men had agreed to put up $15,000 each; "the balance it is hoped will come from people in the state." According to Donovan, "There were a million people in Kentucky who identified the progress of the University with football prowess." McVey questioned whether Donovan had "made a very strong attempt to raise the level of their thinking?" Donovan assured the Rotary audience that "there would be no let down in academic standards in order to get boys or keep them in the University." McVey worried that while thousands of dollars flowed into the coffers to entice a big-time football coach to come to Kentucky, the Frances Jewell McVey Scholarship, named in honor of his wife, languished. The amount received in nearly six months for that scholarship "was less than the three Lexingtonians had subscribed to the football fund," McVey lamented.[21]

With the setup of the new athletics association and a successful fund drive, in 1946 Donovan and the University enticed Paul "Bear" Bryant, a dynamic young coach coming off a 6–2–1 season at the University of Maryland in his first year as a head coach, to come to Kentucky. Bryant brought immediate results that even impressed former president McVey. McVey recorded in his diary on October 5, 1946, that "a long time can be counted between the football games I have attended. I didn't go at all last season tho I did listen to some of the games recounted over the radio." When McVey drove to Stoll Field, he was surprised that he had to park "a full half mile from the gate." "The occasion was the contest with Xavier, a Catholic college in Cincinnati," McVey wrote. "The score was 70 to 0 against the boys from north of the Ohio River. I was interested in the transition that had taken place over the past twenty years. First organization, then money, plenty of manpower, skilled guidance under an expert coach and an awakened interest in Kentucky's hopes and aspirations." The attendance, estimated at 20,200, the largest home attendance to that time, would bring "a considerable sum into the coffers of the Athletic Association." McVey seemed ambivalent about the newfound success of the football program under Bryant. "Big football is now in the field," he wrote, "and the public evidently likes it." Although "no better lighted field is to be found anywhere, in fact I was delighted with [the] clear view, the brilliant light, the green gridiron and large marching band, now the stadium and bleachers are spoken of as meager accommodations for the hosts who come to the games." McVey realized the insatiable appetite that bigness would bring. "Times are indeed changed," he wrote. As for the coach, McVey saw that "Paul Bryant holds sway, maintains discipline, keeps his own counsel, but gets on with the sports writers while at the same time carrying on effectively as shown by the performance of his team."[22]

On October 19, 1946, McVey wrote,

The day turned out to be a fine football day, not too cool, in fact just right. The University of Kentucky was scheduled to battle with the Vanderbilt Commodores who so far this season have not been scored upon. Most people thought the U. of Ky. would go down in defeat, but the game was won by a score of 10 to 7. So this season the new coach has won 4 games out of five. He should win at least 3 more which will be an excellent record. According to reports every seat in the stands at Stoll field have been sold for the season. The University will have some money at the end of the season with which to enlarge the seating capacity.[23]

McVey's take on the football program at UK mirrored the conventional wisdom concerning basketball—that struggling programs with little success had been turned around by charismatic, successful coaches, Adolph "Baron" Rupp in basketball and Paul "Bear" Bryant in football. But Johnny Mauer had fashioned a winning program in basketball before Rupp came along, and in football, the Wildcats had only three losing seasons between 1903 and 1924. It is true that hard times had fallen on the football team during McVey's presidency, but when Bear Bryant became head coach in 1946, a winning football tradition had long been established in Lexington. Like Rupp, Bryant only added to the tradition. In 1924, a running track and permanent bleachers had been added to Stoll Field on

Euclid Avenue to create McLean Stadium, with a seating capacity of 15,000. The stadium was named after Price McLean, an engineering student who had died following a football injury in a game against Cincinnati in 1923. Gilbert Graves, a quarterback for Murray State Normal School and a transfer from the University of Kentucky, had been killed in 1924 in a play against West Tennessee Normal School (later the University of Memphis) on Moore Field in Murray.[24] The deaths of McLean and Graves did not seem to quell the ardor of college football fans in the Bluegrass State.

Alumni Gymnasium had been completed in 1924, along with McLean Stadium. The basketball facility at that time could seat the entire student body, just under 2,000, plus about 1,500 faculty and townspeople. With Bryant's success, the football stadium was expanded to seat 35,000 in 1948.[25] And as Rupp entered the most illustrious period in his coaching career, the golden era of Kentucky basketball, it became increasingly evident, as crowds lined up outside the doors and were indeed turned away at home game after home game, that a new basketball coliseum would follow. In fact, in April 1947, ground had already been broken for a new basketball arena across Euclid.[26]

Ironically, after the football season had been canceled in 1943, there had been talk of abolishing basketball as well. Rupp did everything he could to keep it going. In a faculty meeting, Rupp argued, "We ought to continue it just for the good morale on the campus, for the faculty and for the student body, to give them something to do." Racking up *W*s in the victory column throughout the years of World War II, however, proved to be Rupp's most persuasive argument. "Well, we picked up a bunch of boys that were 4-F kids, and we built a basketball team," Rupp remembered. "We took this basketball team and we made a very fine remarkable record with this team."[27]

While Rupp claimed to have relied on 4-F World War II rejections, Harry Lancaster, Rupp's assistant coach after the war, believed that Rupp depended on younger players who were not yet 18, and that the teams Rupp beat consistently were made up of 4-F players. According to Lancaster, Rupp relied on players who were too young for the draft. "For example," Lancaster recalled, "Parkinson and Brannum had made it in their freshman year while everybody else was in the service. Most of our good players were gone. Brannum was only sixteen years old when he came in here from Kansas and made All-American as a center at the University of Kentucky." Parkinson and Brannum and Jim Jordan, who was named All-American at North Carolina as a Navy Pre-Flight student, played against other teams with 4-Fs, according to Lancaster. "We might as well be honest about it," Lancaster said, "that's what we were playing against. So they are what I would call synthetic All-Americans. When the real All-Americans came back, they couldn't cut it. But this was a great thing in those days. The news media used to say, 'Well, Kentucky ought to have two teams. The A team plays the Southeast Conference and the B team plays in the Big 10. Harry could take one group and Adolph take the other.'"[28]

Rupp fashioned a 19–2 record and won the SEC championship in the 1943–1944 season with a starting lineup of three freshmen and two sophomores, his "synthetic All-Americans." Freshman center Bob Brannum became the youngest player to be named a consensus All-American. After the season, Brannum joined the army along with his brother. For taking such a young team—"fresh out of high school," said Russell Rice—to a conference championship, Rupp was named to the Helms Athletic Foundation's Collegiate Basketball Hall of Fame, the tenth coach to be named by the foundation.[29]

An elated President Donovan wrote to "My dear Coach Rupp" at the conclusion of the season. "You have done it again. In a year when it seemed absolutely impossible to get together a basketball team, you have developed one of the outstanding teams in the nation. We greatly admire your skill and ability as a coach and leader among men. Let me congratulate you and your boys on winning the championship of the Southeastern Conference. The University is very proud of your accomplishment." In a March 10, 1944, reply, Rupp thanked the president: "Naturally we feel very good about the way the boys performed, considering the fact that they were only youngsters and did not have a lot of basketball experience before this year. I only hope that they will be able to continue their winning ways after they get out in the world."[30]

The Wildcats won the conference championship again in 1944–1945, the last year of the war. At the end of the summer in 1945, Rupp left for Paris after the army asked the coach to help initiate a sports program for the troops. En route, Rupp stopped over in New York. There the army made him a colonel and fitted him up with the proper uniform. In France,

Harry Lancaster coached navy softball and baseball teams, preparing them to face the Third Army teams in Reims. Lancaster had been stationed in Exeter, England, where he served as the Recreation Officer. His teams had won the European Theater of Operations Championship in 1945. When Lancaster reported to Major Opperdecker, the USO commander in Paris, "he was flabbergasted to find Adolph in the major's office" wearing a khaki uniform, complete with Eisenhower jacket and garrison cap. "Boy am I glad to see you," Rupp said as he pumped his hand. Rupp asked his fellow Kentuckian two questions: "Where are you staying? Do you have any bourbon?"[31]

"I'm staying in a damn place in Pig Alley [Pigalle] and it doesn't even have a bathtub. I don't have a change of uniform," Rupp told Lancaster. "How in the hell can we win a war this way?" Lancaster made sure Rupp found a bath and a bottle, and the next day the two joined up with fellow coaches John Bunn and Frosty Cox. Rupp wanted to make a trip to the PX. Lancaster told them that he could get in, but that they would have to have special papers. "To hell with that," Rupp said. "We're over here on special business. We'll get in." When the coaches were stopped at the door, Lancaster got in, but Rupp and Bunn and Cox were detained. Rupp wanted to see the colonel in charge. Rupp finagled his way in, leaving the other two coaches at the door. About an hour later, Rupp emerged from the PX, his arms loaded down with shirts, socks, underwear, and handkerchiefs. When Bunn and Cox asked, "What about us, Adolph?" Rupp laughed and said, "You're on your own boys."[32]

With fresh supplies, Rupp stayed on to attend the European Theater of Operations–Mediterranean Theater of Operations track meet in Frankfurt, Germany. There he met several Kentucky boys among the 27,000 GIs. Among the 38 generals in attendance was George S. Patton. Rupp never forgot that afternoon, thinking it odd "that all those Yanks would spend a pleasant Sunday afternoon watching a track meet in the hotbed of Nazism." Rupp worked with other coaches to set up a three-part sports program for American servicemen in Europe. The program included "1) mass athletics, with participation voluntary and open to all men; 2) competitive athletics, including league tournaments, meets, and matches, involving all echelons of command, and culminating in theater championships and inter-theater championships; 3) exhibitions that would send outstanding individuals and teams on tours of hospitals, and command posts."

Rupp held clinics all over Europe and made an impression on the servicemen wherever he went. According to Sergeant Harry Taylor, a football letterman at Kentucky, "some of the fellows" continued to talk about "that coach from Kentucky" long after he had gone back to the states. Rupp must have found it interesting to go back to the land of his parents, in service to his country against the Nazi regime of Germany. "I am glad I had an opportunity to come over here and help in some small way with this program. The point is, the boys have an opportunity to play, and that means a lot."[33]

Even though Rupp, because of age and infirmity, was unable to serve during the war, he found a way after the war to contribute to the armed forces through the development of a sports program. Back at home, it was Rupp's ability to continue his winning ways despite the loss of players and an assistant coach, who were either drafted or volunteered to fight. Paul McBrayer, Rupp's assistant coach since 1934, was drafted in 1943. Despite McBrayer's many contributions to the program and the respect he gained from Kentucky's players, Rupp had told Harry Lancaster, a star basketball and football player at Georgetown College where he had played against Rupp in the Baron's first victory as the Wildcat coach in 1930, that he did not want McBrayer back as his assistant after the war. McBrayer was unaware of Rupp's disenchantment and expected to return to his old position following his stint in the service. Lancaster taught in the university's physical education department, had become "a regular at Wildcat practices," and sometimes scouted for Rupp before he joined the navy.[34]

According to Lancaster, Rupp had told him before he went in that he wanted him as his assistant when he returned from the war, but Rupp had failed to inform McBrayer. Lancaster told the future Kentucky announcer Cawood Ledford, "I got the idea that Adolph thought Mac was after his job." The Kentucky players' devotion to McBrayer and McBrayer's ties to Johnny Mauer—McBrayer was an All-American guard for Mauer and played for Mauer from 1927–1930, during each of Mauer's three seasons as head coach—certainly gave the egotistical Rupp pause. Russell Rice wrote that "some thought Rupp had never gotten over McBrayer's perfect record with the Wildcats when the head coach missed three games with illness in 1940–1941."[35]

"Knowledgeable fans and all the players knew Mac was really running the team," recalled Red Hagan, a star forward in the 1930s. "During a time-out," Hagan recalled, "at least three-quarters of the players turned to McBrayer to find out what to do." Despite his success as Kentucky's head coach, an insecure Rupp feared for his job. As Humbert S. and Steve Nelli put it in *The Winning Tradition: A History of Kentucky Wildcat Basketball*, "Rupp was apparently in constant fear that his job and his reputation were in jeopardy." "Whatever the reasons," they wrote, "several former players have observed that Rupp found it extremely difficult to bear other people receiving publicity he felt should be his. And the Baron was well aware that many people, including some sportswriters, held McBrayer's coaching ability in high regard. Obviously Rupp could not accept the idea of having McBrayer back as assistant coach and thus as rival for control of the team and of publicity."[36]

But Rupp had leaned on McBrayer in practice and games. The Nellis have written about McBrayer's many contributions to the program. Ken Rollins, who played at Kentucky before and after the war, remembered that "Coach McBrayer was at one end of the floor and Coach Rupp at the other and during practice we caught it at both ends. Coach McBrayer had what appeared to me to be a lot of authority. Coach Rupp listened an awful lot to what Coach McBrayer was saying and suggesting." McBrayer, Rollins said, "contributed to everything that was done." Perhaps Rupp, himself having soaked in McBrayer's knowledge, felt that he had learned all that he could learn from his assistant. The Nellis wrote that "although it cannot be proved, another possibility is that Rupp felt he no longer needed McBrayer. A successful program was underway with a style of play that was pleasing to fans and winning games and league titles. Effective drills, plays, plans, and procedures were now in place. Obviously McBrayer had played a major role in standardizing and rationalizing the system but, looked at in a cold-blooded way, he was no longer essential to its continued functioning."[37]

After McBrayer left, Lancaster helped with scouting for a time, and Elmer "Baldy" Gilb filled in ably as Rupp's assistant from 1944 to 1946. Gilb helped coach the Wildcats to three SEC Conference titles and the NIT championship in 1946. Already an assistant on the football team, Gilb was not interested in a full-time assistant's position in basketball, but he continued to scout for Rupp—and socialize with Rupp—after the war.[38] Rupp also called on his friend Lyman Ginger for help, even while Ginger served as the university's dean of the College of Education. "Adolph,

I can't take any money for this," Ginger told Rupp. "I already work for the university." "Oh, I hadn't planned to pay you," Rupp said. Rupp wanted Ginger to help teach Jack Tingle how to shoot a layup going straight to the basket. Ginger worked with the Kentucky guard day after day until he had the shot down to perfection. "Lyman, I bet you that Tingle shoots the way he always had," Rupp told Ginger before the first game. Sure enough, Tingle drove to the basket but veered off to hook it in using his old method. "Lyman, did you see that?" Rupp drawled. "You didn't teach him a damn thing."[39]

Rupp and Lancaster corresponded with each other during the war, but when he received a December 14, 1945, letter from Rupp, Lancaster was disappointed that Rupp did not make clear his determination to hire him after the war. "Frankly," Rupp wrote,

> here is our situation in the Athletic Department. The University has set up a specially chartered Athletic Association and they will hire all the coaches. So far, no one has been hired and I presume we are still working for the University. The Athletic Association hasn't a single employee yet. I haven't appeared before them or talked to them about anything. If you could hold off until March on your decision, I surely will have something by then. As far as I'm concerned, I have told you before that I wanted you here as an assistant and that still goes.[40]

Georgetown College had offered Lancaster the head coaching positions for basketball and football, but Lancaster held out for the UK job. He was not disappointed. Lancaster explained that McBrayer had always worked for the university only three months or so a year, being paid only $500 for his part-time position. Rupp and the university had decided that McBrayer could resume work in another capacity under the same conditions. "Naturally," Lancaster said, "he lost interest."[41]

Lee Huber, a Kentucky All-American before the war, said that he had been "tapped for the job." Huber remembered that Rupp sent Andy Anderson, a former UK player from the 1930s, "to sound him out before the 1946–1947 season." Huber believed that Rupp did not talk with him directly "because he wouldn't risk being turned down." Huber was not interested in being Rupp's assistant. McBrayer only found out the facts of his dismissal "when he came looking for his old job back." According to

Russell Rice, Rupp "sent Bernie Shively to the Kentuckian Hotel to tell him the bad news," and "Rupp and McBrayer remained bitter enemies afterward." Rupp's enmity toward his next assistant coach would come much later. But when Harry Lancaster became Rupp's assistant in September 1946, the golden era of Kentucky Wildcat basketball had already begun.[42]

In 1945–1946, with Baldy Gilb assisting Rupp, Kentucky had gone 28–2, winning not only the conference championship but also the National Invitational Tournament in Madison Square Garden. With Jack Parkinson, Wah Wah Jones, Ralph Beard, Wilbur Schu, and Jack Tingle leading the way, the Wildcats did not lose a game in the conference, either in the regular season or in the conference tournament. Large crowds attended the SEC tournament in Louisville to see Kentucky dispose of Auburn (69–24), Florida (69–32), and Alabama (59–30). In a sold-out final, the Wildcats beat Louisiana State (59–36) for the championship. Russell Rice believed that the big turnout convinced other SEC schools that basketball "could be a paying proposition," and they asked Rupp to play more games with schools in the conference. Rupp was more than happy to oblige.[43]

While Rupp socialized in the hospitality room during the tournament, he learned that his star forward Jack Tingle had settled in to drink beer at the hotel bar. Rupp "eased" out of the room, found his friends Cecil Bell and Bob Sparks, and told them to get Tingle out of there before he found him. "I am going to win the NIT with him," Rupp told them. "If I kick him off the team, I can't win it." Bell and Sparks "hustled Tingle out one door just as Rupp came in the other."[44]

The talented Tingle, a six-foot-three-inch forward from Bedford, Kentucky, had always been a handful for Rupp. Unable to enlist in the army because of a "crushed right elbow" injured in a fall from an apple tree when he was a child, Tingle learned to shoot a flat jumper with a stiff elbow when his mother put up an oat box in the family dining room. At Kentucky, Tingle once asked Rupp if he could borrow his car to visit his sick mother. Rupp called the ill mother, to wish her well, only to find out that Mrs. Tingle was healthy and well and feeling just fine, but ashamed of her son's shenanigans. Rupp called the state police, who tracked Tingle down in Frankfort, telling the basketball player that his mother had made a quick recovery and that his coach wanted his car back.[45]

In the mid-1940s, the NIT in Madison Square Garden was a big deal, more prestigious than the NCAA tournament. A trip to the Big Apple meant national attention for the University of Kentucky and caused more than a little enthusiasm back home. "Now maybe you think that didn't set the people on fire," Rupp surmised in a 1971 interview. The trip to New York City certainly made an impression on President Donovan, who rode with the team on the train to New York along with his wife Nell.[46]

"I'll never forget that," Rupp said toward the end of his coaching career. "We went back there in a Pullman, and Mrs. Donovan held my son Herky on her lap, and read to him until he fell asleep that evening, and of course the next morning, we all got to New York, [the] first time that many of [the players] had been to New York, and we got to the hotel, then we went over to Madison Square Garden and worked out, and we got a lot of nice publicity back there." While Rupp got the team ready, Dr. Donovan and athletic director Bernie Shively met with a group of alumni. After beating Arizona and West Virginia, Kentucky squeaked out a 46–45 win over Rhode Island for the NIT title. Again, Rupp emphasized "that really set the state of Kentucky on fire. I don't think anything ever happened to the state that did more for it than that."[47]

According to Rupp, when the team crossed the Kentucky state line at Ashland, "the people met us down at the platform; it was early in the morning, and they just yelled and hollered, so we got up and all came out, and then we shaved and did everything else. We wanted to make a nice appearance when we got home, hoping the people would be there." The train stopped at Mount Sterling and Winchester, and in Lexington the Fayette County public schools dismissed students to meet the train. Rupp remembered, "Lexington was not nearly as large in those days, and we just had a big time and put the boys all on fire trucks and raced around town and the bands played; everything was just fine."[48]

For many, the perception has always been that Rupp built his reputation by beating up on a bunch of SEC football school patsies year after year, and to an extent that perception is correct. But the bigger, more accurate picture is that Rupp played everyone anywhere. He reveled in going to play the big dogs in the Big Apple, and he won consistently there. In the long run, going to New York and other northern cities proved to be a two-edged sword, however.

Rupp believed that winning the NIT in New York City convinced President Donovan that winning basketball games made for good public relations, especially with the state legislature, "where we had to go to get our funds." Donovan and Rupp had already tried to cultivate the legislators with free tickets to home basketball games. Bernie Shively wrote to Donovan on February 10, 1944, "I thought it would interest you to know the number of guests from the Legislature at our basketball game Monday night with the University of Illinois. There were nineteen members of the Senate, who had twenty-three guests, and seventy-five members of the House, with forty-three guests, making a total of one hundred and seventy." It didn't hurt that Kentucky beat the Illini, 51–40, avenging an early season loss.[49] Now, in 1946, the NIT championship only consolidated the legislators' and the university president's admiration and respect for Adolph Rupp.

President Donovan would stand by Rupp through thick and thin. In 1945, Donovan received a letter from Walter H. Ryle, the president of Northeast Missouri State Teachers College. Ryle wrote, "A matter has arisen between this Teachers College and the University of Kentucky that I wish to call to your attention." Apparently, two athletes, Charles McElroy and Wendell Moulder, had enrolled at the Missouri school, but as Ryle explained it: "Your coach, Mr. Adolph Rupp, has been telephoning and telegraphing these boys trying to get them to leave this Teachers College to play either basketball or football for the University of Kentucky. After a number of attempts he succeeded in getting the boys to leave yesterday afternoon for Lexington. It is alleged that he is paying their transportation."[50]

"President Donovan," Ryle wrote, "never in all my experience have I run across such unethical activities, when one institution attempts to take students from another institution after they are enrolled. As I have known you for many years, I cannot conceive that you would condone such action." Ryle noted the wider implications of such activities: "This type of action on the part of colleges and universities is putting interscholastic sports in disrepute among a number of people to whom we educators must look for support." Ryle was convinced that the Kentucky coach was at fault. "Frankly," he wrote, "I do not think your Mr. Rupp has been ethical toward this college."[51]

Instead of calling Rupp, Donovan went to the dean and to the athletic director, Bernie Shively, before he responded to the complaint. After "a very careful examination of the facts in this case," Donovan determined that Rupp "did not know that those boys were enrolled in your institution." Donovan explained to Ryle that had Rupp known that the boys had enrolled at his school "they would not have been invited to come here." Although McElroy had indeed been offered a scholarship, no offer had been made to Moulder. Donovan assured Ryle that "as soon as Director Shively learned that McElroy had been enrolled in your school, he immediately wrote him withdrawing the scholarship, and stating that he should return to the school where he was enrolled." Donovan quickly placed the blame on the students themselves. "I am confident that our coaches did not know that either of these boys had any connection with your school," he wrote. "The boys evidently misrepresented the whole transaction." As for the University of Kentucky and Coach Rupp, Donovan assured Ryle that the university "will not entice, under any circumstances, young men from other institutions." "It would be a violation of our rules at the University and our Conference rules," he asserted. "We are trying to live strictly by the rules and we are ready at any time to correct anything that is irregular that appears on the athletic scene."[52]

For Donovan's support of his coach, Rupp reciprocated with praise for his president. Of the other five presidents for whom Rupp worked, none measured up, in Rupp's eyes, to Donovan. According to Rupp, Donovan responded to unprecedented opportunity following World War II when former servicemen swarmed to the campus under the GI Bill. "We just had thousands of them," Rupp remembered. Donovan planned and built new dorms and classrooms and offices for administrators. Most important to Rupp, Donovan worked with the legislature to build a new coliseum to replace an inadequate Alumni Gymnasium. Donovan "started this entire program, which was carried out," Rupp said. "I think he had a blueprint of this thing."[53]

Rupp also felt a kinship with Donovan because of the president's interest in farming. "He had a nice farm over at Richmond," Rupp stated. In a 1971 interview, Rupp feigned reluctance to divulge how much the president confided in the coach. "I guess I shouldn't say this, but I'm going to," Rupp said. "I'd be sitting down at my office in the old gym, or over here [in Memorial Coliseum], and he'd call." "Adolph, what are you doing," Donovan would say. "Well, when the president calls, you're usually not doing anything. You ought to be doing something, but you say, 'Well, not anything in particular; what's on your mind?'" Donovan would tell Rupp, "Come and get me. Come and get me right away." "Well, I knew just about what that meant," Rupp drawled. "And so I jump in my car and I go out there, and he's standing in front of the administration building, usually with a cane." "He was headed for the farm."[54]

Donovan would step into the passenger seat and say to Rupp, "Let's go out in the country somewhere. . . . I've got a lot of problems . . . I'd like to talk over with you." Rupp revealed: "Whenever they get after his hide up there in his office, he'd just simply blow and head for the farm, or head out somewhere where he could talk to some of his friends, and think about these problems before reaching any conclusion. When he did reach a conclusion, the old fellow stuck by it. And I'll tell you one thing; he was stubborn at times when he had to be. But he'd stick with his ideas." Donovan would ask Rupp whether he wanted to go to Rupp's farm or his. Rupp had three farms at that time, in Woodford County, Harrison County, and Bourbon County, and sometimes the two would drive to one of those counties. Usually, though, they headed to Richmond. "Well," Donovan would finally say, "I haven't been down to my place for a couple of weeks. How about taking me down to my place." "Well, fine," Rupp said, "I knew that's where he wanted to go anyway."[55]

"I was amazed of the knowledge he had of the farm," Rupp said. "He knew all of the herd bulls. Knew where he got them. Of course, bound to know that. And he knew about his cattle, and we'd go out through the cattle, and he'd have this cane." Rupp knew the solace that a farm could bring. "We'd walk out there, and you could get out there among them; there wasn't any problems at all, and he just was completely relaxed. And we'd usually get back to town about a quarter to six, or six fifteen. I'd take him by his home, then I'd drive over to where I lived, and that constituted a nice day."[56]

Rupp and Esther also socialized with Dr. and Mrs. Donovan at Maxwell Place. "I always enjoyed so much being with him," Rupp said. "And they were so generous. They'd call us in the evening . . . or maybe 4:00 in the afternoon, they'd say, 'We want you to come over tonight for dinner.' Well, we'd come over there, and they'd usually have two or three other guests . . . and we'd sit around and talk, and he'd always like to laugh, and he had a hearty laugh. And he just simply knew how to take his hair down when he wanted to, and enjoy himself, and let these problems that weigh on a president completely disappear." Rupp believed that Donovan was sensitive: "You had to be careful how to handle him. He had his likes and dislikes. And I finally found out how to talk with him, and so I would say that of all the presidents we've had, I was possibly closer to him than I was to any others, and I certainly enjoyed my relationship with he and his wife while they were here on the campus."[57]

Of course, what Rupp liked most about Herman L. Donovan was the president's support of athletics. According to Rupp, "Dr. Donovan came in here, and he realized that in order to have good public relations with the state and with the legislature and the people, it is necessary to have a good athletics program." Perhaps it is no coincidence that it was during Donovan's tenure as president that Kentucky experienced a golden era in athletics. Rupp ticked off the accomplishments: "Before he retired, he found that the University went to four bowl games in football and won three of them. They won the NIT in basketball. They went to the finals one year. They went to three NCAA championships and won all three of them. And I believe it's almost safe in saying that every year won the Southeastern Conference in basketball." "His dream of good public relations certainly materialized during his lifetime. And I don't believe he had a great deal of trouble with the state legislature."[58]

Rupp was wrong on two counts. During the Donovan years, 1941–1956, Kentucky surely dominated the Southeastern Conference, but Rupp failed to win the conference in 1942–1943, 1952–1953 during the canceled season, and 1955–1956. And Rupp had dismissed from his mind the disastrous public relations nightmare of a point-shaving scandal.

With Harry Lancaster as assistant, though, Rupp's Wildcats continued to improve in the late 1940s. Lancaster played the role that McBrayer had played before him. Lancaster had played for Blanton Collier at Paris High School where he had learned a "synchronized and coordinated offense." He also helped Rupp develop the full potential of the fast break and "the sticky defense that distinguished the UK teams of the late forties and fifties."[59] Lancaster would play for Georgetown College in Rupp's first victory at UK on December 18, 1930.

In practice, now in khakis, the practice dress that Rupp took to after the war, Rupp stood at one end of the floor and Lancaster stood at the other end, a place that McBrayer had once occupied. Although the assistant coach was different, the practices remained the same—silent and challenging. Lancaster remembered in a 1980 interview:

If you could stand the two of us and a Rupp scrimmage you found out very quickly whether they could take it or not. And a lot, a lot of youngsters couldn't take it. And of course, with the same token we always felt the same young fellow that couldn't take it if you are up there on the free-throw line with the national championship at stake, you wouldn't walk up [there] and throw in both free-throws. You'd rather walk up there and wouldn't even hit the backboard. You didn't have that inner fiber that would let you go through what we put them through. We did; we worked them hard. We worked, and lots of times if practice went bad, Rupp would call it off. He'd say, "Well, all right, come back tonight at eight o'clock. We'll practice again to-night." And we have had practices after a game. Wasn't satisfied. They looked bad, all right, let's wait till the crowd clears out and we'll go at it again.[60]

"That's right. He worked them hard," Lancaster recalled. "Treated them hard. Gosh the way they travel now and the way they live now compared to the way we traveled." When Lancaster was asked if Rupp had a close relationship with his players, he said, "No. Never had a relationship with his players, nothing close, very, very far removed from anything personal." Rupp's players generally avoided the coach for several years after they graduated. Lancaster remembered, "A lot of the old players, you know, they mellow through the years, too, and they would come back. It took them about five years really to get out of school to find out that we weren't the roughest, meanest two fellows that ever lived. That maybe there was some method in the coaching that maybe was for their good as well as ours. But it usually is about five years after graduation before that seems to dawn on them."[61]

Perhaps Rupp's horrific practices had become more nightmarish during the war when Rupp worked with army trainees at UK. Russell Rice wrote that "Rupp had the same status as a captain, though his exercise sessions more likely made them think of him as a drill sergeant." John Duocomes had already completed basic training at Fort Bragg, before he came to Kentucky in 1943. He thought he was in great shape until Rupp put him to work. Rupp took Duocomes and other trainees to a tobacco warehouse, telling them that "he would show them what calisthenics were all about." Rupp made them duck walk for an hour within a large circle he had drawn on the floor. "He was a madman," Duocomes said. "I wanted to kill him; so did the other guys."[62]

Rupp's draconian methods carried over to the basketball court. Lancaster remembered that in 1944, he saw Rupp slap a player. During halftime in a 1944 game, sophomore guard Tom Moseley talked back to Rupp. After Rupp had sent the team back to the floor, Rupp told Lancaster, "Harry, go get Moseley and bring him back. I'm going to slap the piss out of him and if he raises a hand, you clobber him." Lancaster went out and brought Moseley back. Lancaster remembered that "Adolph gave him hell, then slapped him. Mose bristled, but then turned and went back out on the floor." He claimed, "That was the only time in my long association with Rupp I ever saw him lay his hands on a player."[63]

Apparently, the violence of the war years filtered down in a limited way to the UK courtside.

6

The Fabulous Five

Bear Bryant coached at Kentucky from 1946 to 1953, grumbling all the while that he couldn't get out from under the shadow of Adolph Rupp. Like Rupp, he won year after year, posting records of 7–3 in 1946; 8–3 in 1947; 5–3–2 in 1948; 9–3 in 1949; 11–1 in 1950; 8–4 in 1951; 5–4–2 in 1952; and 7–2–1 in 1953. To Bryant's chagrin, however, Rupp's records were even more spectacular during this period. The Baron's shadow proved to be too long for the Bear.

Bryant's winning ways could not satisfy all of the Wildcat faithful. Even with his concern about the growing influence of athletics at the university, former president McVey sometimes displayed his own fanaticism for winning, especially against Kentucky's hated archrival, Tennessee. On November 22, 1947, when Kentucky went 8–3, McVey wrote wearily in his diary that "again the University of Kentucky football team fell before the prowess of the Tennessee Volunteers. When the game was over the score was 13 to 6. During the regime of General [Robert] Neyland, now 16 years, Kentucky has been defeated. The Kentucky team that stood against the men from Tennessee was not the team that defeated Vanderbilt and West Virginia." Already, disgruntled fans questioned Bryant's leadership. According to McVey: "The fans are asking what is the matter and they want to know. Of course the drug store coaches have the answers or think they have." McVey had heard of Bryant's draconian coaching methods; he wrote, "For myself I ask are the Ky men driven too hard during the week so that injuries are greater? Do other teams have a better type of college men and where do they get them? Can imported youth have enough loyalty to fight for the honor of the University? And finally are other coaches smarter than the coaches here at Kentucky? The young man who is here now has quality no doubt but can he instill his people with great determination to win? I don't know. I ask for the answers."[1]

McVey's questions seem ludicrous in light of Bryant's success at Kentucky and his legendary tenure at the University of Alabama. But even the former president, the leader whose utmost concern had always been the academic integrity of the university, had been bitten by the victory bug. He wanted the university's football and basketball teams to win even as he decried the negative impact of big-time athletics. Although the war placed an obvious strain on college athletics, Kentucky's big-time, professionalized programs in football and basketball grew after the war years.

Bryant's and Rupp's coaching salaries grew steadily in the late 1940s and early 1950s, one coach keeping pace with the other. In those days, the salary for a college coach could not approach the pay for a professional coach. In 1948, for example, Bryant was offered $25,000 to coach the Washington Redskins, double his UK salary. President Donovan, who was constantly under pressure to raise the salaries of Bryant and Rupp, told Frank McVey this "in strictest confidence." The year before, in 1947, Rupp had been offered $15,000 annually by Louisville businessmen to coach a new NBA franchise. McVey wrote in his diary that "Bryant has a ten year contract with Kentucky and it is thought that as an honorable man he will not break the agreement." At the same time, McVey knew that "this shows the demand. The money that can be had and the competition in the football sport." According to McVey, "College teams are now to all purposes professional; basketball is not far behind."[2]

Rupp and Lancaster started practice the first day that school began in 1946. Lancaster recalled, "The practices we had back during the war had been child's play compared to these." The players coming back from the war were older, tougher, more mature. Following Rupp's usual practice, he had 30 or 40 players trying to make the team. And back in those days Rupp could carry 25 players on scholarship. "Those practices were blood baths," Lancaster remembered. "I couldn't understand why the players would go out there and really brutalize each other. It looked like a player felt if he could put the guy that was running ahead of him in the hospital he might get his job while he was gone. Adolph seems to like it that way and since I was his new assistant, I went along with the idea and got to be as bad as he was."[3]

In a 1983 interview with historian Humbert S. Nelli, Alex Groza remembered those practices:

Well, I think some of the toughest games that the teams I played on here happened in scrimmage. I mean it was dog eat dog because that much talent on a basketball team, everybody wanted to start. You could only start five players. And Coach Rupp was not adverse if somebody was good enough to beat out those that he chose to be his starting team, they had to prove it to him and henceforth the scrimmages were very hectic. They were very tough, a lot of pushing, a lot of shoving, a lot of fighting and basically the competition was keen. Then again, I think this viewpoint of having so many good athletes kept those, let's say his starting team, on their toes and we had to be prepared to defend our positions because of the talent that was on the basketball team.[4]

According to Groza:

Coach Rupp certainly watched everything in practice. I think one of his greatest attributes was he was a perfectionist. And he made us work to hone our skills to, I guess, achieve the most success as individuals out of them and through his innate ability he took our raw individual talents and wove them into a good basketball team. And only from the standpoint of him being a perfectionist and making us drill constantly, every drill he had had a purpose. And every drill that he had was a part of his offense so there was no waste of time whatsoever.

You know from the time we walked into the gym we had a lot of fellows on the ball club that were jokesters, pranksters, kidders, all kind of folks. From the time we walked in the gymnasium we zipped our mouths shut. We were there for one thing. We came there to play basketball. We weren't allowed to talk to one another. We weren't allowed to laugh. We weren't allowed to whistle. We came there to hear our coach, Coach Rupp, instruct us on the game of basketball. And we knew that. We accepted it and I think from the standpoint that we didn't do these things that we didn't have to practice three, four and five hours in a practice session. I think the longest we ever practiced was about two and a half hours. I think that Coach Rupp felt that if he's not going to get it done in two hours, he's not going to get it done, because his practices were strenuous. They were hard. They were tough and if he dragged it on longer and longer he wasn't going to get anything out of his athletes and he knew that. So his practices indeed were well-organized, well-structured and well run. And then again I think, ah, his mental toughness, his mental attitude rubbed off on a lot of us and again as I say this is one of the attributes that led to our success. I think that his attributes rubbed off on us and we assumed these attributes and became a good basketball team.[5]

Sportswriter Tev Laudeman believed that the Fabulous Five would have never played together without World War II. The six-foot-one-inch Cliff Barker first came to UK in 1940 from Yorktown, Indiana. After one year under freshman coach Paul McBrayer, Barker left for the service, winding up as an aerial gunner in a B-17 bomber over Germany. After his plane was shot down, he spent 16 months in a German prisoner of war camp. Rollins, from tiny Wickliffe, Kentucky, in far western Kentucky, started for Rupp as a sophomore in 1942–1943, before he was drafted into the service. Groza, from Martins Ferry, Ohio, started out with the Wildcats in the 1944–1945 season but left in the middle of the season for the army.[6]

Kenny Rollins remembered that his teammate Barker

was a good defensive man, very smart, very intelligent. Ah, held his own against the bigger boys, six two and a half. On the boards was very quick to get the ball out once he got the ball [off] the defensive board. And an excellent passer, I think the greatest hands . . . I've ever seen in an individual. He could just do anything with that basketball except shoot it. [Laughter] He lost his shooting touch. He could hit like a son of a gun before the war. . . . Just an excellent shooter, but somehow during the war and his sixteen months of internment in a Nazi . . . concentration camp he lost that shooting touch. Never did regain it. He got most of his points on quick sharp faking rebounds. Every once in a while could hit a little jumper from eight, ten feet away and fast breaks. That's where he got most of his points. Good defensive man, strong.[7]

Barker's years in German POW camps during the war may have had an adverse effect on his shot, but, despite the Nazi guards, he found a way to work on his ball-handling skills. "Well, they weren't too interested in basketball but we were in the various camps out someplace and they'd just let us get together in the compound and the Red Cross would get us athletic equipment," Barker remembered in a 1983 interview. "And of course the guys who had played football they'd have their organization and the ones that played basketball had theirs until the Russians started their offensive and then they started moving us and we didn't have time. Didn't stay in one place long enough to do anything athletically after that."[8]

For Barker, tossing a ball around helped pass the time. "If you were sitting around the prison camp you could go stir crazy," he recalled. "You had to do something to occupy your mind and that was one of the things I did to take my mind off of other things. Trying to get out, we were so far up in east Russia that we didn't know where to go if we had gotten out. So we just did that to keep us from going stir crazy. I mean you'd be surprised; there were some that [never played] any kind of sports in there but guys who were just standing around doing nothing."[9]

Usually a stickler for fundamentals, Rupp allowed more freedom to Barker once he was back from the war. Did Rupp object to the tricks he had mastered in the prison camps? Barker later asserted:

No. No, he never did. I always had good peripheral vision and I could look at you and see; I can see almost parallel. When we played on the road or at home you'd see the color of uniforms; I could look and hit my own teammates. . . . But Rupp never did say too much. The only time he said something to me one time we were playing in the Sugar Bowl game and I don't know whether he had taken me out; no, he was just getting ready to put me in the ballgame. He told me, he said, "Now you get in there and don't play that damn funny stuff." That was the only time, but any other time he never said anything because I knew pretty much what I was doing when I was handling the basketball.[10]

Barker had literally become a man in the service. "Well, when I came back, see I was in the service from '42 to '46," Barker explained, "and fortunately Coach Rupp gave me a scholarship." With the scholarship in hand, he told his wife that he was determined to make the starting lineup: "Well, I'll tell you one thing, if he was good enough to give me this scholarship . . . I'm going to make the first five." "So, I . . . was older than the rest of them," he remembered. "I had to work my tail off to get in shape and make it on varsity. I worked my tail off to do it and then they started calling me the old man because I was older than they were."[11]

Married before he went into the service, Barker's wife Meredith remembered those days well; the months of waiting with her husband in POW camps, and the years together after the war. Meredith Barker especially remembered Barker's year as a member of the Fabulous Five. "Well, Cliff's favorite story," she said, "was he always came down the center of the court and he did that for one reason, Coach Rupp was on one side yelling at him and I was on the other side yelling at him so he stayed in the center and that way he didn't hear either one of us." "No, I've had a lot of thrills, believe me, watching UK basketball," she said. "I really have and perhaps the biggest thrill dealing with basketball was the first time I ever saw the boys play in Madison Square Garden. And I defy anyone to see them play there and not have the same feeling. It's fantastic." Mrs. Barker also knew the price her husband paid to become a member of Rupp's best team. "I want to tell you a little bit about practice," she said. "I never went to a practice but I picked Cliff up after practice every night. And I have seen him walk out of that gym so exhausted that all he wanted was a milkshake. Was too tired to eat. So it was business." Mrs. Barker knew that the hard work paid off. "We've had some real good times," she recalled.[12]

The World War II experience also had an impact on Kenny Rollins. "I started here in the fall of 1941, played my freshman year and one year of varsity and then was drafted into the service for World War II," Rollins recalled. "[I was] drafted into the Navy in World War II and stayed, ah well let's see my service began in April of 1943 and I was discharged in April of 1946 almost three years to the day. And came back and finished my last two varsity years the 1946/1947 season and 1947/1948 season."[13]

The transition from Wickliffe to the mecca of college basketball was at first difficult for Rollins:

[I was] extremely homesick that first year, first time I'd ever been away from home, country boy. I came from a town of one thousand way down in Western Kentucky. Ah, difficult classes, boy, coming from a school that had a total of seventy-five in high school and a graduating class of twelve, [with] a total of four high school teachers. And then coming to the University of Kentucky and trying to pass these difficult courses was tough. I guess that sticks in my mind as much as anything. I almost flunked English. And of course I got along fine that second year but that first year is a difficult indoctrinating period for any young person and especially for one that might be coming from a tiny school with very few courses taught.[14]

The university and even Alumni Gymnasium seemed huge to Rollins:

I think prior to World War II enrollment here was somewhere in the neighborhood of between five and six thousand as I recall. Of course [it] steadily grew as years went by. Old Alumni Gym was our practice floor as well as our playing floor. Total seating capacity was probably near three thousand. People were fighting over tickets then. . . . Students were given tickets, ticket books for each ballgame. And you could see sixty-year-old gray-headed students coming through the line with student ticket books and you knew they weren't students. [Alumni Gym] was as big as anywhere else we played in the Southeastern Conference. It was as big as any other location . . . [and] larger than some. Probably some of the places, well Alabama . . . might have been able to seat more than three thousand but not many more. But Vanderbilt maybe fifteen hundred, Georgia a thousand, Georgia Tech had a pretty good place to play but still I don't believe could seat more than three thousand. Just every place we played was like this.

Rollins also recounted the less-than-favorable conditions in which the team had to play at various schools:

[At Georgia Tech there was] a retaining wall all the way around the floor and as a result the fans could not get close to you which was preferable. Tough place to play, good lighting system. Georgia was a tough place to play down in Athens. Terrible gym, poor lights and the floor was always slick like maybe they'd had dances the night before or something but those kind of things you had to put up with. We played Vanderbilt in a skating rink, the Hippodrome, the old Hippodrome in Nashville. . . . . But again the floors were in terrible shape due to the rollers and the skates and low ceilings. You couldn't arch a shot, very seldom could you get one off twenty-three, twenty-four feet without bumping a ceiling or hitting a light or something.[15]

When historian Humbert S. Nelli asked Rollins about the differences in the game before the war and after the war, Rollins said,

Well there wasn't a great amount of change in the style of play . . . prior to World War II and after. But there was a decided difference in talent. Ah, boys for some reason in just that short of span got bigger, stronger, and quicker. And ah, even when you compare our postwar ball club to the present ball club [in 1983] there is no comparison either because of the increase in the size of each individual and for instance a six-four, six-five guard is almost commonplace now. And back then I am six feet and my running mate Ralph Beard was five eleven. And we weren't exactly tiny back then. So ah, the game has changed considerably, not so much in style of play as I said prewar and postwar but in the size of the individual and the talent and their ability.[16]

Players, both guards and forwards, shot out on the floor during and after World War II, but these shots were of a "different type" than the one-handed jump shots of a later era. According to Rollins, these outside shots were "two-handed set shots from twenty-two to twenty-six or -eight feet even, some that far out. The one handed jump shot just wasn't in existence. And forwards were shooting from farther out on the floor and different type of shots too. . . . They were shooting from the corners. Wah Jones had a . . . two-handed set that he came up over his head with that was very effective. But by and large the shot from any distance on the floor was a two-handed set shot."[17]

Rollins continued:

[We ran] plays that [caused] a lot of what we call picks or blocks. If we could free the guards or free a forward with emphasis always toward driving towards the basket, if we could free that man then it meant the pivot man's defensive individual would have to come over and pick him up. And then we could just lob it over to Groza. Back in those days there weren't any zone defenses played. It was all man to man, so if you were a threat at all from the side in the forward position or from the guard position your man couldn't fall off of you too much. And it made it even easier to get the ball into the pivot man. Once you got it to Groza that's all he needed, just a little operating room.

According to Rollins, Groza was "an excellent faker. He . . . could jump. He could jump hook with either hand. Excellent rebounder, his greatest attribute I still say would be floor balance and his faking ability. He could get defensive men off their feet . . . in no time." With the lane width at six feet before it was widened to twelve feet, Groza had "a lot more operating room, a lot more."[18]

The Kentucky offense always used a lot of picks. Rollins recalled, "We had a total of, oh I have to rely on my memory now, but we had a total of possibly eight basic plays that we could run at any one time. And there were a variety of options off of those eight plays which meant that we were never at a loss to run something in the web of play when we had a set offense but we did a lot of running too, a lot of fast break basketball." Wildcats also relied on "inside screens, certain type passes meant we were going one way." He further explained:

A bounce pass meant the guards were going, ah I've got to stop and think again now. It's been so long. A bounce pass meant that I believe the guards were going outside the forward and a direct pass meant the guards were going inside the forwards. But picking either way if we were outside it meant the forward was picking for us. If we were going inside then we were picking for the forward. And . . . constantly we were looking for the pivot man [to] try to get that ball into him, then we could both cut off the pivot man. And he had the option of giving the ball to either one of us whoever was open or if neither one was open he could take the shot himself. And that went on constantly, all of the time.[19]

Rollins only remembered playing against man-to-man defenses, no zones: "We played Saint Johns. We played CCNY [City College of New York]. We played NYU . . . and Temple of course up in the East. I can't recall ever facing a zone defense. . . . If we did it never gave us any problem. It never stuck in my memory." Rollins did remember a wide range of officiating. "By far the biggest difference was in officiating in the various parts of the country," Rollins recalled.

> There were some parts of the country that you couldn't get near a man on a pick without being called for it. . . . There were other sections of the country that never called picks. You just get very physical. So you had to . . . make game to game adjustments if you went from one section of the country to the other. I don't think that still exists to that degree now. I think it has changed to become somewhat more uniform across the country. And I hope it gets even better because that's difficult for teams to lose their best ball players in a very short period of time in a ballgame. . . . Coach Rupp tried to warn us always if we were going to New York City for instance to watch our picks. This really was a situation up there that was called very closely. Ah, in the Midwest if we were to play say DePaul or to play a Big Ten team, it was just the opposite. Man, you could throw a pick that was near a football block before you'd be called for anything.[20]

Rollins remembered Rupp as "very demanding, very much a disciplinarian, very much unreachable, untouchable from a ballplayer's standpoint." He concluded, however, that Rupp could spot who would fit into his system, and through his tough discipline, Rupp managed to shape his players to become the best that they could be:

> I don't know how far you want to go . . . but this was a very difficult man to deal with. You had to be, I think, a certain type, have a certain type of psychological makeup in order to be able to take all of this and not flip your lid, because he could be extremely unreasonable at times. But he was effective; he was effective. Nobody can challenge that record. No one can dispute what he accomplished. I have the utmost respect for his ability to select ballplayers to fit his style of play. I think that was his great secret, tremendous ability to look at ball-

players, watch them play in high school, bring them up there in try-outs, you know that was allowed back then, and visualize how that kid would fit into his system. He would take some boys that nobody else would look at. That's the only place I got an offer . . . was here.[21]

The same was true for Alex Groza, even though in high school Groza had scored an Ohio state record 628 points his senior year. Martins Ferry's coach, Floyd Baker, a friend of Rupp's, told the Kentucky coach about his star center. Rupp thought the tall, skinny kid would be a good replacement for All-American Bob Brannum, who had been called into the service. Rupp made a trip to Martins Ferry, and visited with Groza's father, a miner and millworker who had come to Ohio from Hungary in the 1920s. Groza's father invested his savings in a poolroom that he later converted into a tavern, and Alex and his three brothers grew up in rooms above the tavern. "Adolph had a few beers with my dad," Groza remembered, "and they had a big time." All four brothers were athletic, but Lou, who had played on the Martins Ferry basketball team with Alex, went on to football stardom at Ohio State, and then as "the Toe" became an All-Pro tackle and place-kicker with the Cleveland Browns.[22]

Ohio State didn't recruit Groza. He instead came to Lexington for a tryout, one of 30 players Rupp had invited in that weekend. "They put us up at the Phoenix Hotel and had the tryout on Friday and Saturday," Groza remembered. "To my knowledge, I was the only guy he invited back." Groza accepted the only scholarship he had been offered and came to Kentucky. A few days before the 1944–1945 season, Groza passed his army examination and was told to report in three weeks. So Alex Groza started his freshman season at UK with the US Army looming ahead. Kentucky met Ohio State in Lexington two days before Christmas. Groza always remembered the Ohio State game "because I was ready to show them they were wrong about not wanting me." Ohio State featured Arnie Risen, a six-foot-eight-inch center from Williamsburg, Kentucky, but Groza outscored the taller and more experienced Risen 16–14, and the Wildcats won in overtime, 53–48. When Harold Olsen, the Ohio State coach, approached Groza after the game and asked him why he hadn't come to Ohio State, Groza told him that "nobody had asked him . . . and it was too late now."[23] As Groza told it in a 1983 interview,

When the game was over I was in the shower, taking a shower and the head coach of Ohio State came to me and wanted to know why I didn't come to Ohio State. I said, "Now, I can't answer that question for you." I said, "You're the guy that does the recruiting, why wasn't I extended a scholarship offer?" And to be honest, my senior year in high school I was six foot five inches and I weighed a hundred and sixty-five pounds and I didn't think anybody wanted to take a chance on me. They probably thought I was going to be a skinny, old, frail kid. So he could not answer my question when I asked the coach as to why I was not extended a scholarship, but he was willing to offer me a scholarship if I was willing to transfer. And I told him, "No, I was quite happy."[24]

After Groza got his induction notice he scored 27 points, including the game-winning shot in a 45–44 win against Temple. Kentucky went to New York City, ranked number one in the nation, and beat Long Island University, 62–52, with Groza scoring 25. After Groza scored another 25 in a January 6, 1945, 59–46 win over Ohio University, he made a trip home to Martins Ferry, missing the 75–6 shellacking of Arkansas State. His last game of the season came on January 13, 1945, in UK's Alumni Gym against Michigan State. "I'll never forget it," Groza said in a 1975 interview. "My train back to Lexington was a few minutes late. They picked me up, rushed me to the gym, brought me out at halftime, and presented me a key to the university and farewell gifts." Groza scored 12 in the second half, and Kentucky won going away, 66–35.[25]

According to Groza, "I was inducted into the service and went away to serve twenty-one months in the Army and came back and I, of course, even in the Army I had many, many scholarship offers. And I said, 'No, there was one school, one coach that was interested in me prior to my entering the service' and I said, 'I feel an obligation to return to that school and play basketball for them.' So I did return to Kentucky. I left here in, oh, December, no, it was January of 1945 and returned September of 1946."[26]

While Groza was away, Kenton "Dutch" Campbell, a six-foot-four-inch freshman from Newark, Ohio, replaced Groza in the starting lineup. Before the Tennessee game on January 20, Johnny Mauer, now the Volunteers coach, asked Rupp why he should miss one player when he had 30 others. "You don't replace a Caruso with a barbershop singer," Rupp replied. Kentucky certainly missed the presence of Groza in the middle. Tennessee beat Kentucky in Knoxville, 35–34. Kentucky would go on to lose games to Michigan State and Ohio State, both teams they had beaten with Groza in the line-up.[27]

Kentucky finished 22–4 in 1944–1945, good enough to win the SEC tournament, but not good enough to advance beyond the first round of the NCAA tournament. In 1945–1946, Rupp won the NIT with freshmen Ralph Beard from Louisville and Wah Wah Jones from Harlan. In 1946– 1947, Barker, Rollins, and Groza had returned. In the service, they had gained maturity and experience, Rollins and Groza played on service teams, and Barker honed his ball-handling skills, sometimes with a soccer ball, in the prisoner of war camps. After the 34–3 season in 1946–1947, Barker moved into the starting line-up and, as Tev Laudeman put it, "the Fabulous Five was born," the best team Rupp would ever coach in Laudeman's estimation.[28] Rollins remembered,

> Well it's a strange thing. A lot of people don't think about this but that crew came about primarily because of the war. Cliff Barker started in 1939, played just part of his freshman year, fell in love, went home, got married, and joined the army. I came along in 1941, played my freshman and my sophomore year, and was drafted into the service. Groza came along in 1944, I guess played one year, and was drafted into the service. And then along comes some great talent out of high school in the persons of Ralph Beard . . . from Male in Louisville and Wah Wah Jones from Harlan. Well, here you've got us all coming back at the same time after the war. You've got Cliff Barker who's a twenty-four-year-old veteran. I'm twenty-two. Groza's twenty or twenty-one and this mixture of this maturity plus the talent of Jones and Beard. . . . This ability, this chemistry, this ability to know each other's moves and be very comfortable on the floor but even that first year we were so comfortable together that three All-Americans had to sit the bench, couldn't get on the club. . . . But that's why it came about. Because of the war, size, speed, unselfishness, in every ball club you've got to have somebody . . . who not only is willing to take a leadership role but is willing to sacrifice his ability to score in

order to feed the others. Well we had two. I was willing to do that. Wonderful, I got just as much of a charge out of a good pass as making a basket. And Cliff Barker was the same way. We had two on the ballclub. The other three were just excellent scorers and . . . fine, fine individuals. And the chemistry worked, the speed, the unselfishness, the shooters, and hard workers. None of us were ever lazy, never slacked off. That combination, the war years, the individuals, and the maturity just put it all together and made it.[29]

Kentucky went 34–3 in 1946–1947, with the nucleus of the team that became known as the Fabulous Five the next year. The Wildcats lost only to Hank Iba's Oklahoma A & M Cowboys in the Sugar Bowl (37–31), to DePaul in Chicago (53–47), and to Utah in the final game of the NIT (49–45). Ralph Beard, Alex Groza, Kenny Rollins, Wah Wah Jones, and Joe Holland, as the starting five, won more games for Rupp than he had ever won. Former president Frank McVey wondered about the effect of so many games on the Kentucky players. "Some of our citizens are staying over in New York City to view the final basketball game in the invitation tournament," McVey wrote in a March 21, 1947, diary entry. "Dr. and Mrs. Donovan are in New York seeing the sights and at the same time waiting for the final game." The Donovans already had a taste of the glamour of the city from the trip to New York the previous year. In a veiled jab at his successor, McVey wrote, "I am quite disturbed that the University has allowed the team to play so many games . . . this season. What is the effect on the boys, how can they keep up their work? In addition it overstresses the game as a factor in college life." McVey also blamed Rupp. "The hopes of fans that follow the U of Ky basketball teams were dashed to the ground when [the] Utah team defeated the Wildcats by a score of 49–44," McVey wrote on March 24. "To my mind our teams have played too many games, traveled too far and so are tired. Part of this is due to Coach Rupp who certainly likes the limelight."[30]

The Wildcats played—and won—even more in 1947–1948, going 36–3, with the Fabulous Five—Beard, Groza, Rollins, Jones, and Cliff Barker. McVey refused to let up on the negative impact of such a grueling schedule. On April 1, 1948, the former president devoted his diary entry, not to the university's first NCAA championship, but to the long season. "During the season the Kentucky team played 38 games and lost two," he wrote. "The boys have been driven hard and kept at the games too long. How can they get an education?" McVey did not count a 53–49 loss to the Phillips Oilers, the AAU champions. This championship game in the collegiate bracket determined who would coach the 1948 Olympic team in London.[31]

Kentucky won the SEC championship and the NCAA championship, beating Baylor in the finals, 77–59. Tev Laudeman, a staff writer for the *Louisville Courier-Journal*, saw every one of Rupp's teams from 1930 to 1972, except for his 1943–1944 squad during World War II. "From my viewpoint," Laudeman wrote, "Rupp's best team was the one that stacked up better against the competition in its time than the others did in theirs," and "that would be the 1947–1948 team—the Fabulous Five."[32]

"It had speed and a marvelous fast break," Laudeman wrote, when Rupp died in 1977.

"It had outside shooting, so far outside that teams now wouldn't attempt such shots, and it ran Rupp's set plays with crisp passes and darting, driving moves to the basket. The team had quickness on offense and defense in three players—guards Ralph Beard and Kenny Rollins and forward Cliff Barker. The other two starters, 6-foot-7 center Alex Groza and 6-foot-4 Wallace (Wah Wah) Jones, were strong and rugged, both good rebounders and able to play the power game. And they could run. [Teams] were astonished to see Groza scoring on the fast break." According to Laudeman, "The Fabulous Five was a blend of finesse and power, and with that had more experience and maturity than any college team has a right to have."[33]

Harry Lancaster agreed. When Lancaster was asked in 1980 if the Fabulous Five were indeed fabulous, he said,

They were, they were. They were a beautiful team to watch. They had the finest fast break I have seen, ever seen before or since. They had some sort of a thing in Louisville four or five years ago where they had all the schools in the state, the teachers colleges. I still refer to them as teachers colleges, Eastern, Western, Morehead, U of L, of course and Kentucky. And they showed films of their old teams, their better teams. And it was just a revelation. You'd see Groza get the ball off the board; he'd hit Jones about the head of the circle; he'd hit Rollins middle stripe; he'd hit Beard going under. The ball might touch the floor once or twice, never more than that. It wasn't this dribble, dribble, dribble. Bing, bing, bing and in it went. And Beard and Rollins were, of course, so fast. They burned rubber. When they cut for the basket you'd just hear their shoes screech just like an automobile going around a curve too fast, you know. And, of course, Jones was a great basketball player and Barker was a great ball handler, fine defensive man. You see some of these fine blacks doing it now but Barker was doing it back then before white boys ever thought about it, you know. . . . I used to kid him during shooting practice. We always shot for thirty minutes, Rupp's students. We went out there at 3:15 suddenly you heard the ball start bouncing because if they got there about a quarter till three or three o'clock they shot free throws until 3:15. At 3:15 everybody started working on his moves and his shots from his particular position on the floor. And Barker . . . I told him "it's a waste of time, don't bother to shoot. Just skip it. Forget about it. Do something else. Work on your passing if you want to," because he couldn't. And then he made one basket in old Alumni Gym that was clear from the free throw line, clear to the other end, you see. And then we had a little fun about that. That was his shot. That was the only one he ever made. He could make a layup but outside of that he was unable to make anything. And Jones was a great rebounder and fine shooter. Fine all around player and Groza, Groza was terrific [and] Ralph Beard was the best small basketball player I've ever seen even today. See he was only five ten and a half, weighed about one hundred and eighty-five pounds. He was strong and stocky built and had blazing speed. Great outside shooter, great defensive man, great ball handler. He could do it all.[34]

Lancaster never tired of talking about those players, even if at times he used politically incorrect language. According to the assistant coach, Beard could hit from the "head of the circle and just a step beyond." Lancaster went on to describe more about the team's extraordinary agility and skill:

See in those days we put it up in a two-hand touch shot. And Jones' spot was over opposite the free throw line, clear to, just as wide as he could get without going out of bounds and he'd just pour the thing in there or out deep in the corner . . . and he was a two-hand shooter.

Barker was a passer. He wasn't a shooter. But Groza had great moves and agility. He was very clever and of course, he was only six seven. You know nowadays he'd be considered very small. But he was strong. He was a Pollock. Brother Lou, you know, played for the Browns. His daddy, his daddy looks like, oh, he must have weighed three hundred and fifty pounds. I never will forget we were in one of the hotels in Cincinnati. We were going to play the University of Cincinnati and Mr. Groza, Mrs. Groza came down. She was a big woman, too. He was sitting there, there used to be a thing in the comics of a Neanderthal man named Thor. This is what Mr. Groza looked like. He had a huge mouth and big teeth. So Rupp was saying, "Mr. Groza, I just don't know now about Alex, how he's going to handle this fellow tonight [for] Cincinnati; he's a very fine basketball player." Mr. Groza said, "Mr. Groza." He called him Rupp (pronounced with a long u sound). He said, "Mr. Rupp, that's your job. You tell him how. He do it." [Laughing] I remember that conversation.

But . . . Kenny Rollins was really the coach on the floor comparable to [Kyle] Macy on this team [in 1980]. Kenny ran the show. He had been in the Navy for two years and came back so he was a little older too. But he had tremendous speed and wasn't a great shooter, but he was a good shooter. . . . Rupp never would admit it but that has to be the best team that he had man for man.[35]

Alex Groza agreed. "Well, in my own personal opinion I thought the Fabulous Five was probably one of the greatest basketball teams put together," Groza said in a 1983 interview.

Now there's got to be a reason for greatness and I think the reason that made us great and when I talk about the Fabulous Five, it's a misnomer because well, we said it takes more than five people, you know. No one guy makes a basketball team, no two. It takes a lot of things. I think we had a great coach. I know we had a great coach. I know we had a great assistant coach. I know we had great scouts in Baldy Gilb and Ed Lander. I know we had great substitutes. I know that we always had somebody behind us pushing us and making us better. And I personally feel if it wasn't for the combination of all of those things, I don't think we could have achieved that success. I think by our playing together as sophomores and as juniors and as seniors, you know, we played together basically for three years and we got to know [each other]. Cliff Barker knew when I was going to move to the basket. He'd say, "Hey, Beak . . ." Everybody called me Beak, I guess because of my nose. He says, "Hey, Beak, you know, the [pass] is going to blind side you, you take it, you help me." If I had . . . a bad night, the other four guys could pick me up. Cliff had a bad night, the other four guys could pick him up. If Ralph Beard had a bad night, the others . . . Kenny Rollins had a bad night, the other guys would pick him up. We always, we had the knack of, you know, picking one another up. If they were a little lax, then we helped one another. We knew what one another was going to do with and without the basketball. I think through the perfectionism of Coach Rupp we developed a lot of skills that a lot of other basketball teams didn't have. Coach Rupp never worried about a zone defense. He said, "I'm not going to worry about a zone defense." He said, "You run your man to man offense and don't worry about it. They can't stop us." So he never practiced against the zone defense. He never believed in coaching his own defense and we played man to man. It gave us great responsibilities.[36]

"When I say the Fabulous Five was the greatest basketball team," Groza said,

it stems from the fact that our substitutes made us hustle. They made us . . . better. And if we fell down they came in and picked us up or substituted for us until we got our breath and came back in. But the whole total thing was meant to be a good basketball team. So, you know, that's what I felt at that particular time [that] we were probably the finest college basketball team of that era.

Of all the basketball players on our team I think Kenny [Rollins] was the unsung hero. [In] 1948 he was our captain and I know of no other basketball player that I have seen prior to that and even to this day, you know, you're covering my playing time I got started as a young kid of, oh, ten or eleven. And I would say in the last forty-seven years I've never seen a basketball player [who] had as quick and deceptive change of pace as Kenny Rollins. And many, many times I saw Kenny come down, give the guy the quick fake on the dribble and go on around him. I can picture his move today in my mind; what a graceful move it was; go into the hoop and land that crib shot in and you kind of sensed when he was going to do it; not only me but the other players on the team. And I would get my man out of the way and just clear the floor so Kenny could make that move and it was a thing of beauty. And to this day I've never seen a guy that could do that. Kenny was a good catch and Kenny was a good leader.[37]

"Kenny and Cliff Barker, I think, were the two oldest fellows on the basketball team and Kenny was indeed a good leader. I mean he just knew the game, knew when you were down, he'd come and talk with you. Kenny and I were roommates in the dormitory and I gained the utmost respect for his ability as a player and a leader and as a human being. Now I'll love Kenny as long as I live and as long as he lives," Groza said in 1983. "He's a great man and a good man and I feel the same way about all my teammates. They were indeed good people and I love them all."[38]

Lancaster stated in his book, *Adolph Rupp as I Knew Him*, that "Rollins, Beard, Groza, Jones and Barker were the Fabulous Five but the firepower on the bench was overwhelming. Bob Brannum had already made All-American at Kentucky, but when he found himself running third string he transferred to Michigan State." UK had two All-Americans sitting on the bench, Jim Jordan—who had been an All-American at North Carolina before transferring to UK—and Jack Parkinson. Joe Holland, who had made All-Conference the year before, also sat the bench. "There was so much talent on that squad," Lancaster said. Lancaster remembered that in some games the score was so lopsided at halftime that "Adolph would order the starters to get dressed and not even show up for the second half."[39]

7

The Golden Era, 1946–1951

By the 1940s, Rupp's routine was etched in stone. According to Kenny Rollins:

To deviate from a routine was excruciating for that man. It literally tore him apart. He wanted the timing to be exact at every ball game when we came off for our pre-game instructions. When we went back on the floor, always to be at the same [time]; if something should happen, if the lights weren't working or the scoreboard wasn't working or we were delayed, it just tore him apart. [Laughing] Of course, everyone knows about the brown suits and the seats on the bus. He always sat in the same place. He always wanted the same driver on our Greyhound chartered buses. One thing you don't hear people talking about was the Southeastern Conference Tournament in those days was played at the old Louisville Armory with a seating capacity of about six thousand. We always had the same dressing room. Rupp had a paper cup that he drank water out of at a certain time before we went on the floor. And after he drank his water out of that cup he hid it up above some rafters at the top of the room some place always in the same identical spot. And as far as I know that thing was still there when I finished school in 1948. Now it had to be filthy. [Laughing] How much dust can accumulate in one of those old, old dressing rooms down there? But he was that kind of a superstitious man. Didn't want to deviate from anything that was making him a winner.

Let's take no chances. Quite a person, I think the mold was broken when he was put together by the good Lord. I don't think there'll be another one come down the pike like him ever.[1]

Joe B. Hall, who played for Rupp, then served as his assistant coach, and then succeeded him as head coach, knew Rupp's superstitions well. In a 2009 interview, Hall remembered that Rupp "had a notebook for the managers that listed all the things, the procedures on game night and practices and everything. And in it were things that had to comply with his superstitions." Everything went according to the book. "On the morning of game day, he got up, and he dressed in a particular sequence," Hall said. "Like he'd put his left sock on first, then his right sock, then his left shoe and his right shoe. And he'd wear the same clothes. And then at lunch, when we would go to the cafeteria, we would have the same thing on game day." After lunch, "he would walk back to the coliseum and there was a manhole cover on the student center side of the street that he had to step on with his left foot before he crossed the street." "Then we always had the same thing to eat for the pregame meal," Hall continued. "On game day he would always drive to the Coliseum by the same route . . . and parked in the same place behind the coliseum. Then the night of the game he always wore his brown suit, and the reason for that was [that] early in his career he wore a blue suit and got beat. So the next game he wore a brown suit and they won, so he stayed with the brown suit."[2]

Before a game, Rupp came into the locker room to talk to the players. Hall said,

When he would go through the door, he would go to the second locker on the right and get a Kleenex out of a box—there had to be a box of Kleenex—it was an empty locker not used by one of the players. And he would wipe his glasses, blow his nose, wad the Kleenex up, and throw it down beside the trash can, never in it. Nobody knows why. Then the manager offered him three sticks of gum . . . and he always took the middle one, which was spearmint. He unfolded the papers, put the chewing gum in his mouth, wadded up [the chewing gum papers] and threw it down by that Kleenex. . . . Then he would take the program and he would stick it in the assistant's outside pocket, and that was the one I always ended up carrying.

The assistant would then report the starters to the scorer's table:

> Then the managers would lay a damp towel out on the floor by the bench and after warm-ups [the players] would come by and wipe their shoes on that damp towel to get the dust off of their shoes. And then . . . Coach Rupp was the only one who could pick up that towel. And when the players left for the jump, he would pick it up and throw it down by the scorer's table where it had to stay until Kentucky scored, and then the managers could pick it up. And when he came to the floor after the talk to the players in the locker room, when they came out to play, there was a little guy who wore a white coat, a little African American, and Adolph always shook hands with him when he went out on the floor. Well that guy got sick and they had to bring him to the coliseum in an ambulance so that Coach Rupp could shake his hand.[3]

Hall remembered, "On game day he would walk the parking lots wherever we were—Starkville, Mississippi, Nashville, Tuscaloosa—looking for hairpins, and he would feel that if he could find a hairpin it would mean a victory. If the open end was pointed toward him when he spotted it, it meant that we would go away with a blowout. And he'd pick that pin up and put it in his pocket, and then it was all right; everything was okay." "And you wonder," Hall said, "if that was his way to get things going right, that he'd have the confidence going into the game in the right frame of mind." "When Rupp had an ulcerated foot and not able to get out and walk," Hall explained further, "the managers would go to Woolworths . . . to get a box of hairpins" to put in his path from the hotel room to the bus. One day the managers got in a hurry, Hall remembered, "and just piled them outside his door; it looked like an anthill of gold hairpins and he opened the door and he says, 'My gawd Joe; look what I found.' He got down and scooped up those hairpins, just like they just happened to be there." "But he was very superstitious," Hall said, "and I guess being in horse country where the horse people are very superstitious" it stands to reason.[4]

The players were all too familiar with the Baron's idiosyncrasies. According to Rollins, to the players it was all "funny." "But you didn't dare laugh," he explained. "Oh, you didn't ever dare crack a smile in the dressing room with Coach Rupp. If you smile you didn't have your mind on the game. [But] we laughed at it. We never . . . felt that superstitious. We never wanted to always do the same thing the same way every place we went. It didn't affect us. We laughed at this privately."[5]

Rollins, however, said,

You had to get up early in the morning to get ahead of Adolph Rupp. He was a sharp, sharp individual. Loved to hear him speak. It was just the most entertaining thing to . . . hear him talk anywhere but on the basketball floor during practice. That wasn't very entertaining. That was sometimes excruciating. . . . Oh my, tear you apart . . . with words, never laid a hand on you. But he didn't have to. He could just cut you to ribbons with words, extremely sarcastic. Never ever, the closest I ever heard him come to a complimentary remark to any of his ball players was the night we played in South Bend, Indiana. We played Notre Dame. We worked our bottoms off, just dug, and aggressive and played hard for forty minutes. We just gave everything we had, couldn't buy a basket, our shooting percentage was terrible and we lost by about, I don't know, six or seven points. And he came down to the dressing room and he says, "I can't complain about this ballgame. Let's get dressed and go home." And that's as close as I ever heard in four years to a compliment.[6]

Rollins said, "I asked him one time. I got real brave and I asked him, I said, 'Coach, why don't you ever compliment a ball player, tell him he did well? He played well, ah that was a good pass or keep up the good work or something?' I said, 'You're constantly berating us, tearing us down but you never compliment us.'" Rupp replied, "By gawd, I brought you here to play a hundred percent all of the time. Hell, you're not supposed to make any mistakes." "I never asked the question again," Rollins said. "And never got a compliment either. . . . Until I left the school and he mellowed a little bit and then he'd talk about some of his former ballplayers and what a defensive job [they] had done on so and so such and such a ballplayer years past. But never ever while you're playing for him would you get that kind of [compliment]."[7]

Normally, Rupp's halftime routine did not vary, at least during the years that Lancaster served as his assistant. Lancaster remembered,

The manager would unlock the dressing room door and Adolph would take off his jacket, hang it up, then go into the room where the urinals were. In a highly vocal and colorful manner, he would begin commenting on team play, individual play, and straightening out various people while still urinating. He got louder and madder as the minutes ticked by. Then he would storm back into the dressing room, go directly to the blackboard and really get down to the business of straightening things out. He'd always save three or four minutes at the end of the tirade for me.

"All right, Harry, what have you got?" Rupp would say. For a few minutes Lancaster would "take over on what we should be doing and what we could do to stop what had hurt us in the first half. Adolph certainly had everybody's attention by the time I got to my part, so I didn't have to worry about whether they were awake or not."[8]

Lancaster admitted that during that golden era, "While we were going so good it was hard sometimes for Adolph to find something to criticize. It might have been difficult, but he always found something." Only once did Lancaster remember halftime laughter. In January 1948, the Wildcats beat Western Ontario 98–41. Already far ahead at the half, as Lancaster told it, "Adolph stormed into the dressing room, hung up his jacket, went to the urinal, and started raising hell." "Who in the hell is guarding number ten?" Rupp bellowed from the urinal. "I am, Coach," Cliff Barker shouted back. "Well, by [gawd] get on him. He's got the only two damn field goals they've got." "We couldn't hold it any longer," Lancaster said. "We all really laughed. He did too."[9]

Lancaster said that Rupp would never admit that the 1947–1948 team was his greatest in later years—the point-shaving scandal marred the team forever for Rupp—but Rupp did admit it immediately after the NCAA championship game against Baylor. In the semifinals Kentucky defeated Holy Cross, a team that rode a 19-game winning streak into the game behind star guard Bob Cousy, a dribbling and passing wizard. Holy Cross was the defending national champion, and Cousy, only a sophomore, was considered the greatest player in the college game. A bedsheet hanging from the Madison Square Garden balcony proclaimed "COUSY—THE GREATEST." Another sign called him the "Best Player in the

World." "We'll see about that," Rupp said. He turned to Kenny Rollins, and told him, "Kenny, he's your man." Rollins had come away from the previous tournament game against Columbia with a badly sprained ankle. Lancaster and Bernie Shively stayed up all night with Rollins, alternating hot and cold towels on Rollins's ankle to bring down the swelling. Rollins and substitute guard, Dale Barnstable, had studied Cousy's moves, and the two decided to force him to the center of the floor because he shot mainly from the sides. Rupp and Lancaster watched Rollins closely during warm-ups and decided to start him and then bring in Barnstable if Rollins had trouble. Rollins and the little-used Barnstable held Cousy to three points, all free throws. Lancaster believed that Rollins "played what I consider to be the greatest defensive game I ever saw." With Groza leading the way on offense with 23 points, Kentucky defeated the Crusaders, 60–52.[10]

Rollins remembered it differently. To him, Cousy was unique: "Oh goodness, now here's another one with a funny body, short, heavy stocky legs, ah, long body and long arms and big long sensitive hands and fingers. That's how he could take that thing behind his back and through his legs just could keep control of that ball because of his build. Sloping shoulders and those hands and arms came way down." "No, I never toot my own horn about this because I think really honestly and truly Cousy was having a bad night," Rollins said. "But he did come in averaging something like twenty, twenty-one, twenty-two points a ball game which was high in those days." "I don't think it was anything exceptional that I did honestly," Rollins said.

> I think Bob just had an off night. I thank God it was that night. Ah, way up in Madison Square Gardens some of his fans had taken an old bed sheet and had written "COUSY—THE GREATEST" and tacked it up on one of those rails, those second or third tier rails. And after the game we were still celebrating on the floor and someone walked up to me and says "Kenny, keep this for a keepsake." They had that sheet. They had gone up there and torn it down and gave it to me. I've still got the thing [laughing] in the attic at home.[11]

Against Baylor in the championship Kentucky led 7–0, 13–1, and 24–7 and won going away, 58–42. Groza had 33. After the game, according to Russell Rice, a teary-eyed Rupp "locked the dressing room door, hung up his coat [and] called that squad the greatest team ever assembled in college sports." "You've done everything you've been asked to do," Rupp told the Fabulous Five and the rest of the team. "You've kept training and made many sacrifices, and I thank you from the bottom of my heart." Rupp had special praise for Groza: "You undoubtedly played the greatest game at center that has ever been seen in the Garden."[12]

With a 36–2 record and with the SEC championship and the NCAA championship already in hand, Kentucky's season was not yet over. The national champions now played a series of games in the trials for a chance to play in London, England, in the 1948 Olympics. In 1948, the Olympic team would be composed of five players from each of the two teams that made it to the finals of the Olympic trials in New York City, plus four at-large players chosen by an Olympic Basketball Committee, made up of politicians and coaches. Kentucky beat Louisville (91–57) and Baylor again (this time 77–59) before losing to the Phillips Oilers, the AAU champions (53–49). The Oilers boasted seven-foot Bob Kurland, who held Groza to one field goal in the championship game.[13] So the Oilers' starting five and Kentucky's starting five would play in the Olympics. A committee would decide the four at-large players. Frank Maggiora, a member of the committee and an Oakland politician, lobbied hard for six-foot-six-inch Don Barksdale, an African American player who had graduated from UCLA in 1947 and now played for the AAU's Oakland Bittners; the pros were yet to be integrated.[14]

Maggiora pressed his case for an at-large berth for Barksdale. Other committee members responded, "Hell no; that will never happen," Barksdale later remembered. But Maggiora would not let up. "This guy fought, fought, and fought," Barksdale said, "and I think finally the coach of [the Oilers, Omar "Bud" Browning] had said, 'That son of a bitch is the best basketball player in the country outside of Bob Kurland, so I don't know how we can turn him down.' So they picked me, but Maggiora said he went through holy hell for it—closed-door meetings and begging."[15] Because of Maggiora's persistence, Barksdale became the first African American to perform on an American Olympic basketball team.

Because the Oilers had beaten Kentucky in the title game of the trials, their coach Bud Browning became the head coach of the Olympic team with Rupp as his assistant. Rupp fumed over the loss to the Oilers, because, as Russell Rice put it, he "was not eager to play second fiddle to Bud

Browning." Ralph Beard remembered that Rupp never forgave the Wildcats for losing to the Oilers. "You all made me the assistant coach because you let the Oilers beat us," Rupp told his players.[16]

Rupp was appeased somewhat when the Wildcats returned home from New York. Fifteen thousand fans greeted the team at Blue Grass Field, then paraded them through Lexington, the players riding on fire trucks and Rupp in the back seat of a convertible next to the mayor. Schools dismissed classes, Warner Brothers recorded the festivities, and Phog Allen spoke at a victory banquet. After Rupp's Kansas coach praised his former player, he took advantage of the opportunity to warn "that gamblers throughout the country sought to control the outcome of basketball and football games." According to Allen, "Colleges and their conferences should do more to protect their athletes from these leeches." Rupp seemed unconcerned.[17] He knew his players and they were winners. That's all that mattered.

The full Kentucky team played against the Oilers in three exhibition games that summer to raise money for the Olympic fund. Barksdale played for the Phillips team and led the Oilers to a 60–52 victory over the Wildcats in Tulsa. Kentucky won the second exhibition in Kansas City, 70–69 in double overtime, when Rollins batted the ball to a streaking Joe Holland who scored the winning goal on a layup. At the end of the game Phog Allen rushed onto the court, grabbed a microphone, and said, "The Kentucky boys fought their hearts out, and I never saw a greater exhibition in my life."[18] High praise from one of the most successful coaches in college basketball history.

Rupp organized a third exhibition game in Lexington. A temporary floor was constructed over Stoll Field. Rupp had dreamed of an outdoor venue under lights since the 1930s, and perhaps his tour of Germany at the end of the war when he often held clinics outdoors for hundreds of servicemen had convinced him that it would work. Fourteen thousand fans gathered in McLean Stadium to see the Wildcats lose to the Oilers, 56–50. The game raised $25,000 for the Olympic fund. Lexingtonians raised an additional $15,000 to send Barnstable, Holland, and Jim Line with the Olympic team, although none of the three played or even dressed for a game in London. Assistant coach Harry Lancaster had to stay at home. Speaking uncharacteristically in the third person, he said, "I felt sorry for Harry Lancaster for awhile since I stayed home, but it was enough glory for me that I had helped in some small way to bring the first NCAA championship to the University of Kentucky."[19]

The exhibition game between the Wildcats and the AAU champions was the first time that a Kentucky basketball team had competed against a black player in Lexington. Don Barksdale scored 13 points, 12 in the second half when the Oilers rallied to beat Kentucky. Larry Boeck of the *Louisville Courier-Journal* wrote that Barksdale "received a big ovation when he was introduced before the game and another one when he left after the tilt ended."[20]

Despite the ovation, Barksdale could not stay with the rest of the Oilers in a Lexington hotel. This was nothing new for Barksdale. He had not been able to stay with his teammates in Bartlesville, Oklahoma, where the Oilers had trained. In Lexington, Rupp contacted local black community leaders to arrange for Barksdale's lodging, and Dr. J. R. Dalton, a local black physician, provided his home, as well as a Cadillac with driver to take Barksdale from the African American side of town to the game. Lexington's black community, about one-fourth of the town's population, treated Barksdale as a hero and held a softball game in his honor. In *They Cleared the Lane: NBA's Black Pioneers*, Ron Thomas wrote that Jack Robinson of Baylor believed that Rupp resisted bringing Barksdale to Lexington, and, at first, refused to let Barksdale enter the state. As Rupp later argued repeatedly, it would be dangerous to bring a black player to a southern state. In the 1960s, when University of Kentucky administrators pressed Rupp to recruit black players, he told them that a Kentucky black recruit would have a hard time on road trips to Mississippi or Alabama. He apparently had reservations, at first, about bringing a black player to Lexington as well. Rupp knew well the continued prejudice of some white Lexingtonians.[21]

Barksdale received a death threat in Lexington. He told only his host family, the Daltons, and he decided to play in the exhibition game despite the danger. During a timeout huddle, Barksdale passed up a water bottle instead of taking a swig before passing it on to his white teammate, "Shorty" Carpenter. Barksdale was well aware of the danger of drinking out of a bottle passed on to whites in the segregated South. "If a black man went to a white fountain, they put his ass in jail," Barksdale later said. "Segregation was segregation all down the line. If you went out with a white, they'd kill you. There's many a black kid dead for doing nothing because some ass just said, 'I'll kill a nigger,' and they didn't go to jail for it. No, I wasn't scared about getting arrested. I was scared I was going to be killed. I was scared to death."[22]

After the three exhibition games, the Americans left for England. In a 1983 interview, Ralph Beard described the team's voyage overseas on the SS *United States:*

> It was a beautiful ship and had great things to eat and we used to go on the top deck and practice. We did lose one basketball off of the top deck. I don't know if somebody threw it over there. But you could see it bouncing on the waves as we just went right on by. But that's where we ran and that's where we'd do some passing drills and stuff like that; couldn't shoot any baskets because there were no hoops. But then we toured Scotland and we did some exhibition games there. And that was fun. Had high tea with the Lord Mayor at Saint Andrews right on that big, that huge eighteenth green, that you've seen on television when they play the British Open there. I was nineteen years old. As much as I love golf now at fifty-nine I didn't even know what golf was. Is that not a sacrilege?[23]

Once in England, the American Olympic team, including Don Barksdale, stayed at the Royal Air Force camp in Uxbridge. They toured Scotland by bus, visiting five Scottish cities, and playing exhibition games "wherever they could find a court." Over 12,000 Scots cheered the American Olympians as they played in Edinburgh in the open air. Earl Ruby, then a sports editor for the *Louisville Courier-Journal,* traveled with the team through Scotland. According to Ruby, it was Rupp, rather than head coach Bud Browning, who held center stage at the various stops. At every Scottish village, "the lord mayor would make a flowery speech and give mementos to the visitors. Rupp would reply in kind, extolling the virtues of Scotland and its people." Ruby remembered that "with that twang in his voice, Adolph was uproarious. Half of them laughed with him, half laughed at him."[24]

The United States team made the most of their Olympic experience. They went to Wembley Stadium to watch other competitions. "Yes, we would go over there and we'd watch track and field on the days that we didn't play," Ralph Beard remembered. "And we'd have practice in the morning and they'd let us go see them. Oh yes, it was wonderful. We all stayed [in] Uxbridge. It was an old ex-RAF camp. And that's where the Olympic Village was. Eat in the mess hall there."[25]

The Americans swept through the international field in London. Beginning on July 30, the United States team defeated Switzerland (86–21), Czechoslovakia (53–28), Argentina (59–57), Egypt (66–28), Peru (61–33), Uruguay (63–28), Mexico (71–40), and France (65–21). Playing before sparse crowds in London's Harringay Arena, Ralph Beard remembered that "the opponents were no better than a good YMCA team back home." All except Argentina, which led the Americans by 7 at the half. In that game Browning and Rupp experimented with a "unit" system with Groza, Jones, and Rollins from Kentucky starting with Ray Lumpp of New York University and Vince Boryla of the Denver Nuggets. Ahead 14–3, Browning put in the second unit. Gordon Carpenter, Lew Beck, and R. C. Pitts of the Oilers played with Don Barksdale and Baylor's Jack Robinson. Beard somehow got lost in the shuffle and with three minutes left the game was tied 55–55. With the Americans ahead by two, a long "buzzer beater" by the Argentines went awry and the United States prevailed. Rupp had not watched the team from Argentina play in earlier games, "one of the few times in Rupp's career that he had failed to scout an upcoming opponent." Browning and Rupp learned that mixing Kentucky's players with those from the AAU simply did not work. When they decided to alternate the Kentucky players with those from the Oilers, placing on the floor familiar teammates, the Americans breezed through the competition.[26]

During the games, Rupp ironically developed a close relationship with one of his players, something he never did with his players back home. That the player was Don Barksdale baffled later Rupp critics. Barksdale might have qualified for the US Olympic team in track and field; he had won the triple jump in the national AAU competition. He decided, however, to place his hopes in the American basketball team, even though no African American had ever made the team. When questioned about why he set his sights on the basketball team, Barksdale said, "You can't be a pro in hop, skip, and jump. Watch it. When I make the team the rest of my life it will be 'ex-Olympic cager.'"[27]

Barksdale faced challenges during his Olympic experience before arriving in London, when the team trained in the United States. Sports editor Murray Olderman wrote in 1968, 20 years later, that at one training site "the rest of the United States Olympic basketball players stayed in the big hotel downtown. Don Barksdale had to stay 'across the tracks' with a Negro family. The rest of the United States team went down the hall to get their rubdowns. Don Barksdale had to take the service elevator up to the 12th floor." "To me," Don Barksdale said in 1968, "being the first black man to play on a United States basketball team was a great honor, something I'd have gone to hell and back for." "But it wasn't until we arrived in London," he said, "that I got away from racial prejudice. I mean I had to leave America, my country, before I was treated equally." Barksdale gave credit to his teammates and to his coaches for making the Olympics a positive experience for him. "The players and the coaches Adolph Rupp and Omar Browning were the only reason that I kept going. They were great." Barksdale remembered, "I had to put up with a lot of horse manure before I got to London. Then the whole thing changed. It was beautiful. All my teammates and I hung out together, went everywhere together. R. C. Pitts became one of my best friends and he was dead out of Mississippi." "It was a breakthrough," he said. "There had been other black athletes on United States Olympic teams—Jesse Owens, Ralph Metcalfe and others—but never one in basketball." Barksdale noted that there were five black basketball players on the American team in the Mexico City Olympics in 1968, "and probably would have been more had there not been a Negro boycott." In 1948, though, he said, "I remember like it was another world. So many fine guys on the American team. I got very friendly with Harrison Dillard and Barney Ewell and some other black athletes. And with a lot of white ones like Bob Richards and Bob Mathias."[28]

Barksdale reserved special praise for Adolph Rupp. He talked as if Rupp ran the team instead of head coach Browning. Barksdale said that "Rupp had each player play about 15 minutes each game." Barksdale was the third high scorer on the team. According to Barksdale, Rupp "was a great coach, amazing at knitting a team." Charles Bricker interviewed Barksdale for a *Philadelphia Enquirer* story in 1984. Rupp "turned out to be my closest friend," Barksdale remembered in the interview. When Barksdale faced indignities at home or abroad, Rupp pulled him aside and told him, "Son, I wish things weren't like that, but there's nothing you or I can do about it."[29]

"The entire U.S. Olympic team came back by boat," Barksdale remembered. "It was a six-day trip. The togetherness really got me. I was a very proud young man. But as soon as I stepped off the boat into New York, I stepped right back into prejudice. For five years I was an All-American college and AAU basketball player, but I didn't get one nibble from an NBA team. The league had an unwritten law: No blacks." Barksdale finally got his shot at the NBA. In 1951, three years after the London games, Chuck Cooper with the Celtics, Nat "Sweetwater" Clifton with the Knicks, and Barksdale with the Baltimore Bullets broke the NBA color line. Barksdale was already 29 and past his prime.[30]

Rupp and his players never forgot their Olympic experience in London. Russell Rice believed that "when the basketball champions received their Olympic medals in Wembley Stadium, it was the proudest moment of his life."[31] For Ralph Beard, too, the gold medal in the Olympics meant everything. "Oh man you don't realize how valuable an experience that really was until you got older," Beard said in a 1987 interview.

> I didn't. And the absolute aura of winning a gold medal is absolutely magic with people. You know they say, "You played in the '48 Olympics and won a gold medal?" Yes. I mean you know even in my business relationships whenever I made a talk they would say, "Bring your gold medal; I want to see it," you know. It is amazing. It is absolutely amazing, but the thrill of being on that podium and let them play the *Star Spangled Banner*; I know everybody that wins a gold medal says that, but that is the truth. There is nothing like it. I mean that means you are the best in the universe. And that certainly meant something. And I tell you what; even Coach Rupp was touched by that you know.[32]

Ralph Beard and his wife visited London on business years later, but it had all changed. "On a business trip my wife and I went back to London a couple of times," Beard said,

> and so I told her one day, you know Bet I'm going to go and try to find Harringay Arena. I know Wembley Stadium is still there. I told the fellow I said I want to go to Harringay Arena and he said "Harringay Arena?" And so he called someone and found out it had been torn down and was a parking lot now. And Uxbridge had been remodeled into either apartments or something. And so, the only three

things that I knew anything about was of course Wembley Stadium and there wasn't any sense in going back out there but I tried to find the other two but they'd long been torn down.[33]

Later, after basketball had been taken away from him because of his involvement in the point-shaving scandal, Beard would still have his Olympic experience to remember and cherish.

Rupp thought his 1948–1949 team could be even better than the year before. Dale Barnstable, a six-foot-three-inch junior from Antioch, Illinois, filled in for Kenny Rollins, the only member of the Fabulous Five lost to graduation. Jim Line and Walt Hirsch proved to be able substitutes. Alex Groza had gained weight in the off season. "Alex was virtually unstoppable," Harry Lancaster remembered. "He was stronger and just as quick as he had been when he was voted the most valuable player in the NCAA the year before."[34]

Kentucky plowed through the first eight opponents, including a hard-fought 51–48 victory at Boston Garden over Holy Cross, their NCAA nemesis from the year before. In the Holy Cross contest, described by Lancaster as "a brutal game," a fight between Barker and Bob Cousy brought Rupp and the Crusaders' coach Buster Sheary onto the court. Wah Wah Jones fouled out, and after he sat down next to Lancaster, a Holy Cross fan sitting directly behind the bench started to berate him. As Lancaster remembered it, "He kept daring Wah to turn around until it was more than Jones could stand." When Jones did turn around, the fan threw a wadded-up cigarette packet in his face. "As strong as a bull," Jones grabbed the fellow by the tie and the front of his shirt and hit him with a hard right to the jaw. When the man's friend jumped in, Lancaster knocked him down. While on the floor, the man's friend kicked Lancaster. "Leaving his footprints on the stomach portion of my white shirt," Lancaster said. After UK won the game, a police escort ushered Wildcat players and coaches to the dressing room.[35]

One player who made the road trip to Boston and the next game to New York against St. John's was sophomore Joe B. Hall. Hall had starred at Cynthiana High School and had met Rupp during his junior year when the Kentucky coach came to watch one of Hall's senior teammates. Rupp "was . . . bigger than life," Hall recalled in a 2009 interview. "He just overpowered any other presence when he came into a gym." After Hall's senior year at Cynthiana in 1947, he was selected for the East-West All-Star game in Alumni Gym. Although Hall turned an ankle in a practice, "and was useless in the game," Rupp invited him for a tryout in the fall after school started. "Where you came with 74 other high school players and you scrimmaged all day," Hall remembered. At the end of the day, Rupp, who sat in the balcony in Alumni Gym with Lancaster, sent Humsey Yessin, a team manager, down on the floor with 15 names to invite back. "The next week we had another 75 guys, and he cut it to 10," Hall said, "and I made the second cut." "Then finally he cut it to 4, and I was one of the 4 that got invited to come on to the squad."[36]

"Coach was the kind of person that stayed aloof from the players," Hall said. "He didn't want to get familiar. You had no personal contact with him. Maybe the members of the Fabulous Five who played at that time had a little more rapport with him, but I'll never forget one time my parents had come up to watch a game, and I met them, I think it was in front of the Lafayette Hotel . . . and we were on the street when I met with them and Coach Rupp walked by, and I thought, 'Oh, I'll introduce Coach Rupp to my parents,' and he just kept on walking." "You very much respected him," Hall said, "but you were afraid of him. He was intimidating, and by him being not close, it made him more of a mystery type person as a coach. And that way he exercised control without being familiar with his players."[37]

Hall said that Rupp only played six or seven players in those days, and it was the trip to Boston and Madison Square Garden that convinced him that he needed to make a move to another college. Twelve players would make the road trip and for the last slots, Hall said, "We drew straws" to see who could go. "I won the trip to New York and Holy Cross," Hall remembered, but when the team went on a road trip in the South, Hall wasn't so lucky. "So that's when I decided to leave and go to Sewanee." Rupp knew Sewanee's coach, Lon Varnell, and Varnell happened to be looking for a guard that could play immediately, beginning in January. Earlier, he had stayed in Lexington for a year to observe the Kentucky program, so "Coach Rupp knew him well." Hall said that it didn't bother Rupp that he left, because his leaving opened up another scholarship for Rupp to award.[38]

In 1948, after Groza scored only 13 points in a 42–40 Sugar Bowl loss to St. Louis, Rupp moved Barnstable to forward and the better-passing

Barker to guard. From then on, Groza became the center of the Wildcats' offense and he usually came through. After a close call against Bowling Green in Cleveland, a game that Kentucky won, 63–61, Rupp brought the team back to Lexington, to, according to Lancaster, "some of the most rugged scrimmages that any team has ever gone through." "At practice each day we would run through our drills to sharpen our ball handling, then we got down to business," he said. "I thought that for the rest of the season the best games I saw were those played during the afternoons in Alumni Gym. When you could split the kind of talent we had into two teams you really had a game in those scrimmages. I never could understand how they would foul each other so viciously then almost never foul out when we played a game."[39]

The tough practices after the close Bowling Green game paid off; Kentucky reeled off 20 straight, to go 29–1 during the regular season and through the SEC tournament. Against Mississippi in January, "in the old downtown auditorium in Memphis," Rupp scheduled a practice the day before the game. The auditorium was so dark that Rupp called off practice, complaining to the press that "he was going to equip our boys with miner's caps and carbide lamps" for the game. Chauncey Barber, the longtime manager of the auditorium, promised Rupp that he would correct the situation. "When we got out to the Auditorium the evening of the game," Lancaster said, "sure enough, they were hanging these lights on cords reaching 40 or 50 feet from the ceiling." A "little custodian in his bib overalls and railroad engineer's cap overseeing the work," came over to Rupp to explain. "Coach Rupp," he said, "I'm doing this for you. There was a fellow who brought his team in here last week and wanted more lighting, but I never heard of him. I'm doing this for you, Baron. I'm doing it for you." When Rupp found out the coach the custodian had never heard of was the legendary Hank Iba of Oklahoma A & M, he couldn't help but laugh. Rupp told the story the rest of his life.[40]

At 29–1 Kentucky became the first school in history to be invited to both the NIT and the NCAA tournament. Rupp reveled in the publicity as Kentucky had a chance at the unheard-of "Grand Slam" of college basketball. The Wildcats faced Loyola of Chicago in Madison Square Garden in the NIT, a game that pitted Groza against Loyola's Jack Kerris, a player that Lancaster referred to as a "mule" player. "I always said you could take a mule and run him three miles a day for ten years, but you couldn't win the Kentucky Derby with him," Lancaster said. "Kerris was big and strong, but he was slow. He was not a clever player at all." Lancaster and Rupp believed that Groza would handle Kerris easily, and by halftime, the Loyola big man had four fouls. At the half, Rupp instructed Jones and Barker to get the ball in to Groza. In the second half, however, Groza simply refused to work to get open. "He was almost hiding behind Kerris when we had the ball," Lancaster remembered. Even Kentucky's players on the bench shouted at Groza to move. Instead Groza fouled out and Kerris played out the game with four fouls. With Kentucky's star being outplayed at every turn, Loyola stunned Kentucky, 67–56.[41]

Lancaster and Rupp roomed together on the road. Rupp usually went to bed early after a game, but Lancaster was known to stay out until late. When Lancaster did get to sleep, his snoring often kept Rupp awake. Rupp mentioned the problem to Louise, Lancaster's wife. Louise advised Rupp to snap his fingers, and her husband would stop snoring. Rupp tried the tactic, and it worked. After the Loyola loss, Rupp and Lancaster went back to their room together, and, according to Lancaster, "We drank a few healthy shots of bourbon and talked into the night." Rupp could not understand Groza's performance. "Harry, what in the HELL was wrong with Alex out there tonight?" Rupp asked again and again. "Why wouldn't he move? With the boys on the bench yelling at him all night, why wouldn't he TRY to get open?"[42] Rupp finally dropped off to sleep with his questions unanswered. It would be two years before he would finally understand. Russell Rice noted the gambling that was rife at each game at the Garden. Rice wrote that the New York writers ignored the gambling on each game: "Betting on the point spread had become a way of life in the Garden."[43]

Following the NIT loss to Loyola, according to Lancaster, "We went back to Lexington and raised hell with the team that whole week. We practiced tough and hard." Lancaster believed that Kentucky played its best basketball of the season during the NCAA tournament. Playing in Madison Square Garden again in the Eastern Regional, Kentucky easily beat Villanova (85–72) and Illinois (76–47). Lancaster commuted between New York and Kansas City, where Hank Iba's Oklahoma A & M Cowboys defeated Wyoming and Oregon State in the Western Regional. Sent by Rupp to scout, Lancaster said, "It seemed like I went a week without sleep flying between Kansas City and New York." Lancaster saw the "very deliberate" play of Iba's team. During the long cross-country train trip from

New York to Seattle, where the final game would be played, Lancaster had plenty of time to go over his scouting report with Rupp. Despite Groza's lackluster play against Loyola's Jack Kerris, Lancaster was convinced that Groza could score at will against the Cowboys. "Adolph," Groza told Rupp, "Iba thinks his center, Bob Harris, is the best in the country, but there's no way in the world he can handle Groza." Rupp and Lancaster decided to use Wah Jones to get the ball into Groza.[44]

With Jones driving to the basket and dumping off to Groza, Kentucky beat Oklahoma A & M, 46–36, with Groza scoring 25 of the Wildcats' 46 points. The team took a train back to Lexington, finishing the season as NCAA champions, for the second time, and a 32–2 record. The Wildcats came home to a huge crowd, with thousands of fans at Union Station. Lancaster remembered that "they had life-size pictures of everybody including the coaches. It was a mass of humanity." In a later ceremony, Rupp retired the jerseys of Beard, Jones, Barker, and Groza, as well as Kenny Rollins, who had graduated the year before. "It was his way of enshrining the Fabulous Five," Lancaster said. In Lancaster's thinking, it was the Fabulous Five that "established Adolph as one of the great coaches in the country," and it was also the Fabulous Five, at least several members of that team, that would later "bring him the greatest humiliation of his life."[45]

With an eye on the main chance, the seniors of 1949 had planned for two years a barnstorming tour after the season. Rollins and Holland joined Groza, Beard, Jones, and Barker and called themselves the "Kentucky Olympians," as they played local athletes before overflow crowds in towns throughout Kentucky and in parts of West Virginia. J. R. "Babe" Kimbrough, the sports editor of the *Lexington Herald,* handled the money at each venue. Russell Rice recalled that "no one had thought of including Rupp in the deal, and he seethed at reports of the tour's financial success."[46] Kentucky players continued the barnstorming practice following their senior seasons, at least in Kentucky, into the 1980s.

Professional teams in both the National Basketball League and the Basketball Association of America coveted the services of the Kentucky players. Eventually, Groza, Beard, Jones, Barker, and Joe Holland formed a team of their own and joined the National Basketball League as the Indianapolis Olympians. Kimbrough became the team's general manager, and, because he was the oldest, they named Cliff Barker as coach of the team, making him the first individual to go directly from the college classroom to a head-coaching position of a professional team. Russell Rice wrote that "the players owned all the common stock [in the team], and Indianapolis businessmen bought thirty shares of preferred stock at $1,000 a share." Again, the players left Adolph Rupp out of the scheme and never considered asking him to coach.[47] Rupp would remain in the college ranks for the rest of his coaching career.

Rupp faced a major rebuilding challenge in the 1949–1950 campaign. He had only Dale Barnstable back from the starters of the NCAA champions of the year before, although Jim Line and Walt Hirsch had valuable experience coming off the bench. To take over at center for Alex Groza, Rupp had signed his first 7-footer, Bill Spivey from Warner Robins, Georgia. According to Harry Lancaster, at 7-feet-¼ inches and 165 pounds, Spivey was a work in progress. Rupp had enrolled Spivey in summer school the year before his freshman year in 1948, while Rupp was in London for the Olympics.

Although he remembered the measurements a shade differently than Lancaster, Kenny Rollins said,

> I'll never forget the first time I looked at Bill Spivey. I thought, my golly, how in the world will that spindly ball player ever play any basketball? He was six eleven and a half, got on the scales and weighed a hundred and seventy-four pounds. Ralph Beard a full foot shorter got on the scales right after him and weighed a hundred and seventy-six, two pounds more. I just thought, my goodness. We watched him that summer before we went to the Olympics. He was here on the campus. The only thing that kid could do was dribble the ball from one end of the floor to the other and lay it in. And once you look back on it you think well, if the kid can do that he's got good enough hands, six eleven and a half can dribble the floor from one end of the floor to the other without kicking it out of bounds. That's something they had to build on. And my, did they ever build on it.[48]

With Rupp away, it was up to Lancaster to see to Spivey, and the assistant coach took him to Alumni Gym every afternoon that summer. "The gym had a metal roof," Lancaster said, "and it must have been 110 to 115 degrees in there. We worked like dogs two or three hours every afternoon. We worked on teaching Bill to receive the pass, to fake, to dribble and slide back to the basket and shoot a hook shot. Bill never mastered the left hand hook, but he was to eventually develop a great hook with his right hand. He was also very accurate with a turnaround jump shot." Lancaster did not stop coaching when they left the gym: "[In the dining hall], we insisted that Spivey eat all the fattening foods we could provide."[49]

All the while, according to Rollins, "the telegrams were being fired from Rupp in London at the Olympics and Harry back here working out and feeding Bill Spivey mashed potatoes and whatever else he could stuff in him to get him some weight. I guess you've heard that story or read about it. Harry would send a wire and say Spivey's doing fine. He's gained five pounds. He's now up to one hundred and ninety." Another would come and after three or four of these telegrams when he got up to 200 pounds or 205, Rupp sent one back and said, "You've convinced me he can eat; can he play basketball?"[50]

Spivey could indeed play basketball. "Spivey went from being a tall boy with no talent to a great basketball player," Lancaster said. "No player ever worked harder."[51] Joining Spivey from the freshman team was five-foot-ten-inch Bobby Watson, a shooting guard from Owensboro, Kentucky. Rupp started Spivey and Watson, along with Line, Hirsch, and Barnstable. Although the young Wildcats lost an early season game to St. John's (69–58), they won the Sugar Bowl in New Orleans with victories over Villanova and Bradley. Rupp addressed his players in the locker room after the championship. "Boys," he said, "I'm proud of you. You've won the Sugar Bowl, something the Fabulous Five never did. We've been riding around since Christmas with a bunch of kids in diapers and winning games."[52]

After beating Villanova (57–56 in overtime) and Bradley (71–66) to win the Sugar Bowl tournament in New Orleans late in December 1949, Rupp was unable to get his entire team on the same train back to Lexington. He decided to have Mrs. Rupp and Mrs. Lancaster accompany the reserves on one train, while Rupp and his assistant coach stayed with the varsity for a later departure. When the second train had left the station, Rupp and Lancaster made their way back to the smoking car. As Lancaster told it, after they had taken their seats "a very distinguished looking gentleman [who] had these bushy snow white eyebrows with dark piercing eyes looking out from beneath them" came into the car. "His hair was full and white" and Rupp instantly recognized the man. "Harry, that's Boss Crump," Rupp said. Rupp would have admired the skillful use of power demonstrated by the political boss. After all, he had witnessed the shenanigans of Boss Billy Klair in Lexington, in the twilight of Klair's long political career just as a young Rupp had arrived in the Bluegrass. But here was the famous Memphis boss in the smoking car of a train headed north from New Orleans. "Let's go back and introduce ourselves," Rupp suggested to Lancaster.[53]

The Memphis politician invited the coaches to join him. Lancaster remembered, "I was totally fascinated as the two prominent men began talking." They discovered that both the boss and the coach had been reared in Kansas, and they learned that both loved poetry. They started quoting "Opportunity" by Edward Sill. As Lancaster recalled, "Crump would take a line, then Adolph would take a line." "The two men had a great visit," Lancaster said, "until Crump got off in Memphis."[54] That Rupp found a kindred spirit in the political boss from Memphis should not be surprising. Both men knew how to get things done. Both men knew how to wield power. And both men knew how to manipulate the press.

After the Sugar Bowl championship, the Wildcats lost in the regular season to Tennessee in Knoxville (66–53), to Georgia in Athens (71–60), and to Notre Dame in South Bend (64–51), and then reeled off eleven consecutive wins to end the regular season. During the streak, Spivey scored 40 points against Georgia Tech to break Groza's SEC record of 38. The Wildcats beat Vanderbilt, 70–66, in the last game played in Alumni Gymnasium. At the half, Kentucky trailed by twelve points. "Boys, a man spends a lifetime compiling a record," Rupp told his players, "and in one given night a group of bums like you are about to tear it down. If it looks like we're going to go down in defeat tonight, I want you to know that I am personally going to do something to this facility before the game is over and before you get out of this gym." Rupp's cryptic message got through, as Kentucky set a national record of 84 consecutive home court wins. Kentucky posted a record of 247–24 during 26 seasons in the old gym.[55]

The Wildcats went on to win the SEC tournament in Louisville with victories over Mississippi State (56–46), Georgia (79–63) and—sweet revenge—against Tennessee in the final (95–58), with Spivey scoring 37 points. Kentucky had won two straight NCAA national championships but failed to get a bid in 1950. Art Tebell of Virginia, the chair of the District Three selection committee, ruled that a playoff game must be played between Kentucky, with a record of 25–4, and North Carolina State, at 24–5, for the district's slot. Rupp argued that Kentucky ranked fourth in the last Associated Press poll, compared to North Carolina State's ninth ranking. Furthermore, Kentucky had defeated Villanova and number one Bradley to win the Sugar Bowl earlier in the year, and North Carolina State had lost to Villanova on the Wolfpack's home court. Rupp refused to participate in a playoff, and Tebell and the committee gave the slot to North Carolina State. Tebell explained, "North Carolina State agreed to play Kentucky anyplace, anytime, but Kentucky declined and asked to be selected outright." Rupp was adamant that the reigning NCAA champion deserved to have the opportunity to defend its crown.[56]

"I think we would have won it in 1950," Lancaster said in a 1980 interview.

> That was a thing that should not have happened. We had won it in '48 and '49. We won the conference again in 1950 but . . . the athletic director of Virginia at that time was on the committee as a representative of the third NCAA district. And he did not invite us. You had to be invited. We were defending champions, two successive seasons and we were not invited. So they skipped that year and then we came back in 1951 and won it. And I'm quite sure we could have won it four times in a row without any trouble. And we might even have won it after the [1951–1952 season] because you know we were suspended because of the scandal.[57]

Rupp used the negative publicity against the NCAA for the snub to bring on a change in the tournament format in 1951. The field doubled from 8 to 16 teams with 2 teams coming from each of eight districts. In 1950, however, Kentucky had to settle for another NIT bid in Madison Square Garden. Rupp predicted another Kentucky championship in a depleted field; some coaches refused to allow their teams to play in the Garden, because of the gambling that had become so evident there. Rupp called such reluctance "poppycock." "He loved the big city," Russell Rice wrote, "and so did his boys. They were always under his wing. He would vouch for them."[58]

Kentucky played unranked City College of New York (CCNY), a team with four black starters, in the first round. In 1998, Marvin Kalb narrated HBO's documentary, "City Dump, the Story of the 1951 CCNY Basketball Scandal." Kalb, a 1951 graduate of CCNY, presented Rupp and his players as evil incarnations of German Nazis. One reviewer noted that "Kalb is still eager to express his manifest distaste for Rupp, spitting out his name as though he were Adolph Hitler." In describing the NIT game, the reviewer said that Kalb "is not generally known for dynamism." When talking about the CCNY team, however, Kalb seemed like "Damon Runyon on a coffee jag." In the documentary Kalb intoned,

Adolph Rupp, Adolfff Rupp . . . was coming into town. And coming into a town filled with Jews, and was about to play a basketball team filled with Jews. And Nat Holman, a Jew, aware of all of this and being very smart in playing psychology, said to the team before the game, "You know, I think it would be a very good thing if you guys just tried to shake their hands . . . before . . . yeah, just kinda sportsmanlike." I watched as Floyd Lane put his hand out and this tall, blonde, gorgeous giant [from Kentucky] turned away from Floyd, which is exactly what Holman wanted . . . to get Floyd very upset . . . to get all of the other players upset. And Floyd hissed out at the guy, "You gonna be picking cotton in the morning, man!"[59]

Racked by flu, Spivey was unable to start. The Wildcats lost 89–50, the worst defeat of Rupp's career. After the game, the Baron congratulated Holman, the legendary CCNY coach, graciously, but when he got back to his players in the locker room, he told them sarcastically, "I want to thank you boys. You get me selected Coach of the Year [by the New York Writers Association] and then bring me up here and embarrass the hell out of me."[60]

Claude Sullivan, the general manager of radio station WINN in Louisville and the "voice of the Wildcats" since 1946, remembered how hard Rupp took the NIT loss. "I remember sitting up until dawn with him in 1950 after City College of New York beat the Wildcats by 39 points,"

Sullivan recalled in 1964. Sullivan said that on into the night Rupp kept repeating, "Thirty-damn-nine points! Thirty-damn-nine points!"[61]

Kentucky began the 1950 season with a 73–43 victory over West Texas State to inaugurate the new Memorial Coliseum on Euclid Avenue, across the street from the old Alumni Gym. World War II had postponed the building of a new "fieldhouse," and, according to historian Carl B. Cone, "by the time the first two postwar legislatures appropriated funds for it, the plans had changed." President Donovan wanted more than a field-house, insisting instead on a "general-purpose" auditorium that would seat 11,000 spectators not only for basketball games but also for other univer-sity gatherings as well. When completed, the structure included two wings, one for a swimming pool, and the other for athletic department offices. Once the cornerstone was laid in 1949, the building was dedicated as a war memorial. During World War II, 7,644 University of Kentucky students, alumni, and faculty, both men and women, served in the armed forces. Of that number, 334 gave their lives. Their names were inscribed in Memori-al Coliseum, "the monument erected to commemorate them." Cone called the coliseum "the most grandiose project in the university's history up to that time." The structure cost about $4 million. The Kentucky legislature paid 75 percent of the cost, and the newly formed athletic association "made itself liable for the bonds sold to pay the remainder, expecting to retire them from athletic revenues." In this way, Cone argued, "bondhold-ers had a stake and the association a sense of urgency in the success of UK football and basketball." Donovan had already become convinced that winning games on the gridiron and court was responsible for the largesse of the legislature. Donovan tried to promote the new building as some-thing more than a basketball arena, but everyone knew it was "the house that Rupp built."[62]

Rupp and the Wildcats won four in a row in 1950 before the Univer-sity of Kansas, Rupp's alma mater, and the Jayhawks' coach, Phog Allen, Rupp's old mentor, came to the coliseum on December 16. Several years before, Rupp had invited Allen to Lexington to speak, and Lancaster re-membered, "We all went out to Rupp's that evening and the two of them did most of the talking that evening. I understood where Adolph got a lot of his mannerisms. The two men were so much alike it was unbelievable.

It was one of the few times I ever saw Adolph intimidated by anybody. Rupp was absolutely in awe of his old college coach."[63]

The Kansas match was, according to Lancaster, "a game that was blown all out of proportion by the fans, the press, and by Adolph." Clyde Lovellette, the Kansas center, and Spivey, the "two premier centers in college basketball," faced each other, and for the first time, Rupp, "Phog's most famous pupil," faced Allen, "the winningest coach in the country." "Adolph was jittery for a week" before the game, and he had already sent Lancaster to New York and Philadelphia to scout Kansas. "We seldom scouted a team twice in those days," Lancaster said, "but it pointed up how badly he wanted to win this game." Lancaster told Rupp that the key to the game was the much-anticipated center matchup. Lovellette knew how to establish position on the block, but Lancaster was convinced that Spivey was quick enough to "step around to the side of Lovellette and swat the ball away."[64]

Lancaster had meticulously cut out clippings from the New York and Philadelphia newspapers lauding the talent of Lovellette. The coaches pasted these on Spivey's locker. "Bill would tear them down," Lancaster recalled, "but when he came in for practice the next day we had a fresh batch right back on his locker door." In the locker room the evening of the game, Rupp told his center, "Spive, you can be the All-American center or you can let Lovellette be the All-American center. It's up to you." When Spivey went onto the court he "was three feet off the ground," Lancaster said. The assistant coach's scouting report proved helpful. Throughout the game, Spivey nimbly slapped away incoming passes to the Kansas center. One play that "brought the house down saw Spivey bat the ball away, run and get it, race to the other goal and execute a slam dunk." "That wasn't done in those days," Lancaster said. "It was the first time I ever saw anyone dunk the ball during a game." Spivey outscored Lovellette, 22–10, and the Wildcats beat Kansas 68–39.[65]

Kentucky rampaged through the regular season, losing only to St. Louis, their old nemesis, in the first game of the Sugar Bowl in New Orleans. The Wildcats defeated Vanderbilt at home on February 24, 89–57, to go undefeated in the conference. In the SEC tournament, however, Vanderbilt got revenge on the earlier two lopsided defeats by winning over Kentucky, 61–57, in Louisville. Under new rules, the regular season champion, not the tournament champion, received the automatic bid to the NCAA tournament, so Kentucky got the bid. After Kentucky beat Loyola of Chicago handily (97–61) in a postseason game, they won over Louisville (79–68) in the first round in Raleigh, and St. John's (59–43) and Illinois (76–74) in the Eastern Regional in New York City. Kentucky headed to Minneapolis to face Kansas State, a team that had beaten Hank Iba's Oklahoma A & M team in the semifinals, 68–44. Iba told Rupp that Kansas State "was the best team he had seen all year."[66]

Rupp had struggled through the season with a recurring eye infection, and during the NCAA tournament a bad knee forced him to wear a steel and leather brace that extended from his hip to below his knee. On the day of the tournament final, Rupp was not well enough to make it down to the pregame chalk talk. Lancaster proved to be more than able to direct the team. But the team he had to work with was also diminished. Senior forward Walt Hirsch could not play in the tournament because he was in his fourth year. Cliff Hagan, a promising forward from Owensboro, took Hirsch's place, but Hagan was running such a high fever that he did not make lunch or the chalk talk either. When the game began, both Hagan and Rupp sat morosely on the bench, while Lancaster ran the team. When Kansas State got up by 6 in the first half, Rupp turned to the team doctor and bellowed, "Hell, Hagan's the right temperature to play." Hagan went in and immediately tipped in a missed shot to bring Kentucky close. At the half, with UK down by 2, Rupp told Hagan that, fever or no fever, he would start the second half. With a sick Hagan and a dominant Spivey playing together, the Wildcats took command of the game in the second half. When Kentucky gained the lead and with his team physically struggling, Lancaster made the decision for Kentucky to uncharacteristically "go to a delay game." Kentucky held the ball, shooting only layups, and won their third national championship in four years, 68–58.[67]

"After the game I went with Adolph back to his hotel room and waited while he put on his red pajamas and got into bed," Lancaster recalled. While the two coaches talked, Rupp turned to Lancaster and said, "Harry, I want to thank you. You won this game for me." Rupp would never say anything like that again during their long relationship together.[68]

The two coaches went their separate ways in the summer after the championship, Lancaster to Greece to coach the national team, and Rupp to Puerto Rico to coach his own team in a series of exhibition games. Rupp had recovered by the summer and proved to be his old, irascible self. The Kentucky coach accused the Puerto Ricans of dirty play and threatened to cancel the next day's contest. Puerto Rico's coach argued that Rupp was the first American coach to question his team's sportsmanship. It would not be the last; three decades later, Indiana's Bobby Knight would be accused of assault during an incident in Puerto Rico.[69]

Although the 1950–1951 championship Wildcats were overshadowed by the Fabulous Five and by later Rupp teams, Lancaster believed that for anyone who saw the team perform, "it was one damned great basketball team." And although Rupp was incapacitated for part of that season by physical ailment, forcing him to rely on Lancaster more and more, Rupp's players would remember the head coach as a larger than life figure. Frank Ramsey, a six-foot-three-inch sophomore guard from Madisonville during that championship season, would later remember that Rupp "convinced us we could do things we didn't know we could do. We were just cogs in the wheel. We were country boys, impressed with what we read about other players and other teams. He made us believe we were as good as anyone. He told us what he wanted done, and we did it."[70]

As it happened, the 1950–1951 season ended the golden era of Rupp's storied career and a golden age for Kentucky Wildcat basketball. In the period from 1941–1951, Kentucky won the SEC championship, either in the regular season or in the tournament, in 9 of the 11 seasons. The Wildcats won the NIT crown in 1946, back when that tournament was as prestigious as the NCAA. They won the Sugar Bowl championship, another big tourney, in 1949. Five of the Wildcats played on the 1948 world championship team in the London Olympics and Rupp served as the assistant coach. And then, Kentucky won the NCAA championship in 1948, 1949, and 1951.

As Alex Groza put it, "I think at that particular time it was probably in my opinion the golden era of all sports. Not only at Kentucky but at every university in the United States because every school had returning veteran athletes that had been in the service that were coming back. Not only in basketball but in football and in baseball and every intercollegiate sport that was played."[71] Groza failed to mention, however, a force Rupp had repeatedly ignored during his years of glory that would mar the golden era. Scandal would threaten to tear down everything that Rupp had built since he came to Kentucky in 1930.

8

Scandal

Adolph Rupp, recognized as Coach of the Year in 1950 by the Metropolitan Basketball Writers Association, coached a group of college all-stars against the NBA champion Rochester Royals on October 20, 1951 (the pros won 76–70).[1] Arriving in Chicago for practice a few days before the game at Chicago Stadium, he shared a room at the Morrison Hotel with Sewanee coach Lon Varnell, his assistant for the all-star game.[2] Rupp used his spare time to contact area high school prospects, remembering with pleasure and pride his years down the road as coach at Freeport High in the late 1920s.

The Monday before the all-star game, Rupp addressed the Chicago Quarterback Club. He reported on Kentucky's prospects for the coming year, then addressed an issue of growing concern among followers of college basketball. As early as 1945, Brooklyn College had expelled five basketball players for taking bribes to throw a game. In 1951 it became clear that players at other schools had agreed to fix games. Junius Kellogg of Manhattan College admitted he had accepted money "to control the point spread in a game." With City College of New York and Long Island University involved as well, it appeared at first that the scandal centered in New York, especially in games played at Madison Square Garden. But when players at Bradley in Peoria, Illinois, were implicated, it soon became clear that the problem stretched beyond the Big Apple. In fact, investigators found evidence of tampering in at least 86 games in 17 states from 1947–1950. Thirty-three players were implicated, and many more were rumored to be involved.[3]

In the summer of 1951, Rupp had weighed in on the gambling scandal, assuring a reporter in Lincoln, Nebraska, that the "fixers couldn't touch my boys with a ten-foot pole." Now in Chicago he took up for the accused players, painting them as victims of the gamblers and, ironically, of the press. An Associated Press story about his Quarterback Club speech reported that Rupp urged the public to "show more leniency with players involved in the scandal" because, after all, they didn't actually throw games. Instead, the New York newspapers should be blamed for publishing odds on games.[4]

In October, Alex Groza and Ralph Beard, former UK All-Americans and arguably the best players Rupp had ever coached, headed for an exhibition game in Moline, Illinois, as players and part owners of the Indianapolis Olympians, a short-lived National Basketball Association team. They decided to stop off in Chicago to watch the college all-star game and perhaps touch base with their former coach. Groza and Beard already had made their mark in the NBA; Groza was recognized as the second-best professional center, next to the great George Mikan. Their futures seemed bright.

After the all-star game, however, instead of dinner with the coach, police arrested Groza and Beard outside the stadium and charged them with fixing college games during their playing days at Kentucky. The police led Groza and Beard away for questioning. Later that night in Louisville, police leveled the same charge against Dale Barnstable, the captain of Rupp's 1949–1950 team and now the basketball coach at Manual High School in Louisville.

According to *Lexington Herald* sports editor Ed Ashford, rumors of UK's involvement in the scandal had circulated since Gene Melchiorre admitted fixing games as a player for the Bradley Braves. Ashford had heard that Nick Englisis, a former UK football player, first contacted Melchiorre about a deal to shave points, telling him that "you boys might as well come in, too; Kentucky is in." Although Ashford thought at the time that Englisis made that claim falsely to pull the Bradley players into his scheme, the rumors continued to circulate from more reliable sources. A couple of months before the arrests of the former UK players, *Chicago Tribune* sports editor Arch Ward wrote in a column, "The simmering University of Kentucky scandal will hit the front pages soon."[5]

Early in September, Ashford learned "from an unimpeachable source" that the next scandal would involve Kentucky. He wrote: "I was told that authorities had proof that the UK-Loyola game [which UK lost 67–56 in the NIT on March 14, 1949] had been fixed and they were holding up making arrests until they had time to investigate the possibilities of other games being involved." Ashford also wrote that "Frank Hogan, New York district attorney, preferred to wait until after the World Series before making any arrests so the story would get bigger play in the papers."[6]

The charges against Groza, Beard, and Barnstable stunned the state of Kentucky from the mountains to the Mississippi. UK president Herman L. Donovan, Rupp's erstwhile supporter, said he was "shocked and grieved over the report." Governor Lawrence W. Wetherby, campaigning in Western Kentucky, said that "all Kentuckians are holding their heads in shame today. Baron Rupp is one of the cleanest and finest coaches in the world, and this must be a hard blow for him."[7]

Rupp did not find out about the arrests until he returned to the Morrison Hotel after the all-star game. He had left Chicago Stadium to attend a dinner, and when he called Lon Varnell to tell him he would be late returning to his room, Varnell told him: "Adolph, I have some bad news for you. You should come over to the hotel as soon as you can." Back in the room, Varnell told Rupp about the arrests. Rupp had him call the newspapers and radio stations to verify the facts. Varnell assured him it was true and told him it might even be worse than it seemed. Shattered, Rupp stood by the phone as the news sank in, then collapsed on his bed and broke down in sobs.[8]

He hurried back to Lexington, for once having had his fill of big-city publicity. The next morning, he huddled with assistant coach Harry Lancaster, and they agreed at first that the charges couldn't be true. Then they remembered back to the Loyola game and two close games against St. Louis in New Orleans, and it all began to become clear. Rupp's emotions and responses ran the gamut from anguish, to anger, to defensiveness, to defiance. He assured the press that "the whole world has known for years how I feel about gambling on athletic contests, and my stand has not changed." When Groza and Beard came to visit, Rupp briefly played the role of sympathetic father, but later he angrily unretired the jerseys of the two stars, removed their pictures from the "Wall of Fame" in Memorial Coliseum, and refused to see them for years.[9] After the players received suspended sentences, Rupp concentrated on his own reputation, defiantly refusing to admit any wrongdoing on his part. The best coach in the country fought to prove he should be allowed to continue to coach the best team in the land.

As it turned out, Rupp had little to fear from his boss. Soon after the sentencing of Groza, Beard, and Barnstable—and a harsh assessment of the coach's deficiencies by Saul Streit, the "graying jurist of New York's General Sessions Court"—President Donovan wrote to "My dear Coach Rupp" on May 6, 1952. Donovan enclosed a copy of his statement of support to a joint meeting of the executive committee of UK's board of trustees, the board of directors of the athletic association, and the executive committee of the alumni association. "I want you to know that I shall not desert you in your hour of need," he assured the coach. "This is a good time for you to find out who are your real friends and who are your fair weather friends."[10]

One individual Rupp certainly did not consider a friend was Saul Streit, who saved his longest diatribe in the New York court proceedings for the Baron himself. The judge specifically praised Donovan, UK's trustees, and the governor, and he began his judgment of Rupp with an admission of his success: "Coach Adolph Rupp, also known as Professor Rupp at Kentucky University, is one of the outstanding basketball coaches in the country and probably the most successful. He has had many, if not more, winning teams and championships as any other basketball coach in the country." Streit noted that Rupp "has written a book on basketball and has taught advanced basketball at the University of Kentucky."[11]

By the end of his assessment, however—some 14 pages later in the sentencing transcript—Streit had made clear his contempt for an individual whose "sanctimonious attitude before me becomes ludicrous and comic." While the judge concluded that "it is unnecessary at this time to decide the issues raised by the coach . . . the undisputed facts are that he aided and abetted in the immoral subsidization of the players. . . . With his knowledge, the charges in his care were openly exploited, their physical welfare was neglected and he utterly failed to build their characters or instill any morals—indeed if he did not impair them."[12]

Streit compared Rupp with coaches such as Knute Rockne and Percy Haughton, who "have been inspirational factors in their students' development." Like Rupp, those coaches were considered members of the faculty, an honor that "ought not to be a mere device for increased salary and 'position' but should connote the coach's place in contributing to the development of the students' character." Streit went on: "How different is the influence of the coach whose ear is cocked for the betting odds, whose view of his players is that of horses who must win even if they are injected with novocaine to dull their pain, whose relationship with his players is almost that of a hostile employer and his employees."[13]

In a devastating critique, the judge stated that "every player-defendant spoke contemptuously of Coach Rupp. His overbearing manner and 'it pays to win' policy marked him as a foreman of a hard-driven working squad, rather than as a teacher and inspirational force worthy of the institution he represented." Streit said his findings "with respect to the corruption of the athlete are only a mere glimpse of the entire picture. This examination has been confined to only 6 of the 113 athletes performing under athletic scholarships at Kentucky University. The deleterious practices involving other subsidized athletes may not have reached the stage of criminality, but there is no doubt that it must ultimately affect their future adult lives."[14]

While the words "People vs. Dale Barnstable, Ralph Beard, Alex Groza" appeared on the sentence issued April 29, 1952, the document was mostly a blistering condemnation of Adolph Rupp. Judge Streit stated that Rupp had "accumulated a moderate fortune" during his tenure as Kentucky's coach: "He owns two farms and an interest in the largest tobacco marketing association in Kentucky." His salary of $8,500, plus an expense account of $1,500, made him the best-paid basketball coach in the nation. Streit also noted that Rupp "receives many invitations to address graduating classes in secondary schools, in some colleges, and at many college banquets, for most of which he is paid."[15]

Rupp found these speaking engagements, especially at high schools, to be opportunities for recruiting. Streit's indictment of his recruiting practices sounds quaint today. The judge expressed his amazement that "on these speaking trips, he also interviews prospective candidates for the Varsity Basketball team and tells them of the advantages at Kentucky and just what an athletic scholarship entails." Rupp had even "taken many trips out of town for the specific purpose of interviewing prospects and on occasions sends his assistant, Mr. Lancaster, out to interview the boys." Streit did acknowledge Rupp's argument, confirmed by the conference commissioner, "that it is not a violation of any of the rules of either the University or the Southeastern Conference or the National Collegiate Athletic Association to actively solicit and recruit candidates and offer them athletic scholarships."[16]

Rupp responded almost sarcastically to the judge's naïve questioning of his recruiting practices: "If that is the rule," he said, "it certainly is not observed, and I have never even had anyone mention it to me." Recalling the "cattle calls" at Alumni Gym in his early years, he stated modestly that, in the current era, "I haven't tried out anybody, although I have gone to see some boys play. That is the way we have to try them out now, go and see them in action." Streit asked, "Well, if you think a boy measures up to your standards of basketball, then you recommend him for a scholarship?" "Yes, sir," Rupp replied. "And that goes on until this day?" the judge asked. "Yes, sir," Rupp assured him.[17]

Rupp readily admitted giving money to players after well-played games, noting that they got $50 after a victory over Kansas. Asked where the money came from, he said it was "left over from the money that was raised to send these boys to the (1948) Olympics. . . . It is money laying around that had not been spent." Obviously, his players had developed a strong sense of entitlement by the late 1940s. He outlined his view of their attitude to Judge Streit:

> I think if you check up you will find that Bobby Watson and some of the boys came and said, "Will you give us $50 if we win the St. John's [game]?" I said, "No, boys, we are not going to give you any money to win the St. John's game, but let's see if we win the game, that is the main thing. . . ." Then they came back from there, they said, "Coach, how about that St. John's game?" I said, "Boys, I didn't promise you I would." I said, "I told you let's wait and see." They said, "Since the football boys did get some spending money at the game, we think we are entitled to it." I said, "I will take it up with the boys who have the fund." I took it up with them and they said give it to them, so they gave the money to Mr. Lancaster and I think he gave it to them, if I remember correctly, but they got it. . . . I am sure it was given to them after we got back from the Sugar Bowl.[18]

When another player claimed the coach had handed out $50 bills after the 1949 national championship game, Rupp said: "I imagine that was that fund that the merchants sent up to those kids at the time we played Baylor in the (NCAA) Tournament. We had to lay over for the Olympic tryouts. . . . That $50 was to be used for those kids to go to shows . . . so the merchants made up that money for those kids to get to those shows."[19]

Rupp acknowledged under oath that he knew Ralph Beard frequently received money from a supporter and that Alex Groza had been given a do-nothing job at a Lexington tobacco warehouse.[20] And although Wallace "Wah Wah" Jones, Rupp's bruising forward from Harlan County, was not involved in the point-shaving scandal, he, too, regularly received payments beyond his scholarship. Rupp readily admitted this in his testimony:

> Q. While he was at college, did he receive any additional monies to your knowledge from any source?
> A. Yes, he did.
> Q. What did he get?
> A. Well, Jones had a lot of sponsors, I think he got some money from people down Harlan.
> Q. Yes?
> A. And I think he had some sponsors in Lexington. I know he did, I know he did.[21]

Of the players indicted for fixing games, only Barnstable did not receive extra cash from "sponsors." "Barney was not good enough," Rupp testified. "I don't believe anybody gave him anything."[22]

Rupp knew that all of these activities were in violation of NCAA rules in force by 1950, but he maintained that the rules had changed. When Streit asked him if he had broken the rules in 1946, 1947, 1948, or 1949, Rupp responded, "I don't think so, I don't think so."[23] He admitted he knew exactly what was going on. Made-up jobs and payments from coaches, merchants, and the UK athletic association had all been provided with his blessing.

Even more damning was Rupp's active role in fostering an environment of acceptance of gambling. He associated with Ed Curd, one of the nation's largest bookmakers. From his perch above the Mayfair Bar on Main Street, within walking distance of the UK campus, Curd operated a lucrative sports bookmaking establishment. His name is misspelled "Kurd" throughout the sentencing transcript, but it is clear that Saul Streit knew the significance of the gambler's close association with Rupp's program.

"Do you know Ed Kurd?" the judge asked. "Yes, sir," Rupp replied. "You knew that Ed Kurd conducted a bookmaking establishment there?" "That was general knowledge," Rupp assured him. Asked if he had dined with the bookie, Rupp gave a reply that was at once confusing and telling. The sentencing transcript, quoted here verbatim, revealed the extent of Rupp's laxity if not his complicity in the gambling scandal that had engulfed the university.

Q. Have you ever had dinner with him?

A. Yes, sir, I have.

Q. Where was this?

A. I had dinner with him only once—no, I had—didn't have dinner with him—I had a—it was not a dinner, it was kind of an after supper snack with him at the Copacabana here in New York one night after a game.

Q. And there were a number of people at this table?

A. That's right.

Q. And some of the players were there?

A. Oh, no.

Q. Weren't some of the athletes at the table?

A. Oh, no, not at that time. . . . Now, I'll tell you the instance you are thinking about. We took the entire (team) and our wives to the Copacabana. . . . Now, we used to have those kids go to night clubs up here. They would go in and get a $2 service charge. I told them we ought to do the boys better than that. We went to the night club, the entire team went there, the University paid the bill.

Q. Mr. Kurd was there at the dinner?

A. He came up there and spoke to us but he didn't sit at the table.

Q. There was another occasion when you had dinner with him?

A. I think about three nights later, Happy Chandler, Mr. Shively and one or two others and I went to the Copacabana. . . . Ed came in and sat down with us.

Q. Did he take the check then?

A. I don't know. I didn't pick it up. I don't know who paid it. I didn't pay it. [Rupp was a notorious tightwad.]

Q. Wasn't he on the train on occasions coming back while the team was traveling?

A. He came up here on the train with us one time. He didn't come with us; he was on the train when we came up here to New York.

Q. And didn't you have a conversation with him then on the train?

A. I imagine I did, yes.

Q. Were you familiar with the point spread while your team played?

A. When we played [in] New York I was acquainted with it, yes, sir.

Q. Weren't you acquainted with it outside of New York?

A. Well, you would be, but then sometimes we would go six, seven or eight ball games and never know what the games were, when we played in Lexington.

Q. Do you remember an occasion in Cincinnati when you came into the room where the players were and you said you had just called Ed Kurd and you got the line from him and (you) were favored by so many points?

A. No, sir, I don't remember the occasion.

Q. Do you remember that?

A. No, sir, I don't remember—I don't remember that at all. Now wait a minute, that is the year Groza played, that is Groza and the three boys talking.

Q. Yes, at the Sinton Hotel, Cincinnati?

A. We always stayed at the Sinton.

Q. You played Xavier then?

A. I don't remember the instance, Judge, I am as honest as I can be.

Q. Did you ever call Ed Kurd and ask him what the point spread was?

A. I did once, yes, sir.

Q. What was the reason for that?

A. Well, we were sitting out in the athletic office one day and I didn't—I don't remember if I called him or called his office. We had beaten—Alabama had beaten us at Alabama on Monday and we were playing them again—Alabama on Saturday and someone came in and said, "You guys will win by"—I don't know how many. I said, "You are crazy." I said, "We can't beat Alabama to-night." He said, "That is what the odds are given downtown," and I said, "That's a lie." He said, "Well, call Ed Kurd and find out," so I called his place, but I don't remember what the points were.

Q. But you don't remember coming into the hotel room and telling the boys that you called Ed Kurd and just got the line?

A. I don't even remember, I don't even remember saying anything to the boys unless it was an occasion to impress upon them the fact that they were a favorite and I didn't think that they could win by that point spread.

Q. Well, Groza goes further. He says "Rupp showed us some slips in every game, how much we were favored by."

A. That is absolutely untrue.

Q. Did you ever visit the Mayfair Bar?

A. Once, yes, sir.

Q. Did you see Mr. Kurd there?

A. No, sir . . . We went in there to solicit an ad for the Shrine Crippled Children's Football Game and he was not there.

Q. Were you ever out to Mr. Kurd's home?

A. Yes, sir.

Q. How many times were you there?

A. I was there I believe twice.

Q. How many times?

A. We went out there to get the ad from him there.[24]

According to Walter Byers's autobiography, *Unsportsmanlike Conduct: Exploiting College Athletes*, "the scorecard read": "Five key basketball players were convicted of fixing points on basketball games over a three-year period; three were sentenced by Judge Streit. Adolph Rupp was condemned by Judge Streit for 'consorting with bookmaker Ed Kurd.' One player testified that before a game in Cincinnati, Rupp came into the hotel and told the team, 'I just called Kurd to get the points. Now these guys will be tough tonight so I want you to pour it on.' Judge Streit blasted the school's athletics policy as 'the acme of commercialism and overemphasis.'" The Southeastern Conference and the NCAA later found that players had received illegal cash payments, some of which were made with the knowledge of Coach Rupp.[25]

Clearly, Rupp's association with the bookie Ed Curd mattered to Streit. The fact that a prominent bookmaker socialized with the Kentucky coach—at least twice at the Copacabana in New York City—and sometimes traveled with the team concerned the judge, as did Rupp's familiarity with the "line" on a particular game and his mentioning it to his players.

And Adolph Rupp was not forthcoming with the judge about the full extent of his relationship with Ed Curd. Rupp owned a tobacco warehouse with Curd, and Curd told investigators of the point-shaving scandal and that he often attended Kentucky practices and that he often took Rupp to dinner.[26]

According to Dale Barnstable, after a Sugar Bowl game in New Orleans in which Barnstable missed a crucial shot, Rupp turned on him and said, "You just cost my friend Burgess Carey $500." Judge Streit asked Rupp if he had indeed made the statement. Rupp admitted knowing Carey but said he wasn't a particular friend of his.

Q. Were you familiar with any bets that Burgess Carey made?
A. Well, he bets pretty heavily at times.
Q. On basketball?
A. Well, he bets on every sporting event I imagine that he attends.
Q. Did you ever say to Barnstable after he missed a shot at the Sugar Bowl, "You just cost my friend Burgess Carey $500?"
A. No, I did not, I think I said that, I remember an instance though that the boys might have thought about. I remember we lost to—I guess it was St. Louis because they always beat us down there in the Sugar Bowl and as we were walking up to the dressing room and Burgess came by he said, "Coach, you just cost me $500" . . . and I was a little peeved at the time and I came in the dressing room and [Bernie] Shively was standing there and Harry [Lancaster] and all the kids dressing there, and I said, "Burgess Carey just got on me for losing $500." I said I told him, "By God I didn't lose any $500" for him, and that was—I remember that instance, yes. . . . I remember telling the boys about it because Burgess jumped on me and I came right out of the auditorium and started up the steps to the dressing room.[27]

Rupp maintained his innocence of any complicity in the point-shaving scandal. Was he naïve? Or did he simply look the other way after making it clear to his players that gambling had become part of the big-time college game? Only when his players were caught, only after his program had been shamed, only after his university had been embarrassed, only after he had been questioned about his role in the sordid affair did Rupp grudgingly acknowledge the extent of the sin:

> Q. Do you draw any distinction in your mind as to the immorality of shaving points and deliberately losing a game?
> A. I don't anymore, no, sir.
> Q. When you made the statement [Rupp's initial statement to the court]?
> A. I didn't exactly, I don't believe I exactly felt that way about it.
> Q. But before you did?
> A. At that time I didn't think it was as serious as going out and deliberately throwing a ball game.
> Q. As you reflect on it?
> A. But now then, since it hit into our family, I think it is a bad thing.[28]

Rupp's systematic effort to build Kentucky basketball into a big-time program produced just that: a program that Judge Streit called "the acme" of commercialism and professionalism. Streit found that "intercollegiate basketball and football at the University of Kentucky have become highly systemized, professionalized and commercialized; covert subsidization of players, ruthless exploitation of athletes, cribbing at examinations, 'illegal' recruiting, a reckless disregard of their physical welfare, matriculation of unqualified students, demoralization of the athletes by the coach, alumni and townspeople, and the most flagrant abuse of the 'athletic scholarship.'"[29]

Streit's conclusions, stated in the court documents in full, indicted not so much the players who had accepted money for fixing games, but the program that alumni had coveted so much, and the very system that Rupp had built during the first two decades of his tenure:

> 1. Intercollegiate basketball and football at the University of Kentucky have reached gargantuan proportions. They have become highly systemized, professionalized and commercialized enterprises.
> (A) The expense of maintaining these teams far exceeds that of the top professional teams in the country.
> (B) College sports at Kentucky have been developed from games

played by students for pleasure and glory into professionalized contests for the prestige and financial profit of the college.

(C) Commercialism has produced huge profits to this University though it has involved the open exploitation of these athletes.

(D) The huge financial obligations on Kentucky's athletic stadia has changed the spirit of the athlete from that of fighting for "Alma Mater" to giving his all to pay off the mortgage and bondholders.

2. By the extensive use of the athletic scholarship the University in effect, through barter and trade and under the guise of philanthropy, exchanged a so-called education for four years of service on the gridiron field and basketball court. This practice in certain American colleges constitutes the darkest blot on American college athletics.

3. The defendants and other athletes on the Kentucky teams with the full knowledge of the coach were covertly subsidized in violation of the amateur rules.

(a) The defendants and other athletes were openly subsidized by the coach, his assistant and townspeople.

4. Athletes were scouted, recruited, proselyted and tried out by the athletic director, the coach and his assistants, and scholarships awarded solely on the basis of athletic ability.

(b) Soliciting and recruiting students solely because of their athletic ability so as to increase the institution's prestige in athletics is immoral, objectionable and sinister.

5. Unqualified students were matriculated on athletic scholarships.

6. Academic standards were ignored and evaded.

(A) Cribbing at examinations by these defendants was encouraged and tolerated by University officials.

(B) These subsidized athletes found themselves under irresistible pressures to give their whole time and thought to their athletic careers, with no time for study—resulting in failures and extended courses.[30]

Although Adolph Rupp was not on trial, Judge Streit specifically lambasted the coach for his complicity in the whole sordid affair, and he offered his own evaluation of a coach's, a university's, and a conference's responsibility in the guidance and oversight of scholar athletes:

7. Adolph Rupp, the head basketball coach, failed in his duty to ob-

serve the amateur rules, to build character and to protect the morals and health of his charges.

(a) The physical welfare of a star athlete was deliberately sacrificed to the putative exigencies of victory.

(b) He openly subsidized players.

(c) He withheld information concerning their covert subsidization.

(d) He aided in their exploitation.

(e) He referred to gambling on the games and the point spread.

(f) He recruited and proselyted the athletes.

> A coach is supposed to take the material his college has to offer and to teach them the decent principles of sports. It is not his concern to go prospecting, subsidizing and proselyting.

8. The University and the coach must share the responsibility with the fixers for corrupting and demoralizing these defendants, and

9. The National and the Regional Conferences lack sufficient impartial, investigatory and enforcement powers.[31]

With these conclusions, Judge Streit made clear that exposing the abuses was not enough. He desired a thorough reform of college athletics. "Again I say, the devastating racket has been exposed," he declared. "The time has come to act. The appointment of committees or commissions can only delay the day of reckoning. There is still time to restore amateur intercollegiate sports and return them to the students." To that end he recommended:

1. That every college and University President, their faculties and trustees forthwith adopt the minimum ten standards approved by the Executive Committee of the American Council on Education.

2. I repeat my earlier recommendation to the National and the Regional Athletic Conferences—to appoint a committee or group of persons on expulsion and suspension, who

   (1) shall be entirely independent of the colleges or any of its officials or employees,

   (2) who shall have power to impose sanctions,

   (3) and who shall have a sufficient force to police and investigate the athletic activities of any of its members,

(4) with ample financial provisions to carry out the letter and spirit
of the amateur code.[32]

Streit adamantly insisted that "there is still time to act." Then he turned
prophetic: "Inertia and fine phrases must inevitably lead to new and greater
scandals, which will rock the world of sport." He noted that "to date, commercialism has driven over 36 colleges to abandon football as part of their
educational program." Now "the very existence of college sports is in the
balance. There will not be many more storm flags to warn us. The banner
of ethical standards must be raised over the championship pennant. Reform
from within or the public will demand correction from without."[33]

In November 1951, the American Council of Education appointed a
committee of 10 university presidents to "study and report on the problems
confronting intercollegiate sports." Although the executive committee of
the ACE unanimously adopted the special committee's report and the
NCAA unanimously endorsed the report "in principle," the NCAA failed
to officially adopt its specific recommendations.[34] Those recommendations
struck at the very heart of what Adolph Rupp had worked to build:

1. Athletic scholarships be abolished.
2. The absolute prohibition of recruiting of athletes.
3. Elimination of postseason games.
4. Athletes be required to make normal progress both quantitatively
   and qualitatively toward a degree, and that
5. Freshmen who are not graduates of junior colleges be prohibited
   from playing on varsity teams.[35]

In his opinion delivered at the end of the former UK players' sentencing on April 29, 1952, Judge Saul Streit wondered whether the NCAA's
failure to act was "an indication that the die hards and forces of reaction
are still in control of the NCAA." He noted that "until now, these regulations respecting academic standards, recruiting and subsidizing were
merely regarded as ideals, which a large number of institutions have not yet
attained." According to Streit, enforcement by the NCAA and the conferences had been "sorely defective" because there was no independent inves-
tigative and enforcement body. He called for a system based on the
recommendations of the university presidents on the ACE special commit-

tee. "The Presidents of the universities have shown the way," he wrote. "They ought to have the power to protect their institutions."[36]

Reaction to Streit's attack on Rupp and on the overemphasis of sports at UK was swift and more diverse than one might assume. President Donovan and university officials scrutinized each of the judge's accusations and issued a point-by-point defense on May 5, 1952. Governor Wetherby, acting as chairman of UK's board of trustees, invited Vincent O'Connor, New York's assistant district attorney, to come to Kentucky and make a complete investigation. O'Connor met with Wetherby, Donovan, members of the board, and alumni. He and District Attorney Frank Hogan praised "the full cooperation" of these Kentucky officials. Board member Robert P. Hobson, Dean of Students A. D. Kirwan, athletic director Bernie Shively, and Rupp traveled to New York to confer directly with Streit, and the athletic department furnished the judge with financial records to give him a more complete picture of the situation.[37]

Despite this cooperation, a joint statement by representatives of the trustees, athletic association, and alumni association said that "much of Judge Streit's statement reflects only his personal opinions based on meager and sometimes erroneous information. Interspersed with his statements of opinion are statements of fact. But these statements of fact, removed from context and taken together with his statements of opinion, have produced a distorted and untrue picture of the athletics program of the University."[38]

The signers specifically took issue with Streit's antiquated view about awarding athletic scholarships, a practice that Rupp had pioneered in the Southeastern Conference and that other SEC coaches and schools around the nation had subsequently followed. And they asserted that "many of Judge Streit's opinions are controversial, even among his colleagues on the bench," citing an April 26 statement by Judge Barrett of the Bronx County, New York, Court in sentencing two Manhattan College players on fixing charges. "I see no harm in athletic scholarships; in fact, I think they are a good thing," Barrett had written. "The fault lies with the public. If they continue to bet on the games, they are responsible."[39]

UK's joint statement then focused on Streit's specific charges. "Charges were made that Coach Rupp discussed point spreads with his teams and there is an insinuation that he was in liaison with gamblers," it read. Although "Coach Rupp has stated that on a few occasions he pointed out to his team that they were favored to win by a lopsided margin," the same information "was published in every metropolitan newspaper in the land for all who were interested to read. . . . We can understand how Judge Streit, from his point of view, might read a sinister meaning into such an act, (but) we can also appreciate that Coach Rupp and other coaches would use this information only to stir their teams to greater efforts."[40]

The statement specifically defended Rupp against one of the most damning charges:

> It appears to us that Judge Streit has labored to establish a relationship of intimacy between Coach Rupp and a Lexington bookmaker. He points to two occasions during a week in New York when this individual [Ed Curd] visited Mr. Rupp's table in a night club and two visits which Coach Rupp made to the bookmaker's home in Lexington. However, Judge Streit's own statement explains that the bookmaker was not a member of Mr. Rupp's party in the night club but that he happened to be there coincidentally with him and called for a short time at Mr. Rupp's table. Judge Streit also explains that the visits to the bookmaker's home in Lexington were for the purpose of securing a contribution to the Shrine Crippled Children's Hospital. While we certainly do not condone even a casual relationship between any University employee and a professional gambler, it appears to us that Judge Streit has taken a rather accidental affair and given it an appearance of evil that is not warranted.[41]

The statement made no mention of Curd traveling on the same train as the Kentucky team on a New York trip.

The only concession the signers made to the judge's criticisms and really the only rebuke—a mild one—of Rupp concerned payments to players beyond their scholarships. The statement read simply, "This practice is not condoned." At the December 1951 Southeastern Conference meeting, UK representative Ab Kirwan moved that all athletes "make affidavit that they have not received and will not accept any inducements beyond the legitimate Southeastern Conference scholarships." Rupp had testified to Streit that "certain players received rather generous expense and entertainment allowances following bowl games." University officials assured the public that "steps have already been taken to eliminate such practices."[42]

Donovan agreed with Streit's conclusion that Kentucky athletics had become "highly systematized and commercialized," but he saw no reason to condemn that. He said that the UK teams "are superbly coached and equipped and are well organized," and "their finances are administered and audited as is proper in the case of any public enterprise." Donovan argued that "the same is true of every department of the University." And because athletics were self-supporting, they must be commercialized. "It might be preferable if this were not so, but opinion in Kentucky and throughout most of the nation holds that athletics as an extra-curricular activity must not be a financial burden on the educational system." Donovan wanted it made clear that "no dollar of taxpayer money goes into our athletics program."[43]

Donovan and the signers of the joint statement sought to transfer the blame from Rupp and the university to Streit himself and the corruption that was so much a part of the judge's home state. Donovan felt that Streit had gone too far, that "it was totally unnecessary to the accomplishment of the purpose of the court for him to attempt to shake the confidence of the people of Kentucky in the entire structure of their University." He lamented the fact that "in sixty-seven pages of the attack upon the athletics policies of the University and upon its faculty, its alumni, its trustees, and its administration not one reference is made to the organized gambling in New York and the criminals that produced this scandal." Donovan added, "We do not contend that our record in this affair is above criticism and we are firmly resolved to make such reforms in our athletics program as will assure the people of Kentucky that never again shall a scandal besmirch the name of their University." However, he made it clear that "our policies will not be dictated by Judge Streit."[44]

In his last salvo, Donovan made no direct reference to Rupp. The blame must be shared by many. Indeed, the blame should be widely shared, according to the University of Kentucky president:

For what has happened in respect to basketball, the administrative officials and the athletics staff are partially responsible, and they are ready to acknowledge that responsibility. But the blame for the tragic events of the last few months does not rest completely on any particular group or individual. It must be shared by the public that persists in gambling and in protecting gamblers, by overzealous alumni, real and synthetic, who place athletics victories above all other considerations, by radio stations, newspapers and magazines that have featured varsity administrative officials and coaches throughout the land. And it would be well for Judge Streit to remind himself that not the least responsible, by any means, are those who have tolerated the unsavory environment in which Madison Square Garden operates. It is a fact of some significance that there were no basketball fixes in America before the game was featured in Madison Square Garden and that no school, whether located in New York City or elsewhere, was ever touched by scandal until its teams had participated in one or more games in that arena. University administrators and coaches have erred in several respects, but one of the gravest errors was in ever permitting a basketball team to play in Madison Square Garden.[45]

Clearly, officials at the University of Kentucky reacted defensively, stung by what they felt to be an overly aggressive indictment by the New York judge. Actually, Streit's writings about Rupp and UK were tame compared with his earlier criticisms of New York schools and other universities already swept up in the scandal. The judge had said it all before.

In November 1951, before the sentencing of the Kentucky players, Streit had blasted the state of intercollegiate athletics in another sentencing statement for fixer Salvatore Solazzo and Long Island University stars Edward Gard, Sherman White, and Leroy Smith. There, for the first time, he laid out his major accusations in a scathing attack on college basketball, accusations that he would repeat in the UK case. "I found among other vices," Streit said of LIU basketball, "that the sport was commercialized and professionalized; devices, frauds and probably forgery were employed to matriculate unqualified students to college; flagrant violations of amateur rules by colleges, coaches and players; recruiting and subsidization of players." He lambasted Coach Clair Bee, who "openly exploited" his players. Among other transgressions, Bee had admitted advancing $75 to $80 loans to players and had created an environment open to gamblers. According to Streit, "The naivete, the equivocation and the denials of the coaches and their assistants concerning the knowledge of gambling, recruiting and subsidizing would be comical were they not so despicable."[46]

After citing a litany of abuses at various colleges—he mentioned Bradley, Toledo, Michigan, William and Mary, Ohio State, Denver, and Pennsylvania in addition to UK and the New York schools—Streit concluded that "the exposure before me is only the lifting of the curtain for a small glimpse of intercollegiate football and basketball, fired by commercialism and determination to win at all costs. . . . It has come to pass that college fame depends less and less on education as a center of learning and more and more on the prominence of its football or basketball teams." He found that commercialism and overemphasis on sports were rampant and bemoaned the fact that "athletes are bought and paid for" and that "the average undergraduate student with athletic ability has not the remotest chance of making the varsity team." Furthermore, college officials resorted to "trickery, devices, frauds and forgery to overcome entrance requirements." Much to blame were coaches hired "at salaries far exceeding professional pay." These coaches were often given "artificial titles of learning and in many instances their tenure depends on winning."[47]

Today such naïve suggestions seem laughable, because all of the above have become so entrenched in college sports. In 1951, however, a respected judge was aghast at the state of things, brought on by Adolph Rupp and other coaches' determination to win.

Streit let the presidents of the New York colleges—LIU, CCNY, NYU, and Manhattan—off the hook, much as he had UK's Donovan. "To the credit of the Board of Higher Education and the presidents of the four municipal colleges, it should be noted that they promptly admitted their culpability in succumbing to commercialized basketball, have since changed the policy of the colleges, have taken the game back to the campus, abandoned professionalized basketball and adopted a policy of athletics for all rather than sports for the few," he wrote.[48] Indeed, changes in the athletic policies of these schools insured that they would never reach national prominence again. Perhaps it was the intransigence of Rupp, his unwillingness to de-emphasize basketball at Kentucky, that riled Streit so much.

UK was not alone in responding to Judge Streit's allegations in his sentencing statement of April 29, 1952. Responses from the press made clear that more was at stake than just the fate of three former UK players. The *Lexington Herald* echoed Donovan and university officials, placing the blame outside the school and even the commonwealth: "The *Herald* believes that steps already taken by the University administration will go a long way toward preventing any recurrence of the regrettable scandals that have haunted the school during the last year." The editorial sarcastically supposed that "it must be our 'provincialism' that causes us to resent some of the pious scoldings that have come out of New York, whose citizens did so much to engineer the whole basketball scandal, and where all who are genuinely interested in the curbing of crime could, if they chose, find such a wide, wide field for their endeavor."[49]

The *Courier-Journal* felt "the judge was off base in some particulars" but also said that Streit's charges "should be investigated thoroughly and any bad conditions found should be rectified." Editors at the *Louisville Times* admitted they didn't know whether the charges were true or false: "But we do know that the people of Kentucky, who support the state university with their tax money, have the right to insist on finding out whether these charges are true or false. . . . We, like other Kentuckians, have been gratified by UK's athletic successes. But we—and we think most Kentuckians will agree with us—don't want that success at the price of dishonesty and professionalism."[50]

Many of the reactions to Streit's accusations questioned everything Rupp had worked so hard to build. The *Paducah Sun-Democrat* believed, "It is up to us as Kentuckians to decide whether winning, big-time athletic teams for our state are worth risking more of the corruption of young people that has resulted from such emphasis in the past." The *Maysville Independent* placed the blame squarely on the shoulders of UK officials, including Rupp. Singling out a statement made by athletic director Bernie Shively that "we did everything in our power to prevent this," the *Independent* stated emphatically: "No, no, Mr. Shively. . . . We—including Shively, Coach Rupp, President H. L. Donovan, the board of trustees, alumni and fans—have been guilty of turning a boys' game into a business of such magnitude that education's foundation stone, the development of Christian character, has been completely lost." Even the UK student newspaper, the *Kentucky Kernel*, acknowledged that Judge Streit's criticisms were in "a great measure deserved," adding that "the real blame for the scandal lies with those who have caused the winning of games to be over-emphasized, rather than with the players themselves."[51]

Rupp stewed in his hurt and anger for more than six months—from the arrests of Groza, Beard, and Barnstable on October 20, 1951, until Judge Streit's sentencing statement of April 29, 1952—knowing all the while that his leadership as Kentucky's coach had been called into question. He wondered if he would be fired. When Donovan assured the belea-

The Rupp brothers from right to left. Otto, Theodore, Henry, and Adolph. Elizabeth and Albert completed the Rupp family.

High school graduate from Halstead High School, Halstead, Kansas, 1919.

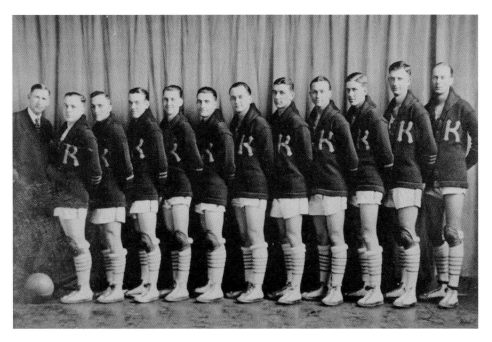

Rupp's senior year with the Kansas Jayhawks, playing for legendary coach Forrest C. "Phog" Allen (*far left*). Rupp, sixth from the right, never scored a varsity point. University of Kentucky Archives, Russell Rice Collection, Box 12, Item 3.

Dapper young graduate from Kansas University, 1922.

(*Above*) Rupp's Freeport Pretzels team with William Moseley anchoring the back row. Courtesy of Jon Scott, BigBlueHistory.net.

(*Left*) "The best damn basketball coach in America!"

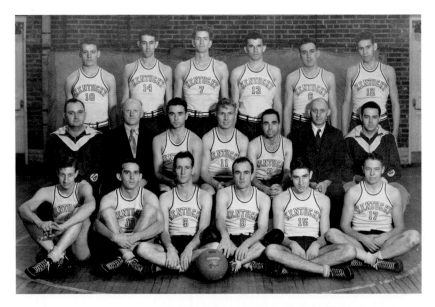

(*Above*) Rupp and his 1930–1931 University of Kentucky Wildcats. His first UK team went 15–3. University of Kentucky Archives, Louis Edward Nollau F Series Photographic Print Collection, Box 7, Folder-Item 253_0022b.

(*Below*) Paul McBrayer with the 1941–1942 freshman team during World War II. McBrayer would not return to coach after the war.

The 1947–1948 University of Kentucky Wildcats, 36–3 (SEC Champions, Tournament; NCAA Champions). The first five also won gold in the Olympic Games in London, England, with Rupp serving as assistant coach. The "Fabulous Five" were Wallace "Wah Wah" Jones (27), Alex Groza (15), Cliff Barker (6), Kenny Rollins (26), and Ralph Beard (12). Rupp is seated far left and Harry Lancaster is seated far right. University of Kentucky Archives, University of Kentucky General Photographic Prints Collection, Box 1A, Item 50.

The 1948 Olympic trials at Madison Square Garden, New York City. The first five would play with the first five of the Phillips Oilers for Olympic gold in London, England.

(*Above*) Rupp coaching five sophomores in 1948. From left to right: Garland "Spec" Townes, Hazard; Walt Hirsch, Dayton, Ohio; Joe Hall, Cynthiana; Bob Henne, Bremen, Indiana; and Roger Day, Frostburg, Maryland. Courtesy of the *Lexington Herald-Leader*.

(*Below*) The 1948–1949 University of Kentucky Wildcats, 32–2 (SEC Champions, Tournament; NCAA Champions). University of Kentucky Archives, University of Kentucky General Photographic Prints Collection, Box 1B, Item 56.

Rupp on one of his cattle farms with a prized white-faced Hereford calf, posing
with Miss Wisconsin Marvene Fischer, 1948. University of Kentucky Archives,
Russell Rice Collection, Box 11, Item 43.

The 1950–1951 University of Kentucky Wildcats, 32–2 (SEC Champions, 14–0; NCAA Champions). University of Kentucky Archives, University of Kentucky General Photographic Prints Collection, Box 1B, item 70.

Frank Barriess, Carl Combs, Rupp, and Ken Kuhn returning home by train from Chicago after the point-shaving scandal broke, 1951.

Rupp and Harry Lancaster looking with concern over point-shaving documents in 1951. University of Kentucky Archives, Russell Rice Collection, Box 11, Item 61.

Paul "Bear" Bryant spent much of his time looking over Rupp's shoulder during his time at Kentucky. Courtesy of the *Lexington Herald-Leader*.

(*Above*) The 1957–1958 University of Kentucky Wildcats, 23–6 (SEC Champions, 12–2; NCAA Champions). University of Kentucky Archives, University of Kentucky General Photographic Prints Collection, Box 1B, item 94.

(*Below*) Rupp with an unidentified colleague in his cluttered, memorabilia-filled office in the basement of Memorial Coliseum. University of Kentucky Archives, James Edwin Weddle Photographic Collection, Box 22, Item 3011.

Rupp in action with assistant Harry Lancaster looking on in the 1960s. University of Kentucky Archives, Russell Rice Collection, Box 11, Item 62.

Rupp displaying a gentle touch with grandson Chip. University of Kentucky Archives, Russell Rice Collection, Box 11, Item 55.

The Man in the Brown Suit in Alumni Gym. University of Kentucky Archives, Russell Rice Collection, Box 30, Item 10.

(*Above*) Concerned coaches at courtside. From left: Rupp, Harry Lancaster, and Joe B. Hall.

(*Below*) A scowling Rupp with (*from left*) Dickie Parsons, Joe B. Hall, and Gale Catlett. University of Kentucky Archives, Russell Rice Collection, Box 12, Item 44.

An aging Rupp with three stars (*from left*): Mike Casey, Dan Issel, and Mike Pratt.

Rupp and Joe B. Hall (*right*) signing Tom Payne in the Payne family's Louisville home. University of Kentucky Archives, Russell Rice Collection, Box 30, Item 28.

(*Above*) A smiling Rupp enjoying popcorn with smiling heir apparent Joe B. Hall. University of Kentucky Archives, James Edwin Weddle Photographic Collection, Box 22, Item 3014b.

(*Below*) Rupp waves to the adoring crowd at Rupp Arena in 1976.

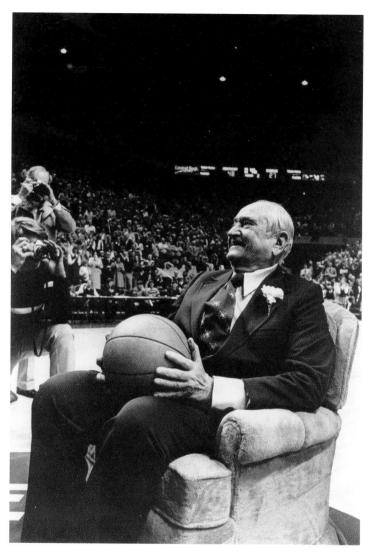

Rupp was honored with a Big Blue easy chair at courtside at Rupp Arena in 1976.

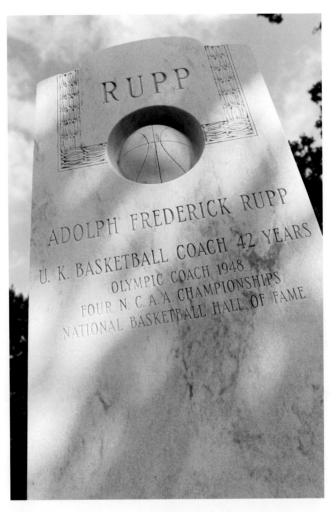

RUPP

ADOLPH FREDERICK RUPP
U. K. BASKETBALL COACH 42 YEARS
OLYMPIC COACH 1948
FOUR N. C. A. A. CHAMPIONSHIPS
NATIONAL BASKETBALL HALL OF FAME

Rupp's memorial monument of white marble in the Lexington Cemetery. Courtesy of Hayward Wilkirson.

guered coach of his support, Rupp took a chapter out of his own playbook and went on the offensive. Speaking at a Winchester civic club the day after Streit's sentencing, Rupp told the crowd, "I am willing for the citizens of Kentucky to be the judge." Referring to Streit's main criticism—the overemphasis of college sports—Rupp asserted his goal of "de-emphasizing de-emphasis. . . . I'm a little tired of this de-emphasis business. Do they want de-emphasis on ability in sports, spectator interest, or on winning games?"[52]

Making his usual spring tour of the high school banquet circuit, Rupp told students and fans at Pikeville that "the only statement to be made (relative to Streit's blast) will be coming from Dr. Donovan's office." In Clark County, local attorney Marcus Redwine criticized Streit as he introduced Rupp—who then used his banquet address to stoke up interest in the coming season. Noting that Linville Puckett, Clark County's three-time all-stater, would enroll at UK in the fall, Rupp told the gathering: "Some say Puckett can't make the team. I told Puckett I hoped he couldn't, because if he couldn't make the team, I certainly would have no more worries about winning games."[53]

Rupp already had determined that the scandal would not keep his 1952–1953 team from vying for another national championship. He would not get the chance.

9

The Businessman at Home

Adolph Rupp led a different life away from the court and the limelight of basketball polls and sports reporters. His family and circle of friends tell of a different man, and his numerous business interests showed that he did indeed have a life apart from basketball—a life of various business ventures, Hereford cattle, and devotion to his wife, Esther, and their son, Adolph Jr. (nicknamed Herky, short for Hercules). Even in his Memorial Coliseum office, Rupp presaged the coach as businessman, a modern phenomenon that would become the norm in big-time college basketball. He ran his office with all of the acumen, efficiency, and political acuity of other top business executives.

"He was the most organized and most delightful person you could ever work for," recalled Jane Rollins, Rupp's secretary from 1955 until his retirement in 1972. "He never said, 'You work for me.' He said, 'You work with me.'" She remembered in a 1977 interview, "He was already well-known when I came. And he wasn't just known here, but was almost known better internationally. . . . He was very interesting to work for. I met, talked and worked with people that I would never have had the opportunity to in any other capacity." But to Rollins, Rupp was "a celebrity of a different phase." She did not know "the gruff Der Baron that the players, the press and the fans in the stands of Memorial Coliseum knew and respected." The Rupp she knew was "sympathetic and considerate, demanding but not harsh." "He was so considerate," she remembered, "that he would call me at home during bad weather and say, 'Just wait until the weather clears, I'll take care of it myself.'" But Rupp didn't want other people to see that side of him. "He wanted them to think he was hard-hearted," Rollins said.[1]

"I always told him he had more P. T. Barnum in him than P. T. Barnum himself," she said. "He was a real showman." In the office, however, Rupp went about his work and expected his secretary and others to do the same. "He delegated responsibility and never asked you later if you did it or not," Rollins said. "He just expected you to do it. He expected a lot of everybody around him, and he knew how to get the best out of those people. They bent over backwards to carry out his requests because that's what Coach Rupp expected." Apparently, Rupp displayed the same knack in the office that he did with his players. "The greatest thing he did for me was the tremendous amount of confidence he gave me with his trust and faith," Rollins said. "The fact that he respected me as a person and my capabilities meant so much." Upon learning of Rupp's death in 1977, Rollins said sadly, "There's no way I can express my feelings. The words can't even say what I feel. . . . Not anything he saw was too great for him to achieve. He was the most remarkable individual I've ever been around. He had more in his head than businessmen have in books."[2]

Rupp did indeed have a lot in his head, and it wasn't all basketball. He was a businessman himself in an astonishing array of ventures. Many were connected to his primary employment, of course—author of books on basketball strategy, popular speaker at high schools and colleges on the banquet circuit, conductor of lucrative camps and clinics in Kentucky and around the world, radio and television personality—but the longer he stayed in Kentucky, the more he became involved in business ventures unconnected with basketball. Many of them—cattle ranching, insurance, tobacco farming, warehousing, and whiskey distilleries—have long been associated with life in the Bluegrass. Rupp became a prominent Kentucky entrepreneur.

By his side, or more accurately in the background, was his wife. Rupp met Esther Schmidt when he was coaching at Freeport High School in Illinois, and she was studying at a business college there. He was attracted to her not only by her beauty, but also because of the German heritage they shared. Rupp left for Lexington in 1930, but he did not forget the girl back in Freeport, Illinois. The couple married on August 29, 1931, after Rupp had spent his first year in Kentucky as a busy but lonely bachelor. A Rupp biographer and friend believed that "marrying Esther turned out to be one of the smartest things he ever did. She was the centerpiece of the puzzle, the glue that held them together. If there is such a thing as a perfect marriage, Esther and Adolph—living proof that opposites attract—had one."[3]

From the outset, Esther lived quietly at home, first in an apartment near campus, then at 175 Eastover Drive. She attended games, met new friends, and always stayed in the shadow of her increasingly famous husband. "Esther was one of the most beautiful women I have ever seen, but she was completely submissive to Adolph," said Ruth Shively, wife of longtime UK athletic director Bernie Shively. "She was a charming and delightful person to be with. Her personality changed when she was around Adolph."[4]

Esther attended all of UK's home games and many of the away games. Mary Phyllis Riedley of the *Courier-Journal* in Louisville, who wrote several articles about the Rupps' home life, believed that at games Esther was "as serious about watching as the team is about playing." One friend remarked that she "would sooner burst a balloon in church than talk to Esther at a basketball game." Rupp sometimes chided referees with the line, "My wife knows more about basketball than you do!" Esther did indeed come to learn the game. "She should know it all by now," Rupp said in 1966. "She even brought Herky to the games when he was a baby. She was always behind the team 100 percent."[5]

At home Esther concerned herself with other things, and apparently her husband did, too. According to Esther, "The coach does all his fussing and fuming on the bench or in the dressing room and is nothing but agreeable at home." One sportswriter observed that "Wildcat fans who enjoy 'Der Furor's' fussing, feuding and fidgeting as part of the game would scarcely recognize the husband that Esther Rupp describes." She once said that "basketball is rarely a topic at home. He never brings the game home." Of course, he was away from home a great deal, on road trips during the season and speaking at clinics and banquets in the off-season. Esther once said that she attended the banquets in order "to eat a few meals with my husband."[6]

At home Rupp talked more about his farms and his cattle, although these were topics, unlike basketball, that Esther learned little about. If someone asked her about the farms, she insisted, "You'll have to ask Adolph." "I know more about basketball than I do about cattle breeding and bloodlines," she said.[7]

When they first met, Esther thought Adolph was "the kindest, most thoughtful young man I'd ever met," and she remained impressed with his thoughtfulness throughout their life together. She said he never forgot "a birthday, an anniversary or a promise. He just always remembers to remember." For her part, Esther faithfully documented his achievements, clipping articles from newspapers and magazines. "Esther clips them all," Riedley noted, "and, if she would prefer to put them to use, she could paper every wall in the house and have enough left for a wall-to-wall carpet." Some sportswriters wished she would do just that, because it would squelch rumors of Rupp's imminent departure to another college or a professional team. After all, "Adolph would hardly leave his clippings."[8]

Rupp appreciated Esther's devotion. He often quoted a verse from the Old Testament book of Proverbs: "A prudent wife is from the Lord." He recognized that being the wife of a coach, especially one so famous, was not an easy assignment. In 1966 he said he knew that Esther had "the worst life in the world." That year Herky was coaching at Lexington's Lafayette High School, and Esther dutifully attended all of his games in addition to UK's. "She has about 50 games to worry about every season," Rupp said. "That's a double dose." Searching for the words to describe the household during basketball season, Esther finally settled on "a state of confusion."[9]

In 1970, two years before Rupp was forced to retire, he paid tribute to his long-suffering wife:

I don't know how Momma has lived through this many years in coaching with me. I don't know who else would allow a guy to be away from home for as long as 91 days straight sometimes and let me conduct those overseas tours. All the time she was sitting back home with Herky. She wasn't only a basketball wife. She was also a basketball mother. She saw Herky through his athletic program and cooked for us whenever we were home. She was very patient. She went to see all his games when he played at U High. Then she'd come over and see all my games. When he started coaching, she ran to see him and then ran back to see me. I imagine she's had her fill of basketball. She played it as a girl, but I don't think she had the disease like she does now. She's a wonderful woman.[10]

When she died in 1998 at the age of 95, the Kentucky Senate passed a resolution that "when the Senate adjourns this day, it does so in loving memory and honor of Esther Rupp." The resolution stated that she "exemplified what a wife, mother, and friend should be," and remembered especially that she had "Christmas dinner at the Rupp home for her husband's players who were unable to go home for the holidays. . . . Kentucky basketball was fortunate to have Esther Rupp as first lady for so many years, [and] all who knew and admired [her] will grieve over their loss, and she is mourned across the length and breadth of the Commonwealth."[11]

Described as "a shy, quiet woman who was the opposite of her extroverted husband," Esther said in a 1966 interview: "Adolph speaks for himself. I think two personalities in one family are enough, don't you?"[12]

Esther and Adolph were married for almost a decade before Herky, their only child, arrived on June 30, 1940. Born with a triple hernia, the baby stayed in Lexington's Good Samaritan Hospital for 91 days before he was finally released to go home. Esther's friend Judy Crouse remembered that "she was a very good mother to Herky and tried to keep him shielded from the media enough to lead a normal life."[13]

As for the father, Rupp must have remembered his own hard life growing up without a father and working in the Kansas wheat fields. Like Esther, he wanted to shield Herky from hardships. On the other hand, there apparently were times when he remembered his years in Halstead with a sense of nostalgia. Lyman Ginger recalled that Rupp often spoke fondly of life back in Halstead. Ginger served as director of the University School at UK and later as dean of the College of Education. Rupp had a master's degree in education from Columbia University, so sometimes their conversations turned to matters of education. "I was never sure whether he was really sincere or whether he meant it," Ginger said, but Rupp would insist that "what we need in the state is to go back to the one-room school." Rupp told Ginger that he had gone to a one-room school in Kansas and "got an education that was good enough to put me in the University of Kansas."[14]

Ginger also recalled that after "a couple of bourbons" at a party one night, Rupp told him: "You know, they drive that great big yellow bus in front of my house and load it up with kids and haul them two blocks. They ought to be walking to school. . . . We're wasting the taxpayers' money. I don't see why you don't do something about that." Ginger said Rupp "went on for 10 minutes talking about the noise they make. They wake people up when they want to be sleeping."[15]

Rupp considered himself an authority on education as well as basketball, and he thought of himself as a teacher. He told a breakfast gathering at the state Lions Club convention that "too many are being misled by the thought that a good school system exists when it has new school buses, new buildings and when it pays its teachers well." "We are being misled into thinking that if you pump enough money into a thing, it's good," he proclaimed and said that an education system "is best built by having teachers who can inspire and challenge the students to better work. It doesn't matter whether the teaching is done in a modern building or in a tent." Of course, Rupp would not settle for a subpar facility for his basketball players.[16]

He told a crowd of more than 6,000 at the Minnesota State Teachers Convention: "We are teaching masses instead of individuals," and instead of challenging youth, "we merely try to do the routine because it is inevitable. . . . Still another paradox is the image of the educator in modern America. We're going to have to decide, we teachers, whether we want to be skilled technicians or learned scholars." In his rambling address, he also weighed in on the proper role of the school superintendent. In the old days, the superintendent "knew very little about acoustic tiles, standard deviation or dry-wall construction. Perhaps he was not as good in public relations, but he could read Latin, he possibly could read Greek, and in those days was respected precisely because he was educated."[17]

Rupp then seemed to argue against his own assertions. "America doesn't need any more 'well-rounded' people produced by our colleges and universities," he said. "A well-rounded person is like a ball, (which) rolls in the first direction he is pushed. We need more square people who won't roll . . . restless men and women with imagination, balance and courage, ready to move into untried fields."[18]

Rupp defined such a "square" precisely: "A guy who volunteers when he doesn't have to . . . gets kicked for trying to do a job better than anyone else . . . hasn't learned to cut corners or goof off . . . gets all choked up when he hears children singing, 'My Country 'Tis of Thee' . . . believes in God and says so in public . . . lives within his means whether he wants to or not." Then the kicker: The "square" tells his son "it's more important to play fair than to win. Imagine."[19]

He challenged his audience: "Will all you gooney-birds answering this description please stand up? You misfits in this brave new age. You dismally disorganized, improperly apologetic ghosts of the past, stand up. Stand up and be counted! You squares . . . who dignify the human race. You squares . . . who turn the wheels and dig the fields and move mountains and put rivers in our dreams. You squares who hold the world in place."[20]

Quite a performance. And it was a performance. Rupp rarely voiced such sentiments to the press, to his players, or even to fathers and sons at basketball banquets. But in a speech to thousands of teachers, he hammered out ideas that his audience surely wanted to hear, whether he spoke sincerely or not. His admonitions almost seemed more suitable to teachers in the old one-room schools rather than practitioners in large, modern, brick and glass facilities.

Despite his devotion to the one-room school, Rupp sent Herky to UK's University School, where Lyman Ginger was director. One morning Rupp picked up the phone and called Ginger. "By gawd, Lyman, what's going on?" When Ginger asked what he meant, Rupp said, "That g——d—— teacher said that Adolph couldn't go to New York with us." Rupp wanted to take young Herky with the team to Madison Square Garden, and he had sent a note to the kindergarten teacher asking for permission. She said no. Ginger tried to kid the distraught father: "Why, you don't want him to go up there with you, that bunch of roughnecks, that bunch of drunks. You don't want to put him in that." Rupp was not amused. "He'll learn more up there in one hour than he will in kindergarten in one week," he argued. "Now, Adolph, just relax," Ginger said. "When are you leaving?" "I'm leaving this afternoon," Rupp replied. "You take Herky and you go right on," Ginger said. "It'll be all right when you come back. They may put him back [a year, but] he can work his way back up." By that time Rupp knew his friend was joking, but he told him, "By gawd, it would be just like you to do that." Herky made the trip, and after they returned to Lexington, Rupp called Ginger to his office, pulled out a drawer with a dozen or so watches—gifts from tournaments—and told him to take his pick. Apparently, the kindergarten teacher did not receive one.[21]

Rupp introduced Herky to basketball early on, but at eight years old, Herky told a newspaper reporter that he didn't want to become a UK player. "I want to be the coach," he said. He eventually did play for his father, and even though he rarely saw action, he came to be popular with UK fans. Of course, he always was popular with one particular fan. Ask Esther Rupp who her favorite player had been over the years, and she would not hesitate to name Herky. And she wasn't particularly happy about his lack of playing time. "You can't become an All-American sitting on the bench," she once said.[22]

Herky played at University High School. Lexington sportswriter Billy Thompson observed that Herky "tried hard, but he spent much of his first year on the bench. . . . Perhaps the pressure was too much for the young teen-ager." Everywhere the Purples played, the fans would whisper, "There's Adolph Rupp's son." "This was bound to make it rough on a mere kid," Thompson wrote, "and he was younger than most of his classmates." As Herky got older and more experienced, though, he "rapidly began rounding into a real, real good player," and by his senior year he "was one of the top scorers in Lexington prep circles."[23]

In August 1958, rumors were circulating that Rupp planned to retire. Thompson said those rumors were premature by at least four years. "Why four years?" he wrote. "Well, his son, Herky, will be enrolling at UK next month, and it so happens that his son is rapidly becoming a pretty good-size boy. And since pretty good-size boys are handy to have around on a basketball floor, it may be that one of Adolph Rupp's chief desires is to coach his own son." In the next four years, according to Thompson, "the Rupps are going to gang up on the opposition. They both have set a big goal, and knowing Adolph and Herky Rupp, I wouldn't bet against their reaching that goal."[24]

Thompson believed that "whether he will admit it or not, [Rupp] wants son Herky to be an outstanding basketball player." Coach Rupp indicated, however, that "Player Rupp is going to have to be better than the other cagers to make the team. This means that Papa Rupp is going to have to work hard . . . and so is Son Rupp." It didn't work out exactly as both might have wished. Undoubtedly, Rupp worried about playing his son ahead of more talented teammates. And, of course, he wanted to win. All of this was hard on Esther. In at least one instance she took up for her son forcefully and publicly. Mary Boeck, wife of *Courier-Journal* sportswriter Larry Boeck, remembered one incident in particular. "I was sitting next to Mrs. Rupp for this one game, and he was like 30-something points ahead of this other team, UK was," she recalled. "He had cleaned that bench off, and there sat Herky." That was when the chants began in the student section: "Send Herky in," "We want Herky." "He was stubborn, you know," Boeck said of the coach. "Nobody was going to yell from up there and tell Adolph Rupp what to do."[25]

Kentucky won by 30, but there sat Herky until the final horn. Just as Rupp was to go on the air for his postgame radio show with Claude Sullivan, Esther walked over and told him, "I'm leaving." "What do you mean, you're leaving?" Rupp asked. "I'll be through in a minute; you can go home with me." "No, I'm not," she said. "I've got a ride, and I'm not going home with you. Let me tell you something. You put everybody but the water boy in that game, but you didn't put Herky in there." "Well, now Esther," Rupp began, but she cut him off. "If you're such a damn good coach, why can't you teach your own son to play basketball?" Esther then "flew out" of there, Mary Boeck remembered. "She was not about to leave until she told him off, and she flounced out of that thing, and everybody was standing there and two or three people applauded. . . . But that was the only time I ever saw her do anything in public that would detract from Adolph."[26]

Herky did not hold his lack of playing time against his dad. "Naturally, my father expected me to act in a certain way," he said, "but he wasn't harsh or unreasonable about it. He made no excessive demands of me." The media's portrayal of Rupp's "Prussian personality" was considerably different. *Lexington Herald* sportswriter D. G. FitzMaurice described this typical view: "The massive head, the stern demeanor, the uncompromising perfectionist, the ultimate disciplinarian all helped to portray Rupp as the Bismarck of basketball. It is a portrait of as intimidating a person as ever chalked a play on the board, yet Herky sees as much pussycat as Prussian in his father."[27]

Rupp always sympathized with other coaches whose sons chose to play for them. In the 1960s, Rob Vanetta played for his father, Bob, at the University of Missouri. "We had some problems before we came to the MSU Classic," Bob Vanetta explained to a *Memphis Press-Scimitar* reporter. "A small group of students were against Rob playing for me, but I think this is the usual thing, especially if you don't have a good year." Rupp took the time to write Rob a note of encouragement:

I have just learned you are playing basketball under your father. I think it is commendable, and I cannot tell you how happy I am for you. Dr. (Phog) Allen's son, Bob, played for him; Henry Iba's son, Moe, played for him; and my son, Herky, played for me. Although he (Herky) did not get to play very much, the crowd always cheered for me to put him in. He was not a strong athlete. He has always been happy that he played under me, what he considered "the best," and I was always happy that he decided to play for me.

Rupp assured Rob that he had made a good choice to play for his father. "I know your father well," Rupp said. "He is the best and can teach you more basketball than any other man. When you decided to play for your father, you paid him the finest compliment that any boy can pay his dad."[28]

Rupp's sensitivity about coaching his son carried over to the home front. When he wasn't traveling for a game, a clinic, or a speaking engagement, he made it home for supper each evening. At Christmastime the Rupps hosted players who were unable to go home. Herky remembered, "One of our traditions was to have a family photo taken each Christmas and reading 'Twas the night before Christmas.'" He said his dad "loved Christmas, I guess because my father had so little when he grew up, and he enjoyed the tree and the exchanging of presents. My father would hold off opening some of his presents so that he'd still be enjoying Christmas by the time New Year's rolled around."[29]

Rupp sent out a yearly Christmas letter to family and friends, although he sometimes didn't get it mailed until after the first of the year. Those letters combined reports on the basketball team with family news and descriptions of the weather, crops, and livestock on the farm. On January 3, 1967, for example, he wrote:

Dear Family:

Now that the holidays are over I want to wish all of you a Happy New Year.

1966 for us here in Kentucky was not a bad year. Until December came we were very fortunate with our basketball. I stated before the season started that we would not have a great team and I think that is coming true. However, December brought us a grandson so the name of Rupp will carry on. Don and Bob fell down on us in this department. The youngster is fine, weighed 8 pounds 3 ounces and seems to be getting along nicely. We, naturally, are so happy with him.

Our team this year is even smaller than last year. They shoot well and handle the ball well but we have trouble getting it in the rebound department.[30]

Rupp told about his August trip to the "Near-East." "We have 1,200 feet [of film] in color and I hope some day to be able to show it to you," he wrote. "It was certainly a wonderful trip." Most of the rest of the letter concerned farm news, where he showed his usual attention to detail:

The year has not been bad on the farm. So far this year we have had 46.38 inches of rain, which is two inches over our season's norm. We normally get about 44 inches. Eight of these inches came in August when I was in the Near-East and it brought a marvelous tobacco crop to Kentucky. The rain was general, falling over some eight days so you can see how valuable it was. We have had late winter moisture which has caused all our creeks to flow rather freely. Since we depend on this source of water for our livestock you can see how fortunate we are. Our corn was also good. Our pastures are still good. We haven't opened our three silos so we have over 600 tons of feed there when we need it. Our winter has been open. We had a wet snow in November but it only lasted a few days. As long as the weather is open it is satisfactory to me from a farming standpoint. We had several pastures of grass that had no livestock on them at all so the grass is knee high.[31]

Addressing his brothers back in Kansas, he wrote, "[I'm] sorry to hear you have had so little moisture and that the wheat is going into the winter in such bad condition. Nothing beats the rain at the right time." He told his readers, "We have some 14,000 students on campus and 9,000 in our Community Colleges. We have been off since the 20th as we are on the trimester basis and we will begin again on the 12th." Rupp's holiday letters revealed his interests, and his life seemed to be divided in about equal parts: basketball, family, and farm.[32]

He communicated regularly with his family back in Kansas, especially his sister, Elizabeth. When the point-shaving scandal broke in 1951, he wanted his family to know that things weren't as bad as they might appear in the papers. "This thing is beginning to work out," he wrote in 1952, "and I think a few of the sports writers are beginning now to see that the judge was just trying to get a lot of cheap publicity by tying himself in with one of the outstanding schools in the nation. As our President said, 'McCarthy is a gentleman compared to that guy.' The implications in all of this were what was hard. In other words, as you well know, if you don't tell the truth or the whole truth about things the story doesn't make sense, and the judge put statements out in such a way as to make himself look good."[33]

Rupp visited when he could. In April 1953 he wrote, "Our plans now call for a hurried trip early in June to visit Esther's mother and to run out to Kansas for two or three days. Would it be convenient for us to stop for a day—possibly around June 4 or 5? We want to get our visit over before the hot weather sets in."[34]

Like Herky, Rupp's closest friends remembered a kinder, gentler Rupp than the caustic Baron of court and press. "There was a lot of compassion in Adolph," said Dr. V. A. Jackson, UK's team physician from 1965 until Rupp's retirement in 1972. "I remember seeing him on the road, going over to talk to kids who were trying to watch practice. He would go over and make them feel at ease." Cawood Ledford, the radio voice of the Wildcats following Claude Sullivan, remembered how easy Rupp made it for him during interviews. "It didn't matter what you asked him," Ledford said. "He always came up with something to say, and after that he'd come back and say, 'What was it you asked me?' Sometimes neither of us could remember." Ledford was impressed with Rupp's turn of phrase. "I remember one time they had lost a game at Auburn and he was telling me how it was in the locker room," Ledford recalled. "It was so quiet in there, 'You could hear 'em breathe.' I liked that. I thought that was a nice way to put it."[35]

Soon after the Rupps set up housekeeping in an apartment in Lexington, Esther began playing bridge with a group of women, and the friends met once a week for the next 40 years. Although several acquaintances did not believe that Adolph himself had many really close friends, the Rupps forged several advantageous friendships. Paul and Jeanette Nickell often hosted parties at their home. Esther had met Jeanette when the future Mrs. Nickell lived in a sorority house next door to the Rupps' apartment. Paul was a salesman for the Graves-Cox men's clothing store. "I patched (Rupp's) brown suit at least a half-dozen times," Nickell told Russell Rice in a 1994 interview. "He was only making $2,800 a year and didn't have the money to buy a new one." The store sponsored Lexington's first sports radio program on WLAP. Nickell lined up the guests for the show, but he needed someone to serve as the interviewer. He asked Rupp, and the young coach, always eager for attention, agreed to do it for free. Nickell remembered that "the program was so popular that people would stop dinner to listen to Adolph, [who] became known as the Will Rogers of Kentucky radio." Although the coach was not paid, the company told Nickell to take care of him, so he outfitted Rupp in "the company's most expensive brown suit and matching accessories: brown hat, brown shirt, brown shoes, brown socks and a brown tie."[36]

Some of Rupp's closest friends—the Nickells, Mr. and Mrs. Cecil Bell, Mr. and Mrs. Rob Sparks, and Dr. and Mrs. Lyman Ginger—all remembered good times at after-game parties and summer cookouts. The couples would meet at a different home on a rotating basis, and the Rupps took their turn. "What I remember is how we would all come over here after games," Mrs. Bell recalled. "The rest of us would be making small talk, but Adolph would turn on the TV and three radios so he could get all the scores. And woe be unto you if you made him miss something."[37]

Teddy Roosevelt's daughter once said that her father "has to be the bride at every wedding and the corpse at every funeral." Rupp's friends knew he was like that, too. According to Lyman Ginger, Rupp "would take over a party and be the center of attention, no matter who else was there. He knew many things and had opinions about most of them." Baldy Gilb, one of Rupp's early assistant coaches, and his wife Stella remembered those after-game parties well. "Many times after basketball games we'd end up going to Rupp's house . . . or the Shivelys' house, and we'd all get together," Stella said. At one party in Bernie Shively's home, Cleveland Browns coach Paul Brown was the honored guest. "Shive had a big crowd there," Baldy Gilb recalled. "Of course, Paul Brown was kind of the center of attention." Brown held forth, sitting in a chair near a fireplace in one room. "Adolph didn't stay in that room with him very long," Gilb recalled. "The next thing you knew, Adolph was in another room with his old . . . group."[38] Stella remembered another dinner party at their house, when the Gilbs invited a prominent retired football player. After dinner someone else took over the conversation in the living room, and Stella found Rupp sulking, nursing a bourbon in the den. "He wasn't going to share the limelight with anyone," Baldy said. "He was top dog." Other than basketball and the parties, the Gilbs found little in common with the Rupps. "They didn't belong to a country club and they didn't dance and they didn't play golf, and we did all those things," Stella said. "So we drifted apart."[39]

According to Russell Rice, when Adolph and Esther came for dinner at the home of Cecil Bell, Rupp always sat at the same place at the table. They called it "Adolph's Chair," Rice said. Attending a cookout at the Nickells', Rupp would prop his feet up on a porch railing, take a large glass of bourbon from the host and say, "By Gawd, Paul, let's get that incinerator going." Rice believed that in such a state of relaxation, "the group talked about everything but basketball." Rupp and Ginger argued good naturedly about school consolidation—Ginger was for it and Rupp against it—and invariably Rupp would bring up stories of his one-room school back in Halstead.[40]

Rupp proved to be a loyal friend, especially in times of difficulty. When Rob Sparks's lumber business burned, a Lexington newspaper reported he "had a $100,000 loss and only $80,000 in insurance." When Rupp and Esther came to visit two days later, Rupp asked if he could see a new room that the Sparkses had added on to their house. Sparks knew Rupp had already seen the room, but he took him down the hall anyway. When they were alone, Rupp said, "Hell, I don't want to see the room. I wanted to tell you that I have $20,000 that you're welcome to."[41]

Rupp also took care of his friends in other ways. Before Memorial Coliseum was completed and the Wildcats were still playing in 5,000-seat Alumni Gym, Rupp's friends asked him to get them into games. According to Rice, the gymnasium had two scoreboards with two control buttons each. "There are four buttons," Rupp told his friends. "That will take care of four of you." Sparks fired a blank pistol at halftime and at the end of the game, another friend kept the locker-room keys, yet another served as the public-address announcer, and Ginger kept the scorebook. Even after the move to 11,500-seat Memorial Coliseum, Rupp kept his "support staff" with a few changes. Sparks kept the new game clock, but because Ginger had become dean of the College of Education and no longer had time to keep the scorebook, Rupp recruited Jim Robinson, his banker. Another bank official, J. D. Reeves, charted rebounds.[42]

Rupp rewarded these friends with a close association to his storied program. He, however, expected them to perform in their various capacities, and sometimes his friendship bumped up against his competitive nature. In one game, with Kentucky leading by 14 points, a Mississippi player hit a shot at the halftime buzzer (Sparks by then had upgraded from his blank pistol). The referee came to the table and said, "Just tell me where the ball was when the horn blew." Sparks replied that the ball was indeed in the air, so the basket counted. After the halftime break, Rupp approached his friend and said, "Bob, I knew everybody else in this gym was against me, but I didn't think you were." Sparks replied: "If you want me to steal for you, turn out the lights. I won't steal before 11,500 people." Rupp quickly backed down, saying, "Oh, you know I didn't mean it." "What difference did it make?" Sparks asked. "You were so far ahead they didn't have a chance." To which Rupp responded: "Every time they score, my heart bleeds. I don't care what the score is."[43]

Another group of friends, not associated with the university, often traveled with the team. This extended entourage—Rupp called them his "Deadheads"—included local printers, motel owners, druggists, builders, a news vendor, and a doctor. Two of the Deadheads, Bob and Lula Mae Lutes, usually invited Rupp and his friends to their room, where the coach would "have two or three shots of bourbon, relax, go to his room, put on a pair of red pajamas and worry about the upcoming game." Rupp presented the Lutes with a "Most Valuable Deadheads" plaque.[44]

His associations were not always so positive. When Ed Curd, a Lexington bookie and one of the most infamous gamblers in the United States, traveled with the UK team to Chicago and New York in the late 1940s, his connection with the Wildcats and their coach would come back to haunt them.

Stories also circulated about Rupp's drinking, though for years he tried to maintain the façade of clean living. After his first NCAA championship and the Olympic gold medal in 1948, Rupp's photograph and message accompanied an advertisement for the state Woman's Christian Temperance Union. "The one basic rule that every boy and girl—athlete or otherwise—should abide by is never drink alcohol in any form," Rupp warned. "Alcohol is a menace to the body. It destroys coordination between mind and muscle, and severely impairs judgment and timing. In return, alcohol offers absolutely nothing. So why put something into your system that merely serves to damage it?"[45]

But the longer he lived in Kentucky, the more he enjoyed one of the state's most famous products, bourbon—although his taste seemed to lean more toward a sourmash distilled in Tennessee. Asked whether Rupp drank, Lyman Ginger rolled his eyes and nodded his head, then tried to remember the brand. "He liked Jack Daniel's," he said. Asked if the coach was a heavy drinker, Ginger replied: "Yeah, at parties he was. . . . Once in a while a vodka, but he liked bourbon. He liked as much bourbon as he could get." He added: "I never saw him when I thought he was drunk. I've seen him when I've thought he was kind of thick-tongued, you know, talking."[46]

The sportswriter and Rupp admirer Earl Cox said that when the East-West high school all-star games were moved from Lexington to Richmond and Bowling Green, Cox began to host "a little social for all of the state's college head coaches." At the social in Richmond, Rupp headed "straight to the bar I had set up and inspected all of the bottles of bourbon." "Where the hell is the Jack Daniel's?" Rupp asked. "Can't the *Courier-Journal* afford good whiskey?" Cox said his "last memorable experience" with Rupp was in 1977, when the coach went with a Lexington delegation to St. Louis to try to persuade the NCAA to bring the 1982 Final Four to Lexington. Cox had dinner with Rupp and UK sports information director Russell Rice. After dinner, although it was still early, Rupp asked Cox to take him to his hotel room. Once there, Rupp turned to him and said, "Now stay with me until I get in the bed." Cox reminded him of the "cheap whiskey" story and told him "that I was prepared this time, that I had a bottle of Jack Daniel's in the room." "Oh, no, thanks anyway," Rupp said, "but I'm tired and sleepy." Cox went off to join some friends at another hotel, leaving the old man to dream his dreams. The next morning Rupp "was roaring at me," Cox recalled. "'Where in the hell were you? I couldn't sleep and I kept thinking about that Jack Daniel's, and I kept calling your room.'"[47]

Rupp might have told the Woman's Christian Temperance Union that "alcohol offers absolutely nothing," but clearly it offered a degree of comfort and solace that he found nowhere else.

In the summers, the Rupps, Bells, Nickells, and Dr. Escumb Moore and his wife went fishing in Florida. Bell and Moore operated the boat and caught most of the fish, but Russell Rice noted that "when they caught a big fish, Rupp was first in line to have his picture taken with it." Rupp actually was a poor fisherman. He went regularly to Herrington Lake, where some of the UK coaches had put up a fishing camp. Bob Sparks recalled that Rupp "had a rusty little steel rod, a knobby reel and a silk line that was rotten because he never dried it. Rupp would fish for about 15 minutes and say, 'Well, they're not biting, let's go.'"[48]

On one such group fishing trip to Florida in the early 1950s, he became ill and spent most of the time in his cabin. Paul Nickell said that "was the first indication that Rupp had a blood sugar problem."[49]

His health deteriorated throughout his career at Kentucky. As early as the 1930s, chronic back pain caused him to be hospitalized. Tim Cohane, a writer for *Look* magazine, suggested that Rupp's back problems resulted from hard work as a young man in the Kansas wheat fields. In 1935 he had an operation to remove two disks, keeping him in the hospital for 35 days and at home another eight weeks. He "wore a reinforced corset nine months and couldn't move around too well for another six." Cohane believed that it was during this extended period of incapacity that Rupp "had a lot of time to worry about his future. He was more determined than ever to achieve financial security."[50]

Billy Reed's description of Rupp's Memorial Coliseum office at the time of his death in 1977 portrayed the Baron best. The office, which Rupp had continued to maintain after his retirement, "is a sort of self-made tribute to himself," Reed wrote. "The walls are covered with plaques and awards, along with some photographs of some Shriners and some of Rupp's prized Hereford bulls." Reed noted that "the office has a comfortable, cluttered atmosphere. One of Rupp's raincoats is draped over the back of a chair. And amid the pile of mail and papers on his desk is a pair of glasses, almost as if the owner laid them down momentarily while he stepped out to get a cup of coffee."[51]

The private Rupp was certainly different from the public Rupp. It was not unusual for his schedule to add up to a 14-hour day, but when he came home in the evening, he found time to live quietly with his wife and son. "I'm not a country clubber," he said in a 1964 interview. "When I'm done at the office, I go home and I'll devour three magazines a night." *Courier-Journal* sportswriter Larry Boeck said Rupp "reads a great deal—rapidly —and is quite a literate man, something disguised by his speech. When he talks in his Kansas twang, he often uses country idiom. When he writes an article, he is fluent and shows a versatile vocabulary. His writing reflects the range of his reading." Rupp subscribed to the daily *Wall Street Journal*, the daily *Drovers Journal*, other farm publications, and *Forbes* and *Fortune* magazines. "I get 26 magazines or periodicals a week," he said, "and I read them all."[52]

New York writer Jimmy Breslin, who visited Kentucky while working on a 1952 profile of Rupp, left the state with an impression of a larger-than-life figure who lived simply despite his great wealth. "The Baron is a big man in the Blue Grass," Breslin wrote. "He has farms which total 1,280 acres. He is a Hereford breeder, with 130 head, and he fattens 450 hogs a year. He is on the board of directors of a large tobacco auction warehouse." Breslin tried to describe a typical day for the coach: "Rupp lives simply. Each morning he drives his handsome limousine to Memorial Coliseum at 9 a.m., gripes about the lack of parking space, then goes in to begin his day's work." Breslin learned that Rupp received "dozens of letters every day from throughout the world requesting information on his system," and that his book, *Championship Basketball*, after its translation into Japanese, had sold an additional 6,000 copies. "Lunch for the Baron," he wrote, "consists of a stroll across the street to the campus bowling alley for a 20-cent bowl of soup and black coffee. He'll dip down into his pocket for the correct change rather than break another bill. Rupp does not give the impression of being an extremely wealthy man, which he certainly is."[53]

If Rupp didn't have lunch at the bowling alley, he walked down to 504 Euclid Avenue. He had discovered Brookings Restaurant in 1946 or 1947, after George "Mr. B" Brookings founded the place in 1938. Rupp tried Brookings's chili, declared it "the best chili in town," and usually ate there several times a week—at least in "chili season"—for 30 years. "Adolph hardly ever missed a week being here," said Harold Brookings, who took over after his father's death. Rupp always sat at the same booth in the tiny, 24-seat joint. "It's a big part of my father's life," Herky once said. "My father brought me here sometimes when I was quite young." Rupp never invited Esther, however. "I think everybody has been, but I have never been there," she said. "I don't know why. I understand their chili is really good."[54] Even years later, Rupp's booth was easy to find, with framed articles and pictures of the Baron on the wall above the table.

In his early years, Rupp took an active part in university life. In 1937 he was named the faculty adviser of the Nu chapter of Omicron Delta Kappa, the national leadership fraternity.[55] In those days it was not unusual for Rupp to drop in unannounced at some faculty office for a chat. "He used to come up to our office and sit around and talk about history," said Thomas D. Clark, head of the history department. Along with classes in business and economics, Rupp had studied under Frank Hunter, a history professor at Kansas, and he always liked that subject. "As I recall, he had a notion that he was going to go on and do graduate work in history," Clark said. "But he became a successful coach and later forgot about it." Rupp had been a serious student at Kansas and Columbia, and he insisted that his players perform in the classroom as well as on the court. Clark remembered that Rupp would send around a helper named Buckshot Underwood to check on the boys' academic progress.[56]

"A lesser-known side of Rupp was his mother-hen approach to the academic success of his players," said *Courier-Journal* writer Richard Wilson. Dr. M. M. White, dean of the university's College of Arts and Sciences, remembered that "Adolph always insisted that his boys keep up their academic work." White, who also came to UK in 1930, said the players usually responded to the coach's demands out of fear. "So far as academic work was concerned, he certainly backed me up with every boy I ever had a problem with, even his own son," said White, who remembered Herky as "not too good a student." Lyman Ginger said Rupp sometimes called to check on a player's standing. "He was very interested that they keep their academic work up and that they graduated," he said.[57]

Frank Dickey, dean of the College of Education and later UK's president from 1956 to 1963, remarked that Rupp was simply a perfectionist "in everything that he did, and he expected everyone else to be one too in everything that they did. I think I can say with some degree of certainty that he never asked for any unusual breaks for his boys, because he believed they should be expected to meet the same requirements as any other student." At the same time, Rupp displayed little tolerance for professors he felt did not measure up. When one of them refused to tell him about a player's progress, arguing that "an athlete's grade was a private matter between the professor and the student," Rupp responded that his boys "were used to being graded publicly. Their grades as basketball players came twice weekly during the season, usually before 11,000 people."[58]

Rupp's relationship with the faculty, usually cordial in the early years, soured after the point-shaving scandal of 1951. Thomas Clark wrote to the Appalachian writer and activist Harry Caudill on October 22, 1951: "Now comes the basketball scandal. I have always been of the opinion that athletics had too much to do with the university." Clark imagined that "a lot of people who embarked on this program now feel the same way about it. Most of the faculty is, I am sure, deeply regretful of this, and they see it as a needless criticism of the university. That is the way I view it. Universities all over the country are making the mistake of overemphasizing their athletic program. I think this is going to have some real repercussions in that area." Even after Rupp retired, Clark bemoaned his legacy for the university. In a 1976 letter to writer A. B. "Bud" Guthrie Jr., Clark wrote that "the basketball season has begun, and as you know, this is the season of the idiots. The university has moved its games to the damned Rupp Arena, where all the idiots of Kentucky can jam in and create an unbreakable traffic jam."[59]

Clark once found himself sitting beside Rupp on a flight to Chicago. Clark was en route to Grand Rapids, Michigan, to speak at a conference of Phi Alpha Theta, the history honor society. Rupp was on his way to deliver an address at a father-son banquet. "Adolph was a winning speaker. He could keep an audience interested," Clark said. "He was a great one for telling stories on himself." According to Clark, he and Rupp "disliked Jack Oswald [the UK president] so much that that's what we talked about. I don't remember any mention of basketball on the way up there."[60] Clark remembered that the coach talked nonstop about his numerous speaking engagements and asked the professor how much he would make for his history talk. When Clark said he was doing it for free because of his love of the subject, the Baron laughed and bragged, "Hell fire, they're paying me a thousand dollars." Clark never forgot Rupp's interest in his speaking fees and his appraisal of the comparative worth of professors and famous coaches. "My answer was I don't have the *Courier-Journal* and the *Lexington Herald* and the *Lexington Leader* and every other paper in this country running a section telling me what a wonderful man I am," Clark said. "Once he became . . . the Baron, then he became the Baron."[61]

When Otis Singletary sought to force Rupp out in 1972 because of the university's mandatory retirement policy, Clark wrote the UK president about the controversy. "I see by the paper that the animals are at you to allow Adolph Rupp to continue after he is 70," Clark wrote. "This sort of thing came up with this stuffed shirt when I was on the Athletic Board." Clark noted that in 1960 Rupp refused to pick up his paychecks for a time when he felt he was not being paid enough. According to Clark, "I proposed that the university follow the same rule with Rupp as with any other cantankerous tenured professor. You would have thought I had proposed overturning the Throne of God." Clark said he turned to Frank Dickey, the UK president, during an athletic board meeting and said, "Frank, if I refused to pick up my check, you'd fire me, wouldn't you?" Dickey told him that indeed he would. "And I said that we should fire Adolph Rupp," Clark recalled. "Don't deal with Adolph in one way and the faculty another. Well, if I had advocated tearing up the charter of the university, I couldn't have caused any more consternation than I did."[62]

Rupp's 1960 salary dispute would not be the last time he complained about his paycheck. Clark was still on the athletic board when Rupp made public his frustration about not getting a raise in 1962. Rupp called a press conference to vent his anger at the board. "I've got only three or four years left here at Kentucky, and I'm getting too old to pull any punches," he told reporters. "I've got some things I want to get off my chest. What do I have to do to make these guys happy? Everybody in the state appreciates me, everybody at the university, just about everybody that is appreciates me. But what about the athletic board?"[63]

"Last year, gentlemen, I took a bunch of boys who weren't expected to do much and built them into one of the best basketball teams in the country. So what does the board do? They give the groundskeeper here a raise; they give the man who parks the cars a raise; they give everybody on the athletic staff a raise. But what do they do for me? Nothing." Hardly pausing to catch his breath, he went on:

When we took in all that money last year, some $250,000, Mrs. Rupp and I expected we would get a raise, but it never came. We were hurt deeply. I don't know what they expect. Now you gentlemen know we were 23–3 last year. This is a great record for a team that wasn't rated in the top 50 before the season started. We even went to the NCAA Tournament. Just what does this board expect me to do before they give me a raise? It beats me how a man can be so mistreated. And when you run the only department at the university that operates in the black, it hurts all the worse.

He insisted he wanted more money "just so I know the university appreciates me.[64]

The situation must have been awkward for Lyman Ginger, a member of the athletic board and a close friend and ally of Rupp's. Ginger said that he had not been at the spring meeting when other raises were handed out and that he didn't "know exactly what happened to Rupp's." Neither did Dickey, athletic director Bernie Shively, or athletic board vice chairman Leo Chamberlain. "I for one genuinely appreciate him," Ginger said, insisting he was sure the rest of the board did as well, "or it wouldn't have given him consistent raises year after year after year. Maybe the board can take up the missed raise at its next meeting and salve the coach's feelings."[65]

Rupp probably already was the nation's highest-paid basketball coach. A *Louisville Times* report in November 1962 made clear that money was not the issue, although Rupp was always concerned about money. The article noted that the coach owned a cattle farm and that "during the off-season he conducts scores of basketball clinics and gives scores of speeches, for which he commands a fee."[66]

The issue would not go away. In letters to the editors of the *Lexington Leader* and the *Lexington Herald*, fans and critics expressed a wide range of opinions about the Baron. A "BASKETBALL FAN" wrote to the *Leader* that "the recent press release by Coach Adolph Rupp made him sound like a peevish child. I suggest a simple solution. Instead of money (which admittedly he doesn't need) present the unhappy Mr. Rupp with a huge scroll inscribed, 'Adolph, we love you and we DO appreciate you.' And have every cotton-pickin' member of the Athletic Department sign it." Apparently, Rupp had also complained about certain interruptions during home games, and the letter writer could not fathom the coach's arrogance. "His unwarranted attack on the paging of doctors at games was inexcusable," the letter said, adding with dripping sarcasm that "people do have heart attacks, even during basketball games; and while this would indicate they are insensitive clods, perhaps we should permit them to have immediate medical attention. On several occasions fans attending the games have had heart attacks right in the Coliseum and it will be interesting to see how Coach Rupp deals with these characters. One assumes his next edict will be that they die quietly, lest attention be distracted from the game." The writer concluded that Rupp "has done a magnificent job for UK, but he has not gone unrewarded."[67]

Another wrote that "it is of course not the love of money which is behind the coach's plea for a raise, but it is a sense of the eternal fitness of a proper emolument for a man whose work has been well done." According to this writer, Rupp "has a salary larger than that of 97 percent of the professors at the University. He has many possessions. But these things are for him, without the love of the Athletics Board, like the apples of Sodom, full of dust and ashes." The writer believed that "the coach should get as much as the president of the University." After all, Rupp had "done more for the University than any forty of its professors. He is not preaching free love and communism, rather he is promulgating practical Christianity." Apparently, UK professors had recently been in the news for a "handbill episode." If the professors were intent on disseminating handbills, the writer suggested that they should "band together and distribute handbills at local churches advocating a substantial raise for Coach Rupp by Christmas." It is hard to tell if the writer was serious or sarcastic. He ended his letter by writing that "my heart goes out to this great and noble man, even as I am blinded by my tears and choked by my sobs."[68]

Yet another writer used the salary controversy as an opportunity to call for the coach's dismissal. "After the Wildcats' poor performance last Saturday night," he wrote, "I cannot see Coach Rupp's continued usefulness at Kentucky. Coach Rupp has earned the acclaim of thousands in the past but can no longer produce a winning team, in my opinion." According to this critic, "His request for a raise emphasizes the commercialism rather than sportsmanship that dominates collegiate games." The letter concluded: "Coach Rupp has had his day and should quit while he is ahead. He well deserved the past honors, but should not allow them to become tarnished by an unrealistic view of his position when he can no longer do the job."[69]

Rupp's demands seemed to bring out sarcasm in more than one Kentucky fan. Another critical letter suggested that Rupp be included in a local charity drive: "Wouldn't it be a more generous gesture to drop all those others [those high-salaried professionals] and just make Mr. Rupp a one-man United Fund? After all, what comes before 'character building'?"[70]

Other writers supported the coach unabashedly. "Some persons feel that Coach Rupp has plenty of money and doesn't need a raise," a fan from Georgetown wrote. "Well, it's the principle of the thing. And that is exactly what Coach Rupp told me." According to this fan, Rupp said, "If they had sent me a card and said, 'Thanks for a job well done,' I would have appreciated it a great deal. But they didn't say one earthly thing." The writer concluded that Rupp "has done more for basketball—not only in Kentucky, but in the nation as a whole—than any man, alive or dead."[71]

Another supporter put it in verse. In a poem titled "Up the Pay of Mr. Rupp," Jim Honaker lauded "the finest fans in all the land," and noted their trust in God as well as their faith in the UK coach:

There the greatest players have often been applauded
Amid excitement's clamoring din,
But the noble Baron has not been amply lauded
Although we win, and win, and win.

According to Honaker, the only just solution would be to pay the coach what he was obviously worth.[72]

Clearly, Rupp's salary dispute rankled fans for different reasons. Supporters could not believe that the university would hesitate to reward a coach who had won more national championships than any other. Critics saw Rupp's concern with money as another example of the rising commercialization of sports, a phenomenon for which he was largely responsible.

Surely the coach's pride was hurt, but his concern for money was real, too. His hard upbringing made thriftiness important to Rupp and his brothers and sister. After their father's death when Adolph was nine years old, the children all shared a responsibility to supplement the struggling family's income. In a 1953 article headlined "Rupp Isn't Exactly Speedy with a Buck," *Courier-Journal* sportswriter Larry Boeck suggested that "it was as a student at Kansas University that Rupp first revealed his frugality, which has been a lifelong trait."[73]

"I worked my way through college," Rupp told Boeck, admitting it was true that he entered the university in midsemester with five cents and still had five cents at the end of the term. "And it was the same nickel," Rupp declared. "I came from a thrifty family. We had to be." As a seventh- and eighth-grader, he walked a mile and a half to school, arriving early. "I made $1.25 a month by sweeping out the classroom every day, cleaning the blackboards and building the fire each morning," he recalled. He carried over that personal thriftiness to his basketball program. According to Boeck, Rupp was "never a spender nor one to indulge overmuch in luxuries." He lived in a modest home and only recently bought his first auto-mobile "outside the low-priced field." He was just as parsimonious with the university's money. His teams often traveled by bus and sometimes by train—at least until center Bill Spivey arrived. Then Rupp had to resort to airplanes because the seven-foot Spivey "was cramped in a bus and couldn't find a berth to fit him on a train."[74]

Boeck discovered how carefully and cheaply Rupp provided for his team. He had heard the story about a trip to Knoxville when Rupp had the bus driver stop at a country store so the coach could buy his players a lunch of bread, cold cuts, and cheese. Boeck knew of another trip to New York City with the Fabulous Five, when Rupp called Ralph Beard and Wah Wah Jones to the front desk as the team checked out of its hotel. "You boys have radios sent to your rooms?" he asked. "Yes," they answered sheepishly. "Well, boys, you each owe $1 a day for the three days you had the radio. That's $3 each you owe the university."[75]

Boeck experienced Rupp's penny-pinching firsthand after covering a game at Ohio University in Athens. After paying his own hotel bill and boarding the team bus, Boeck was told by Beard with "a wry smile" that Rupp wanted to see him at the hotel desk. "Larry," Rupp said, "there are three telephone calls from your room charged to the team's bill. You owe 18 cents." Boeck paid up. Although the coach gave liberally to charity and could be a solicitous host, he always knew the bottom line.[76]

One UK athlete told Boeck he was amazed at accusations that Rupp had lavished money on his players after games. Aside from the $50 he re-ceived from the coach at the Sugar Bowl in New Orleans, one player could not "remember Rupp's passing out money," although "the alumni often did." "I can't remember Rupp being lavish with dough," the player said. "If anything, I always thought we weren't getting as much in the way of enter-tainment and other things as players on other major teams were getting. No, sir, I can truthfully say that Coach Rupp never impressed me with his generosity."[77]

All-American Frank Ramsey recalled the night after an NIT game in New York when Rupp treated the team and the media to the musical com-edy *Gentlemen Prefer Blondes*. "Remember we were way up there in the balcony?" Ramsey told Boeck, who was on the trip. "We even had to rent those binoculars for 25 cents so we could see the stage." Rupp, standing near his former star, cut in, "Now, Frank, maybe the tickets weren't the best, but the show was a sellout and we were lucky to get in the balcony."[78]

Red Auerbach, the legendary Boston Celtics coach, told matter-of-factly of his own experience with his friend's stinginess. "Once I'm in New York and I go to lunch with Rupp," he said. "We went to the old Gayety Deli, which was a few blocks from the old Garden. I think we each had a couple of hot dogs. The bill came to something like three bucks. I paid it and then left a fifty-cent tip. That was pretty standard in those days." Rupp looked at him and said, "Fifty cents! That's way too much." "Before I can argue with him," Auerbach recalled, "he picks up one of the quarters—and puts it in *his* pocket. Never said a word. I was so stunned I let it go. I kept thinking he was joking and was going to give it back to me. He never got around to it." Auerbach always defended Rupp against accusations of racism. "Now cheap," he said, "that was another story. He was the single cheapest person I've ever met in my life."[79]

But Rupp's thriftiness did not stop him from taking part in charity work, which sometimes evolved from his position as the UK coach. Russell Rice told of Rupp's encounter with Wayne Walker, the athletic director and coach at Kentucky Village, a state-run juvenile facility. For Walker's team to compete on the high school level, he needed uniforms and equipment, so in 1957 he asked Rupp for assistance. "I'll never forget walking into his office with all the sports pictures on the wall and his delightful handshake," Walker said. "I went over my needs with him, and he sat there with his hand over his mouth for a moment. Then he got up and put his arm around me." "By Gawd," Rupp swore, "anybody that has the nerve, patience and guts to work with these kids, I'm going to help. Let's go see the equipment manager." He took Walker straight to George Hukle, who loaded him down with "shoes, athletic supporters, practice shorts, shirts, uniforms, warmup pants and jackets." The name "KENTUCKY" was stitched to the back of each warmup jacket, so Walker had "VILLAGE" added underneath, and his team became the Kentucky Village Wildcats. "When my season started, all the opponents were complimentary of our uniforms," he said.[80]

Rupp would eventually have a falling out with assistant coach Harry Lancaster when the latter became athletic director, but during their long partnership Lancaster came to know Rupp's softer side. Lancaster was in

New Orleans to scout teams at the Sugar Bowl Tournament when his mother died. Rupp called him to break the news and also made arrangements for his quick return to Kentucky. He called the hotel, had Lancaster's baggage delivered to the airport, bought him a ticket for the next flight to Cincinnati, and met him there at 4:30 a.m. Rupp drove Lancaster the 75 miles from Cincinnati to Lexington, then lent him his car for the short trip to Richmond, where his mother had lived.[81]

In 1937 Rupp was initiated into the Ancient Arabic Order of the Nobles of the Mystic Shrine at a Thanksgiving-eve ceremony of the Oleika Temple in Lexington's Woodlawn Auditorium. W. Emmett Milward, the Illustrious Potentate of the Oleika Temple, and several hundred Shriners from central, eastern, and southern Kentucky gathered for the ceremony, which was preceded by a torchlight parade through downtown Lexington.[82] Rupp had always been a joiner. As a young man in Freeport, Illinois, he joined the City Club and the Elks Club, and he especially enjoyed the camaraderie of the Germania Society, where he played cards and socialized, sometimes speaking German at the meetings.

In the Shriners, Rupp found the perfect combination of elite, if wacky, male comradeship with a focus on good works and charity. Along with his farms, he found the secret society of the Oleika Temple to be a perfect antidote to his very public and often volatile professional life. When he put on his Shriners fez—"a rhinestone-studded red tower rising half a foot above his crown with a long black tassel that dangles to his neck"—he entered a different world. Founded in 1920 as a suborder of the Masons, the Shriners boast thousands of members throughout North America. Well known for their philanthropy, they sponsor children's hospitals, burn centers, circuses, and parades.[83]

Rupp took his membership seriously. He promoted the Shriners' circus, giving out tickets in Pralltown, a poor African American neighborhood in Lexington. He helped found the Shriners Hospital for Crippled Children and became its chairman in 1942. "The world at large thought that, other than family, Adolph's two loves were basketball and Hereford cattle," said Marvin Whitton, the recorder of the Lexington Shriners for more than 35 years. "The Shriners Hospital for Crippled Children was his third love." Perhaps Herky's problems at birth helped prompt Rupp to make this his special project, but for whatever reason, he helped raise $1.1

million for the building and a 28-acre tract on the outskirts of Lexington. Once it was built, "Uncle Adolph" often visited the children there.[84]

Rupp rose through the Shriner ranks, eventually serving as potentate of the Oleika Temple and as national membership chairman, among many other titles. He finally was nominated for Imperial Potentate, the Shrine's highest office, but he failed to win the post. As Russell Rice put it, "A majority of the voters were not UK basketball fans."[85]

"I guess you could say he was a sort of Dr. Jekyll and Mr. Hyde type of person," Whitton said. "I got to see the better side of him that a lot of people didn't really know about." Rupp impressed him with his dedication to the hospital. Whitton remembered that Rupp often mentioned to the other governors of the hospital board "how seeing the needs of crippled children in the hospital made him dedicated to their cause."[86]

Rupp's coaching exploits, coupled with his civic activities, gave him a rising stature as a Kentucky ambassador and leader. In 1948 he received the Lexington Optimist Club award as the community's Outstanding Citizen. Club vice president A. D. "Ab" Kirwan, the Dean of Men at UK, presented him with a sterling silver pitcher and said: "Like Alexander the Great, Rupp can weep because he, too, has no worlds to conquer. He's conquered them all in the basketball world—Southeastern, National Collegiate and Olympics." Kirwan lauded Rupp as "a master salesman and master advertising man, selling Lexington and the University of Kentucky all over the sports world—a messenger of friendship and ambassador of good will." In accepting the award, Rupp expressed his gratitude to the club and the community and especially to his players, "who have taken us a long way." He also said, "I think a man who loves his work lives a good life, and I love basketball. A man didn't have to be crazy to coach basketball, but it helps."[87]

Rupp had spent the previous summer with his players on a tour of the Middle East, "passing out keys to Lexington." In 1959 his friend Governor Happy Chandler awarded him the Governor's Medallion. UK vice president Frank Peterson called him a man who "is loved, feared and respected by millions of people."[88]

Those words came a year after Rupp had won his unprecedented fourth national championship. His position in basketball history was secure, but he did not rest on his laurels. He used his fame to promote worthy causes but also to make money and to explore other opportunities away from the college ranks.

Rumors circulated year after year that Rupp would jump to the pros. Long before Rick Pitino, John Calipari, Brad Stevens, and other successful college coaches signed lucrative contracts to coach professional teams, Rupp had several opportunities to do the same. As early as 1947 the Associated Press reported that Rupp "will be offered one of the highest salaries ever paid a professional basketball coach." A new pro team planned to seek incorporation in Louisville, and team president Wilson W. Wyatt said Rupp would be offered the coaching job. Sponsored by Dad's Root Beer, the Louisville Dads would be granted the first franchise in the National Professional League. The root beer company planned to open a bottling plant in Louisville, where the players would be provided off-season employment.[89]

"We are out to get the best coach in the business," Wyatt said. "Rupp is our first choice. We are willing to pay him more money than any other basketball coach ever has received. We will offer him at least 50 percent more than he is making at the University of Kentucky. With salary and bonus, he could make $15,000 a year." According to Wyatt, if Rupp declined the head coaching job, he would offer to make him an "advisory coach" who "would have the privilege of naming our coach for us and assisting himself whenever time from his college duties permitted." Wyatt and his lawyers planned to present the proposition to Rupp in Lexington. Rupp had just returned from Tuscaloosa, where the Wildcats had handed Alabama its first loss, when the story broke. Asked about the offer, Rupp said: "I'm in the middle of a fairly successful season here at the university and have no comment to make on any offers at the present time."[90]

Out for the main chance and always concerned with what he considered to be his low pay at Kentucky, Rupp entertained the idea of jumping to the new professional league. As it turned out, Louisville never got the franchise and Rupp stayed at Kentucky, leading the Wildcats to three NCAA championships in the next four years. Those titles in 1948, 1949, and 1951, coupled with the point-shaving scandal that occurred in the 1947–1948 season and came to light in 1951, would represent both the heights and the depths of his career.

It seemed that with every successful season, new rumors of professional offers surfaced. The year after his fourth national title in 1958, yet another opportunity came his way. Rupp had known Tom Wood, owner of the Cincinnati Garden and the NBA's Cincinnati Royals, for years because both raised Hereford cattle. "Mr. Wood and I have had mutual interests in livestock for many years and have swapped bulls on numerous occasions," Rupp said. "I have advised him; he has advised me. If I can help him, I'll be glad to do so. As for helping me, he already has done so." Noting that Wood "certainly has an investment I think is wonderful," the coach caused fans to wonder when he added, "I would do anything to help him."[91]

Rupp knew that pro basketball needed a lift. "Professional basketball is like watching 'Gone With the Wind,'" he said. "It could be boring."[92] Billy Thompson of the *Lexington Herald* found it impossible to get Rupp to commit on the Cincinnati offer one way or the other. At one point in an interview, Rupp said, "I in no way have been contacted, and I do not want to jeopardize the fellow who is now coaching the Royals (Tom Marshall, a former Western Kentucky University star). But when and if Mr. Wood calls, I'll answer the phone. That's all I will say."[93]

Thompson was convinced Rupp would leave Lexington, having already accomplished more than any other college coach. "If a bomb had been dropped in the center of Lexington yesterday," Thompson wrote, "it wouldn't have stirred up much more noise than the article stating that Adolph Rupp may become a professional coach. You've heard and will hear pros and cons on the subject, but take this friendly bit of advice. If 2 and 2 equal 4, Rupp will be coaching the Cincinnati Royals when the 1959–1960 basketball season gets under way."[94]

Thompson gave several reasons for his prediction: "There is little question that Rupp is the best basketball coach in America. He has never turned his back on a challenge, and professional basketball now is one of the biggest challenges of all. The game ranks in a mediocre category, just as pro football did 12 or 13 years ago." Thompson gave credit to Cleveland Browns coach Paul Brown for having "picked up pro football by its shoelaces," and he was convinced that for pro basketball, Rupp "could toss his famed brown suit into the ring and pull the sport out of the red and into the black."[95] "Certainly we're interested in Adolph Rupp," Wood said. "We'd be willing to give him $40,000 a year and part ownership of the club." According to Wood, Rupp "could put this team over. However, Adolph may be too big a man for us; he means so much to the Bluegrass."[96]

This period marks the beginning of Rupp's intense expressions of displeasure with his salary at UK. Rupp made $18,500 as UK's coach in 1964, and when Dr. Otis A. Singletary became president of the university in 1969 he expressed amazement to Cawood Ledford that the coach's salary was still only $19,500; Singletary raised it to $32,000. Before Singletary, previous president John W. Oswald had been reluctant to raise his pay very much.[97] At the same time, Rupp's stock as a pro coach multiplied dramatically. Still, he stayed at UK, finding other ways to make up for any lack of appreciation by the administration.

One way was to pound the banquet circuit during the off-season. He gave speech after speech at high school banquets, teachers' conventions, farm meetings, and businessmen's luncheons—for example, the 1959 annual meeting of the Kentucky Society of Certified Public Accountants. He would go anywhere for a price. *Courier-Journal* columnist Joe Creason reported that within days of the heartbreaking loss to Texas Western in the 1966 NCAA championship game, Rupp began a string of 19 banquet appearances in 22 days.[98]

"Tables are being set in his honor," Creason wrote, "from one end of Kentucky to the other, and in other states as well, as Ladies Aid Societies, Cub Scout troops, alumni clubs and high schools want him to dine with them and tell in his own words how it all was done. This, I hold, is paying dearly for success. Not only will he hear his praises sung until his ears ring, he'll also wind up burdened with enough plaques and scrolls to stagger a pack mule." Creason also worried that "it takes a man with a cast-iron stomach to withstand so many testimonial-style meals which always seem to feature vulcanized steak and/or chicken a la Goodyear, boiler plated rolls, watery peas and melted ice cream with a chocolate-sauce toupee."[99]

Creason failed to mention how many of the coach's appearances were paid gigs. Rupp began a rigorous speaking schedule early in his tenure at UK. It mattered not where or to what group. He also spoke and instructed at basketball clinics in Kentucky, around the nation, and overseas. As early as 1933, he conducted a weeklong "coaching school" for college and high school coaches at Morehead State Teachers College in eastern Kentucky.[100]

In 1946 he followed up his NIT championship by being the guest of honor at the Boston Quarterback Club, stayed on for two days to conduct a clinic at Holy Cross, then flew to St. Petersburg to speak at the Florida State Coaching School. In 1947 he again made the rounds, speaking at

Marshall College in Huntington, West Virginia, winner of the small college national tournament in Kansas City, and at Cumberland College in eastern Kentucky, winner of the state junior college championship and the Southeastern Junior College Tournament. It seems that champions wanted to hear champions. Also in 1947, Rupp took his team to the Woodford Club at the Woodford County courthouse, where they were honored and shown motion pictures of the NIT. "Coach Rupp owns one of Woodford County's farms and therefore is considered to be a Woodford Countian," explained the club president.[101]

In 1949 Rupp participated in the "world's largest coaching school" in Beaumont, Texas (the third time he had spoken there) and at the University of Mississippi football-basketball coaching school. While Missouri football coach Don Faurot covered the split-T offense he had originated, Rupp "discussed individual fundamentals, offensive drill and building the basketball offense."[102]

Rupp's clinic talks were not unlike his banquet addresses. He combined humorous anecdotes with sage advice about strategy and fundamentals, with a mention of his own team's prospects for the coming season. At a 1961 clinic in Cookeville, Tennessee, he covered a wide range of topics. He told the coaches that "action and competition are necessary to make basketball, or any sports program, successful." He also compared college basketball to professional football: "Fifteen years ago I wouldn't have gone to a pro football game if someone had given me a ticket. Today, with emphasis on moving the ball, I go every chance I get." He emphasized that "you must play teams that are capable of beating you, because the fans won't come out just to watch your players shoot baskets." Rupp backed up his argument by noting that in the previous year his UK program "made over a quarter-million dollars," and "that much money . . . makes 'em happy." Noting that his 1961–1962 squad would be the shortest in recent years, he added: "Overall height doesn't mean that much anyway. I'd like to have Jerry Lucas of Ohio State to go with four short ones if I could."[103]

It didn't matter who called, Rupp would answer. He gave a commencement address at Bald Knob, Arkansas, and conducted clinics in Europe and Asia. After his trip to the 1948 London Olympics, he became more comfortable traveling overseas. He first went to Germany in 1951, when he and Yale coach Howard Hobson put on a two-week clinic for the armed forces stationed there. By 1961 he had worked clinics for troops stationed in Germany five times. In 1959 he spoke at a Shriners convention in Memphis the night before flying to Hawaii for a vacation and a clinic. From there he flew across the Pacific for other clinics in Japan and South Korea. He was gone for a month, returning to Lexington in time to start practice in October.[104]

All those clinics and speaking engagements provided Rupp a hefty income beyond his coaching salary, but they weren't his only sources of revenue. From the beginning of his tenure at UK, he dabbled in various business interests. In a 1947 *Saturday Evening Post* profile titled "The Crafty Wizard of Lexington," Rupp bragged that even if they "fire him tomorrow," he still would have "a 200-acre farm twelve miles from Lexington, a thriving insurance business and a substantial block of stock in . . . a tobacco warehousing corporation that bills itself as the largest in the world." And, of course, he was in no danger of being fired tomorrow.[105]

After a decade in Lexington, Rupp began to acquire farmland, and it was his devotion to the land that colored his conservative politics and tied him deeply to Kentucky soil. Tim Cohane, the sports editor of *Look* magazine, wrote in 1951 that the land "has always been close to him, has steered his economic beliefs." A registered Democrat, Rupp represented the more conservative wing of the party. Like his friend Happy Chandler, he was no New Deal Democrat. "He voted for Roosevelt once," Cohane wrote, "but the Tennessee Valley Authority, among other things, upset him." Rupp simply "couldn't abide good soil being put under water." Cohane told of a road trip to Knoxville when the UK team bus passed over a TVA dam. Muff Davis, a little-used substitute, looked out the window and murmured, "Roosevelt's folly." "Dammit, Davis," Rupp roared, "I'm a-startin' you tonight."[106]

Rupp even toyed with the idea of taking up politics himself. A March 26, 1953, article in the *Lexington Herald* proclaimed: "Rupp Reported Considering Race for Lieutenant Governor." He refused to confirm or deny his intentions but agreed that "there have been efforts made to bring me into the political picture." Chandler, who had already made it clear that he would run for governor in 1955, acknowledged his close friendship with the coach but said the two had never "talked about running for public office as a team." The *Herald* reporter wondered if Rupp's political ambitions would end his coaching career, though the university had set a precedent in 1951 when it didn't require the resignation of a UK employee who ran for the legislature.[107]

Rupp's conservative politics mirrored the way he wanted to run his basketball program: free from interference. A student of economics, he favored a laissez-faire, free-enterprise approach to government. When sportswriter Larry Boeck asked him to define "free enterprise," Rupp replied: "It means that a man has a right to go as far as his ability and industry will take him. This is true in sports as well as business. It's one reason I went into the coaching field. And in sports, like business, you have to expect some people to take potshots at you when you're on top. Everybody's trying to knock down the champion. That's natural. In the end, though, a man or a team makes himself or breaks himself through his use or disuse of free enterprise. It's the greatest thing we've got." Rupp related his philosophy to another sport: "You know, when a man is at bat at Ebbets Field with the bases loaded, his team behind by two runs and two men out, no government subsidy is going to help him. He's on his own. That's free enterprise in its purest form."[108]

Discussing his own sound investments, centered on his shrewd acquisition of land, Rupp said to Boeck: "You know what 'baron' means, don't you? It means 'landowner' in German."[109]

Rupp considered his farms to be the best of his many investments. "Farming is the safest investment a man can make today," he said. "In fact, everyone ought to have a farm, a place where he can look over the rolling hills and call the soil his own." He had bought his first farm in 1941, the year after Herky was born, and began investing in registered cattle in 1944. "I'm fulfilling an ambition that goes back to 1920," Rupp told a reporter in 1953. He had grown up working in the Kansas wheat fields, of course, but during college he learned about another kind of farming. "When I was a student at the University of Kansas, playing under Phog Allen," he recalled, "I skipped school one day to go to Kansas City, where the American Royal Livestock Show was being held. I took one look at those white-faced Herefords, and I made a resolution. I told myself that if I ever had a farm, and if I had enough money, I was going to raise Herefords."[110]

"My objective," Rupp said in 1953, "is to build a herd of Herefords that I can be proud of, just like I am proud of a standout basketball team that I had a hand in building." He even referred to his cattle in basketball terms: "After I build my herd to the point where I think the animals are good enough for tournament play, I'm going to shoot for the big shows, including the International and the Royal, just like I shoot for the top with my basketball team."[111]

In 1948, after Rupp had won his first national championship and added the Olympic gold medal, he headed west for a well-deserved vacation—and to meet with cattlemen to pick their brains about the business. He also went to nearby Sunnyside Farm in Paris, Kentucky, to buy his first bull, Milky Way Domino 65th, who was sired by the famed Colorado Domino 159th. One sportswriter reported, "Adolph revels in a platonic friendship with probably his most prized possession, a complacent, benign, but thoroughly competent white-faced Hereford bull named MW Domino 65." Before a game against St. John's, Rupp turned to assistant coach Harry Lancaster and said: "Harry, there must be easier ways of makin' a livin.' I wished I was back in Lexington. I jes' know ole' Domino would be glad to see me." Lancaster once pulled a gag on his boss that Rupp didn't find a bit amusing. After a big road victory, Lancaster "gravely informed him of a wire from Lexington that said Domino had caught his posterior elements in a wire fence."[112]

Rupp eventually raided Sunnyside Farm again, this time hiring away Chester Jones as chief herdsman for his own Four Leaf Clover Farm. The *Kentucky Hereford* announced that "Chester, better known as 'Chet,' is reported to be greatly pleased to be back with MW Domino 65, that good son of Colorado Domino 159 which now heads the herd at the Four Leaf Clover Farm." In 1951 Rupp added H. P. Baca Larry, another prized bull for which he shelled out $3,000 at the American Hereford Association sale at the International Livestock Exposition in Chicago. It was the top price paid in an auction that sold 31 bulls for a total of $49,405.[113]

Rupp was convinced that Kentucky, long a showplace for thoroughbred racehorses, would one day become a leading cattle state, too. "I think the future is more than bright," he said in 1951, a decade after he had bought his first farm.[114] He joined the Kentucky Hereford Association, subscribed to the *Kentucky Hereford* magazine, and carefully worked to build up his herd.[115] The February 1948 issue of the magazine stated that Rupp's herd would "rank with the tops." In 1949 the Kentucky Hereford Association named him as a director, and five years later he became president.[116] He would serve another term from 1958 to 1970.[117]

In the late 1940s and early 1950s, Rupp advertised his Four Leaf Clover Farm regularly in the association's magazine. His ad in the January 1951 issue featured a half-page photograph of MW Domino 65 and hailed the farm's stock as "traditionally good Herefords." "We have 18 excellent heifer calves," he said with pride, "and 19 nice bull calves for your inspection."[118]

His fame as a cattle breeder spread outside the Bluegrass. A photograph of Rupp looking over some prized calves graced the cover of the April 15, 1951, issue of the *American Hereford Journal*, which had a feature story about his farm. The press much closer to home took note, too. In a 1953 issue of the student newspaper the *Kentucky Kernel*, cartoonist Woody Huston had a sketch of the coach with his arm around Domino as the two looked out onto a basketball court filled with Kentucky stars. "There! There! Dom," Rupp comforts the bull, "don't be jealous. You're as famous now as they are. . . . You're an All-American too!"[119]

Rupp attended cattlemen's meetings, livestock shows, and auctions, and he carried on a lively correspondence with breeders from several western and southern states. He also hit the road to inspect other herds and acquire stock. Upon his return from one such trip in 1950, he wrote a lengthy letter that was published in the *Kentucky Hereford*. "I have just completed a 7,000-mile tour of the West," he wrote, "and it was a privilege to see some outstanding Hereford cattle. I drove out by way of Kansas, Oklahoma, New Mexico, Arizona, to California, and then came home by way of Oregon, Washington, Montana, South Dakota and Iowa. It is certainly gratifying to a Hereford man to make such a tour. Some days I would drive an entire day and not see a single cow except a Hereford." He also noted that "the crops along the way are excellent except in Western Kansas, the Panhandle of Texas and New Mexico." He found South Dakota's crops "very outstanding," adding, "I was glad to see those folks getting a break after their many bad years."[120]

Just how immersed Rupp was in the cattle business is evident from his account of a visit to Milky Way Farm in Phoenix, the original home of his prized bull Domino 65. "The thing that impressed me the most was the good condition of the cattle and the economical operation that they have for their setup," he wrote. "They have two pastures of 40 acres of irrigated alfalfa. They place the entire herd they said numbered at 240 cows with their calves in one of these pastures just before the alfalfa gets into bloom. Then they irrigate the other field. In eight weeks they change. Pasturing the entire herd on approximately 80 acres of land they experience little bloat, which surprised me. Their buildings are practical and their entire setup is well thought out." He also spent an afternoon at the 2,400-acre A. H. Karpe Ranch in Bakersfield, California, where he saw the bull Baca Duke 2 "being mated to the outstanding females in the herd." Rupp later purchased one of that bull's offspring, H. P. Baca Larry.[121]

Because the NCAA canceled the Wildcats' 1952–1953 season as punishment for Kentucky's involvement in the 1951 point-shaving scandal, Rupp had plenty of time on his hands, and he devoted it to his Hereford operation. "This is the first time in 37 years, ever since I played my first game of high school basketball, that I'm not competing in athletics," he told Larry Boeck of the *Courier-Journal* in January 1953. "It's pretty hard to find any solace in anything like that. If there is any ray of sunshine, it's in my cattle. . . . My one ambition now is to someday produce just one national champion Hereford. Then I'll consider myself a successful cattle breeder."[122]

Rupp still held several basketball practices a week, and he seemed to look on the suspension as a blessing in disguise. "We have a real unity now—and throughout the state, I believe—that we didn't have before the NCAA suspension," he said. "I don't think a team in the country has the closeness that exists between the players and the coaches here. . . . They're practicing with the same determination and zeal that they would if they were going to play for the national championship tomorrow night." Boeck interviewed Rupp in the coach's dressing room, and when the two of them headed toward the court, they passed All-Americans Frank Ramsey and Cliff Hagan. "Great players," Rupp said. "I've been blessed with a lot of great ones. Now if I can only get one championship Hereford out of the lot."[123]

Carl Hay, whose farm sat across the road from one of Rupp's, knew that "farming was always on the coach's mind," even at the end of his life. "About a month ago," Hay said the day Rupp died in 1977, "he called me to his house in Lexington to talk about his cattle and tobacco. He must have had farming on his mind, because that's all he wanted to talk about. To me there wasn't a better fellow. Never had a word of trouble about money or agreements—he didn't back off on anything."[124]

J. D. "Doug" Gay Jr., a Pine Grove cattle breeder and one-time president of the Kentucky Hereford Association, first met Rupp in the early

1940s. Rupp bought bulls from Gay, and Gay purchased cows from Rupp. One day sparks from a railroad steam engine set one of Gay's fields afire. In the neighborhood visiting friends for Sunday dinner, Rupp saw the blaze. "It was one hell of a fire," remembered Gay, "and we were all out there fighting it. I looked up and saw Adolph, and he was fighting it just like everybody else."[125]

Bernie Milam, a Bourbon County agricultural agent, said Rupp's place was "not a hobby farm. I don't believe the coach ever had a hobby." However, he did recall that the farm "at least once turned into a proving ground for a basketball prospect. He had a potential player on the farm once and told him to chase a bull up to him. He didn't want the bull. He just wanted to see how fast the boy could run."[126]

Fellow Bourbon County cattleman Walter Meng argued that, while the livestock business gave Rupp great satisfaction, the Baron contributed much in return. "He tried to improve the breed by supplying good seed stock to breeders who wanted to improve their herds," said Meng, who both bought from and sold stock to Rupp. "He was a great lover of the breed, but when basketball practice started in the fall, somebody else had to take care of the cattle." Meng added that Rupp was always in control on the farm as well as the court. "I'm certain he was never chased out of a field by a bull," he said. "More than likely, it would have been the other way around."[127]

Rupp wasn't afraid to take any bull by the horns. In a 1959 editorial in the *Kentucky Hereford*, he wrote that children of wealthy parents had a distinct advantage in 4-H and Future Farmers of America (FFA) livestock shows. "How many 4-H and FFA youngsters went out, bought the calf, fed the calf and cared for the calf?" he asked.

> Or did their father go out, buy the calf, feed it most of the time, or have it fed by another, and then let the youngster, dressed in cowboy attire, lead the calf into the show ring? I'd say it is done too much of the time. The little boy back off in the hills who didn't have the benefit of a father who raced all over the countryside for a top-flight calf, spend the money for it, then feed it, came away heartbroken and discouraged. I know of a sale that was held two years ago where four of these calves that went out as club calves brought over $450. What chance does a youngster have who is really trying to learn how to feed

a calf? He was beaten before he started, and he was beaten by a pocketbook rather than by effort.[128]

Rupp's published criticisms drew an instant response. *Courier-Journal* reporter Joe Bright wrote that "Kentucky farm leaders, both young and old, think that Adolph Rupp isn't as faultless when commenting on cattle shows as he is when directing the University of Kentucky's basketball team." Said George D. Corder, chairman of the 4-H extension program: "I don't see how favoritism can take place in the 4-H ring. Our rules are strict regarding ownership, and all the showers have to prove that they actually raised the cattle themselves." "Whenever there's competition, people are going to form opinions," said H. C. Brown, Jefferson County's extension agent. "There's keen competition between breeds and also among breeders, but I don't think there's favoritism." One concerned father took Rupp's accusations personally. "My kids have won out over kids from farms that have 20 times the cattle we do," he said. "Their fathers have also had political connections. The integrity of 4-H shows is high, and the kids are rewarded for the effort they make."[129]

By 1953 Rupp owned four farms totaling close to 1,000 acres with an estimated value of more than $250,000 (his base coaching salary at the time was $11,000). He had a 200-acre tract in Woodford County, 187 acres in Scott County, 266 in Harrison County, and "a 283-acre Bourbon County showplace." He bought that 283.4-acre John H. Bell Sr. estate in Bourbon County for a little over $115,000, or $410 an acre (he was looking to sell the Woodford County property to help pay for it). Located on Russell Cave Pike 15 miles from Lexington, it provided pastures for his cattle as well as a 9.8-acre tobacco base.[130] His first farm, for which he paid $15,000 in 1941, was reported to be worth $65,000 in 1953, and land that he bought at auction for $38,000 in 1946 was worth more than $80,000. Still, he laughed off any suggestion that he was a rich man. "I am comfortable," he said, "but I'm not wealthy. I'm selling one farm, maybe two, to help pay for my last purchase. And like most everybody else, I have had to borrow money from the bank to help me make purchases and investments."[131]

Rupp grew burley tobacco—Larry Boeck wrote that "35 acres of this precious federally limited commodity are spread over his farms"—but his passion remained Hereford cattle. In 1953 he had 160 head of registered stock on two farms. A photograph accompanying a 1953 *Courier-Journal* article shows a pensive Rupp in gloves, overcoat, and fedora leaning on the rail of a pen, admiring four white-faced calves. And just as he was a coveted speaker at basketball banquets and coaching clinics, he was sought after by farm groups wanting to know the secret to his success in that field, too. During that canceled 1952–1953 basketball season, he kept busy by addressing numerous Farm Bureau and cattlemen's gatherings and "getting quite a kick out of it," according to Boeck.[132]

Rupp incorporated his farms and other businesses in the name of Adolph Rupp and Son, and he put all of the stock in Herky's name. In addition to insuring financial security for the family, it provided opportunities for father and son to share time with each other.[133]

Larry Boeck attributed much of Rupp's success to an energy that "allows him to combine high-pressure business with coaching, which in itself is a killing ordeal for many men. This same drive also has allowed him to carry on such money-making sidelines as conducting basketball clinics for coaches and making speeches." The going rate for a Rupp clinic was $500, and he averaged $100 per speech. Boeck estimated that Rupp's earnings from clinics and speaking engagements in 1953 probably exceeded his coaching salary.[134]

Rupp found other ways of turning a buck. Dick Robinson, a member of his first UK teams in the 1930s, remembered that soon after he graduated in 1938, Rupp phoned him to inquire whether he had a car—which Robinson did—and to ask him for a ride to Louisville. Robinson explained in a 1984 interview that Rupp had borrowed $5,000 from a bank to invest in "whiskey warehouse receipts," or warrants, which give the holder the right to buy a certain number of shares at a later date for a set price. The gamble is that the value of the shares will have gone up by then, so they can be bought and immediately resold at a nice profit.[135]

Robinson recalled that they drove to the A. J. Cummings Company in Louisville, where Rupp bought $5,000 worth of receipts at 55 cents a gallon. Before they left for home, "the guy that waited on Adolph gave him a pound of coffee and gave me a pound of coffee," Robinson said. When Rupp got out of the car back at his apartment on Forest Park, he reached behind the seat and gathered up both pounds of coffee. "Coach, he gave us one each," Robinson objected. "He did not," Rupp replied. Robinson, who had had several run-ins with the coach during his playing days, now threatened, "I'll whip your ass for it." Rupp told him he was being unreasonable. "Well, look," Robinson said, "I drove you down there for nothing, and I'm going to take this pound of coffee." Rupp finally gave in: "Well, if that's the way you feel, you take it."[136]

Larry Boeck wrote in 1953 that Rupp "got a big financial push in 1943," at the same time that "he bought and then sold stock in a distillery." Rupp said his distillery investment was just one of several deals in which "friends helped me to invest wisely."[137]

Early in his UK years, Rupp also began to invest in the Central District Tobacco Warehousing Corporation, which operated 16 warehouses in central Kentucky. By 1953 he had become one of the corporation's three largest shareholders, and he owned a tobacco warehouse himself in partnership with Ed Curd, the Lexington bookie who operated out of the Mayfair Bar. Curd cultivated a wide array of friends, including actor George Raft, oddsmaker and TV sports commentator Jimmy "The Greek" Snyder, Governor Happy Chandler, UK football coach Paul "Bear" Bryant, and, of course, Adolph Rupp. During a televised Senate committee hearing in the early 1950s, the gangster Frank Costello was asked with whom he gambled. "With my little friend Ed Curd in Lexington, Ky.," he replied.[138]

Curd began booking bets for a living in the 1920s and soon acquired a reputation for the connections he made between betting and sports. In 1945, Phog Allen, Rupp's old coach at Kansas, warned a Lexington reporter about Curd's "gigantic handbook agency" at the Mayfair Bar. "As long as we have places like the one there in Lexington, the threat to our colleges and college boys will continue," Allen said. He proved prophetic, and when the point-shaving scandal broke in 1951, investigators looked closely at Curd's relationship with the Kentucky program. Curd admitted his friendship with Rupp, telling investigators that "he was able to glean some information by attending practices and taking Rupp to dinner," but he claimed that he "never asked a player to shave points" and that "Rupp was totally ignorant of the scandal." Curd actually took credit for bringing the scandal to light. After losing a large bet on a UK game, he decided to keep a close eye on the Wildcats. Sportswriter Billy Reed wrote that when Curd "finally compiled enough games that didn't pass his smell test," he called UK athletic director Bernie Shively to tell him the games had been fixed.[139]

Though Rupp wasn't a gambler per se—he was "too cheap to bet," Curd once said with a chuckle—some of his business ventures carried risk.[140] Rupp's investment of $5,000 in the Great Depression in whiskey warehouse warrants was suspect; one newspaper dubbed it "a get rich quick scheme."[141] In 1959 he filed incorporation papers for the Rupp Oil Company in partnership with son Herky, at that time a sophomore at UK, and former UK basketball player Roger Layne of McKamie, Arkansas. With the purpose of "drilling for oil in Kentucky and elsewhere," the corporation was capitalized at $100,000, divided into 1,000 shares of stock at par value of $100. Layne held 500 shares, Rupp 480, and Herky 20.[142]

A few years later Rupp served as president of Pioneer Cable Vision Inc., a firm planning to start a cable television system in Lexington and Fayette County in 1964. Rupp asked the city for a 20-year permit to erect the necessary towers and wiring. His friends Thomas Bell and Happy Chandler were stockholders in the company, which already had a "financial commitment" of $1 million, according to the *Lexington Herald*.[143]

In 1960 Rupp teamed up with thoroughbred breeder Leslie Combs II to form the Valiant Annuity Life Insurance Company, which made a public stock offering of 1 million shares at $5 apiece. Combs and Rupp served as directors of the firm, headquartered in Louisville.[144] Rupp already had been involved in selling insurance of another sort. His friend Lyman Ginger remembered that in the early years Rupp "was selling farm insurance primarily" and was having trouble peddling much tobacco insurance. One evening Rupp turned to Ginger and said, "You know what we need in this county more than anything else? We need a damn good hail storm."[145]

He might have been joking then, but he was dead serious about his various business interests. "Rupp is as capable a businessman as he is farmer and coach," Larry Boeck wrote in 1964. "Economics, as well as the desire to bow out with a fifth national championship quintet, motivate him." Talk of retirement from coaching came up as early as the 1950s, but by the 1960s sportswriters were wondering each year when he would quit. "I'm on professional status," Rupp said in 1964 at age sixty-three, "and that means that I can retire at the age of 65 with 75 percent of my pay as retirement. I could retire now, but at 68 percent." UK was paying him $18,500 in 1964, and he now seemed reluctant to give up a salary he had complained about year after year. His close friends wondered why he would worry about finances. He was a man of means, as his will attested when he died in 1977.[146]

What do we make of Rupp the businessman? It should not be surprising that he made such a mark in farming, having been raised on a Kansas farm. Of course, farming in the Kentucky Bluegrass, with his livestock and tobacco, was considerably different than laboring in the wheat fields of Kansas. Yet he yearned for the country life with which he was intimately familiar. It shouldn't be surprising, either, that he proved to be such a successful businessman. For Rupp, agriculture became a sort of conglomerate involving Hereford breeding, farm insurance, and tobacco farming and warehousing.

But he proved to be a businessman in another sense. It was Rupp, more than any other coach, who transformed college basketball—in the South specifically but also in America as a whole—into a big-time, big-business phenomenon. It must be said, too, that the business of basketball resulted in many problems—gambling, commercialization, and professionalization—that university administrators are still grappling with today. Only after his death would other coaches and players capitalize on the foundation that Rupp had built. And long after his death, American society continued to struggle with changes that he had initiated.

10

From a Canceled Season to the Fiddlin' Five, 1952–1958

Herman L. Donovan stood behind Adolph Rupp in the days and weeks and months after the point-shaving scandal broke. Donovan steadfastly refused to fire his coach, even when, in the words of historian Bert Nelli, "It became evident that such action would spare the team punishment by the SEC and the NCAA." Donovan and the university paid a high price for such unwavering support. On August 11, 1952, the executive committee of the SEC announced its punishment. In its decision, the committee referred to Judge Saul Streit's indictment of the UK program, which alleged payments to players by boosters and a general "commercialization" of UK athletics. Because of the accumulation of infractions, the committee ruled that Kentucky could participate in no conference games or postseason tournaments in the 1952–1953 season. Rupp and assistant Harry Lancaster scurried around to piece together a schedule of non-conference opponents and somehow came up with 21 games. Then in November, the NCAA instructed all member schools not to schedule UK that season. As one writer put it, "Kentucky was in such bad odor that the NCAA discouraged those teams from playing the Wildcats."[1]

On Monday, November 3, 1952, the day before the presidential election in which Dwight Eisenhower defeated Adlai Stevenson, Rupp and athletic director Bernie Shively summoned team members to a meeting in Memorial Coliseum. Frank Ramsey and Cliff Hagan sat in the front row of a section of coliseum seats, along with fellow starters Gayle Rose, Bill Evans, and Lou Tsioropoulos. With Rupp standing by his side, Shively informed the players that the decision had been made to cancel the season.[2]

The NCAA's injunction for schools not to play Kentucky amounted to a death sentence for the coming season. "That was the first death penalty they ever had, and we were shocked," remembered Ramsey. After writer C. Ray Hall interviewed Wildcat players who had experienced the canceled season for a 2002 *Courier-Journal* piece, he concluded that "officially it was about the money that changed hands between UK boosters and players. Unofficially it was about UK players' involvement in the point-shaving scandals of the late 1940s. Perhaps it also was about Coach Adolph Rupp's imperious attitude toward the NCAA and other keepers of the flame." Ramsey concluded that "the NCAA was mad at Adolph for saying the gamblers couldn't touch his boys with a 10-foot pole."[3]

President Donovan conducted an internal investigation, which totally exonerated Rupp. "From all we could learn," Donovan said, "Coach Rupp is an honorable man who did not knowingly violate the athletic rules." Apparently, Donovan's support was not shared by Paul "Bear" Bryant, UK's highly successful football coach. Bryant felt his program and his own accomplishments were not fully appreciated. He mirrored Rupp in more ways than one. One writer suggested that "both Rupp and Bryant were coaching geniuses, both had enormous egos, and both needed a large stage on which to perform. It proved impossible for them to coexist on the same campus."[4]

Some thought Bryant was under the impression that Rupp would be dismissed. When Donovan continued to support Rupp and gave the basketball coach a vote of confidence, even after the forced cancellation of the season, Bryant understood that he would never be out of Rupp's shadow. Bert Nelli noted the irony of what would eventually transpire: "Thus, instead of forcing Rupp's departure from the university, the basketball scandal precipitated Bryant's departure."[5]

"I don't think I would ever have left (Kentucky) if I hadn't gotten pigheaded," Bryant wrote in his autobiography, *Bear: The Hard Life and Good Times of Alabama's Coach Bryant.* "It was probably the most stupid thing I ever did. I could have had about anything I wanted, and Mary Harmon (his wife) loved it. We had a social position coaches seldom have—good friends with Governor [Lawrence] Wetherby and all—and we lived right there near the Idle Hour Country Club."[6]

"When I try to put my finger on it, I can't say exactly why I left Kentucky," Bryant said, "but one thing I want to make clear. I never tried to get the late Bernie Shively's job as athletic director, and the athletic directorship had nothing to do with what you could call a clash of objectives between me and Adolph Rupp. I guess, to be perfectly honest about it, that was the crux of the matter, me and Coach Rupp." Bryant admitted, "If Rupp had retired as basketball coach when they said he was going to, I would probably still be at Kentucky. The trouble was we were too much alike, and he wanted basketball number one. In an environment like that, one or the other has to go."[7]

"Rupp and I never had a cross word, actually," he added. "I just got tired of seeing the papers full of basketball. There has to be two sides to it. I probably went there for more money than he was making. I was at $8,500, then $9,000, then they raised me to $12,000 when Alabama offered me a job after the first year. Basketball made money at Kentucky, though, and everywhere I went trying to sell the football program it was 'basketball and Rupp, basketball and Rupp,' and I was jealous."[8]

During Bryant's first year at Kentucky, he went on a recruiting trip to Harrodsburg, Kentucky. He was told there would be a big crowd to greet him, but when he arrived only 20 people showed up. The fellow who introduced him said, "I'm sorry we couldn't give Coach Bryant the key to the city, but we have given one to Coach Rupp for all the championships he's had. We'll save one for when Coach Bryant wins as many games." "I got up burning," Bryant remembered. He told the crowd, "I don't want a key to the city. When I win as many games as Coach Rupp, I'll be able to buy the damn city and never miss the money."[9]

Bryant recalled, "You either liked Rupp or you hated him. There didn't seem to be any middle ground. Some of my friends who were high in the university administration didn't like him, and I probably let them know how jealous I was. He had that abrasive way of talking and dealing with people, and if you didn't like it you didn't like him."[10]

Bryant's office was next to Rupp's in Alumni Gymnasium, and Bryant could hear Rupp interviewing players. "Funniest thing in the world," Bryant said. "He called the door to his office the 'pearly gates,' and he would announce to a kid in that Kansas twang, 'By gad, you just walked into the pearly gates of basketball!' And he'd give them the darnedest talks you ever heard, all about how good he and his program were. All the truth, too." One prospect, Forrest Tucker, a future movie star, did not make the grade. Bryant heard Rupp tell Tucker, "Only trouble is, son, you're just too damned short. I don't think we'll be able to use you around here. But here's a dollar. Take this and get yourself something to eat and go get the bus home."[11]

Bryant might have resented Rupp, but he also respected how he "took the bull by the horns." One year a faculty group investigated the athletic department. They asked Bryant about finances and budgets. When they got to Rupp, he was ready for them. "I could hear it plain as day," Bryant recalled. Rupp greeted the faculty group by bellowing, "By gad, come on in here! I been waiting for you bastards! I wanta know what the hell happened to my basketball player over there in your English class. By gad, you expect me to take these pine knots and make All-Americas out of them and I send you a B student and he's making a goddamn D!" An admiring Bryant recalled that Rupp "just ate their fannies, and they haven't sat down yet. They haven't even opened their mouths. They're in there trying to investigate athletics and he's attacking academics. They got out of there in a hurry." After the move to Memorial Coliseum, Bryant "got an office as far away as I could, at the other end of the hall, away from Rupp and all that traffic."[12]

"They hated each other," said Ruth Shively, wife of Bernie Shively. "Only Bryant was more subtle. Each was afraid one would make a nickel more than the other. Bernie had to bear down on them all the time to keep the peace. They would go out in public, put their arms around each other and pretend they were the best of buddies. Either would do his best to stick a knife in the other's ribs. It was no joy living with them. They took ten years off my husband's life."[13]

"I didn't appreciate Adolph until I left," Bryant admitted. "If I had to do it all over again, I would have gone in there and asked Rupp to do something for me. He'd have liked that and he'd have done it, and he'd have been my friend."[14]

Bryant kept a photograph in his den of Bud Wilkinson laughing over a story that Bryant told at a banquet. Bryant had just won the SEC championship, "the only time a Kentucky football team ever has," and Rupp had won it "for the umpteenth time." They gave Rupp a big blue Cadillac with whitewall tires. Bryant rose to speak at the banquet and said, "And here's what I got." He held up "this little old cigarette lighter. Well, when the thing came to a head I remembered that cigarette lighter, and I knew I was too far behind to ever catch up."[15]

C. M. Newton—who played for Rupp, was hired by Bryant to coach basketball at Alabama, and still later became UK's athletic director—was in a good position to compare the two icons. "Both coaches cared about their players, but they had a different way of showing it," Newton said. "Bryant was outgoing, while Rupp had a hard time expressing his feelings. Bryant worked to build loyalty; Rupp expected it. Bryant could practically kill his boys on the practice field and they would take up for him. Let Rupp do the same thing, and his players would bitch and moan. Say something about Bryant, and the football players would challenge you in a minute. That wasn't true of Adolph's players." Newton believed that "Bryant always took the blame for his losses, saying he hadn't prepared his players properly. Rupp was never at fault; if Johnny didn't guard his man, he heard about it, and so did fans tuned to Rupp's postgame radio shows."[16]

The basketball scandal had an impact on Bryant's football program. Gene Donaldson, a star football guard, was accused of being hired by a Lexington architect for work he didn't do. In the investigation following the scandal it was found that a local merchant had given clothing to football player Chet Lukawski. Both Donaldson and Lukawski were suspended and the university fined $500 for each violation. Nick Englisis, another UK football player, quit the team to work for gamblers in Brooklyn. The *Louisville Courier-Journal* later published a photograph showing Englisis, nicknamed "The Greek," sitting on the UK bench during a basketball game in Louisville. Although Rupp claimed he was unaware of Englisis's presence and did not even know him, the newspaper's revelations embarrassed the Baron.[17]

Bryant believed that the basketball scandals hurt his football program by keeping athletes from coming to Kentucky. Donovan hinted to Bryant that Rupp would soon retire, but when that didn't happen, Bryant himself tried to resign in 1952 and again in 1953 before leaving for Texas A&M in 1954.[18] In Texas he lost nine games his first season. "You think he's down a little bit now," Rupp said, "but I'll tell you, he *will* win. He will win. Make no mistake about it, and don't forget Uncle Adolph told you." Rupp warned Bryant's opponents to "get your old buggies together and grease them up and go out and start recruiting, because he's gonna do it night and day and he's gonna beat you." "He sure didn't have to say that," Bryant wrote years later, "but, boy, I appreciated it. Practically every paper in Texas picked it up, and a whole lot of eyebrows were raised." Rupp proved prophetic. After that 1–9 start at A&M in 1954, Bryant went 7–2–1, 9–0–1, and 8–3 before moving on to Alabama.[19]

Although Kentucky could not compete in SEC or NCAA basketball games in the 1952–1953 season, Rupp and Lancaster told the players they would have "occasional practices." Those practices soon became a daily affair. "Shoot, we didn't miss a day," said Bill Bibb, a substitute on the team who later became commissioner of the Atlantic Sun Conference. "We were lucky to get to go home for Christmas."[20] Phil Grawemeyer, a freshman forward from Louisville, remembered that "it was a long year. When we started out, I think Coach Rupp said we'd practice two days or three days a week. And then it became four. And then it became five."[21] Rupp already was looking ahead to the 1953–1954 season, and he wanted to make sure his team would be loaded.

In 1952, however, there seemed to be much work to do. "We wouldn't have beat many people that year," said Frank Ramsey, one of the team's stars. "We only had six (varsity) people on scholarship. We sat out. We practiced the whole year. It was a shock, but it was a very enjoyable year." Bill Evans, a junior guard from Berea, agreed. "I'm sure a lot of fans look on it as 'what a terrible thing to happen,'" he said, "but as it worked out, it wasn't. The story is not one of disaster. It was a . . . fun year." Cliff Hagan, Ramsey's roommate and an All-American, remembered it all differently: "Coach Rupp worked us pretty hard every day. It was the longest season I've ever been through."[22]

Hagan and Ramsey teamed with Lou Tsioropoulos as the senior stars of the team. And despite Ramsey's claim that the squad was relatively weak, others disagreed. Grawemeyer remembered the merits of his three older teammates: "Lou Tsioropoulos was strong and a great rebounder and a good defensive man. Ramsey was a kind of a rock-'em, sock-'em type guard. He got everything just by working hard at it. And Cliff Hagan was a natural—he had a sixth sense about him." Grawemeyer recalled that after practice Hagan "would get out on the floor and shoot hook shots without looking—and hit them. He had that uncanny ability that he knew exactly where he was on the floor." Ramsey remembered one "jaw-dropping moment" when Hagan tipped in a jump ball—"not clowning around after practice. In a game."[23]

Ramsey, Hagan, and Tsioropoulos were joined by junior guards Bill Evans and Gayle Rose, along with a talented freshman class. Writer C. Ray

Hall described the team's quality in no uncertain terms: "They were college basketball's royalty, under house arrest in a palace, the 2-year-old, 11,500-seat Memorial Coliseum."[24]

"House arrest" described it well. The players recalled the intensity of those Memorial Coliseum practice sessions. Apparently, they were no different than they had been during a regular season. "It was very silent during practice, naturally," Tsioropoulos recalled. "No one talked" except for Rupp and Lancaster. With no games to prepare for, practices had a different feel altogether. "The temperature was cool in there," Tsioropoulos said. "It was quiet, and it was a controlled practice, and it was fundamentals." The only break in the routine came with "congratulations and criticism and maybe some stories that [Rupp] would tell." As always, Lancaster "was the tactician on court and the mediator off court, listening to players' complaints about all things great and small, right down to the milk ration: only a pint with each meal." Rupp "was autocratic. He was almost above the fray."[25]

Ramsey gave it his all during those workouts, driving relentlessly to the basket. One day Rupp shouted, "Ramsey, by God, if the Maginot Line was in front of you and you had a basketball in your hands, you'd try to dribble through it. There must be some insanity in your family." After practice, Ramsey confided to Lancaster that he did indeed have an aunt who suffered from mental illness, and he wanted Lancaster to tell Rupp that his barb had hurt. "Hell, I knew it," Rupp said. "This just confirms my judgment."[26]

The coach continued to demand perfection. "Somebody would blow an assignment," Ramsey said, "and he'd stop and he'd chew their butt out there. All you could do was kind of drop your head, because everybody was [thinking], 'Thank God that's not me.' He would point out your mistakes in a way that you'd never forget. But at the same time, you respected him. He had an aura about him." The practices must have seemed pointless at times, but Rupp did not allow the players to lose focus. "If Adolph Rupp and Harry Lancaster had a talent," Evans pointed out, "it was to drive and require perfection—every day. They didn't let up." Rupp "never tolerated less than perfection, and he drove [us] unmercifully. The whole deal at Kentucky was not how you played in games, but whether you got into his top six or seven, because that's all he played—seven or eight. The other guys played miniscule minutes."[27]

At least the players were "mercifully spared the sight of the SEC gyms," as writer C. Ray Hall put it. Said Ramsey: "You go to Tennessee and you played in a gym that was like old gyms in little rural towns, which had a stage on the side. . . . Vanderbilt had a gym so small that we played at David Lipscomb College. Mississippi would always be paid to change their [home] game to the Owensboro Sportscenter. . . . We went to play Tulane and we played in something that had a balcony around it. Small. Georgia Tech . . . had a little gym that was almost like an operating room." Ramsey remembered a game at Mississippi State when the students had gone home for Christmas and the heat was off in the gym, so the Wildcats warmed up in sweat suits and overcoats.[28]

During the canceled season UK played four intra-squad exhibitions in front of large crowds in Memorial Coliseum. About 6,500 fans braved a treacherous ice storm on December 13 to watch the varsity dismantle the freshmen 76–45. "It was solid ice on the road and about six inches of snow," Ramsey recalled, and even the players had trouble getting there.[29]

After that lopsided varsity/freshmen game, Rupp decided to split the team between the "Ramseys" and the "Hagans" for a January 19 exhibition. With Hagan scoring 8 early points, his team led 10–0. The *Lexington Herald* reported that "the count reached 18–3 and the crowd began pleading for the Ramseys to rally." The Ramseys did just that and ended up winning 71–50 before 8,500 fans.[30]

On February 4, the Hagans got their revenge, 68–55. Hagan scored 28 and Pete Grigsby had 10 for the winners. (Grigsby became a legendary coach at McDowell High School in Floyd County, Kentucky, and Grigsby's daughter, Geri, became the greatest scorer in Kentucky high school basketball history for McDowell High School. Geri Grigsby still holds the national career scoring average of 46.1.)

Before the game on February 4, Rupp conducted a lengthy clinic for the 10,000 fans, so the quarters were cut from 10 to 8 minutes. The last intra-squad game took place before 9,000 fans on February 28. Rupp put Hagan and Ramsey on the Blue team, but the Whites, coached by Harry Lancaster, won 49–47.[31]

Phil Grawemeyer noted that those intra-squad games "were kind of fun compared to what we had gone through [in practice]." The fans "were appreciative and they cheered," Tsioropoulos said, "but it wasn't the intensity, naturally, of a game. It gave the people a good idea of just what the entire squad was like. Before, if they could see Adolph's teams play, they would see maybe six players. . . . The only way they would see those [other] guys play was if Adolph was ahead by 20 points with less than two minutes and he said, 'By God, I think I'll take a chance.' He didn't believe in substituting frequently or too early."[32]

The "Lost Season" of 1952–1953 prepared the Wildcats for the following campaign. Hagan, Ramsey, and Tsioropoulos had been drafted by the Boston Celtics, but they decided to stay in Lexington. Only an NBA rule change initiated by Rupp's friend Red Auerbach, the Celtics' coach, allowed the three to be drafted. The rules stated that a player could not be drafted until his college eligibility had been completed, but Auerbach proposed that players should be allowed to be taken four years after they graduated from high school. The league accepted his proposal, enabling him to draft the Kentucky players.[33]

Auerbach and Rupp admired each other's success and became friends. Auerbach made it a point to watch UK play in New York, then socialized with Rupp after the game. He came to Kentucky in the off-season and once traveled with Rupp for clinics overseas.[34]

With Hagan, Ramsey, and Tsioropoulos back, UK went 25–0 in the 1953–1954 season. Hagan scored 51 points, at that time a UK record, in the season-opening victory over Temple. When highly rated Tulane visited UK on January 16, Rupp focused his pregame talk on Green Wave coach Cliff Wells. According to little-used UK sub Dan Chandler, the son of A. B. "Happy" Chandler, "Coach Rupp had come to the locker room early and had plastered the walls with the New Orleans papers of the previous year. In these papers we learned that Cliff Wells had voted to suspend Kentucky. We read the clippings but missed the message . . . until the coach came in. Rupp was unusually serious, almost grave. A pin dropped at that time would have burst an eardrum."[35]

"He's out on the floor now," Rupp told his players, "the man that led the fight against you last year. For every blister, every bruise, every black eye, every tooth knocked out last year—that little runt of a coach owes you. This is the night you have waited for! Tonight you pay 'em back for all of last year." With that he left the locker room. The players were left to remember what he had told them the year before: "You boys don't deserve this suspension, but if you are willing to work and work hard, we will turn this terrible blow to our advantage." Chandler mused that "several of us must have wondered if Cliff Wells, mild-mannered and reserved, ever had the slightest idea why all twelve of us stared at him before the game with vengeance, almost a hatred, that had been turned into a fiery desire by a very determined individual." Kentucky won 94–43.[36]

As in the past, Rupp rarely used his substitutes—his "turds," as he called them. Dan Chandler recalled the 97–71 rout of Tennessee on January 23:

> The game was less than five minutes old when Hagan drove hard on the last leg of a fast break and was hit hard and knocked to the floor. Hagan lay on the floor and Rupp stood, but didn't move. "Chandler!" he yelled. I had settled back and was not expecting to hear my name for quite some time. I was, at that time, seven miles mentally, and almost that far physically, from the coach. Rupp called again, "Chandler!" It was so early in the game that my ears wouldn't inform the rest of my body that the coach was actually calling for me. A chain of elbows from teammates, equally eager to play but hiding their eagerness with half-smiles for my benefit, started shoving me and patting me encouragingly as I moved toward the coach. Already I was late. I ripped every button off my warm-up jacket in removing it, and discarded my warm-up trousers in the rush to Rupp's side. I got down on one knee, looked up into Coach Rupp's eyes for instructions and listened intently as Rupp put one hand on my shoulder and said, "Go help Hagan to the dressing room."[37]

Kentucky reeled off 24 straight wins before Ramsey scored 30 points in a play-off victory over Louisiana State for the SEC title. Hagan, Ramsey, and Tsioropoulos had earned their undergraduate degrees during the canceled season, and according to an NCAA rule that has since been changed, they were ineligible as graduate students to participate in postseason games. With their three stars out of the picture, the other players voted to compete anyway, but Rupp overruled them and kept the team home. Tom Gola led LaSalle, a 73–60 loser to UK in the regular season, to win the NCAA championship.[38]

Rupp was simply unwilling to compete in the tournament with a diminished squad even though he had other capable players. Gayle Rose, for example, was a small, flashy guard whom Rupp once labeled with one of his favorite epithets: "Gawddammit, Rose, you really do look like a Shetland pony in a stud horse parade." Rupp likened Tsioropoulos to his pet bull. "You are just exactly like Domino," Rupp told him. "You are big and slow, but you can get up on the boards and get on top of everybody."[39]

With the canceled season and no postseason play the next year, some Kentucky fans thought it was time for the Baron to retire. He would have none of it. "I'm not retiring," he said. "I'll not retire until the man who said Kentucky can't play in the NCAA hands me the national championship trophy." In a defiant address to the Lexington Rotary Club, Rupp said, "We at the university do not seek your sympathy, and we have no apologies to make."[40]

He also blasted "some stupid jackass" for criticizing the new Memorial Coliseum as "just a basketball building." "It's not just a basketball building," Rupp claimed. "It's a state memorial building" honoring Kentuckians killed in World War II. A *Lexington Herald* writer said that "in his hour of trouble, at a time when he is a victim of vicious and unwarranted attacks, Basketball Coach Adolph Rupp of the University of Kentucky is discovering that he has many faithful friends, and their friendship may turn out to be his best defense against the criticism he is receiving in the nation's press."[41]

The 1950s proved to be a decade of great lows and great highs for Adolph Rupp. The repercussions of the point-shaving scandal dominated the early years of the decade, and he won his fourth national championship toward the end of it. In the years in between, he solidified his reputation as the best coach in America. After the 25–0 season of 1953–1954, his next four teams went 23–3, 20–6, 23–5, and 23–6 in 1957–1958, when he won his last national title.

On a personal level, Rupp's mother died of a heart ailment on her eighty-ninth birthday in May 1954. Rupp himself suffered from stress-induced heart trouble, but he flew to Halstead, Kansas, to be by his mother's side during her last days. In January 1959, Mary Schmidt, the mother of his wife Esther, suffered a cerebral hemorrhage and died in Streator, Illinois.[42]

On January 8, 1955, Rupp saw his 129-game, 12-year home winning streak come to an end against Georgia Tech, which won 59–58 when Joe Helms stole the ball in the backcourt and hit a jump shot with 11 seconds left. It also snapped the number-one-ranked Wildcats' overall winning streak at 32.

The loss was the first for the Wildcats on their home floor since January 2, 1943, when Ohio State won 45–40. Ed Ashford of the *Lexington Leader* wrote that "pandemonium reigned when the ball went through the net" on Helms's shot. The Wildcats rushed down court and Linville Puckett shot from the top of the circle, but the ball bounced off the front of the rim. A desperation tip by Phil Grawemeyer also fell short. Ashford wrote that "when the game ended, the Georgia Tech reserves all but pummeled the life out of the five Yellow Jackets who went all the way in the most surprising game ever played in Lexington." For the hometown fans, "Memorial Coliseum was a dreary place. . . . It was the first time most of the fans in the gym ever had seen a Kentucky team beaten."[43]

John "Whack" Hyder, the Georgia Tech coach, said, "We will live on that one a long time. What is there to say but 'wow.'" Part of the credit went to future UK assistant coach Lake Kelly, who played on that Georgia Tech team. During a Christmas trip back home, Kelly's father, Ed, a Kentucky state senator, had gotten him tickets to a UK game. "I took a few notes," Kelly said. "I noticed a lot of screen and roll." When he returned to Atlanta, he met with Hyder, who drilled the team on how to stop the screen and roll. "It really hurt Kentucky," Kelly remembered. "It just bottled them up. We kept talking to each other and thinking any minute now Kentucky was going to beat us to death. It just didn't happen."[44]

Ed Kelly refused to attend the game. "I don't want to see you all get beat by 50 points," he told his son. "After the game," Lake Kelly recalled, "I called him and said, 'Hey, you're not going to believe this. We beat them.'"

"What a hell of a way to start the new year," Rupp groused. "These turds are making me old before my time."[45]

UK played Georgia Tech again on January 31, in Atlanta, losing 65–59 this time. After the first game, Kelly had talked with Gerry Calvert, a friend on the UK team. "I bet old Adolph went nuts, didn't he?" Kelly asked. "Oh, let me tell you what he did, Lake," Calvert replied. "He told us if we go to Atlanta and get beat there, none of us have scholarships anymore." The Wildcats "were so uptight," Kelly remembered, "they couldn't do much. They just didn't play well. We were loose and happy."[46]

Calvert saw it differently: "No matter how much Coach Rupp screamed and hollered and tried to get us ready, we were all overconfident. We went into both of those games knowing very well if we went on a sandlot and played those guys, it'd be a matter of how bad we wanted to beat them." After the second defeat, the players were able to retain their scholarships but lost something else. When they sat down for their post-game meal, which usually included a salad, steak, honey, and toast, Calvert finished his salad and waited for the next course. "What are you waiting for?" Rupp asked. "I'm waiting for my steak," Calvert replied. "Steak, hell," Rupp said. "You guys played like rabbits; you'll eat like rabbits."[47]

The first defeat had had its own aftermath. Although the next day was a Sunday, Rupp held practice anyway, and the players showed up ready for a grueling punishment. But instead of chewing them out, Rupp walked onto the court calmly and called them around him. "Now I want you boys to listen to me carefully," he said. "I want you to go out and buy a copy of the paper with the headline saying, 'Georgia Tech Beats Kentucky.' Then I want you to tuck it away safe some place so's it won't ever be lost. It is a famous clipping. There have been two catastrophes of our time. One was Pearl Harbor and the other was last night."[48] There was another "famous clipping" after the second loss to the Yellow Jackets.

Between 1940 and 1958, Georgia Tech beat the Wildcats only in those two 1955 games. They were Kentucky's only regular-season defeats that season, but they were so devastating that they led to a shake-up in the roster. After the team returned to Lexington, several of the players went home—a violation of training rules—when they found out there would be no practice the next day. When Rupp learned they were gone, he promptly called another Sunday practice.[49]

Linville Puckett had not gone home because, as he remembered it in a 1983 interview, "The girl I was dating, who is now my wife," lived in Lexington. On Sunday afternoon Puckett went to the Jack Cook Service Station, a hangout for the players just down the street from Memorial Coliseum. "Well," he remembered, "I was sitting there at the service station and the players came in and told me that Adolph had found out they had left town, and would I say I had left town, too? So I agreed to say I had gone home." The players had heard that Rupp planned to take their privileges away, so they all agreed to quit the team if he followed through with his threat.[50]

Before practice, Rupp held a team meeting and told the players he had learned that some of them had been breaking training rules. The *Louisville Courier-Journal* reported that as punishment he informed them that he planned to take away the four complimentary tickets each player received for every home game, along with their free theater passes. Puckett's younger brother, Omer, later explained what happened next: "When Rupp announced what he was going to do about the tickets, Linville said if his were taken, he'd quit the team. Rupp got angry. He told the team that members who wanted to stay and follow the rules should go out the door to the left and those who couldn't abide by this could go out the door to the right. Linville was closest to the door and he went to his right."[51]

Omer Puckett said "Rupp seemed to be shaken up" by Linville's departure. Rupp and Lancaster promptly left the gym, telling team captain Billy Evans to take charge. "Evans started talking," Omer said. "During the meeting, he put all the blame on Linville. He said it was Linville's fault Kentucky had been beaten by Georgia Tech. Linville was hurt and left school." According to Omer Puckett, it was Evans, not Rupp, who caused Linville to quit the team.[52]

Linville Puckett insisted at the time that "this isn't something that just happened; it's been brewing all season." In one interview, he said he decided to leave the team because basketball "was overemphasized at Kentucky. It isn't regarded as a game, but as a matter of life or death with resemblance of one going to war." Puckett's remarks carried a remarkable resemblance to the accusations of Judge Saul Streit during the point-shaving trials. Puckett claimed that "Adolph didn't treat his boys like he loved them." When Rupp heard that, he responded, "We don't go out there to make love."[53]

Bill Bibb, a substitute, eventually left the team along with Puckett— the two went on to play at Kentucky Wesleyan—but Rupp seemed unperturbed. He said Puckett left the team after breaking training rules. "I have only one training rule," Rupp said, "and I think it is very simple. All I ask is that each boy live just as his family expects him to live when they send him here. That's all." Harry Lancaster weighed in: "We've had trouble with Puckett and training before. He's a boy who tells you the truth, and he didn't deny that he'd not always kept to the rules. . . . Bibb was his buddy and went with him. . . . That's all."[54]

Ed Ashford of the *Lexington Leader* devoted a long column to the affair. "Puckett admitted breaking training," Ashford wrote, "but he was not dismissed from the squad. He walked out of the meeting voluntarily, making his own decision." After Puckett failed to report to the next practice, he issued a statement claiming that "it was impossible to get an education at Kentucky and play basketball at the same time." Ashford argued that the fallacy of this statement is evident to all acquainted with the facts, because Puckett's running mate at guard, Capt. Billy Evans, not only has played basketball a year longer than Puckett at UK, but also has been on the baseball and tennis teams and has made straight A's. The Puckett incident will go down in history as the only time a coach has been criticized and berated in a nation's press for asking that his players keep training. All Rupp asks of a player is that he keep himself in condition to play the best basketball he is capable of playing, and that he do his best at all times—on the court and in the classroom. The UK curfew of 10:30 for cage players is not at all severe.[55]

"I feel sorry for Puckett," Ashford wrote. "He is a fine basketball player and had the makings of a great one. He could have been an All-America player at Kentucky next year, if not this. He would have helped the team immeasurably, had he taken it upon himself to observe training rules. I think Puckett was ill-advised by his so-called friends who, I have reason to believe, urged him to issue a statement before Coach Rupp made one and suggested that he make it to a Louisville paper—not a Lexington paper." To Ashford, the most "unfortunate thing about the whole affair is that it gives anti-Rupp and anti-Kentucky sports columnists an opportunity to bring up the old basketball scandals again. Every time something unusual happens at UK, these scribes rehash the scandal and repeat Rupp's quote: 'They can't touch my boys with a 10-foot pole.'" Ashford concluded that "it appears that no matter what UK does, it still will be considered a 'basketball factory' as long as it wins basketball games."[56]

Despite the loss of Puckett and Bibb, Kentucky continued to win, marching to its sixteenth SEC title. The 1954–1955 season represented Rupp's silver anniversary at Kentucky. Following the final victory of the regular season, a 104–61 thrashing of Tennessee, he was honored for his 25 years of service to the university. The *Kentucky Kernel* reported that "former lettermen from all over the country assembled to help honor the world-renowned Coach, whose teams have compiled a fabulous 496–82 won-lost record during his tenure." Players lined up to greet their former coach as they were introduced by athletic director Bernie Shively. Former team manager Humsey Yessin stole the show with a vivid imitation of Rupp's "halftime oratory." With wife Esther and son Herky looking on, Rupp was surprised with a 1955 two-tone blue Cadillac.[57]

Kentucky entered the NCAA Eastern Regional at Evanston, Illinois, with a sterling 22–2 record, marred only by those galling losses to Georgia Tech. But the Wildcats fell in the first game of the tournament to Marquette, 79–71, then beat Penn State 84–59 in the consolation game for a final record of 23–3. Phil Grawemeyer remembered that "the team really missed Puckett because he was a terrific passer. No one else we had was as good." Even more devastating was the loss of Grawemeyer himself. The six-foot-eight-inch forward had suffered a skull fracture in a preseason practice and played with specially designed headgear. Then in a game against DePaul on January 10, he was lost for the rest of the season with a broken leg. The Wildcats sorely missed his 13 points and 13 rebounds a game.[58]

Kentucky had solid seasons in 1955–1956 and 1956–1957, then returned a veteran lineup for the 1957–1958 campaign. The Wildcats won an early match with Temple in what Vernon Hatton remembered as "Rupp's most dramatic victory ever," 85–83 in three overtimes on December 7. Hatton hit the winning shot from midcourt with one second on the clock. The next morning he went to Rupp's office, thinking he should be given the game ball. "Give you the game ball?" Rupp said. "Just because you scored two points from 47 feet with one second to go, you want me to give you the game ball? How would I explain that to the Athletic Board, giving away a $35 basketball? What would they think of me spending all that money? Anyway, if you hadn't scored that basket, it would have been one of the other boys. It was just one of our plays we've been practicing for occasions like that." Hatton "was furious, red as a beet, almost ready to quit the team and definitely ready to leave Rupp's office" when the coach reached under his desk, pulled out the ball, and tossed it to him. "Congratulations, son," he said. "You're sure tough in the clutch. You may have this ball. Tell your grandchildren about it."[59]

After early losses to Maryland and Southern Methodist and a first-round loss to West Virginia in the UK Invitational Tournament, however, Rupp became disillusioned with the prospects for a successful season. "We've got fiddlers, that's all," he said. "They're pretty good fiddlers; be right entertaining at a barn dance. But I'll tell you, you need violinists to play in Carnegie Hall. We don't have any violinists."[60]

Harry Lancaster remembered that the success of the 1957–1958 team was unexpected because the players could not compare with previous national championship squads. "We had no real ability at all, but we had everybody doing the thing he could do best," he said. "Team members played their roles well. Ed Beck, for example, could defend and rebound well. He couldn't score, but if he could cut that high-scoring center on the other team down from twenty-five or thirty points to eight or nine, which was about Ed's average, why, it leveled things down beautifully." The Wildcats depended on Johnny Cox, Adrian Smith, and Vernon Hatton to score. According to Lancaster, John Crigler was "the unknown and unsung player on the team. He had no particular abilities, but he was the only true driver we had." It was Crigler's ability to drive that proved so effective in the championship game against Seattle.[61]

After the Wildcats drubbed Miami of Ohio and Notre Dame in the first two rounds of the NCAA Tournament and nipped Temple again, 61–60, in the national semifinals in Louisville's new Freedom Hall, Rupp and Lancaster rose early on the day of the final to devise a scheme to beat Seattle. Bill Surface and Jimmy Breslin wrote in a feature article for *Time* that "by lunchtime their mimeographed diagrams were distributed to the team." By dinnertime, however, Rupp had "decided to change everything. So three hours before game time he locked his team in the dressing room and announced that every defensive assignment which had been given out should be ignored." "The scouting report says Elgin Baylor is the finest defensive man in the country," Rupp said. "Well, Harry and I question that. We don't think so. We are going to prove it, too. We are going to throw everything at Baylor. I believe we can get him to foul out of there and then we'll be home free."[62]

When the game began, Baylor guarded Crigler, so "Kentucky immediately set up its pick-offs and weaves and cuts and the other things basketball teams do with the single purpose of getting Crigler the ball. Crigler, moving to the corner, would take a pass from outside and then drive along the baseline of the court toward the basket. It is a difficult play for the defensive man because it is too easy to foul a man. Crigler made it easier for Baylor. He drove through and then went up for twisting under-the-basket layups. Baylor fouled him three times at the start and the game was virtually over right there."[63]

Forced into a sagging zone defense, Seattle gave Kentucky the outside shot, and the Wildcats made the most of it when Hatton and Cox, "a couple of lean, crew cut kids with those fantastic eyes college basketball players have, tossed up a couple from outside and they hit." Seattle went back to a man-to-man defense, and the Wildcats went to work on Baylor again. Surface and Breslin wrote, "Rupp's kids started to work their guard-around plays. This is a pick-off play worked methodically by any Rupp team. Down at Lexington, they say, 'The schedule for any basketball game is: Star-Spangled Banner, tipoff, number seven and eight guard-around.' It is an uncomplicated play, but worked to perfection it is murder to stop."[64]

"A Rupp-trained basketball team plays the game automatically," they wrote. "The kids all have the same style. They work their plays with a simple but flawless style, and they follow orders as if they were in the Army." With machine-like precision, the Wildcats ran the guard-around play directly at Baylor. He picked up his fourth foul when he hit 6-foot-7 ½-inch center Don Mills on the elbow. With free reign to drive to the basket, Hatton scored 30 points and Kentucky won the national championship, 84–72. "When we got the four fouls on Baylor," Rupp said, "we had him at our mercy, boys."[65]

The championship was no fluke. In *The Rupp Years*, Tev Laudeman wrote that in 1957–1958 Kentucky played "the toughest schedule in the school's history up to that time. Almost every non-conference opponent was a veteran team, on the way to winning a conference championship or finishing high in the race." Kentucky also benefited from the setup and the location of the tournament. Only 24 teams were invited to the NCAA Tournament at that time, and the Wildcats' four games were all in the state of Kentucky. The first two were against Miami of Ohio and Notre Dame, within the friendly confines of Memorial Coliseum, and the semifinals and final were in Freedom Hall.[66]

Rupp already had dubbed the starters on his 1958 championship squad the "Fiddlin' Five." "Coach Rupp gave it to us because he said we fiddled all the game and finally toward the end we made up our mind we were going to win and gave him heart attacks," recalled John Crigler, adding that Rupp finally had to admit: "I guess they turned out to be concert pianists playing at Carnegie Hall."[67]

Surface and Breslin had a different term for Rupp's winning ways: "Murdering you is closer to it." Seattle got a taste of what Southeastern Conference teams had endured for years. "In fact, perhaps the oldest joke told in the area concerns the time a report got around that Rupp had died. A coach immediately asked his athletic director for permission to go to Kentucky for the funeral. The athletic director thought it was a fine gesture. 'Tain't no gesture,' the coach said. 'I just want to make damn sure he's dead.'"[68]

With the 1958 national championship, Rupp cemented his place as the greatest college basketball coach in America. Surface and Breslin wrote, "Right after bourbon whisky, the biggest thing in Kentucky is a basketball coach named Adolph Rupp. And if you don't think he's the greatest one who ever lived, just ask him. His name has a fantastic draw on people from every walk of life in Kentucky. Whether you are in the governor's office at Frankfort or a diner in Lexington, people talk of 'Ole Adolph' in words normally used for the President of the United States or maybe Robert E. Lee."[69]

Rupp's businesslike approach was admired in Kentucky. "He was strictly all business back in those days when most coaches weren't," Crigler said. "When almost all the [opposing] teams came to UK, they went out to visit the horse farms. We didn't go any place but the gym." Surface and Breslin wrote that "Rupp is quite certain that playing basketball his way is the most important business in the world."[70]

Dan Chandler and Vernon Hatton noted in *Rupp from Both Ends of the Bench* that "Adolph Rupp is an administrator, a leader, a motivator of men. If he had been born a Russian, then Russians would have dominated basketball all these years. He would have been a great football coach, and if he had chosen politics, he would have been Governor or even President." And Rupp always had "a knack for stepping in front of the camera," according to Linville Puckett. "You can lead Coach Rupp all around town with a flash attachment."[71]

Not only was Rupp intent on publicity from the press, but he also furbished his reputation through his own publications. In 1957 a revised edition of his textbook, *Rupp's Championship Basketball: For Player, Coach and Fan*, appeared. The first edition had come out in 1948, the year of his first national championship. Rupp dedicated both editions "To the Memory of My Mother, Greatest and Best of All My Teachers, and To My Boys, Wherever They May Be." He then listed five former players who had been killed in the European and Pacific theaters during World War II. In the preface he displayed his penchant for poetry: "Since this book covers a subject in which there is so much change, I necessarily have been reminded of a poem that has come to my desk which I believe illustrates perfectly that, as time goes on, this book too shall pass away."

A mighty monarch in the days of old
Made offer of high honor, wealth, and gold
To one who should produce in form concise
A motto for his guidance, terse, yet wise;
A precept, soothing in his hours forlorn,
Yet one that in his prosperous days would warn.
Many the maxims sent the King, men say,
The one he chose . . . "This too shall pass away"![72]

Rupp said that he had received "hundreds of requests during the past few years to write a book on basketball so that coaches might have an exact picture of our style of basketball." He included chapters on "Getting Ready for the Season," "On Watching Basketball: A Word to the Fan," and on various "Fundamentals." He also wrote about "Diet and Training Table," the "Duties of a Manager," "A Coach's Relationship to His Players," and "Scouting." The second edition added game and practice photographs of his Kentucky players, illustrating skills and drills.[73]

Sports Illustrated asked Rupp to write a feature article, and "Defeat and Failure to Me Are Enemies" appeared in the December 8, 1958, issue. "The philosophy that has governed the lives of the boys here at the University of Kentucky in the past 28 years may not have been different from that which has been employed elsewhere, but its application may have been better," Rupp wrote. "Unfortunately, today in the sports world too many coaches are constantly worrying about what the other coach is doing rather than spending their time in a constructive way developing talent that is at their disposal."[74]

Not bashful about his success, he alternated between the practical and the philosophical. He returned to several favorite themes: a comparison of a coach to a teaching professor, team unity, overcoming difficulty, a comparison of success in basketball to success in other sports, and a recitation of the tenets of free enterprise and Social Darwinism.

"We here at the university," he said, "believe that every coach should have a definite plan and that every practice session should have an aim and a purpose. It is my opinion that if you have a well-organized practice, conducted along the same lines as those employed by a successful professor in chemistry, law or medicine, and if the boys see that there is a reason for them to repeat hundreds of times the fundamental details that are essential in developing a good basketball player, the work will not only be done well, but will also be done with enthusiasm."[75] Rupp demanded full attention to the game whenever his players were on the court:

> He was greatly amused at a sportswriter who visited us here this past winter. He came out to watch our practice. My boys shot their free throws, took their warm-up practice shots and then went to our fundamental drills and to our organized play. When the practice was over, the sportswriter said, "Don't these boys ever talk?" I said, "Yes, they talk occasionally, but it is generally understood out there that no one is to speak unless he can improve on the silence!" He said, "Don't your boys ever have any fun?" I said, "Yes, they have as much fun, or more, than any other players. Why should boys constantly chatter in a class in basketball any more than they do in a class in English? Why should they whistle and sing? I don't believe that you can get the maximum efficiency from a boy and have his undivided attention whenever you have a lot of noise at a practice session."[76]

During the national championship run, Rupp wrote, "We told our boys [when] everyone prophesied that we would not win, that if we would all get together and work as a unit, pay careful attention to fundamental details, that, possibly, we could become the Cinderella team of all time. Up to that time, the praises that were passed out to our boys were not great. Our boys were considered average in ability by everyone. However, you cannot measure the desire in a boy, you cannot measure the heart in a boy. I told them that if we would all work together as a unit, we could win." "Boys," he told his team, "it is just this simple; individually we will not go anywhere; as a unit, we can. The time has come when either you have to fish or cut bait."[77]

Rupp outlined for his readers a typical road trip, emphasizing that all attempts were made to minimize the time the athletes were away from the campus and classes. "On our trips we try to relax as much as possible," he wrote.

> Most of the boys take books with them. We usually like to practice at home on Friday night, then have our dinner at Lexington and catch a plane at 7 o'clock, say, to Knoxville. By the time the boys get to the

hotel and check in, it is bedtime. We get up in the morning at 7:45 and have breakfast together. We give the boys freedom until about 10 o'clock, then we go out to the gym and shoot baskets for about 30 minutes. This serves a twofold purpose: it breaks the monotony and it accustoms us to the place where we will play that night. We eat at 12 o'clock, have a short chalk talk to go over our last-minute notes, then the boys retire to their rooms from 2 to 5, where they can either study or rest, whichever they prefer. The main thing is that they are relaxing and are off their feet. After the game we fly back to Lexington, eat on the plane, and usually are home in bed by midnight. We lose very little time from school on these trips.[78]

Despite the 1958 championship, Rupp still smarted from the repercussions of the point-shaving scandal at the beginning of the decade. He always assumed that he and his teams were victims rather than perpetrators of the offense. "Unfortunately," he wrote,

the road to anywhere is filled with many pitfalls, and it takes a man of determination and character not to fall into them. As I have said many times, whenever you get your head above the average, someone will be there to take a poke at you. That is to be expected in any phase of life. However, as I have also said many times before, if you see a man on top of a mountain, he didn't just get there! Chances are he had to climb through many difficulties and with a great expenditure of energy in order to get there, and the same is true of a man in any profession, be he a great attorney, a great minister, a great man of medicine or a great businessman.[79]

Whether writing a basketball textbook or an article for *Sports Illustrated*, Rupp often found solace in the lines of some poem. In his article, he concluded that "any man who is successful in life will be envied by those less successful. I have always thought that an excerpt from Pakenham Beatty's *Self Reliance* contained a good philosophy for every coach":

By your own soul learn to live,
And if men thwart you, take no
heed,

If men hate you, have no care;
Sing your song, dream your
dream, hope your hope and
pray your prayer.[80]

Rupp likened success in basketball to success in other sports, but he also mixed in patriotism as he compared his success to free enterprise in a competitive world. "We do not wish merely to *participate* in sports," he wrote. "We wish to be *successful* in sports! In order to be successful we must create within these boys the competitive spirit that will bring success." He then made the statement that became the title of his *Sports Illustrated* article. "Defeat and failure to me are enemies. Without victory, basketball has little meaning. I would not give one iota to make the trip from the cradle to the grave unless I could live in a competitive world, and by competitive world I mean a democratic world where every boy has an opportunity to become the greatest in his chosen profession." Rupp made no place for girls and women in his competitive world. "When a boy lines up in the 100-meter dash in the Olympic Games and finds a Russian, an Englishman, a Frenchman and a German in the starting lanes next to him, when the gun is fired there is not a single subsidy in Washington which is going to bring him in first. When a man stands at the home plate with the bases loaded and two out, there isn't anything that anyone can do to help the pitcher or the batter. It is a competitive world," he concluded. "It is free enterprise and it should be encouraged."[81]

Rupp likened his philosophy of life to that of Etienne Gilson, who wrote: "True democracy in education certainly consists in insuring the intellectual survival of even the unfit; it cannot possibly consist in preventing the natural superiority of the fittest from bearing their fruits to the greater benefit of all." Rupp would agree. "Again let me repeat," he wrote, "it is the exceptional performances of the few which act as a challenge to all."[82]

It was in the area of race that Rupp's personal philosophy of democracy and success for all broke down.

11

Rupp and Race

T he *New York Times* hailed Mississippi State's participation in the 1963 NCAA tournament as "an important breakthrough in Southern race relations." The newspaper—just as the segregationists predicted would happen—had identified the "next logical step" for colleges in the South, the recruitment of black players.[1]

Texas Western College in El Paso, a member of the obscure Border Conference, took that next step before schools in the Southwest Conference, ACC, or SEC. Texas Western had admitted its first black students in September 1955, becoming "the first four-year Texas school to publicly do so." It was only one more year before two black basketball players, Charles Brown and his nephew Cecil Brown, enrolled as transfers from Amarillo Junior College. In November 1956, Charles Brown became "the first African American to play Division I basketball for an historically white university in the ex-Confederate South."[2] Texas Western recruited more black players when Don Haskins became coach in 1961.

Other schools followed suit. Murray State University in western Kentucky became the first school in the Ohio Valley Conference (OVC) and the first school in the southeastern United States to integrate in basketball, with Stewart Johnson in 1963.[3] Houston recruited Elvin Hayes and Don Chaney in 1964, the same year Louisville signed Wade Houston, Sam Smith, and Eddie Whitehead. Western Kentucky also integrated its basketball team that year. The three major southern conferences finally desegregated in the mid-1960s as well. ACC members Maryland and Wake Forest signed black basketball players in 1964, and Texas Christian broke the color line in the Southwest Conference in 1965. In the SEC, Vanderbilt coach Roy Skinner—with the full support of Chancellor Alexander Heard, who "had been quietly working to liberalize race relations" on campus—landed Nashville high school star and class valedictorian Perry Wallace in 1966. Wallace played in his first game in November 1967, and it was two more years before another African American, Auburn's Henry Harris, played in an SEC contest. Also in 1969, Wendell Hudson (Alabama), Ronnie Hogue (Georgia), and Tom Payne (Kentucky) were awarded scholarships. Those three would compete for the first time in 1970.[4] It took almost a decade after Adolph Rupp first recklessly stated in April 1961 that he would integrate the UK team before Payne took the floor in a blue and white uniform against Northwestern on December 1, 1970.

In 1966, Kentucky lost the NCAA championship game to Texas Western, the first Division I team in the South to integrate. That game proved to be a turning point in the integration of the SEC and its most prestigious member, whether or not people realized it at the time. But what about Rupp? What did he really believe? What did he really want to do? Was he a racist who failed to act, a man who held back the process of integration, as his critics claim? Or was he actually progressive in his views for the time, someone who often came to the aid of African Americans, as his friends and family attest?

Some sportswriters such as Billy Reed, Dave Kindred, and Earl Cox defend Rupp as a great, if curmudgeonly, coach whose reputation as a racist is unwarranted. Cox—the "dean and most honored sportswriter in Kentucky," according to a blurb on the back of his book, *Earl Cox: Calling It Like I See It*—argued that "Rupp was NOT a racist, now [sic] matter what others say."[5] The media depicted him that way "because UK had no African Americans on its team when it played all-black Texas Western and lost 72–65." If lily-white Duke had beaten UK in the semifinals and gone on to play Texas Western, "would its coach (Vic Bubas) have been considered a racist?" Cox asked. He cited Rupp's advocacy for a player at all-black Paris Western High School, helping him land a scholarship to another college, along with the coach's oft-cited work for the Shriners Hospital for Crippled Children, raising money "which helped many black children." According to Cox, Rupp knew the trials that a black player would face at Deep South venues. "Rupp was treated badly enough at some SEC schools. No telling what would have been done to a black Wildcat," Cox mused.

And "when St John's came to Lexington in 1951 with Solly Walker, the first black to play against UK in Lexington, the crowd treated him well because Rupp had arranged for *Herald* sports editor Ed Ashford to write a column asking UK fans to behave." What Perry Wallace went through at Vanderbilt, Cox argued, "was evidence that Adolph Rupp knew what he was talking about when he feared for a black player's safety in the SEC." "Say it over and over," Cox demanded. "Rupp was not a racist."[6]

Dave Kindred and Billy Reed echoed those sentiments. "Rupp has been cast as the racist villain," Kindred wrote, "but I've never bought into that point of view. . . . I'm not buying it."[7] Through the years, Reed, Cox, and Kindred maintained that the Rupp-as-racist line was a recent phenomenon. "This ugly and unfair misconception," Reed wrote in a 2006 essay, "is the work of revisionist historians who have taken the 1966 NCAA championship game between Kentucky and Texas Western and twisted it into something it wasn't." Chief among the revisionists, according to Reed, was Curry Kirkpatrick, whose April 1, 1991, *Sports Illustrated* piece titled "The Night They Drove Old Dixie Down" vilified Rupp. Reed contended that the 1966 game "was a terrific story, no question, but not because of race. Nobody wrote or talked about that aspect of it at the time." Instead, the game simply represented a "David vs. Goliath" spectacle with Kentucky and Rupp—once described by Rick Pitino as the "Roman Empire of college basketball"—pitted against "an upstart program from El Paso, Texas, that had never been even a blip on the national radar screen." Only later, Reed said, did the game become "a morality play" with Rupp as the villain. He argued that both ESPN and CBS "blew it." Reed said he agreed to be interviewed by both networks for documentaries, but "every time, the editors left out my comments defending Rupp and used only the stuff they thought would flesh out their one-dimensional stereotype."[8]

"The truth is," he wrote, "nobody knows what was in Adolph Rupp's heart. Of course, it's also true that nobody knows what was in the hearts of every man who coached football or basketball in the Southeastern Conference or Atlantic Coast Conference at that time. No university in either league recruited African-American athletes." Reed admitted that "Rupp was—and is—the perfect villain" for what he calls "this morality play" concocted by revisionist historians. "He has been likened to Eugene 'Bull' Connor, the bigoted public-safety director of Birmingham who laughingly ordered fire hoses and attack dogs to be used against civil rights protesters in 1963," Reed complained. "Bull and the Baron. Two of a kind, right? Absolutely not. But who in the media wants to let the truth stand in the way of a good storyline?"[9]

Reed made a list of "what we know about Rupp," including that he coached an African American player at Freeport High School; wrote a letter published in the *Lexington Herald* in 1951 asking that UK fans treat St. John's Solly Walker with respect; told Julius Berry, a black player for Lexington Dunbar in 1959, that he wished he could recruit him "but couldn't because of unwritten SEC policy," then helped Berry secure a scholarship at Dayton; "thought seriously" about recruiting Jerry Thurston from Owensboro in 1967; scheduled nonconference games against teams with black players, unlike any other team in the SEC except Vanderbilt; sent his team to the integrated NCAA Tournament when the Mississippi legislature forbade Mississippi State from participating; and offered scholarships to Louisville Seneca's Westley Unseld and Breckinridge County's Butch Beard.[10]

Reed cited these as examples of Rupp's progressive racial views. He said that *Sports Illustrated*'s Frank Deford was so convinced that Kentucky would sign Beard that he traveled to Lexington in 1965 to write a story "lauding UK's leadership in integration." Rupp liked the story so much that he welcomed Deford back in 1966 for another article that became a cover story, featuring the Baron himself. Reed also asserted that he never heard Rupp utter a racist remark and that he never heard any of his players in the mid-1960s—"Rupp's Runts"—claim the coach ever made a racist remark. (Deford would later claim that he witnessed a Rupp halftime harangue laced with racial epithets.)[11]

According to Reed, Rupp's role as an integration pioneer was usurped in the SEC when Vanderbilt coach Roy Skinner signed Perry Wallace in 1966 and in the ACC when North Carolina's Dean Smith signed Charlie Scott that same year. (Actually, ACC rivals Maryland and Wake Forest had signed black players in 1964.) Reed also argued that, when Smith's Tar Heels arrived at Standiford Field in Louisville for the 1967 Final Four, the players got off the plane waving Confederate flags, an action that at that time "was considered to be only an innocent display of regional pride, not a racist statement." When Rupp Arena was dedicated in 1976, UK athletic director Cliff Hagan arranged for an aging and ailing Rupp to sit in a big blue easy chair at midcourt. This was four years after he had coached his last game but before the revisionist historians had done their work. Reed argued that "nobody protested naming the arena for Rupp because nobody had yet bought into the Texas Western myth."[12]

Reed concluded that it was time to correct the misconceptions about Rupp and race. "The most significant way to honor the 30th anniversary of Rupp Arena," he wrote in 2006, "would be for all friends of the University of Kentucky to band together in a concerted effort to officially refute the widely accepted idea that the man for whom the building is named, former UK Coach Adolph Rupp, was the most vile racist in college sports."[13]

For Cox and Kindred and Reed, the idea of a racist Rupp didn't ring true.[14] Thousands of diehard UK fans concur. And for Rupp's family, what is to them the undeserved stigma continues to rankle. In 1992 Carlyle Farren Rupp, the coach's granddaughter, responded to columnist George Will's contention that Rupp was "a great coach, but a bad man." "I realize that his knowledge of my grandfather was limited," she wrote. "Consequently, truth can be an evasive and suppressed factor when it is not sought. . . . The insinuation that my grandfather was a racist could not be further from the truth." She pointed out that the fact that the SEC remained segregated until 1966 "never prevented him from actively seeking to help young black players receive scholarships to major universities in conferences that were integrated." In 1950, for example, Rupp helped Jim Tucker, a basketball star in Paris, Kentucky, get a scholarship to Duquesne, where he became an All-American.[15]

Farren Rupp described her grandfather's fundraising for the Shriners hospital, which treated "all crippled children, regardless of race, color, creed or ability to pay." She remembered seeing him "leave his home to attend a Shrine Hospital board meeting when he was dying of cancer." She brought up his trips to the Pralltown neighborhood to distribute circus tickets to black children. "I am proud to say that my family and I enjoy close friendships with many minority friends, especially blacks," she wrote.[16]

Herky Rupp, Farren's father, echoed her sentiments, saying that his father's "reputation for not wanting blacks on the team was undeserved." He argued that Rupp recruited players such as Westley Unseld, Ron Thomas, and Jim McDaniels, but they didn't want to become the school's first black player. "He wanted to recruit players that could play," Herky said, "not because of their color. Daddy tried to recruit quality."[17]

Even former Boston Celtics coach Red Auerbach weighed into the debate. In his collaboration with John Feinstein, *Let Me Tell You a Story: A Lifetime in the Game*, Auerbach said that winning basketball games trumped all other priorities for Rupp:

> Let me tell you something about Rupp. All I ever hear from people is that he was a racist. You know what? He did hate black guys—who couldn't play! He also hated white guys who couldn't play, blue guys who couldn't play and green guys who couldn't play. He hated Jews who couldn't play, Catholics who couldn't play and Muslims who couldn't play. That was it. All these people who never met the guy said he was a racist. I *knew* the guy. I traveled with him, I spent time with him. I never saw any sign from him or heard anything from him that indicated to me that he was a racist or a bigot in any way.[18]

Auerbach recalled a 1955 trip in which he, Rupp, and Celtics star Bob Cousy conducted a series of clinics in West Germany. Sidney Cohen, "an Air Force guy," helped with the clinic. "He was a good player," Auerbach said, and "without saying anything to me, Rupp recruited him—convinced him to go to Kentucky. Now, if he were anti-Semitic, why would he recruit Sidney Cohen?"[19]

In December 2005, Dick Gabriel, the sports manager at WKYT-TV in Lexington, produced a documentary to try to set the record straight. In *Adolph Rupp: Myth, Legend and Fact*, Gabriel asked, "Who was Adolph Rupp, and why have people been saying those horrible things about him?" Although he grew up in Louisville rooting for the Wildcats while at the same time believing that Rupp "was an avowed racist who wound up losing his job because he refused to recruit black players," Gabriel heard a different story after enrolling in the UK School of Journalism and embarking on a career in broadcast journalism.[20]

Gabriel set out to find out for himself. He assured his audience that his documentary was not a response to the movie *Glory Road*, the movie about the Texas Western game, and that it was not "warm and fuzzy." Instead, he claimed that it delved "into some of the ugly things said and written about Rupp, and about his own failings, which were common to people of his era." Gabriel's research convinced him that "Rupp *was* trying to change—himself, his program, the league, but always within the confines of the rank and file."[21]

At the outset of the project, Gabriel asked his 15-year-old son what he knew about Rupp. The reply: "Great coach. Won a lot of championships. Didn't like black people." Gabriel asked why he would say that. "I don't know," his son replied. Gabriel wanted the documentary to help his son and others understand the origins of the legend, to understand Rupp better. "I remember how much I knew about Rupp when I was [his son's] age," he said. "And changing my own perspective took me on an interesting journey."[22] In the end, Gabriel's documentary comes off as little more than an apologia, a string of interviews designed to ward off the criticism that *Glory Road* would bring to Rupp and his program.

Many of Rupp's supporters present more compelling arguments in his defense. Dave Whitney, the longtime coach at Alcorn State, grew up in Midway, Kentucky, in the 1930s but attended high school in Lexington. He and his high school teammates attended UK games in Alumni Gym and tried to meet the players. Apparently, Rupp "took a liking to" Whitney and one of his friends and allowed the two teens to attend practices. "A lot of kids didn't like me because of that," Whitney said. "We were 14, 15 years old and the only black faces in the place." But that's where Whitney learned how to run a practice. "Rupp's practices ran just like clockwork," he said. "Every minute was detailed. I think he is one of the all-time great coaches." As for Rupp's faults, he said, "I didn't care about the other stuff. I know what I got from him."[23]

Regardless of all that testimony, some of the evidence against Rupp is damning. His language at times suggested at least a troubling attitude toward African Americans, even if that language was common for the times in the South. According to Alexander Wolff's book *Raw Recruits*, Rupp called Jimmy Breslin, at that time a young sports reporter for the *New York Journal-American*, in the early 1960s and asked him to "kindly indicate 'colored' high school players with asterisks so Rupp would know where not to bother to send his recruiters."[24] It is unclear whether he made this request so that he wouldn't waste time recruiting blacks or because he simply wanted to know if a player was black.

Harry Lancaster attributed another remark—this time in a Memorial Coliseum office—to Rupp in his book, *Adolph Rupp: As I Knew Him.* Following a meeting with UK president John Oswald in the mid-1960s, an agitated Rupp returned to his office and told Lancaster: "Harry, that son of a bitch is ordering me to get some niggers in here. What am I going to do? He's the boss."[25] Lancaster remembered: "Oswald was putting on the pressure for us to integrate the black player into our program. I didn't see where we had much choice, but Adolph had never been around blacks, and I think he worried about the unknown." Lancaster wrote that Rupp told him "one time that he had told Oswald he would sign a black player as soon as he could find one that was sure to start. He didn't want the blacks sitting on the bench." "He told me that Oswald told him the blacks could sit right there on the bench with the white players," Lancaster explained. Only after the president's repeated urgings, Lancaster wrote, did Rupp recruit "a few blacks," but "without any success."[26] Lancaster's candor is telling, especially in its published form. But in a 2003 interview, former University of Kentucky president Frank Dickey stated that the "real racist" on the UK basketball staff was Harry Lancaster and not Adolph Rupp.[27] Lancaster's book was published in 1979, after Rupp's death and after Lancaster's tenure as UK's athletic director. His acrimonious relationship with his former boss led to such strain that they barely talked to each other in the last five years of Rupp's coaching career. Lancaster had no scruples in refusing to protect Rupp against an increasing barrage of racist accusations at the time his book came out.

After he retired, Rupp remembered one particular meeting with Oswald. "Finally, it came time for another conference up there, at the president's office," Rupp told Russell Rice. "The president I don't think liked it too well, but he said, 'I'm just going to tell you what I'm going to do. I'm going to demand that you get some colored boys.' He says, 'You're keeping us, and probably jeopardizing us from getting us all this federal help which amounts to some 11 million dollars,' and he said, 'If we don't get this through, it's because basketball is the last segregated department that we have here in the University.'" Rupp said he responded with sarcasm: "'Well, Doctor, if you can help me any, suppose you help me go and recruit then. It's just that simple. I made an effort.' I says, 'I brought you the list and told you the times, and we made an effort to go get these boys and we haven't been able to get them.' And I said, 'I can't get them. I had Bernie Shively go with me and we couldn't get them.' I said, 'Now, if you and Bob Johnson [UK's vice president for student affairs] can get them,' I says, 'hop to it.' I said, 'It's going to suit me fine.'"

By the 1960s, a hierarchy of sorts had been established to deal with the university's segregated athletic program. Rupp's assistants answered to him, of course, and Rupp reported any efforts he made to recruit black players to Bernie Shively, who then reported to Robert Johnson, who reported to the president. With the death of Shively in 1967, Johnson was named the acting athletic director, and he also was chairman of the athletics committee. Rupp surely bristled at the involvement of the administration in his basketball program. He especially resented the meddling of the new president. John W. "Jack" Oswald became UK's sixth president in 1963.

In a series of interviews in 1987, Oswald discussed his desire to integrate the university fully. "I felt that the university, in an area where it was so highly visible, should clearly make some kind of major effort with respect to minorities," he said. "Keep in mind that the nation's eyes were focused in the summer of '63 on Bull Connor and Alabama and George Wallace standing in the door and . . . the problems in Mississippi with Ross Barnett and (James) Meredith. There was so much focus on those institutions that weren't integrated." Oswald remembered that "there was no affirmative action program, and the Civil Rights Act wasn't signed by Johnson until 1964. There was very little discussion about what positive steps should be taken on behalf of the total black population." Oswald believed that Kentucky was situated well to make advances in integration because there was no "external pressure" in a border state, unlike Mississippi and Alabama.[28]

Soon after arriving at UK, Oswald announced, "We ought to be responsive to *all* the qualified citizens of the state." Even though the student body had been integrated by then, there still were no black faculty members. That soon changed when Oswald hired Joseph Scott as an assistant professor of sociology. He also decided to "make this special effort in athletics." He admitted: "I knew that's where we were so highly visible." Thus began his meetings with Rupp. "I tried to convince Adolph Rupp and Harry Lancaster that UK ought to be *the* leader or at least one of the leaders, being in a border state, in this area." In his very first discussions with Rupp, however, Oswald claimed, "[The coach] sounded to me like a bigot. . . . I guess primarily it was his language and expressions. He tended to refer to blacks in terms which are now considered derogatory, but which in prior years would more or less have been accepted without notice."[29]

At that time New York center Lew Alcindor (later to become Kareem Abdul-Jabbar) was widely regarded as the best high school basketball player in the nation. Oswald said that when he asked Rupp why he wasn't recruiting Alcindor, the coach replied, "First of all, if some of my coaches were to go down and talk to some good player in Louisville, he'd find the player had already been talked to by Purdue, Indiana, and Illinois." Rupp told Oswald that recruiters from northern schools would tell a black prospect, "Now look . . . if you go and play for Kentucky, you're going to have to go out on the floor in Alabama and Louisiana and Mississippi and Georgia, but if you come with us, you're going to go out on the floor in Minnesota, Michigan and Iowa." Rupp told Oswald, "This was a very powerful argument to these kids. Secondly, if I get one, he's got to be the best. Suppose I got one not quite good enough so that he would have to sit on the bench. They'd all give me hell every day for not sticking this black boy in there. So I cannot have one unless he is absolutely going to be among the top five, but better, the top one or two, and that's why I'd take Alcindor if I could get him."

When it became clear that Alcindor was heading to UCLA, Oswald encouraged Rupp to set his sights on Louisville Seneca center Westley Unseld, the best player in Kentucky.[30] Both Rupp and Oswald visited Unseld's home, but at separate times, "a symbol," according to Billy Reed, "of the differences between them." Oswald did not remember that Rupp made it to the Unseld home—"He didn't get into the recruiting, you know"—but he did recall the particulars of his own visit. He said he told Lancaster: "Harry, I'd like to take a shot at it. I wonder what this boy'd say if I went in there as president of the university." "Anyway," Oswald remembered, "I went to his home, and the mother and father were very gracious to me, and he was, too. He said, 'Thank you for coming, but I've already decided to stay here in Louisville.' He had an opportunity to say some nasty things about Rupp and Kentucky, but he did not say them. I was halfway expecting him to say, 'I wouldn't play under Rupp,' but he didn't. It was a gracious visit."[31]

Unseld contended that Rupp visited his home when he knew the Seneca star would be away. When Rupp finally began to recruit black players, "there was always some excuse," Unseld said. "The player didn't have the grades. The player didn't have the skills. At least those were excuses that couldn't be used [in Unseld's case]."[32] Articulate, polite, and a good student with sound basketball skills, the 6-foot-8-inch, 230-pound Unseld would have made Rupp's Runts even more formidable. Rupp must have recognized that fact.

Unseld remembered, "There was a lot of pressure brought to bear from the black community" for him to go to UK, and "there was a lot of pressure brought from (he laughed) a lot of people that I better not do it." Although his family received threatening letters and phone calls from white racists, other reasons helped him make his decision. In a 1992 *Lexington Herald-Leader* article headlined "Spurned by UK in '60s, Wes Unseld to Coach in House that Rupp Built," about his return to Lexington as head coach of the NBA's Washington Bullets, Jerry Tipton wrote that "Unseld once embodied Adolph Rupp's reluctance to recruit black players for the University of Kentucky." But Rupp did at least go through the motions of recruiting him in 1964. A misunderstanding marred Rupp's visit to the Unseld home—"or something more sinister," Tipton wrote—that indicated to Unseld that the Kentucky coach did not really, earnestly want him. Unseld notified the university that he would not be home the night of Rupp's scheduled visit because he had accepted an invitation to speak at the LaGrange Reformatory. "That was OK with them," he recalled, because "they wanted to speak to my parents." The next day, though, Unseld heard the nasty rumor that he "didn't have the courtesy to stay at the meeting."[33] Rupp offered him a scholarship, but the family understandably wondered if Oswald had just pressured Rupp.

On the Friday morning of the high school state tournament in UK's Memorial Coliseum, Unseld met with what Russell Rice called "Kentucky's inner ring," a group who tried to persuade him to enroll at UK. But when Seneca played Breckinridge County in the championship game the next evening, Billy Reed remembered that "the capacity crowd booed Unseld and his Seneca teammates." Reed acknowledged that "some of that may have come from racists," although Breckinridge County star Butch Beard also was black, but he concluded that "most of it probably came because state tournament crowds in Lexington historically cheered against the big-city Louisville teams and for the underdogs from out in the state." Beard and Breckinridge County "perfectly fit the profile for a Cinderella team," not Unseld and Louisville Seneca.[34] "I remembered being booed," Unseld said in a 1980 interview, "but at that time I attributed that to the Breckinridge County people and not the UK fans." More important, perhaps, was his memory of how he was treated there: "I couldn't eat in the restaurant across the street from our hotel, because they didn't serve black people. That sort of thing might have been going on in Louisville at the time, but I didn't know about it if it was." Lexington remained segregated in 1964; the *Lexington Leader* still carried a daily column titled "Colored Notes and News," by Gertrude Moberly.[35]

Ohio State soon became Unseld's first choice, and he also considered Kansas, where his older brother had played, and Illinois. When his father suffered a heart attack, however, the University of Louisville came more clearly into focus. "I thought Louisville was close by," he said, "and he'd get to see me play."[36] All of these factors convinced him he should play for Peck Hickman at home in Louisville.

Larry Conley remembered visiting Unseld and trying to persuade him to become a Wildcat. "His first words to me," Conley recalled, "were 'Larry, I don't want to be the first.'" Unseld remembered it differently. "I don't think that Kentucky had to wait until I came along to have a black player," he stated in a 2006 interview. "And, yeah, I get angry when I see people trying to rewrite that. I think with as much power as [Rupp] had, if he wanted someone with as much intelligence and skill as some of those white players, he could have had them long before me. They never seriously recruited me, and those who say they did are not dealing with the facts."[37]

Eventually, Unseld's "favorite niece" would enroll at UK. "I thought, 'How could you?'" he said, "but I realized that had nothing to do with her. She wasn't even born when most of that happened. You're talking about a different time and different people. . . . There's no sense dwelling on any of that."[38] In retrospect, Rupp's inability to sign Unseld in 1964 probably cost the Wildcats a national championship two years later, and it cemented his legacy on the issue of race.

It was Charlie Bradshaw's football program that integrated athletics at UK and the Southeastern Conference. Bradshaw signed Nat Northington of Louisville's Thomas Jefferson High School and Greg Page of Middlesboro in 1965. President Oswald had played a role in the signing of Northington by visiting his home, just as he did with Unseld. An elated Oswald wrote to his friend Clark Kerr, president of the University of California at Berkeley: "Through my efforts we have now awarded a football scholarship to a Negro, the first in the history of the SEC, and I expect other schools in the conference to follow suit shortly."[39] It is evident how important Oswald deemed this event for the state. Kentucky's governor, Edward Breathitt, also helped recruit Northington and Page, making telephone calls to both. Northington's mother felt that the governor had put too much pressure on her son and told Breathitt, "If I find that his life is in danger by playing football in the Southern states, I will be forced to take action to haul him somewhere else where he won't be abused."[40]

Her concern proved to be well-founded, but not in the way she had envisioned. Northington suffered a dislocated shoulder in a 1967 home game against Mississippi, and Page was paralyzed from a neck injury in a preseason practice. Page died a month after the injury, and Northington left school midway through his sophomore season.

With what appeared to be the successful integration of the football team, pressure mounted on Rupp to follow suit. The *Kernel*, UK's student newspaper, published articles about the issue, and the Black Student Union and others picketed outside Memorial Coliseum during games.[41] Rupp turned his attention, again belatedly, to Breckinridge County's six-foot-three-inch guard Butch Beard, now the state's best player. His team lost to Unseld and Seneca in the 1964 state final, then won the championship in 1965 when Beard was a senior.

To the irritation of University of Louisville coaches and officials, Breathitt again played a leading role in the recruitment of a black athlete for UK, even giving Beard a tour of the campus. It was part of the governor's larger plan to promote integration throughout the commonwealth. At a time when he was pushing strong civil rights legislation, he was convinced that the integration of basketball at the state's flagship university would benefit the entire state. "Not only will it help the image of the state, but it is the right thing to do," he said. There were financial reasons, too. Federal dollars from Lyndon B. Johnson's programs to build new college classrooms and dormitories flooded the state, and Breathitt did not want racial recalcitrance to retard any Great Society largesse.[42] All this information filtered down to Rupp through his talks with Oswald. And if Rupp hated the involvement of the university's administration with his team, he certainly resented any interference by the state or federal government. He understood the larger implications of integration, but he resented them nonetheless.

Butch Beard had grown up listening to Cawood Ledford's broadcasts of UK games. He realized later that the radio "happens to be a terrific cloaking device for segregation," and "it never dawned on Beard that Rupp's program wasn't one he could aspire to."[43] By the time he reached his senior year, UK's signing of two black football players, the push by Breathitt and Oswald, and Rupp's overtures, however reluctant and belated, seemed to open the way for his enrollment. Beard talked with his parents, consulted with Unseld, then called Peck Hickman at Louisville, just as Unseld had done.

Beard decided to go ahead with a campus visit in Lexington. There he talked with the Kentucky players. In Beard's opinion, Pat Riley, a sophomore from Schenectady, New York, "was different, even then." *New York Times* sportswriter Harvey Araton believed that Riley "was most likely chosen to usher Beard around the Lexington campus precisely because he was no farm boy, because he was different." Riley remembered that race was not "a factor with the players, at least not that I knew, but it was a big deal for others." He recalled that Unseld had gotten death threats when he was being recruited by UK.[44]

An issue for Beard and his family—as it was for Nat Northington's mother, and even for Adolph Rupp—was how a black player would be treated at games in Mississippi and Alabama. Rupp failed to convince Beard and his family that all would be well. "I didn't know if that meant he really didn't want me, or if he was just being honest," Beard said.[45] Tommy Kron, another UK player, remembered going with Rupp to Hardinsburg to visit Beard. Kron later contended that although Rupp was "a difficult man" who was "hard on his players and others, he was no racist." "I never saw that side of him or heard him act in a racist manner," he said.[46] Beard remembered Rupp in his living room, "sipping his mother Maybel's iced tea, bragging about how reviled he was in a Southeastern Conference sick of being dominated by his Wildcats." "He told us how they cursed him in Tennessee and threw bottles at him in Alabama," Beard recalled. His mother asked Rupp, "If that happens to you, then what's going to happen to my son?" Beard remembered that Rupp smiled and said, "Miss Beard, A'hm gonna take real good care of yoah boy." Those assurances seemed insincere to the Beards. "We decided that Rupp was under pressure to recruit a black player, but he really didn't want to," Beard concluded.[47]

Sports Illustrated sent a young reporter named Frank Deford to cover UK's recruitment of Beard. "Beard could have been the SEC pioneer had Kentucky—and particularly Coach Adolph Rupp—acted earlier," Deford wrote. "Not until after Beard had signed a secret letter of intent to go to U of L did Rupp convince him that the school really wanted Negro athletes.

That almost made him change his mind." Deford was convinced that by this time Rupp's efforts were sincere. "In the future," he contended, "Southern Negro youngsters are going to find it easy to stay close to home. The motives of the men involved in lifting the last barrier to Negro participation in college athletics may be purely pragmatic. They want their schools to be a winner. But the results are nonetheless beneficial. Beard was recruited as an athlete and became, only incidentally, a Negro. Henceforth, on these terms, Southern schools will recruit other Southern Negroes."[48] Deford proved prophetic. Nonetheless, the pioneer would not be Butch Beard, and the coach would not be Adolph Rupp. Beard followed Unseld to Louisville, and it would be another few years before the first black basketball player would hit the hardwood at Memorial Coliseum in a Kentucky Wildcats uniform.

In 1966, at the end of his freshman year at U of L, Beard sat in his dormitory room and watched Texas Western defeat Kentucky for the national championship. A sportswriter wrote that "the lifelong Wildcat fan was beside himself." "I felt like they had proved, once and for all, that black players could win big games at that level," Beard remembered.[49]

Rupp failed to lure Unseld and Beard to Lexington, but in the early 1960s he also lost out on white players that he coveted, including Lexington's Jeff Mullins, a high school All-American in 1960. "Rupp wanted him in the worst way," John Oswald said. Mullins, however, decided that he wanted to play for a school away from Lexington. Oswald remembered that an exasperated Rupp said, "Well, you know, we could move the university to Paris or to Georgetown."[50]

Oswald's desire to recruit African American athletes was obvious. Terry Birdwhistell, a UK archivist who interviewed the former president in 1987, understood the importance of the issue in the 1960s: "This shows the degree of the pressure that was mounting that you have the university president and the governor both involved in trying to recruit black players." Birdwhistell asked Oswald, "Do you think that Rupp was doing what he should in trying to integrate his basketball team?" "No," Oswald replied bluntly. His opinion of Rupp soured soon after the two met, and it wasn't just from Rupp's perceived bigotry. He instead described Rupp as arrogant:

I just feel that he was the biggest egotist that I've ever known. He is the only person, in my experience, who wanted to have a bigger office so that he'd have more wall space upon which to hang the plaques honoring himself. I think I made Adolph angry when I asked him if he'd ever been to an art museum. He said, "What do you mean?" And I responded, "In an art museum they have dividers that are on wheels and you can hang pictures on both sides. And you can walk around it and see the pictures on the other side. In your office you could have three of those dividers [laughter by interviewer Birdwhistell] and you could triple the plaques you've got in there."[51]

"What was it he said when he heard you were coming?" Birdwhistell asked. "I believe he said, 'It looks like our new president is a —— lover,'" Oswald replied. "One of the first things I told Rupp was that I had heard so much about him and his success in basketball, but that it seemed to me that one of the things facing us as a border-state, public institution at that time was clearly the recruitment of some black athletes." He added that he told Rupp that he understood UK's reputation in the area of basketball, which meant that he surely could attract the best black players: "They had already demonstrated that they're right at the top. I told him that it seemed to me that he should have an interest from the standpoint of talent, if for nothing else, and that I certainly had an interest and I thought he should, too. I felt UK should be able to recruit some of the better black players." "But he had strong feelings about this," Oswald said. "Apparently there had been some efforts in this direction by whoever recruits for him—either his assistant coach, friends of the team or alumni—and they sensed that the black players didn't want to go to Kentucky because of the schedule and the places they would have to play. As I said earlier, Rupp felt very keenly about not recruiting a black that might sit on the bench. Because, he said, 'I can just hear them booing me for not putting this guy in.'"[52]

Oswald said the coach and his reputation had not been an issue in his own hiring in 1963. He admired Rupp's players—Pat Riley, Louie Dampier, Larry Conley, and, before them, Cotton Nash. "They were all fine youngsters," he said. "The players were not ruffians. He did not go out and get some kids off the street. If you want to look at his better side, he might have felt that the blacks might be disruptive in that they might not be as well-mannered and as well-disciplined. And he was a great person on discipline of his boys—what they did and how they looked and so forth."[53]

On the other hand, Oswald believed that Rupp "had very little interest in the basic purposes of the university. I went to one alumni meeting with Rupp, and he spent most of his time telling the alumni that the faculty was overpaid." Rupp had long abandoned his leisurely talks in the offices of various faculty members. Oswald remembered that by the 1960s the faculty was "on him all the time." Oswald eventually left UK to become president at Penn State, home of another coaching legend in football's Joe Paterno. Oswald remembered that the UK faculty loved Rupp's teams, "but there was about as much anti feeling toward Rupp as there [was] pro feeling toward Joe Paterno at Penn State." "I mean, they knew Rupp didn't tune in to the academic area," Oswald said. Rupp came to UK with a master's degree, but Oswald doubted that he "knew UK had a library, or if he did, where it was." At the alumni meeting, Rupp made his harangue about the faculty being overpaid just after Oswald had "made a plea about the needs of the university if one wished to build excellence." "I was presenting the average of the salaries at the universities in the states surrounding Kentucky," he asserted.[54]

Oswald's struggles were reminiscent of the concerns of President Frank McVey during the 1930s. Even then, while McVey wanted to emphasize the academic mission of the university, Rupp was beginning the process that would lead to bloated athletic budgets and an unhealthy devotion to athletics by alumni and fans. Judge Saul Streit had referred to UK basketball as "the acme of professionalism" in the 1950s, following the point-shaving scandal. In the 1960s, UK athletics had only gotten bigger, often at the expense of academics. After Oswald left the university, Rupp's friend Happy Chandler criticized the former president after a basketball victory against Missouri. "Our team beat Missouri," Chandler said, "but we have been defeated by Oswald." He was referring to Oswald's appointment, just before he left, of four professors to the athletics board.[55]

Chandler never criticized Oswald's efforts to integrate UK athletics, which Oswald took as "in a sense a compliment, because he was critical of most everything" he did. The former governor did criticize him for not emphasizing athletics enough. Oswald recalled that Chandler once had gone through the minutes of the board of trustees and found "that two years had gone by and I'd never mentioned athletics once to the board." Oswald told Chandler, "Governor, I didn't have any reason to." As a student at DePauw, Oswald had captained the football team, lettered in track, and played on the freshman basketball team. He loved college athletics, but he maintained that rather than de-emphasizing sports at UK, he was "re-emphasizing the role of the athlete as a student." Rupp's players were usually good students, and they attended class faithfully (on the 1965–1966 team, only Louie Dampier failed to complete a degree). Oswald praised the coach for this, but at the same time he concluded that "Rupp didn't really care, except that he was smart enough to know that if he had a guy for three or four years, he was going to improve each year."[56] It became obvious, at least to Oswald, that Rupp did not understand or care to understand the purpose of a university and the subordinate role that athletics should play in its mission.

During a 1987 interview, Oswald at first could not recall an instance when he publicly criticized Rupp, but then he remembered that he did so just once, though he couldn't recall the details. The incident led to a *Louisville Courier-Journal* editorial congratulating him "for taking Rupp on." "This was another evidence of my 'courage,'" Oswald joked.[57]

He had even more trouble with Charlie Bradshaw, whose talk of "total athletics or total football" rankled Oswald. Bradshaw's reputation for his almost inhumane treatment of his players during the season and in the off-season was well-earned. "My own conclusion on these two people as professionals is that Rupp was a great coach," Oswald said, "and part of his effectiveness was the great discipline that he maintained, as difficult as he was at times to deal with." As for Bradshaw, "he was not smart and certainly had no creativeness."[58] And as for the athletic director who ostensibly was the boss of both coaches, Oswald said: "Oh, Bernie Shively was a gentleman all the way. I had an excellent relationship with him. I think he learned to tolerate Rupp and Bradshaw in a way. And he could be persuasive with them on certain matters that I'm sure I couldn't have been without just a direct order. I thought Shively was one of the real gentlemen in the field."

In a later recruiting effort, Shively referred to a black prospect as "a high-type Negro"—his way to praise the student—but Oswald did not think Shively shared Rupp's reluctance to recruit African Americans.[59] "Oh, I don't think he was against it," Oswald said, "but Bernie was not aggressive, you know, 'Let's go out and get 'em' kind of person. So I think he was philosophically for it but not aggressively for it. It was not in his nature to go on a crusade." Oswald concluded that Shively "was not the blockage." "No, in fact, he encouraged me in this visit to Unseld," he said.

As for Shively's relationship with Rupp, Oswald believed "it was pretty much understood that Rupp went his way as long as he didn't arbitrarily break conference rules or NCAA rules." "I used to worry about Charlie [Bradshaw] sneaking in somebody who had no business being at UK," Oswald remembered, "but I never worried about Rupp on that."[60]

Bradshaw knew he did not have the confidence of the president. "He was always angry with me for doing away with his football houses, the 'ape houses,'" Oswald said. Bradshaw housed his football players in separate dormitories away from nonathletes. With the building of new, larger dorms, Oswald informed Bradshaw that his players "should be scattered," and he denied the coach's request to at least house them in a block within the dorms. This had not been a concern with Rupp and his basketball players. Rupp "didn't want them to get in trouble together," Oswald said. "I didn't agree with some of his ideas, but I think Rupp's record shows that he was smarter than Bradshaw. But I must say, neither of them was pleasant to deal with."[61]

When asked to compare Rupp and Joe Paterno, Oswald made some interesting observations (of course, long before the revelations of the Jerry Sandusky pedophilia scandal at Penn State):

Well, they were both, technically, people who know their sport and they are very smart people in their respective fields. They were both good disciplinarians and they both demanded respect from their players. Beyond this, they were totally different in almost every aspect. Joe achieved respect through teaching, demonstration and persuasion, whereas I feel Adolph was much more rough, demanding and at times crude. Paterno is first and foremost an educator, and I mean an educator with a capital E. He is fundamentally interested in education. He truly respects the value of a university and what it means to a state. He really is interested in the quality of the institution of which he's a part, as well as the quality of the team that represents it. On the other hand, Rupp was not an educator other than that he was a teacher of basketball. But I don't really feel that he cared much at all, except possibly nostalgically and politically, about the University of Kentucky. He certainly didn't care about the quality of its faculty, the stature of its library, what was going on in research or any of that. At least I never saw any sign of that.[62]

Whereas Rupp was forced to retire at 70, Paterno continued to coach at Penn State into his 80s and, after weathering some lean years, was named National Coach of the Year in 2006. The humiliation of the Sandusky scandal followed.

Rupp's racial views apparently became more regressive as he grew older. After he retired, another documented instance of his using a racial slur occurred just a few years before his death. In his book about the American Basketball Association titled *Loose Balls*, Terry Pluto related a conversation that an inebriated Rupp had with attorney Ron Grinker in the mid-1970s on a flight to Memphis to promote the American Basketball Association Memphis Tams franchise. Owner Charles O. Finley had made Rupp the Tams' president and general manager, and the aging coach flew down to look over the operation.[63] Grinker told of his disappointment in a coaching legend whom he had admired:

> Once I was on a flight with Rupp and sat with him in the first-class section. He had about six Kentucky bourbons in less than an hour and was about halfway to the wind. I told him that I was an attorney who represented some basketball players. Now, I had never met the man, and the first significant thing he said to me was, "The trouble with the ABA is that there are too many nigger boys in it now." I sat there just stunned. That just killed my image of Adolph Rupp the great coach. Maybe it was because he had too much to drink, but even so.[64]

It would be difficult to dismiss Rupp's repeated use of racial epithets as the innocent ramblings of a curmudgeonly, and sometimes inebriated, rascal. His comment to Grinker appears eerily similar to a statement made more than a decade later by Happy Chandler, who as baseball commissioner oversaw the integration of that sport by Jackie Robinson in 1947. In a 1988 meeting of the UK trustees' investment committee, the discussion was about the university's decision to divest its South African investments. An aging Chandler remarked that "the question of Zimbabwe has arisen, and you know what's happened there. It's now all nigger. There are no white folks there anymore. The streets of Salisbury are boarded up. Grass is growing in the streets. And it's all changed."[65] The "Zimbabwe ruckus" or "nigger flap," as the newspapers dubbed it, sullied Chandler's earlier achievements in civil rights and followed him to the grave. Rupp's indiscretions have been resurrected again and again after the grave.

The relationship between Rupp and Chandler was an important one. They were very much alike in many ways. Controversial and disdained by eastern sportswriters, they both craved power and accomplished much, although their failures proved to be enormously consequential. Unlike Rupp, Chandler's courage left a lasting mark in the struggle for integration, and his role in the desegregation of baseball cannot be downplayed. By giving Brooklyn Dodgers owner Branch Rickey his blessing to sign Robinson, Chandler allowed baseball to lead the integration of American professional sports. Robinson endured the same punishing racism in park after park that Rupp claimed a black basketball player would face in the arenas of the Deep South. In Ken Burns's documentary history of baseball, the narrator praised Robinson's contribution: "This is a man who carried the future participation of his race in baseball on his shoulders. This is a man who led the civil rights movement in this country. It wasn't the armed forces. It wasn't a school bus. It wasn't a lunch counter. It wasn't a school. It was baseball that got integrated first. And when he trotted out to first base on April 15, 1947, Martin Luther King was a junior at Morehouse College."[66]

It would be another 22 years before Rupp signed a black athlete at UK. As governor in 1956, Chandler sent troops to Clay and Sturgis to carry out the integration of high schools in those small Western Kentucky towns. But the "Zimbabwe ruckus" suggested that his moral courage was nonetheless tempered with a paternalistic attitude toward African Americans. Said S. T. Roach, who served on the UK board with Chandler in 1988: "All he had to do was tell me that he was sorry. When he didn't, that told me he meant it."[67]

Certainly, Rupp and Chandler encouraged and influenced each other. Chandler said in 1989 that he treasured Rupp's "autograph in a book." Rupp wrote in it that he "was his best friend throughout all the years." Chandler acknowledged that Rupp "drank some" during his later years and "that caused him some trouble." "I worried about that a whole lot," the former governor divulged, "but there wasn't much I could do. Once or twice I remonstrated with him, but he didn't want anyone to tell him what to do. He was hard-headed and wanted to do what he wanted to do." Chandler admired Rupp's superior coaching skills: "Those qualities you've got to have in order to be a good coach. He was wise. He knew the game better than anybody. And he knew how to recruit, knew what to do with 'em after he got 'em. He was a special fellow." At the same time, the governor noted—with his own special brand of Kentucky candor: "Every now and then he got his tit in a wringer, and I got it out." With that statement, the candor ended. Chandler concluded that most of Rupp's problems were personal, and "it's better to let his troubles die with him."[68]

In the end Rupp signed only one black player, Tom Payne from Louisville's Shawnee High School. After his only varsity year—1970 to 1971—Payne entered the NBA draft as a hardship case. Payne's story would be painful and tragic.

12

Rupp's Runts and Runners-Up

At the end of the 15–10 season of 1964–1965, critics argued that an aging, mellowing Rupp had lost the fierce drive and sheer love for winning that had been evident in his heyday. "It appeared that the machine might be running down," one writer said. "Adolph looked poorly," another observer said. "He looked old and said he didn't feel good, and he looked it." One fan argued simply that "losing makes Adolph look old and poorly." Looking back on the 1964–1965 season, Rupp said: "I'm sure some folks thought last year, well, 'He's getting old, he's slowing down.' But I guess this season will show them that age can be an asset."[1] He did indeed answer his critics with his team's phenomenal performance in 1965–1966. And winning seemed to rejuvenate the coach, bringing a satisfaction that nothing else could produce.

The Wildcats sailed through the early season and were not seriously challenged until it took them two overtimes to win 69–65 at Georgia in their eleventh game. They followed that with an easy home victory over third-ranked Vanderbilt, 96–83. With star center Clyde Lee, Vanderbilt had joined number-one Duke and number-two Kentucky at the top of the polls. Unlike coaches who claim they pay no attention to rankings, Rupp apparently did. James Dickenson of the *National Observer* wrote late in January that Rupp was especially interested in the numbers one, two, and three: one for Duke, two for Kentucky, and three for "the margin between the two in the weekly Associated Press sportswriters' poll," a mere 12 points (Duke led UK 398–386 in the voting). Kentucky fans argued that although the Blue Devils had won 12 in a row, they also had lost 1, and they hadn't beaten anybody as strong as Vanderbilt. During a luncheon after the commanding win over the Commodores, Rupp expressed his dismay at not being voted number one. "That was as flawless a game as a Kentucky team has ever played," he told an applauding crowd. "We picked up 87 points in the ratings from the week before. Now we go after those other points." More applause.[2]

In the old days before the point-shaving scandal, Rupp made sure his players knew the point spread before games. Now, perhaps as a motivational tool, he made sure they knew the poll rankings. Apparently, he was aware of another fact he considered to be important concerning the polls. One day he halted practice, gathered his players around him, and told them: "Boys, when you go home tonight, I want you to look long and hard at these rankings. One. Two. Three. Kentucky. Duke. Vanderbilt. All from the South. And all white. Read it and remember. You'll never see it again." According to *Sports Illustrated*'s Curry Kirkpatrick, "The old man was right on the mark."[3] All-white teams would never again dominate college sports.

In game after game, Kentucky seemed to become more and more invincible. Opposing coaches and sportswriters became convinced that the Wildcats would go all the way to the NCAA title. On February 21 they beat Ole Miss 108–65 in the Rebels' first game in their new "swank and spacious" coliseum. Rupp's success had made it necessary for UK to build Memorial Coliseum to hold the Bluegrass masses, and now it had convinced other SEC schools that they should take the game more seriously. George Bugbee, a sportswriter for the *Memphis Press-Scimitar*, wrote that "they unofficially dedicated [the new Ole Miss coliseum] last night and looked officially dead doing it. It took $1.8 million and 18 months to build this 9,000-seat facility, and it will take time and money to build a team suitable to the surroundings." The old cracker-box gym seated only 2,400, "all uncomfortably," but the new place gave promise of "bringing their basketball prowess into some degree of focus with their football and baseball fame." Following the Ole Miss game, Bugbee all but gave the national title to the Wildcats: "But from last night's half-gala, half-tragic experience, the Rebels can take this comforting thought: They are not apt to often face such a wondrous Wildcat team as they encountered in this initiation of their new cage. They just don't make college teams like this anymore."[4]

Sometimes Rupp derided other SEC programs for their primitive facilities and then took personal credit for their improvement. For years he refused to play in Georgia's bandbox gym. His Wildcats wound up playing there one last time a few months before the Bulldogs' new coliseum was completed, because Rupp had thought the new place would be ready in time for the game. "If I'd been the coach here at Georgia," he said, "there would have been a fire on the campus long ago. I would have gone over there and burned down that old gym. That would have started the wheels of progress working."[5]

James Dickenson believed that "basketball would rate a lot lower in the South except for Rupp, although he hasn't made himself the most popular man in Mississippi, Alabama, Georgia and Tennessee by his efforts. He has publicly criticized opposing teams, coaches, fans and some of the primitive facilities in the SEC. And to salt his insults home, he won, year in, year out, game in, game out. As a result, in part at least, Georgia and Alabama have new field houses and Auburn is planning one."[6]

Rupp did not forget the treatment he received at the hands of other SEC coaches and writers. In 1964 Jack Williams of the *News and Observer* sat with Rupp and other members of the press in his hotel room before a game against Georgia. Rupp and Harry Lancaster often entertained the press at these "stag parties" before games. On this afternoon, though, Rupp was in no mood to butter up the writers. "'The Man in the Brown Suit' didn't have on a brown suit at all," Williams wrote. "He was sitting in the middle of a bed wearing bright red pajamas and with corpuscles to match." One has a feeling that Williams cleaned up the language for his article. "You darned sportswriters are all alike," Rupp told them. "Every time I come to Georgia, you misquote me in the papers. You get the fans riled up with lies, and then they come out and boo me." "That's right," agreed Lancaster, "and what a shame they boo a man who's done so much for basketball. It ought to be against the law."[7]

At that time Rupp was struggling through what was for him a mediocre season, and he remained unpredictable. "One minute, he flashes fire and fury," Williams wrote. "The next minute, he is a gentle man, talking about the registered Herefords he breeds in Kentucky, or about how much he enjoys a cold beer on a hot summer day." In 1966 Rupp seemed to sprinkle in references to cattle and beer with increasing frequency as the victories piled up, but he could still find time to recall slights, both perceived and real. "The fans are real bad some places we play down South," he told Williams. "They're worse than anywhere else at Mississippi State. The last time we played down there, they put a dead skunk under my bench. I know that boys will be boys, but must idiots always be idiots?"[8]

"Outside our conference," he continued, "the fans are very bad at Duke. They say ugly things to visiting teams there. And they're real bad at Georgia Tech, too. But it's not the fans who bother me at Georgia Tech. It's that awful ramp that leads from the playing court up to the dressing rooms. Tarzan wouldn't have the strength to make that climb. The first time I did it, I turned to a fellow and asked him was it possible that a bunch of Damn Engineers constructed that gym?"[9]

A reporter asked Rupp if there hadn't been more cheers than boos over the years. "Oh, yes," he answered. "And one particular game I remember more than any other. After we were put on probation by the NCAA and had to sit out the 1952 season, we went to Tennessee the next year to play a game. When they introduced us, the fans gave me a standing ovation that I'll never forget as long as I live." He remembered other times when fans and coaches honored him. But he chafed when someone compared other coaches to him. He especially resented suggestions that Western Kentucky's Ed Diddle was a worthy rival. "All my victories are legitimate," Rupp snapped. "We haven't beat any YMCAs. We've never played Southeastern Louisiana or McNeese State like so many of the southern teams do. We play teams from the Big Ten and the Missouri Valley Conference who have Negro boys who can jump a mile. And we hold our own."[10]

Ironically, other coaches often criticized Rupp for playing most of his games against weak southern teams, and schools like Western Kentucky and Murray State had been playing integrated teams for years. In 1990 Clarence "Big House" Gaines, the longtime coach of NCAA Division II power Winston-Salem State, joined Rupp as the only college coaches at that point who had won 800 games. A native of Paducah, Kentucky, Gaines was aware that Rupp refused to integrate his teams until the end of his career. "I don't think Rupp even had a black dog in his house," he said. Billy Reed, writing for *Sports Illustrated*, noted the irony that Gaines and other coaches at predominantly black schools profited from Rupp's recalcitrance. Until the mid-1970s, Reed wrote, "many of the best black players opted to stay home and play for the black colleges." After the full integration of college basketball in the South, however, Gaines found it increasingly difficult to sign players who now could opt for larger, more recognized programs in the SEC and ACC. "Rupp had a heck of a record," Gaines said in 1990, "but who else was recruiting players in the SEC besides him all those years? No one. They need to put an asterisk beside Rupp's name. It's pretty easy to dominate when no one else is offering much competition."[11]

Rupp insinuated that other schools sometimes failed to play fair in the recruiting game. "I just read in the papers this morning where North Carolina has a fellow named Bob Lewis who is averaging almost 40 points as a freshman," he said. "That young man stood in my office and told me how he'd always dreamed of playing at Kentucky. I figured we had him sewed up. The next thing I know he's down at North Carolina."[12] Lewis played for the Tar Heels through the 1966–1967 season, averaged 22.1 points a game in his career, and set the school's single-game scoring record at 49. No wonder Rupp expressed resentment.

Jeff Mullins, Bob Lewis, Wes Unseld, and Butch Beard were not the only star players Rupp missed out on. By 1961 Bill Bradley had amassed 3,066 points in his high school career in Crystal City, Missouri, and Kentucky and every other basketball power wanted him badly. One *Washington Post* writer said that Rupp "cooled his heels for more than an hour when he turned up without an appointment at the Crystal City State Bank," where Bradley's father was president. "Warren Bradley had never heard of him." Bradley wound up at Princeton.[13]

Following an impressive 105–90 victory over third-ranked Vanderbilt in February 1966, a jubilant Larry Conley raced toward his grinning coach. Rupp extended his hand to shake, but Conley embraced him with both arms, laughing. Larry Boeck of the *Courier-Journal* wrote that "it was hard to tell whether the white-haired Rupp was startled or embarrassed." Never before, "as far as veteran followers of the UK basketball team could recall, had a player embraced the often-flinty and always-precise Rupp— whether after winning four national championships or innumerable other titles."[14]

In response, Rupp "put a bear hug around the senior and patted him paternally before they both strode jauntily, as conquerors should, off the Vanderbilt court." Another reporter said, "There's something I haven't seen in 20 years of following his teams—a real emotional display." Edgar Allen of the *Nashville Banner* agreed: "The Fabulous Five and the unbeaten 1954 outfit were machine-like, unemotional, and went about the business of destroying the opposition as calmly as today's supermarket butcher. The current clan may or may not be Rupp's greatest, and they certainly go about the business of destroying a foe as previous clubs, but they are also the most inspired, emotional UK crew this writer has seen." After the Vanderbilt game, "the jubilance carried into the locker room, where the lively back-slapping and hand-shaking was a departure."[15]

Rupp also uncharacteristically heaped praise on an individual player. Louie Dampier, a six-foot sharpshooter from Southport, Indiana, hit 18 of 29 shots and all 6 free throws against the Commodores. "Dampier is the finest shooter I have ever seen in college basketball," Rupp said, "and this includes 36 years of coaching. He is a very intelligent ballplayer. He has a native basketball sense that a lot of players don't have." Said Vanderbilt's Keith Thomas, who had to guard him: "The amazing thing about Dampier and the rest of those Kentucky boys is that they never slow down. They shoot on the run and fire out on the court and still wear out the net. They are not only the best shooting team I've played against, but absolutely the best shooting team I've ever seen." By February, Dampier's shooting and the ball-handling precision of the team as a whole made people forget the Wildcats' lack of size, which earned them the "Rupp's Runts" moniker. Vanderbilt coach Roy Skinner already conceded the NCAA crown to them. "I believe Kentucky can go all the way, and I don't mean all the way in the SEC, either," he said. "I mean all the way to the NCAA championship. If Duke . . . has a better team, it must be the greatest team ever assembled." Tennessee coach Ray Mears called the Wildcats "the greatest offensive show I have ever seen." Mears's Volunteers upset Kentucky 69–62 in Knoxville on March 5, the Wildcats' only loss in the regular season. (On that same day Texas Western lost to Seattle, the Miners' only defeat.) Still, almost everyone considered Kentucky the favorite to win the title. Fred Russell, sports editor of the *Nashville Banner*, said, "Kentucky of 1966 is, I do believe, the best college basketball team I have ever seen. Some teams have been as quick, some have been as effective rebounding, some have been as deadly shooters, but I've never watched a fivesome combine all these qualities so successfully. Imagine, Vanderbilt shooting 50 percent of its field-goal attempts and getting beat by 15 points. This was one of the Commodores' top efforts."[16]

In city after city throughout the South, newspaper columnists delighted in covering the Baron's progress. David Bloom of the *Memphis*

Commercial-Appeal wrote early in March, "Nowadays the name of the game is Rupp." At 23–0 and with only Tennessee and Tulane left to play in the regular season, "even a card-carrying member of the Tennessee Marching and Rooting Society harbors a sneaky hope that Adolph Rupp will slip his Cats through successfully." Bloom interviewed Cliff Hagan, a star on the 25–0 UK team of 1953–1954. "I can't wait to see the scores," Hagan told him, "and I'd sure like to see Adolph pull them through. The old college spirit comes right out with a team like that." Hagan noted, "What you get from Rupp is superior coaching. I'm sure this Kentucky team is disciplined. That's Rupp's secret. You have to have sense enough to go along with it. I know we did."[17] But in contrast to the coach's almost fatherly treatment of the current team, Hagan said: "In college Rupp wasn't very close to us. He kept a respectable distance, and I'm sure that's the way it should be."

The national media conceded that Rupp had outdone even himself in the 1965–1966 season. Just before the NCAA tournament, United Press International (UPI) selected him as the National Coach of the Year by the largest margin ever. The panel of sportswriters, editors, and broadcasters gave him 168 of the 238 votes cast. Don Haskins of Texas Western and John Bennington of Michigan State tied for second with 12. Such an award seemed unlikely a little more than three months earlier, when the Wildcats, coming off a 15–10 season, were picked third in the SEC and had no starter taller than six feet five inches.

After Kentucky ended the regular season with a 103–74 rout of Tulane, *Cincinnati Post* sports editor Pat Harmon wrote, "This is the slickest team I ever saw on a college basketball floor. They pass the ball like five magicians and they all shoot like pros." Rupp could not argue with that. In addition to praising Dampier's shooting, he likened Conley to the great Bob Cousy of the Boston Celtics. "We played against Cousy twice when Cousy was at Holy Cross," Rupp said, "and Conley is better. Not better than Cousy when he developed in the pros, but a better passer than Cousy of Holy Cross." The Wildcats led that weak Tulane team 52–36 at halftime but had thrown the ball away repeatedly. They picked up the pace in the first few minutes of the second half, prompting Happy Chandler to leap out of the stands and run down to press row to tell Harmon, "Mister Rupp told those boys something at the half."[18]

Harmon had spent the afternoon before the game with the Kentucky coach and found him "the most gracious host [he had] ever met. He bragged about his players excessively, like a fond father." "They're No. 1 in the ratings, Rupp is No. 1 in the coach-of-the-year poll," Harmon proclaimed, "and don't you forget they're marching along together. They're a family. Rupp knows why, and he tells you why. He tells you what they did—and what he did, if you ask. He must know all basketball by now." That being said, Harmon suggested that Kentucky lost to Tennessee because Ray Mears used a 1–3–1 zone defense. "Hadn't Rupp, in his vast experience, seen that before?" the writer asked. "Seen it?" Rupp snapped. "I invented it!"[19] Harmon also wrote that folks in Cincinnati were retelling the story of when Rupp taught classes at UK and every student got an "A." "I'm a great teacher," he explained. "My students learn."

Kentucky started the NCAA tournament by beating Dayton and Michigan in the Mideast Regional in Iowa City, then traveled to College Park, Maryland, for a hard-fought 83–79 semifinal victory over Duke, the team that led the Wildcats in the polls for most of the season. The next evening, March 19, they met upstart Texas Western for the title.

Did the 1966 NCAA championship game, when five black starters for Texas Western defeated Rupp's lily-white Wildcats 72–65, focus attention on the question of race? Some argue that such attention didn't come until years later, when Rupp became a sort of icon for racism in college sports. In 1978, for example, sportswriter David Israel called the game "the Brown vs. Board of Education of college basketball." In his 1998 book *And the Walls Came Tumbling Down*, Frank Fitzpatrick presented it as "the game that changed American sports."

Billy Reed disagreed, contending that sportswriters didn't make an issue of race at the time of the 1966 game.[20] He has maintained since then, however, that "the worst thing that ever happened to Rupp was beating Duke in the '66 semifinals. Had the Blue Devils prevailed, then it would have been all-white Duke of the ACC taking on Texas Western, not all-white Kentucky of the SEC. And the revisionist historians wouldn't have made it such a big deal because Duke coach Vic Bubas was younger and more 'media friendly' than the scowling, autocratic Rupp, a German-American (many still spell his first name 'Adolf,' as in Hitler, which has to be more than a Freudian slip) who was known as 'The Baron of Basketball.'"[21]

Reed especially railed against Curry Kirkpatrick, whose 1991 *Sports Illustrated* piece presented Rupp in a less-than-favorable light. Kirkpatrick quoted players from both UK and Texas Western as saying race was not a factor at the time, yet he was determined not to downplay the issue. Like Reed, Kirkpatrick lamented the work of "revisionist historians," but he had a different idea about who the revisionists were. To Reed, revisionists like Kirkpatrick used the 1966 championship game to paint Rupp as a racist villain. To Kirkpatrick, revisionists like Reed downplayed the significance of Kentucky's defeat at the hands of Texas Western. He wrote: "Revisionist historians maintain that black development in basketball, from the touring professional New York Rens in the 1920s and '30s through the glory years of the Harlem Globetrotters in the '40s and the college stardom of Bill Russell, Wilt Chamberlain, Elgin Baylor and Oscar Robertson in the '50s, had already reached a crescendo by the mid-'60s." After all, Cincinnati started four African Americans in the 1962 championship game, as did Loyola of Chicago in 1963.[22]

Never, however, had five blacks played against five whites in a national championship game. To Kirkpatrick, Rupp represented racism in the segregated South: "'TWC . . . TWC?' Kentucky coach Adolph Rupp supposedly said, spitting out the initials of Texas Western College after his most harrowing defeat. 'What's that stand for, Two White Coaches?'" Although Kirkpatrick admitted that "the story may be apocryphal," he quoted it nonetheless. "Rupp's feelings were always simmering right there for all the world to know," he wrote. "Rupp usually was a charming p. r. rogue, brimming with diplomacy and psychology; regrettably, his politics leaned more toward the KKK." Kirkpatrick situated the 1966 game within the context of the assassinations of the Kennedys and King and the racial tension of the nation, especially in the South. "In Lexington, Ky.," he wrote, "the tenor of the time was manifest the previous summer when the publisher of the *Lexington Herald-Leader*, Fred Wachs, a drinking buddy of Rupp's, had refused to print a word about the riots in the Watts section of Los Angeles, for fear that local blacks would get ideas." One Kentuckian remarked, "Ol' Fred couldn't comprehend blacks might have access to a TV."[23]

Back in Lexington a week after the loss to Texas Western, the Wildcats held their postseason banquet, with *Herald-Leader* sports editor Billy Thompson as master of ceremonies. "At least we're still the No. 1 white team in the country," he said.[24]

In Kirkpatrick's eyes, Thompson, Wachs, and Rupp represented everything bad about the old southern racial attitudes, and the 1966 game was the fulcrum that changed all that. He praised the players for the fact that the game went off without incident, for "the class and attitude and style of both sides." To Kirkpatrick, however, Rupp was the exception. His pregame comments, halftime locker-room tirade, and postgame remarks made his beliefs clear to the *Sports Illustrated* writer.

The 2006 movie *Glory Road*, which was about that Texas Western team, had actor Jon Voight portray Rupp as, if not a racist, at least as an arrogant, overconfident egotist mystified by the changes that had come to the college game. Before the movie opened on January 13, Voight phoned Herky Rupp, not to learn more about his father, but simply to inform him that he doubted the movie would be very popular in Kentucky.[25] Herky revealed that in their 20-minute conversation, Voight assured him "he was a sports fan who saw the UK coach as more well-rounded than it might appear in the movie." Herky said, "He wanted me to know he'd do everything he could to portray my father accurately." Voight, however, admitted, "I can only do what I can do. I can't tell directors and producers what to do." When Herky asked if he could have a copy of the script, Voight said that would not be possible, but the actor warned him, "It's absolutely horrible. You wouldn't like it." Herky knew that "no matter how the film goes, it's going to resurrect idiots out there."[26] Actually, the movie went easy on Rupp. The most egregious documented stories of his racism were left out.

Like Billy Reed, Herky Rupp said it was "media people" who made the 1966 game "something it wasn't, and [his] father something he wasn't." He refused to see the movie because, "No. 1, I know the result," but also because "my father is my father."[27]

Larry Conley liked the movie. "I thought it was pretty good," he said. "I thought it was fair. I didn't see anything negative about Coach Rupp. All of us who knew him knew he had a gigantic ego. You know what? He deserved to have that." Tommy Kron said the film "made (Rupp) look a little arrogant, (but) he could be a little arrogant."[28]

Producer Jerry Bruckheimer and director James Gartner said they wanted to present a fair, accurate portrayal of Rupp. "I didn't want to do a number on Adolph Rupp; I know Jerry didn't want to do a number on Adolph Rupp," Gartner said, "and I don't think we did." Both were influenced by Pat Riley, a consultant for the film. According to Gartner,

"Whenever someone asked Riley, 'Why are you involved?' he said, 'I'm involved to protect Coach Rupp.'" "There's lots of opinions out there," the director said, "but I know Riley said he never once heard any racist comment that came out of Rupp's mouth." Voight studied audio tapes of Rupp and tried to portray him with sensitivity. In the end the actor, director, and producer concluded that Rupp and Haskins "were both competitive coaches who wanted to win," Gartner said. Rupp "seemed to . . . be a man with a huge personality and bigger than life, and a large man in terms of his confidence."

As for Haskins, he had been portrayed for 40 years as a coach who simply wanted his five best players on the floor; it didn't matter that all five starters and two substitutes were black and that no white players appeared in the championship game. But Gartner said, "You talk to those players and they'll tell you Don knew exactly what he was doing." Gartner said he was drawn to the story because of what Haskins and his players accomplished. "What I did respond to was that we were in a period of time that was not allowing certain people—because of the way they looked, because of their skin color—to execute their talents properly," he said. "And these walls, these racial walls, largely came tumbling down during the season, and specifically because of this game and this coach, Coach Haskins."[29]

For Texas Western player Willie Worsley, *Glory Road* evoked another emotion. Worsley—who as a five-foot-six-inch sophomore was surprised when Haskins told him before the Kentucky game that "you're starting, too"—became a successful coach at Spring Valley High School in his home state of New York. He saw a screening of the movie near the campus of his old college, now known as the University of Texas–El Paso. "A 92-year-old white lady was sitting next to me," he said. "She grabbed my hand during the movie and we both started crying."[30]

Much has changed in sports since 1966. According to a 2006 *USA Today* commentary, Worsley felt "that old rush of pride rising from his toes when he turns on the TV. Three black head coaches in the NFL play-offs. Three black quarterbacks on an NFL contender based south of the Mason-Dixon Line. One black quarterback leading the college football juggernaut from Texas, which last won an undisputed national title with an all-white team." When he saw all that, "I'll get real emotional inside," he said. At the same time, Worsley, then 60, was aware "that basketball has been kinder to Kentucky's three best players, Pat Riley, Louie Dampier and [Larry] Conley, who scored far more playing, coaching and TV opportunities than the winners of their landmark game." For example, Ed Sullivan never offered the Miners a guest appearance on his TV show, which he did for most national champs. Still, Worsley has made a mark of his own counseling disturbed children, serving as dean of students for the Choir Academy of Harlem, and coaching boys and girls at Spring Valley. He still remembers that the UK players were "amazed at how disciplined and structured we were. . . . You could see it in their faces. Black teams were supposed to run up and down . . . and we'd pass the ball five, six or seven times. What bothered us was how people perceived us."[31]

The contrast between Rupp, 64 at the time, and Haskins, 33, was certainly compelling. Rupp already had won four national championships; Haskins had coached a girls' high school team and sometimes drove the Miners' team bus. Haskins differed from Rupp in his determination to recruit black players, of course, but in other ways the two were remarkably alike. Both "the Bear" and "the Baron" thought nothing of berating their players unmercifully if they did not meet expectations. Although both exhibited a penchant for the bottle, their teams were extremely disciplined on the court. Many fans must have thought that Texas Western, with players from urban playgrounds, would have a playground style, but Haskins hardly ever allowed them to run. Like Rupp, he had played in college for one of the giants of the game, in his case Hank Iba at Oklahoma State. Kentucky's fast-breaking style had long been associated with Rupp. Haskins preferred "a deliberate, Iba-style protect-the-ball attack."[32] Both had long and illustrious careers at one university, and both were inducted into the Basketball Hall of Fame. And both received pressure from their university presidents: Rupp for not recruiting and playing blacks, Haskins for recruiting and playing too many of them.

Haskins surely respected Rupp as a coach. And because Texas Western was tucked down on the Mexican border, he had avoided the Baron's usual barbs reserved for his SEC coaching rivals. He had never played or coached against Rupp, so all that he knew came from the media. In private, however, Haskins resented Rupp's well-known arrogance. He read that when Rupp had been asked if his 1965–1966 team was his best, he responded that it would be if it won the championship on Saturday night. To Haskins, Rupp "sounded as if he meant when, not if." "I played for the best coach who ever lived," Haskins said. "I wasn't intimidated by Adolph Rupp."[33]

The histories of their universities also bear comparison. Kentucky was the land-grant institution in a border state and historically had been for white students. Texas Western played in the Border Conference and didn't admit its first African American undergraduates until 1955, one year after UK. For years after the 1966 game, however, many basketball fans thought Texas Western was a black school. "They must not have looked at our bench," guard Bobby Joe Hill said, noting that the team had seven African Americans and five whites, one a Mexican American. While Kentucky's players had a collective nickname that season—Rupp's Runts—Texas Western's black players sported colorful individual nicknames: Tyrone Bobby Joe (Slop) Hill, Orsten (Little O) Artis, Willie (Iron Head) Worsley, Harry (The Cricket) Flournoy, Nevil (The Shadow) Shed, Willie (Scoops) Cager, and David (Big Daddy D) Lattin.[34] The two teams took different roads to the pinnacle of college basketball in 1966.

The Texas Western game, rightly or wrongly, cemented the identification of Rupp with racism, and an alleged incident occurring sometime before the game certainly fueled the fire. Rupp supposedly informed Haskins that "no five blacks are going to beat Kentucky."[35] Another version has it that Haskins "had heard before the game—not directly from Rupp, though—that Rupp had said something along the lines of, 'There's no way I'm going to let five black players beat my Kentucky team.'"[36]

Regardless of how—or even whether—he heard it, Haskins used it to motivate his players when they gathered in the hotel before leaving for Cole Field House. Lattin remembered it well: "Haskins said, 'I heard him say it, and I couldn't believe he said it. It's up to you to do something about it.'"[37] According to Harry Flourney, "From that point on, Kentucky had as much chance of winning that game as a snowball had of surviving in hell."[38]

Kentucky supporters claimed that other circumstances spelled doom for the Wildcats. Dr. V. A. "Doc" Jackson, the Wildcats' team physician, remembered the physical condition of the players. "We had beaten Duke in the semifinals on Friday night," he said. "The boys had been sick all week. I'd been going over to the dorm every night, giving them shots. After the Duke game, Larry Conley had a fever of 102. Thad Jaracz's temperature was 101." Jackson decided to try a new drug, and the next morning they still felt ill, although their fevers were down. Pat Riley had developed a foot infection, and Jackson didn't find out about it until game time. Someone had told Riley to soak his foot in hot water, which only made the swelling increase. "We were sick and hurting," Jackson said, "and we still only lost by seven points."[39]

The Wildcats would replay that game in their minds again and again for years. When they gathered for a fortieth anniversary reunion in 2006, Conley brought up the 15–10 season of 1964–1965. "I didn't want to go out of there with a bad record," he said. "That was the last thing we wanted." Tommy Kron said the lack of height caused them to compensate in other ways: "If we didn't play together, if we didn't block out, we'd get beat." He remembered that assistant coach Joe B. Hall introduced a conditioning program in 1965–1966 that got the players "in really good shape. That really made a difference." Jaracz said: "A lot of it was that we were happy to be there. It was an honor to play for Adolph. You wanted to do the right thing and you wanted to be successful."[40]

Louie Dampier said Rupp "had a set plan. A lot of ball movement. He just worked on fundamentals. We always ran drills with a ball in our hands." Said Bob Tallent, a substitute on the team: "Everything you did had to be so precise. He watched everything like a hawk. He knew if you crossed your fingers incorrectly. You had to do everything correctly or you wouldn't be around long." Tallent recalled a 10-minute drill in which the players were allowed only four mistakes. "That's in probably a thousand passes," he said. "If we made five mistakes, we had to do it all over." Conley began to believe in the team's prospects during the fall semester. "At Thanksgiving I thought, 'You know what? I think we're going to be pretty good,'" he said.[41]

For the Texas Western players, the game and the season would be rehashed again and again as well. "In your wildest, wildest dreams you could never expect to win a national championship," David Lattin said in a 1988 interview. "Before the season Coach Haskins told people at a banquet that 'these guys are special.' But even Coach Haskins never dreamed we'd win it all. Those last three games he didn't know what to say." The Miners defeated Cincinnati, Kansas, and Utah to make it to the final. "Nobody had ever heard of us," Lattin said. "We were about 16–0 before they knew we were out there. Even when we went into the tournament, Kentucky was still No. 1."[42]

African American students back at UK gathered in dorm rooms to watch the championship game on black-and-white television sets. William

Turner, head of the Black Student Union, said he and his friends rolled up towels and stuffed them on the floor against the door so that other students could not hear them rooting for Texas Western. Seventeen-year-old James McGuffey watched the game on television, too. "The black boys were slamming and jamming," he said. "Rupp's boys couldn't dunk—it was a huge moment in black history." McGuffey stayed in Lexington and eventually owned the Exquisite Belvedere Barber Shop, "where Muhammad Ali and Malcolm X stare down from the walls." "I rooted for Texas Western," he said. James Baker Hall, later to become Kentucky's poet laureate, filmed UK's basketball games as a student. He believed that "real integration couldn't have happened absent that game and its symbolism." At that time in Lexington, he said, "It just seemed like you couldn't appeal to anyone's sense of social justice and get very far." The game spurred on the integration of Kentucky's program, he argued, and "the basketball team integration led the way in that whole part of society around here." "When all that started, as a black person you couldn't go to the Phoenix Hotel and get a room," he explained. "When the racial barrier was broken in athletics, the rest of society had to fall in place around it because winning was *that* important."[43]

David Lattin faced Pat Riley for the opening tip. Riley had not lost a tipoff all season despite standing just six feet three inches. "I could've never gone back to the playgrounds in Houston and faced all the guys if I'd let Pat Riley get the tip from me," Lattin remembered. "Pat had been stealing the tap (hitting the ball on the way up before the opponent could jump). I knew he was doing it. Coach Haskins warned me about it. Hey, I'd done it a few times myself, but Pat had practically been knocking the ball out of the ref's hands. And he did it on me. I couldn't believe he did it. But I was sure relieved when the ref called it. I'd have had a tough time going home letting a 6'3" guy outjump me."[44] It was Lattin's thunderous dunk over Riley in the first minute that set the tone for the rest of the game.

Rupp believed the game actually turned on two steals for breakaway layups by guard Bobby Joe Hill, a defensive artist from Detroit. Haskins warned Hill before the game that it would be useless to try to steal the ball from the Wildcats because they handled it too well. Hill proved him wrong. Some fans seem to recall that the steals came late in the game, but both occurred in the first half, the second coming near halftime against

Louie Dampier. "I was just reverse dribbling," Dampier recalled. "I was pivoting to my left. It was in my left hand. He got behind me and took it away. Even at that time, it was real big."[45] Kentucky went into the locker room down 34–31 at halftime.

Sports Illustrated's Frank Deford wrote decades later that he stood in the Wildcats' dressing room in Cole Field House at halftime and heard Rupp admonish his team with the words: "You've got to beat those coons." Then, turning to center Thad Jaracz, the frustrated coach said, "You go after that big coon." Deford wrote, "He talked that way all the time. A chill went through me. I was standing in the back of the room, and I looked around at the players. They all kind of ducked their heads. They were embarrassed. This was clearly the type of thing that went over the line."[46]

By the 1990s Deford had concluded that Rupp "hated black people. I mean he was a virulent racist."[47] He said he didn't write about the incident at the time because he'd "gained entry to the locker room for background purposes only, and then only in the event that Kentucky won."[48] Deford later refused to talk about Rupp's halftime language, but something must have taken place in that locker room. Weeks before the tournament, Deford had spent several days in Lexington, watching UK practices and talking with players and coaches. According to a *Lexington Leader* report, "Frank Deford came, saw and was apparently very impressed," and he "carried back to New York a glowing report on the Wildcats."[49] Deford's article, published a few weeks before the championship game, portrayed Kentucky and Rupp in superlative terms.[50]

At the time of Deford's visit, Kentucky was sailing along with a perfect record. He explored the local idea that Rupp had mellowed and concluded that the rumors were true. Still, the coach's new demeanor had little effect on his legendary practice sessions, "those taut lessons in efficiency which the Baron and his assistants preside over, all dressed in outfits of starched khaki." Deford reported that Rupp's sarcasm, "which used to endanger sensitive eardrums, is being held to a minimum" and that "off the court, the players, a remarkably intelligent and personable bunch, are accorded attention and solicitude that no other Rupp team has been granted." He quoted Alex Groza, a member of the Fabulous Five of the late 1940s. "With us," Groza said, "there was no joking, no laughing, no whistling, no singing, no nothing. Just basketball. When we traveled, for instance, he often communicated with us through the team manager." But on a trip to Alabama in the 1965–1966 season, "Rupp positively enthralled some of the starters with an enchanting discourse about how his mother used to prepare fried chicken." There had been times during the season when Rupp had solicited and even used advice from his players. "He has gone so far on some occasions as to ask the players if they approved of his strategy," Deford wrote. "There is virtually no precedent for this."[51]

Deford singled out Larry Conley for special praise. Conley was "a frail and unusually perceptive young man who is that rarity, a playmaking forward," he wrote. "More accurately, he plays smart and is what the NCAA means when it uses the term 'student athlete.'" Conley leaned toward becoming a dentist but majored in political science and took classes in Russian, art, music, "and most anything else he thought might be interesting." He told Deford, "I came to college thinking that I should make it as broadening, as enlightening an experience as I could." Clearly, Deford was taken with Conley and his teammates, and especially with Rupp.[52]

"A governor cannot succeed himself in the Commonwealth," he wrote, "and a horse can run only once in the Derby, but as long as Adolph Rupp is around the Bluegrass will never suffer from a lack of continuity. For 36 years in a land of colonels, he has been the only Baron, a man of consummate pride and well-earned privilege." With all of his success, "one might think that Adolph Rupp would be satisfied now to retire to his estate in the pleasant, rolling country outside Lexington, there to tend his prize Herefords and burley tobacco, to rest amidst his affluence and such souvenirs of glory as no other basketball coach ever has gathered. Instead, at the age of 64, he continues to pursue the only challenge left—trying to top himself. And that is some tough act to follow." Deford's lengthy article was titled "Bravo for the Baron," and a shot of Rupp was on the cover of the March 7 *Sports Illustrated*.[53]

In another *Sports Illustrated* piece following the 1966 game, Deford failed to mention Rupp's language in his halftime tirade, and indeed he did not mention the issue of race at all.[54] In fact, even in 1991 Deford downplayed the issue. "I don't know," he said. "I was always surprised at the significance placed on that game. . . . The Loyola-Chicago team that won it a few years before was virtually all black. That had been the big fuss. Not much was made of Texas Western being all black at the time. It was sort of a discovery by the outside world that came a little bit late, as is often the case."[55] The Kentucky locker room was apparently a different matter, and something had happened to turn Deford—an award-winning, respected journalist—from glowing praise of Rupp to caustic criticism of a coach who "hated black people . . . a virulent racist."

The aftermath of the 1966 game remains a point of contention. Did Rupp and others cast aspersions on Texas Western, its players, and the team's accomplishment? In his book, *And the Walls Came Tumbling Down*, Frank Fitzpatrick praised the Miners and argued against the myth that they were little more than thugs, hired guns who won a national championship and left the school soon afterward. The movie *Glory Road* laid to rest this myth, adding interviews with surviving, articulate Miners at the end of the film. At the time, however, the players were ridiculed. "Here comes this team out of El Paso with these black kids and everybody says, 'Well, there's a bunch of renegades,'" said Moe Iba, who was Haskins's assistant. "They didn't know the kids individually, so it was easy for them to say." Fitzpatrick argued that Rupp "welcomed the targeting of Texas Western." He claimed that Rupp called the Texas Western players "a bunch of crooks" and would "erroneously claim the school had been placed on probation soon after the championship. [Rupp] even said one of the Miners had been recruited from prison." Without citing sources, Fitzpatrick quoted Rupp as saying, "I don't think Duke and Kentucky had to apologize to anybody for the way we played without 'em [blacks]."[56]

Dave Kindred, a Rupp defender on the issue of race, wrote that the coach dearly wanted to win the 1966 title because he knew "he might never get that close again." (He didn't.) "It hurt to lose that one," Kindred wrote. "The coach later told me Texas Western used a player it had gotten out of prison." Rupp apparently was referring to Lattin, who had spent a semester at Tennessee State University, not the Tennessee state penitentiary. Kindred brushed off Rupp's fabrication: "Well, he no more believed that than he believed Louie Dampier was born in a manger. And he said it knowing I wouldn't believe it, either. He just needed to feel he hadn't been beaten fairly or it wasn't his fault anyway—a feeling he tried to engender every time Kentucky lost a game to anyone. For 42 years it was his way of dealing with defeat. Adolph Rupp won 875 games and lost none. It was his players who lost those 190."[57]

In 1976 the prolific Pulitzer Prize–winning novelist James Michener published *Sports in America*, in which he included a chapter on "Sports and Upward Escalation." Michener wrote about what he considered to be the Texas Western debacle. After he had watched an entertaining performance of the Harlem Globetrotters, he realized that "what these blacks were doing for money was exhibiting proof of all the prejudices which white men had built up about them. They were lazy, and gangling, and sly, and given to wild bursts of laughter, and their success in life depended upon their outwitting the white man. Every witty act they performed . . . was a denigration of the black experience and dignity."[58]

Michener likened Texas Western's performance in the 1966 championship game to a Globetrotter act and, in effect, advanced the myth of the players as little more than hired guns rather than student athletes. According to Michener, "White Kentucky ran onto the court tall and beautifully coached and impressive in their pregame drills." In contrast, "the Texas Western blacks straggled on, a bunch of loose-jointed ragamuffins ready for a brawl." It was a foregone conclusion that Kentucky would defeat them, but the Miners prevailed miraculously—and, according to Michener, tragically. "Within a few minutes," he wrote, "Kentucky was demoralized by this swarm of gangbusters." Michener turned to the man sitting beside him at a bar watching the game on television and said, "If Kentucky doesn't stomp on those little bastards, this is going to be a rout." Texas Western won, and "the following year Kentucky started recruiting blacks."[59]

Michener derided the Texas Western players, and especially the coach and administrators who he claimed used them to win a championship and then discarded them. "Later in 1967 stories began circulating to the effect that of the seven blacks who had won the championship for El Paso, only a few had stayed in college after the tournament," he wrote. "The others had no intention of coming back for a degree." He concluded that "the El Paso story is one of the most wretched in the history of American sports."

Fitzpatrick quoted a particular passage from Michener to make a contrast with the real story of the Miners' triumph. "I have often thought," Michener wrote, "how much luckier the white players were under Coach Adolph Rupp. He looked after his players; they had a shot at a real education; and they were secure within the traditions of their university, their community and their state."[60] Michener had gained erroneous information from a five-part piece by Jack Olsen in the July 15, 1968, issue of *Sports Illustrated*. After reading the article, Michener concluded, "The rumors I had been hearing were confirmed."[61] Only later did he admit that his conclusions about the Texas Western program had been based on faulty research.

Even UK president and Rupp critic John Oswald bought into the myth. "Well, I'd like to have been able to state it as well as Jim Michener did in his book," Oswald said in a 1987 interview. "You know he devoted a whole chapter on sports and the exploitation of blacks. . . . But as I reflect on it, I think what happened to that Texas Western team was really pretty outrageous. None of those players, as I understand, ever went on even for another semester, much less graduate. I think that is what Michener found out. None of them were from west of the Mississippi."[62]

Oswald didn't think of any of that while he was watching the game from the stands in Cole Field House. Instead, he thought immediately after the defeat:

> This ought to have some influence on Rupp. I was glad Rupp didn't recruit those kinds of people, but as far as talent, they surely were a talented group. Not very well-disciplined, but talented as all get out. I often wonder what Rupp really felt about that game. It certainly should have convinced him that many blacks have exceptional ability basketball-wise, but it could have had just the opposite effect on Rupp. He might have thought if you're going to get guys that are going to be there only one term and you've got to go all over the U.S. to get them, is that what I really want?

With Rupp, "the boys you'd see as sophomores you'd see as seniors on his team."[63]

For Oswald, the Texas Western championship remained "one of the most blatant exploitations of black athletic capability that, probably, has ever been on the front burner in collegiate athletic history." "Now that's very strong," he argued, "but I think it was."[64] Fitzpatrick wrote *And the Walls Came Tumbling Down* to set the record straight. Certainly, the racial climate in El Paso was more advanced than at UK—or anywhere in the SEC, ACC, or Southwest Conference, for that matter—but Texas Western had its own struggles on campus. James L. Kurtz-Phelan, the student body president in 1967–1968, remembered that the campus "wasn't this idyllic setting people had this impression of. There were undercurrents of racial problems." Olsen's 1968 *Sports Illustrated* piece quoted Texas Western athletic director George McCarty as saying: "In general, the nigger athlete is a little hungrier, and we have been blessed with having some real outstanding ones. We think they've done a lot for us, and we think we've done a lot for them."[65]

Elsewhere in Olsen's *Sports Illustrated* piece, he wrote that Texas Western was the first campus where some black athletes became "so incensed at their treatment" that they gave up their scholarships. Lattin and teammate Willie Cager told Olsen that it was time McCarty stopped "referring to them as niggers." They wanted to be treated like the white athletes; school officials should help them find campus housing and summer jobs. They also demanded that the coaches "stop lying to recruits about how racially sensitive people in El Paso were." Cager, cocaptain of the championship team, said, "We were suckered into coming here."[66]

In a 2005 interview, Don Haskins called the *Sports Illustrated* portrayal "a bunch of garbage." "El Paso was a very tolerant town," he argued, "and we had no racial problems." A writer for the *Chronicle of Higher Education*, however, revealed that "two other people who lived there at the time said the problems described in the article were accurate, but they asked not to be identified." *Sports Illustrated* has refused to apologize and continues to stand by the Olsen series. Perhaps Olsen, Michener, and Oswald raised legitimate concerns after all. At least it is clear that for all of the significance of the Texas Western victory, the "glory road" for the players was not without detours even close to home.

In 1991 Curry Kirkpatrick tried to correct what he thought to be an erroneous interpretation by Rupp, Olsen, Michener, and Oswald. According to Kirkpatrick, Olsen's accusation that none of the Texas Western players had graduated was true in 1968, but many of them graduated later. In bulleted points, he noted:

- Texas Western was not placed on probation after its championship season, nor had it been before, nor has it been since.
- Nine of the 12 Miners on the championship team graduated, compared with 10 of the 14 Kentucky players. Three of the seven black Miners received degrees from Texas Western/UTEP, and a fourth, Worsley, graduated from the State University of New York.
- Lattin is a public-relations executive for Tarrant Distributors in Houston.

- Shed is the head of intramurals at Texas–San Antonio.
- Flournoy is a sales rep for Entenmanns Oroweat in Hawthorne, Calif.
- Cager, who has recovered from his stroke but walks with a limp, is director of the Each One, Teach One foundation for underprivileged children in El Paso.
- Artis is a detective in the Gary, Ind., police department.
- Worsley is deputy executive director of the Edwin Gould Academy for emotionally disturbed children in Chestnut Ridge, N.Y.
- Hill is a senior buyer for El Paso Natural Gas.[67]

Ironically, Jerry Bruckheimer, producer of the Disney movie, took the title from a short speech that Adolph Rupp gave in 1972 at his last basketball banquet as the UK coach. At the end of the evening, a tearful Rupp looked out at his players, friends, and boosters and said, "For those of you who have gone down the glory road with me, my eternal thanks."[68] In 2006, four decades after that famous championship game, Bruckheimer's film gave a decidedly new meaning to the term "glory road" for a new generation of college basketball fans.

Another irony is how the UK–Texas Western saga came full circle when Orlando "Tubby" Smith, an African American, became Kentucky's head coach in 1997. He had been 14 in 1966, "old enough," as one writer put it, "to have felt the injustice of segregated water fountains, bathrooms and schools." On that March evening in 1966, Smith rooted for Texas Western against the team he would come to coach. Smith said the game "had a major impact on me and what I wanted to become, being involved with athletics, being involved with basketball, being a player and a coach."[69]

So what do we make of Adolph Rupp and the issue of race? The debate will continue between his supporters and critics. "The truth is," Billy Reed wrote, "nobody knows what was in Adolph Rupp's heart." Regardless of what the Baron thought and felt about bringing African Americans into the Kentucky Wildcats family, one fact remains: It was not until 1969, after coaches farther to the South had integrated their teams, that he signed a black player. No other coach in the South was as powerful and influential as Rupp, yet for all those years he chose not to "turn his hand."

13

Transitional Times, 1966–1972

Kentucky's defeat at the hands of Texas Western in the NCAA championship game in 1966 ended a phenomenal season—a season that, despite the loss in the finals, had reasserted Adolph Rupp's place at the top of the college basketball world. Rupp would never again get his team to the final game, however. Rupp would never again, in fact, return a team to the Final Four, losing in the first or second game of the regionals in each of his last five seasons. In 1966–1967, the season following the run of Rupp's Runts, Rupp failed to make the NCAA tournament at all. In that year, the Wildcats went 13–13, the first and only time Rupp did not register a winning season. Although Kentucky went 22–5 in 1967–1968; 23–5 in 1968–1969; 26–2 in 1969–1970; 22–6 in 1970–1971; and 21–7 in 1971–1972, Rupp's final season, Rupp found himself faced with a growing—and increasingly vocal—sentiment that it was time for the old man to retire. Rupp also found that he could not escape the issue of race raised—some say after the fact—by the Texas Western loss. The question of whether Rupp would or could sign an African American player continued to linger, even as a longer string of southern schools broke the color line.

In 1984, Knight-Ridder writer Mark Whicker remembered the Texas Western game and its impact on Rupp. According to Whicker, Texas Western's Miners were the national champions, "the ones that took apart Kentucky in the finals." "Black kids running, white kids chasing, and Adolph Rupp aging visibly on the bench. It was probably the most socially influential NCAA final ever," Whicker wrote.[1] The 1966–1967 campaign

312

would indeed be the most difficult year for Rupp since the canceled season in 1952–1953 following the point-shaving scandal.

The season was hard on Rupp as the losses piled up, but it was especially difficult for star Pat Riley, the SEC Most Valuable Player, the MVP of the NCAA regional at Iowa City, a first team All-American, and the leader of Rupp's Runts as a junior the previous year. For Riley, the discouragement of the loss to Texas Western only deepened in his senior season. Years later, in 1984, Riley, at that time the coach of the Los Angeles Lakers, found "himself confronted by a rather bulky figure standing at arm's length" at Madison Square Garden. The Lakers had come to New York to play the Knicks, and, according to sportswriter Phil Straw, "This guy had obviously come to the Garden to see Riley, to somehow make an impression on the coach." Straw believed "he was there to remind Riley of the past."[2]

"Do you remember me?" the man bluntly asked Riley. According to Straw, "There was a spooky guess-who hint of anticipation in his husky voice. His eyes, stone cold, pinned Riley to the wall and left him speechless." Riley looked at him intently. "I drove the lane on you guys and stuffed it in your face," the man told him. "Willie," the man said, and Riley suddenly realized who he was: Willie Cager, a member of the Texas Western team. "Yeah, I told him," Riley said later. "Yeah, Willie, I remember you." How could he forget? Although Cager only scored 8 points to Riley's 19, his dunk put an exclamation point on the Miners' victory. "Can you imagine?" Riley said in a 1984 interview. "All those years, all that time and distance between us, and Willie shows up like a bad dream."[3]

"If we played them 10 times, we'd have beaten them eight," Riley said years after the game.[4] Probably not, if the games had been played the following season. Riley never forgot that game, and he never forgot the heartbreak of the following season when Kentucky went 13–13. In 1965–1966, Riley as a junior had been what Tev Laudeman called "a 6-foot-3 superman: leading scorer and rebounder on the team; a 51.5 percent shooter from the field, many of his shots taken under the toughest defensive pressure; a streak on the fast break."[5] For Riley, however, what had seemed effortless in 1965–1966 became frustratingly laborious in 1966–1967.

Early in the summer of 1966, Riley suffered a back injury, a slipped disc, while water skiing. Reluctant to tell Rupp, Riley traveled with the Wildcats later in the summer in August to the International Universities

Tournament in Israel. "The trip was wonderful," Rupp later wrote to his family back in Kansas, but he also attributed his team's "sluggishness" in the 1966–1967 regular season to the "fact that we had too much basketball during the summer."[6] The trip overseas certainly came at a bad time for Riley. The pain in his lower back did not go away. Laudeman wrote that in 1966–1967, "if the season was painful for Rupp, it was sheer agony for Riley—physically and mentally." As the season wore on, the pain extended down his left leg. According to Laudeman, "Riley took pills all season. Pills for pain, pills for relaxing the muscles and pills for sleeping. Every night when he went to bed he pulled on a corset attached to weights and pulleys. All night long he would stay 'in traction,' easing the pain."[7]

Riley had come to Lexington, sight unseen by Rupp and Harry Lancaster, as a heralded freshman in 1963. Taking the recommendations of other coaches, Rupp and Lancaster knew that Riley had scored over 1,000 points in his high school career at Linton High School in Schenectady, New York. Barry Kramer, a star at Linton two years ahead of Riley, had gone on to a stellar All-American career at New York University.[8]

The New York schoolboy felt at home immediately in Kentucky. He came to respect his famous coach, a respect that continued and deepened into his playing and coaching days in the NBA. He agreed to serve as a consultant for the movie *Glory Road*, so that, more than anything else, Rupp would get a fair shake. Despite his later devotion, Riley would remember his mixed feelings about the Baron during his college days. Phil Straw described the eerie quiet at the beginning of a Kentucky practice. "There was a time each afternoon during the basketball season at Kentucky," he wrote, "when all the busy sounds of Memorial Coliseum would stop at once." "There was no dwindling down or fading away. Silence simply set in and basketball practice under Rupp began. Except for the annoying sound of rubber soles and the swish of nets, the vacuum surrounding Rupp, the coach, and Riley, the player, was devoid of any noise, making it possible to hear the impossible: heartbeats, the floor breathing, bodies sweating."[9]

Riley remembered well the aura that surrounded his college coach, an aura produced by years of success. "Rupp came to practice for four decades with little patience, ample sarcasm and wearing starched khakis," Straw wrote. According to Straw, "He meant to be meticulous, with every minute, every drill, every lesson listed on a card. He controlled the silence as if his hands were on a light switch." "He reduced the game to a science," Riley remembered. At times, Riley resented such attention to detail. Such control. Times "when he doubted Rupp, thinking him to be, perhaps, too old-fashioned, too autocratic and out of touch." Still, Riley responded to Rupp's discipline, and "his demand for sharpening of individual skills," even though he resented along with other players the ordeal of harsh practice sessions.[10]

Harry Lancaster sometimes served as Rupp's straight man, at times teaming up with the Baron in "an interrogation tactic" that the players referred to as "cross-firing." During these "cross-firing" sessions, Rupp bore "in from the north while Lancaster closed in with hot breath from the south." "There was no escape," Straw wrote, "just as there weren't to be any folds or margins or wrinkles in the Kentucky basketball philosophy. It was Rupp's way or else." As Riley later remembered, it was either "Amen" or "Oh, my." Lancaster agreed. After Rupp died, the longtime assistant coach and later Rupp's athletic director remembered, "We put so much pressure on our kids in practice that some folded and transferred. Others gritted their teeth and closed their ears." Riley gritted his teeth. "He rode me, yes," he recalled, "but I was the kind of player who needed that. If there were any gifts, they came from Harry." Lancaster "handed out the goodies," Riley said. "Silence from Adolph was consent."[11]

After his stellar campaign in 1965–1966, Riley's back injury put a damper on his senior season. Preseason polls ranked Kentucky third, and Riley scored 23 points to go along with 11 rebounds in the season opener, a 104–84 thrashing of Virginia. At the time, Riley thought, too optimistically it turned out, "We're a little better than we were in our first game last year." But Kentucky lost three in a row at home, the first time that had happened under Rupp. In all, Kentucky lost four overtime games at home, and during one disastrous stretch, lost six of nine. In the end, Kentucky tied for fifth in the conference.[12]

It was not just a healthy Riley that Rupp missed, however. Although Rupp knew that Riley could not play up to par with the injury, and although he considered asking him to quit, he never did. Instead, Rupp blamed Kentucky's disaster of a season on two factors: "lack of height, lack of leadership." "I knew it was going to be a long year when we lost to Cornell, by 15, in December, at home," Riley said. Rupp placed the blame on the replacements for Tommy Kron and Larry Conley, two important cogs in the success of Rupp's Runts. Gary Gamble and Bob Tallent failed to fill in. According to Riley, "I also quickly realized how much we missed Tommy (Kron) and Larry (Conley). They were the spirit of our team. I didn't appreciate the sacrifices they made for us—especially for Louie (Dampier) and I—until they were gone. Then, it was too late." Riley played in all the games, not missing a one, but his averages slipped, from 21.7 points per game to 17.4; from 8.9 rebounds per game to 7.7; and from a shooting percentage of 51.6 to 44.2. He was a step slow on the fast break and opponents were able to outjump him, unlike the previous season. "I didn't want my injury to become an excuse for a disappointing year," he said.[13]

Rupp knew what Riley was going through. Rupp's own operation in 1935 mirrored the operation that Riley would endure after the season: the removal of two discs from his lower back. In 1935, at the beginning of his UK coaching career, Rupp had spent 35 days in the hospital and then another 8 weeks at home, wearing a corset for 9 months, and incapacitated for over a year. Now, Riley suffered with the same malady with which his coach was all too familiar. Clearly, Pat Riley was not the reason for the Wildcats' horrors in 1966–1967.

Instead, Rupp placed the blame on poor Bob Tallent, a six-foot-one junior from Langley, Kentucky, and an excellent long-range shooter. During a late season 76–57 loss to Tennessee, Tallent dribbled up court and then nonchalantly passed over to Louie Dampier, who, looking straight ahead, did not see the pass. The ball went out of bounds, and a furious Rupp immediately yanked Tallent from the game. Reaching the bench, Tallent and Rupp exchanged bitter words. There was another exchange between coach and player in the locker room after the game. The next day Tallent reported to practice but was informed by equipment manager George Hukle he was no longer allowed to issue equipment to him.[14]

Thomas D. Clark, the head of the history department, wrote to A. D. Kirwan, a fellow historian and dean of students, to gloat over Rupp's recent problems. "Maybe the most sensational thing," Clark wrote, "is the fact that Adolph has now experienced a ride over the public's barrel, and he has proved a rather poor loser." According to Clark, "He fired a boy named [Bob] Tallent from his team and has been threatened with life and death by mountaineers from the Paintsville area [Tallent's home town]." Clark told Kirwan that "the *Courier-Journal* gave both Adolph and Shively [the

UK athletic director] a ride the other day in a biting editorial." "I knew Bernie Shively was stupid," he wrote, "but I did not know he could say to the newspaper boys that they shouldn't have asked the boy about his side of the fuss."[15]

Of course, Tallent was stunned. And Rupp received criticism from several quarters other than Dr. Clark, including John W. Oswald, the UK president, who reprimanded the coach, and from the *Kentucky Kernel*, the student newspaper. Rupp claimed that Tallent had been unable to play well under pressure, but a reporter for the *Kernel* asked, "Did Rupp Choke?" A bitter Rupp completed the SEC conference schedule with an 8–10 record.[16]

Many of Rupp's critics—and supporters too—always claimed that Rupp won all the victories, but that the players were always responsible for the defeats. Certainly, Rupp wondered how the 1966–1967 season could have gone so wrong, especially after his beloved Runts had been so successful the year before. For the players' part, they remembered the slights and mental abuse that the Baron put them through. Vernon Hatton, a star on the Fiddlin' Five, the 1958 national champions, once said, "It takes six to eight years to get over playing for Coach Rupp." "Once you get over it," he said, "you get to like him." A reporter asked Riley if he liked Rupp. "Well," he conceded, "I respected him. I feared him a little." And then he said, "There were times I hated him." According to sportswriter Phil Straw, Riley concluded that "neither castor oil nor Adolph Rupp . . . were necessarily pleasant, but both made you better."[17]

Despite the 13–13 record, the 1967–1968 season had not been a complete disaster for Rupp personally. When Kentucky beat Mississippi State, 103–74 in Starkville on February 18, he passed Western Kentucky's Ed Diddle as the all-time winningest coach with 760 victories. Rupp continued to make his mark in the college game, and he continued to make his mark on Pat Riley. After the final game of the season had been played, a 110–78 victory at home against Alabama, Riley had surgery to repair two slipped discs. With the escalation of America's involvement in Vietnam, Riley received a medical reprieve because of his back problems, but his injury did not prevent a draft of another sort. Riley went in the first round to the San Diego Rockets. He played for the Rockets for three years before being traded to the Lakers, where he played for five and a half seasons before finishing out his playing career with a half-season at Phoenix. Although he endured a nine-year career as an NBA journeyman, his professional career had been less than stellar. Too short for forward, not quick enough for guard. Still, Riley used what he had learned from Rupp in his playing career and later in his coaching career.

By Rupp's last few years as UK's coach, Kentucky basketball had become one of the few unifying factors in a poor—and in many ways divided—state. For thousands of adolescent Kentucky boys, devotion to Kentucky Wildcat basketball was necessary to be accepted by peers and teachers alike; basketball took on a level of meaning not as evident in Tennessee or other southern states. Only in Hoosier high schools in Indiana did basketball reach the level of adulation and respect as in the Bluegrass State. Loyalty to Kentucky basketball marked acceptance and gave identity in tiny west Kentucky county-seat towns and in the hollows of eastern Kentucky. One west Kentuckian, Stan Key, who lived out his dream of playing for Kentucky and the school's legendary coach, remembered following Wildcat greats like Louie Dampier and Pat Riley in the 1960s, mimicking them in playground games.[18] Courthouse crowds—the whittlers and the gossipers—in any of Kentucky's 120 counties regularly ambled across the street to community drugstores to discuss the previous night's game—UK had probably won—and discussions of game results and individual play preceded the Sunday school lesson at church on Sunday mornings.

For many, however, Rupp's last teams in the late 1960s and early 1970s lacked the excitement and exotic appeal of other college players and teams. The Kentucky faithful could certainly admire the play of Dan Issel and Mike Pratt and Larry Steele, but after they were gone, Rupp's final teams were not as glitzy or as successful. Rupp's first and only African American recruit, Tom Payne, showed promise, but only played one year before being drafted as a hardship case by the Atlanta Hawks. Lefthander Tom Parker was a fine shooter, but his steady play simply did not elicit the same excitement as did other SEC and Big Ten players. Jim Andrews was at once solid and boring. Local Kentucky boys such as Stan Key—and Rupp still recruited high school stars from his home state—merited praise, but that was primarily because he hailed from Calloway County in western Kentucky.

Instead, on outdoor concrete courts behind grade schools and in driveways and barnyards with their ubiquitous backboards and hoops, youngsters imitated more exciting players to the south and to the north and to the west of the Bluegrass State. In the pre–Michael Jordan era, before young players yearned to "Be Like Mike," and before LeBron James and Steph Curry, Pete Maravich, coached by his father at Louisiana State University, battled Dan Issel for scoring records. "Pistol Pete's" floppy gray socks and longish hair at once mirrored the freedom of his style and the protest of the 1960s, and the plodding Issel was no match for that.

In one game between Kentucky and LSU at the Tigers' "Cow Palace" in 1970, Issel scored 51 points, only to be outdone by Maravich who had 64. Kentucky won, of course, but that didn't matter. Maravich was the player to watch and imitate. At Purdue University in West Lafayette, Indiana, Rick Mount, the "Rocket," launched his elegant jumpers while falling out-of-bounds in the deep corners of Mackey Arena. His jump shot was pure beauty, and after every Purdue game—carried conveniently for western Kentuckians over an Evansville, Indiana, television station—it was Mount that boys imitated on the concrete court behind the old school.

Mount played against UCLA and Lew Alcindor in the NCAA Final in 1969.[19] John Wooden's Bruins prevailed and indeed UCLA won championship after championship—10 national titles in 12 seasons, from 1964 to 1975, including 7 straight from 1967 to 1973. UCLA went undefeated a record 4 times, in 1964, 1967, 1972, and 1973.

No, Adolph Rupp's faded glory during his last years could not match the appeal of Maravich and Mount and the UCLA Bruins, but Kentuckians rooted for the Cats all the same. A 78-rpm recording of a terrible tune repeating the awful refrain, "Remarkable Rupp, Remarkable Rupp, the Basketball Whiz," came out in the early 1970s, and schoolkids played the thing over and over again on living room stereos. They believed, and were taught by their parents, that it was Rupp and his insistence on a fast-paced style that made the careers of Maravich and Mount and Alcindor possible.

The question of race continued to hover over the Baron during his last decade as UK's coach. In Kentucky, Murray State University's Stew Johnson broke the color line in basketball in the Ohio Valley Conference in 1963. Fellow OVC member Western Kentucky University integrated its basketball team the following year. The University of Louisville signed Wade Houston, Sam Smith, and Eddie Whitehead in 1964 as well. The three major southern conferences finally desegregated in the mid-1960s.

ACC members Maryland and Wake Forest signed black basketball players in 1964; Texas Christian integrated the Southwest Conference in 1965; and in the SEC, Vanderbilt coach Roy Skinner—with the full support of Chancellor Alexander Heard, who "had been quietly working to liberalize race relations" on campus—landed Nashville high school star and class valedictorian Perry Wallace in 1966. Wallace played in his first game in November 1967.[20] It was two more years before another African American, Auburn's Henry Harris, played in an SEC contest. Also in 1969, Wendell Hudson (Alabama) and Ronnie Hogue (Georgia) were awarded scholarships.[21]

And then there was Adolph Rupp at Kentucky. It took almost a decade after Rupp first recklessly stated in April 1961 that he would integrate the UK team before Tom Payne took the floor in a blue and white uniform against Northwestern on December 1, 1970.

Kentucky president John W. Oswald continued to work with Vice President Robert Johnson and Athletic Director Bernie Shively to spur Rupp along to recruit African American basketball players in the 1960s. In a memorandum to Shively after Rupp's Runts had lost the national championship to Texas Western, Johnson wrote on March 29, 1966: "Following the basketball banquet last Thursday evening President Oswald indicated to me that Coach Rupp said he was actively recruiting two Negro student athletes, one from Harrison County, and one from Nashville, Tennessee. I did not see either of these young men at the basketball banquet or at any of the other functions which were arranged for prospects this past weekend." Johnson said, "I am very sure that our posture towards prospective Negro basketball players is going to receive considerable public attention within the next few weeks." Several individuals already had made it a point to tell Johnson that Coach Rupp would never have a Negro basketball player. "The University is being hypocritical when it says it is trying to recruit such young men," they argued. "Needless to say," Johnson told Shively, "I have taken exception to these remarks and stated my conviction that Coach Rupp means what he says when he states that he is recruiting Negro basketball players." "Nevertheless," Johnson wrote, "I think it extremely important that we give some tangible public evidence that we are recruiting in good faith and regardless of race. It seems to me that a visit to the campus, similar to that arranged for the other young men this past weekend, for the young men from Harrison County and Nashville, Tennessee, is very much in order."[22] Contrary to the opinion of prominent sportswriters after the fact, race was clearly a factor immediately after the Texas Western game in 1966.[23]

Assistant Coach Joe B. Hall and Rupp eventually gave up on Fielding "Toke" Coleman from Harrison County because of poor ACT scores. In an April 6, 1966, memorandum to Rupp, Hall wrote, "I, personally, have been close to Toke and his family since recruiting his half-brother, Louis Stout, to Regis College when Toke was in the 8th grade." Hall had visited Coleman during the summer at Harrison County High School, and Coleman made a campus visit to see UK play Vanderbilt, meeting with "friends and coaches in the Blue Room following the game."[24]

The other African American basketball recruit missing from the UK basketball banquet following the Wildcats' defeat to Texas Western was Nashville Pearl star Perry Wallace. Both Lancaster and Hall had recruited Wallace. "They were just great," Wallace recalled. "I really liked them."[25] As for Rupp, according to Wallace's biographer Andrew Maraniss, Wallace "was only vaguely aware of the Baron's reputation." Oh, he knew all the rumors about the coach's reluctance to recruit black ballplayers, but he knew firsthand only when he made a road trip to watch the University of Louisville play Wichita State, preceded by a freshman game against Kentucky Wesleyan.[26]

Louisville freshman Butch Beard battled Kentucky Wesleyan guard Mike Redd in the freshman game, and then superstar Westley Unseld played in the varsity game. Wallace talked with both Louisville stars afterwards. "Wes was a great player," Wallace said, "but most important, he made a huge impression on me as a role model. He was quiet, polite, and yet ferocious on the court." While both Beard and Unseld had been recruited by Rupp, neither came away with positive feelings about the experience. Both felt the UK coach was being pressured to recruit black players, but that the coach did not really want to do so. And Unseld received death threats from UK fans.[27]

Still, both Unseld and Beard took the high road in their conversation with Wallace. "They were measured," Wallace said. "They didn't talk down Kentucky, but they didn't have a lot of good stuff to say, either. What they did say was that just in general, you'd want to be careful going in there integrating, being a guinea pig." Although Wallace liked Lancaster and Hall, what eventually helped him decide against UK was the lack of Rupp's personal contact. Wallace never met him. According to biographer Maraniss, Wallace "determined that he couldn't put his fate in the hands of a man who hadn't bothered to visit him."[28]

As it turned out, perhaps it was less embarrassing that Toke Coleman and Perry Wallace did not attend the banquet. Billy Thompson, the sports editor of the *Lexington Herald*, served as master of ceremonies of the event. The Wildcats, he said, should not be ashamed of their second-place performance to Texas Western in the NCAA Final. "At least we're still the No. 1 white team in the country."[29]

Toke Coleman went on to Eastern Kentucky University and Perry Wallace made history at Vanderbilt as the first African American basketball player in the SEC. It would not be until 1969 that Adolph Rupp signed a black basketball player to a grant-in-aid at the University of Kentucky.

Born in 1950 in Louisville, Tom Payne grew up as an army brat, living in Europe, but moving back to Louisville to graduate from Shawnee High School in 1969. At 7 feet 1 inch and 215 pounds, Payne was a formidable presence on the court, but like Toke Coleman, low ACT scores did not qualify him for immediate scholarship aid.

"It was kind of a rash decision really," Payne told a *Louisville Courier-Journal* reporter in 2001. "I wanted to make my own personal trail. I was trying to carve out my own identity." Payne grew up in the integrated environment of US Army bases around the world and went to high school in Louisville's west end. He had never really experienced racism before coming to the University of Kentucky. After playing for an AAU team coached by former UK player Scotty Baesler in what would have been his freshman year, Payne joined the Wildcats as a sophomore for the 1970–1971 season. He later claimed that the UK coaches arranged for others to take correspondence courses in his name to make him eligible.[30]

Like Perry Wallace at Vanderbilt, Payne faced abuse on the road in the Southeastern Conference, but he said that "the home crowd wasn't much kinder." According to Brian Bennett, writing for the *Courier-Journal*, "Threatening phone calls, broken car windows and eggs smashed on his front door became routine." Payne "feared for the safety of his wife—whom he married right after high school—and their infant daughter." When UK fans booed him during a December UK Invitational Tournament loss to Purdue in December, Payne thought seriously of transferring. His father, however, ordered him to finish out the season. Payne ended up averaging 16.9 points per game and 10.1 rebounds on a UK team that went 22–6.[31]

After the season, Payne joined five other players who were the first college players to claim financial hardship in order to join the NBA draft. Payne signed with the Atlanta Hawks for $750,000. Playing little during his only season with the Hawks, Payne was arrested by Georgia police in May 1972, in connection with a series of rapes in the Atlanta area. He served all but four years in correctional institutions.[32]

Stan Key from Calloway County, Kentucky, played with Payne during the seven-footer's lone season as a Wildcat. "That 1970–71 season wasn't really much different from my other three years at UK," Key said.

Tom Payne was a very talented basketball player, and he contributed significantly to the team's success that one year. He proved that talent by having an opportunity to play in the NBA the following season. During the year I think the coaches and players went out of their way to help Tom develop his basketball skills and assist him in his adjustment to college life. The season did have its normal ups and downs, with the usual minor team rule violations by various players that can occur throughout a long basketball season. Those situations were always handled individually and appropriately by the coaches and, as the season's record suggests, didn't affect the play of the team in any way. I don't think that there ever were any feelings among the players that Tom, as the first and only African American on the team, was treated differently from the other players.[33]

For his part, Rupp lamented the loss of Payne in the coach's final two seasons and blamed the NBA for stealing his best player.

14

Forced Retirement and
Post-UK Years

A writer for the *Louisville Courier-Journal* argued in 1972 that SEC schools paid an odd sort of compliment to Adolph Rupp simply by building new basketball arenas. At the Rebel Coliseum at Ole Miss (8,500 capacity), the Georgian Coliseum in Athens (10,400), the Stokely Center at the University of Tennessee (12,400), Auburn's Memorial Coliseum (13,000), LSU's Assembly Center in Baton Rouge (14,300), Alabama's Memorial Coliseum (15,000), and Vanderbilt's Memorial Coliseum in Nashville (15,600), SEC schools built bigger and bigger arenas for their basketball teams, "most with plush theater seats and other elegant refinements." Even Florida eventually gave in and moved from its 3,800-seat cracker-box gym to a new 6,500-seat arena.[1]

The fact that so many of Rupp's old rivals built—or had to build—new arenas for larger crowds served as eloquent testimony that keeping up with the Baron and the dynasty that he had built in the Bluegrass was necessary. And when it became known that Rupp would be forced to retire on July 1, 1972, the crowds came out in game after game to pay tribute to the coaching legend. Such was the case at the University of Florida on January 15, 1972, when Rupp traveled with his team to coach his last game in Gainesville. According to one sportswriter, "At Gainesville tonight, when Adolph Rupp follows his University of Kentucky team out of the dressing room for its game with Florida, the people will nudge each other and point and wave and shout their greetings to him." "And after it is over," he wrote, "when he is going through the motions of his radio show, the people will crowd up close, straining to hear what the great man is saying."[2]

The sportswriter stated that "it is strange, this empathy the folks in Dixie have for Rupp." He admitted: "I have seen it and wondered about it and, finally, have likened it in the more narrow sphere of sports to the respect that the Japanese developed for Douglas MacArthur." According to the writer, "Like MacArthur, Rupp crushed. But in so doing, also like MacArthur, he uplifted. He forced the rest of the Southeastern Conference to recruit and to build and to play nationally competitive basketball." Now, the writer mused, "unless there is a last-minute reprieve, he is making the initial thrust of his final tour through the precincts that he conquered."[3]

The writer pointed to the retirement rule of UK's governing regulations that university employees must retire at the age of 70. The lone exceptions to the rule applied to the university president and vice president, and as the writer stated, "Rupp is neither of these." "The governing regulations regarding retirement were set up by the Board of Trustees," said Glenwood Creech, the vice president for university relations, "and I assume that a board that creates could also change, if it wishes to. But there have been no waivers to the rule to date. At least, I have no knowledge of any."[4]

Back home in Kentucky, Wildcat fans seemed to be divided on the issue of Rupp's forced retirement. Bob Cooper, an Associated Press writer, said that "the man on the street, in a brief survey, was somewhat more than split on the question. Some noted Rupp's contribution to the game and said he should be retained; others said it was time for him to rest from his efforts." The same division of opinions could be found in the state legislature in Frankfort. According to Cooper, "One man in particular is lobbying hard for a resolution favoring retention of Rupp; another is trying just as hard to defeat any such measure."[5]

Apparently, several "key legislators" felt that the Kentucky General Assembly should not meddle in the internal regulations of the state's flagship university. They knew the subject of Rupp's retirement was a touchy issue, and when reporters asked them where they stood, senators and representatives made sure that they would remain anonymous, if they expressed any opinion at all. One unnamed legislator, for example, stated, "If a resolution to keep Rupp were introduced I'd certainly vote for it. I couldn't vote against it of course. But I'd just as soon not have to vote on that at all." A university official said, "We've really got no reason not to keep him if he wants to stay. . . . But if we do, we've got to realize that there may be some senile professors here and there who have reached retirement age and may want to stay on, too." "We'd just be setting a precedent," he argued.

One writer used Phog Allen, Rupp's mentor at the University of Kansas, as an example, as a precedent. When Allen faced the same mandatory retirement rule at Kansas that Rupp faced at Kentucky, he asked for an extension. "The basketball season just ended was disappointing," he said. "It would be the thrill of my life to end a long coaching career . . . with a truly great team." Allen especially wanted to have the opportunity to coach Wilt Chamberlain, a player he had recruited, eligible to play the next year. The Kansas board said no, not wanting to set a precedent.[6]

As for Rupp, he "keeps his own counsel," wrote one sportswriter. In his own way, however, Rupp made it more than clear that he wanted to keep coaching. Bob Cooper could only guess at what went on behind the scenes. "Will he quietly initiate something which might put the board under pressure to make him an exception and, in so doing, open the floodgates to similar appeals by other university employees?" asked the sportswriter. "Or will he formally announce his retirement some day near the end of the season? Or, instead, will he merely walk off the court after the final game and quietly let the string run out July 1?"[7]

Former UK president and Rupp nemesis John W. Oswald remembered that he had tried to get Rupp to retire back in the 1960s. "Well, you know, I made a stab, but it didn't get very far," Oswald said in a 1987 interview. "You know," he recalled, "there was a regulation when I was there that administrators retired from their administrative positions at 65, and from their faculty positions at 70." Oswald reported, "While I was there, Rupp turned 65 and I took a position that didn't last very long, that Rupp was an administrator. And some of my good friends on the board and I sat down and had a long talk about it." Several of the board members said, "Well, you know, we've heard you say that to be a good coach, you've got to be a good teacher. And that's going to fly right back into your face, because no matter when Rupp's time comes to retire there's going to be a problem."[8]

Oswald knew that the board members made a good point. "They were clever," he said. The president's plan to classify Rupp as an administrator didn't get very far. After Oswald resigned as president at Kentucky to go to Penn State, Otis A. Singletary, a respected historian, became UK's president. It would be Singletary's responsibility to enforce the board's retirement regulations. He inherited the Rupp retirement dilemma. Oswald told Singletary, "Otis, now don't think I left this for you. . . . I put up a balloon and it got punctured . . . before the string got out of my hand." Oswald should have anticipated the controversy that developed when Rupp came to retirement age, but he was amazed from his new perch on the Penn State campus to learn about the extent of the conflict. "I thought that was outrageous what went on down there," he said, "for the legislature to get involved and all that; it was just unbelievable."[9]

Oswald's successor was indeed stuck with the Rupp retirement controversy. He heard both sides of the issue, but as the university's chief executive officer he knew that he had a responsibility to enforce the policies and regulations of the board of trustees. Thomas D. Clark, the former head of the history department, whom Oswald had dismissed from his duties, wrote a letter to Singletary expressing his feelings on the Rupp matter. "I see by the paper that the animals are at you to allow Adolph Rupp to continue after he is 70," Clark wrote on February 5, 1972. "This sort of thing came up with this stuffed shirt when I was on the Athletic Board." Clark remembered the time when Rupp "refused to pick up his checks because he felt he needed more salary." Clark told Singletary, "I proposed that the university follow the same rule with Rupp as with any other cantankerous tenured professor." "You would have thought I had proposed overturning the Throne of God," Clark remembered. "Now you are faced with a mean decision which should not be yours," Clark wrote. "In my private opinion, Kentucky needs some fresh air over in the neighborhood of the Coliseum."[10]

In his early public announcements, Rupp simply put off reporters. "I've made it plain before and I'm making it plain now that I won't make any announcement about that until the end of the season," Rupp asserted on January 28, 1972. Just two weeks earlier, however, a reporter chatted with Rupp over the telephone, the evening before the NCAA amended its rules to allow freshmen to play in varsity competition. "Any news from the NCAA convention?" Rupp asked the reporter. "No," came the response. "Oh," said Rupp. "I was hoping they might have made freshmen eligible . . . immediately, that is." The reporter wondered, "Was he trying to tell us something?"[11]

Several of Rupp's former players made it clear that they wanted the coach to have the opportunity to continue coaching the game that he loved. Gerry Calvert, an attorney in Lexington—Rupp's attorney—and a former Kentucky player, took it upon himself to organize a drive to keep the coach. Three American Basketball Association Kentucky Colonels team members signed a petition to allow their former coach to continue on the job. Former Wildcat star Dan Issel was happy to sign his name to the petition. "I think that a rule that says a man has to retire because he's reached a certain age is, to put it quite frankly, ridiculous," Issel argued. "I think his health seems better now than at any time since I was a sopho-more." Issel said, "I've read where coach Hall is being talked of as the next coach and, quite frankly, it would be difficult for anyone to follow coach Rupp."[12]

Issel knew that Rupp was "a legend." "We just don't think he should be forced to retire, especially in light of all that coach Rupp has done for Kentucky." Mike Pratt, Issel's teammate, agreed. "Why should he be forced to retire if he can still do the job? Why should he be made to retire because of some standard set a long time ago?" Pratt asked. "When he had the blood clot in his foot, he didn't look good. But I think he looks good this year." Fellow Kentucky Colonels teammate and former member of Rupp's Runts, Louie Dampier, said, "I have a million reasons that I wouldn't want known, that I wouldn't want to see in print. But I think it's discriminatory to make him retire if he doesn't want to."[13]

Along with the former players, Rupp rallied other supporters to plead his case. Russell Rice remembered that John Y. Brown Sr. and John Y. Brown Jr., two Kentuckians active in politics, business, and senior citizens' causes, met with the UK board of trustees, along with Harland Sanders of Kentucky Fried Chicken fame, to ask for an exception. The board refused to budge but tried to appease Rupp in other ways. They assured him that he could continue to use his Memorial Coliseum office and that he would be paid a consulting fee of $10,000 a year. That, along with his pension from the university that would pay him 60 percent of his salary, insured that he would not go hungry after retirement. The board also had Harry Lancaster, Rupp's former longtime assistant coach and now athletic direc-tor, place a $10,000 bronze plaque "listing Rupp's accomplishments" in a prominent place in the coliseum.[14]

Assistant coach Joe B. Hall had been chosen as the heir apparent, and Rupp resented Hall's usurpation of the job that only he could fill. Rice wrote that Hall "was in Rupp's direct line of fire." Hall's recruiting class, including Kevin Grevey and Jimmy Dan Conner, was billed as the best freshman group in the country, and Rupp, realizing that he would never be able to coach this talented group, wondered out loud why his assistant had not recruited such players for him. Rupp had brought in Gale Catlett from the University of Kansas as an assistant coach, and, in Rice's words, "Rupp began to praise Catlett and slight Hall."[15] Rupp was unable and unwilling to hide his bitterness at being forced out.

Despite the efforts of Rupp's former players, loyal friends, and many Wildcat fans appreciative of all that the Baron had accomplished at Kentucky, President Singletary made it clear to Rupp that there would be no exception to the retirement rule. And as this became increasingly apparent to the aging Kentucky coach, his last season became a bittersweet reminder of all that he had been through in his illustrious career. If they forced him out, Rupp said, "they might as well take me out to Lexington Cemetery." Rupp knew, however, that he would have to go. "Of course," he suggested, "they said they retired me because of the mandatory age of 70. That is not true. They retired me because of ill health. The athletic board got damn sick of me."[16]

Although he must have known that the inevitable would happen, that he would be forced to retire at the end of the 1971–1972 season, Rupp maintained a caustic wit, and continued to respond to his players' foibles in characteristic Rupp fashion. At 70, Rupp was still unwilling to allow for anything less than perfection in his practice sessions. Sportswriter Dave Kindred attended a practice session during that last season, when, as he put it, "some poor sinner had hesitated momentarily on a layup, allowing the shot to be blocked." "And even at 70," Kindred wrote, "in his last season, the sight of a blocked layup moved him to anger, sarcasm and inimitable theatrics."[17]

Dressed in his practice khakis, Rupp called to the player, showing to him his unforgivable mistake. "You get the ball like this," Rupp said, and then he reenacted his egregious error, holding his hands "waist high, hefting an imaginary basketball which he raised slowly overhead as he spoke again to the sinner." "And then you say, 'Our Father Who art in Heaven, hallowed be Thy name, Thy kingdom come, Thy will be done, I am now going to shoot the damned basketball!' "[18]

Denied a really stellar year without Tom Payne, Rupp lashed out at the professional league that had drafted Payne as a hardship case. "If we had Tom Payne," Rupp said, "we'd be undefeated. The pros don't care whether they destroy a good college team or not."[19] Rupp knew that with Payne alongside Jim Andrews, a 6-foot-11-inch junior center, he might be able to make some noise in the NCAA tournament. Even without Payne, Kentucky finished at 21–7, won an SEC championship, and ranked fourteenth in the UPI and eighteenth in the AP polls. Andrews averaged 21.5 points a game and the rest of the starters all averaged in double figures as well. Kentucky beat Marquette 85–69, in the first game of the Mideast Regional in Dayton, but then lost to Florida State, 73–54.

Although no announcement had been made, the university honored Rupp before his last home game (a 102–67 win over Auburn). Harry Lancaster unveiled a bronze plaque dedicated to Rupp's accomplishments, as many former Wildcat All-Americans looked on. After the playing of the national anthem, a spotlight illuminated a circle in front of the home team's bench. Even though Lancaster did not mention that this would be Rupp's last home game as the Wildcat coach, he made it clear that the night had been set aside to honor the Baron. "Coach Rupp," Lancaster spoke into the microphone, "we want to thank you for what you have done the past forty years for college basketball. We want you in the spotlight." According to Russell Rice, Tom Parker, a senior forward, "regretted that the crowd—uncertain whether it was indeed his last game—didn't give Rupp the applause that was his due." Parker knew that if the crowd had known for sure, "they would have blown the roof off the place."[20]

Parker recorded in his diary that Rupp's "retirement wasn't mentioned until the last game of the season," but the senior remembered that there had been "certain games—Georgia, Ole Miss, Mississippi State, Tennessee—that we thought had to be Coach's last at those places." At all of these "last stops," Parker recalled that "everywhere he went was uncharacteristically warm." According to Parker, "The Mississippi State crowd that hates everything about Kentucky gave him a standing ovation." "They honored him for what he had done for basketball."[21]

"What he had done for basketball." Over the span of his 42-year career at Kentucky Rupp had indeed changed college basketball in the Bluegrass State but also in the South and in the nation. Away from the game—as either a player or coach—for the first time in almost six decades, beginning with his first tentative shots at an old hoop on a dirt court in

Halstead—Rupp faced a tough transition, despite the fact that he certainly had interests outside of basketball. The university administration did indeed give Rupp a consulting job for an annual salary of $10,000 a year, and he kept his Memorial Coliseum office, but it of course would not be the same. "I am a consultant," he told Russell Rice, "but nobody wants to consult with me."[22]

Rupp found some solace on the farm. And he had more time to devote to his Hereford cattle. Rupp began stocking his farm with purebred Hereford cattle in the early 1940s, and he had learned the business in much the same way he had learned basketball, through research and personal experience. Rupp impressed visitors with his knowledge and with the care he devoted to the details of the business. He met Tom Lord, a salesman for a men's clothing firm in New York, through his friend Paul Nickell. At a get-together at Nickell's house, Rupp invited the New Yorker out to the farm. "Let's get together tomorrow, Tom, and go to my farm," he offered. "You damn Yankees don't know what farming means." The next day, Rupp took Lord around the farm, stopping from time to time to identify a bull or a heifer. "Now, Tom," Rupp told him at one point, "this one is by Domino II." All the animals looked the same to the easterner, and he was amazed that Rupp could identify each Hereford by name. According to Russell Rice, Lord "went back to New York and told his friends of the prodigy he had met in Kentucky"—speaking of Rupp, not Domino II—a basketball coach "who had a hundred head of cattle and knew them all by name and could even tell you who their parents were." Only later did Lord find out "that he had been the victim of a con: each cow had its vital statistics imprinted on one of its horns."[23]

With his retirement, Rupp had more time to get to know his cattle, but in a way he felt that he had been put out to pasture too. Furman Bisher, the *Atlanta Journal*'s sports editor, visited Rupp's farm when he came to do a story for *Sport* magazine. "We had gone out to look at his farm and were driving around the pasture with Chester Jones, his foreman," Bisher said. "Adolph was admiring the bovine lines of the herd as if it were a basketball squad when we came upon a heifer lying on the ground. Adolph said to Chester, 'What's wrong with her?' Chester replied, 'She just lays down and coughs all the time. I can't find a thing wrong with her.' Adolph said abruptly, 'Get rid of her. She is not a credit to the place. She's like a sub sitting on the bench rooting for the other team. Get rid of her.'"[24] Rupp likened the heifer to an unproductive sub, but now that he had been forced to retire to the farm, he wondered if his productive years were over too.

At first, Rupp felt that he still had something to contribute to college basketball. Some others agreed. At Duke University, Bucky Waters abruptly resigned as coach just before the 1972 season. Terry Sanford, the former North Carolina governor, United States senator, and now the Duke president, talked to Rupp about coaching the Blue Devils. According to Rice, Rupp "said that would be fine." He would come to Duke and bring along Herky as his assistant coach. Herky worked at a Lexington bank, having gotten out of coaching after successful stints at Louisville Atherton, Lexington Lafayette, and Shelby County in the high school ranks. Now he was ready to join his father as a college coach. Just two days before the start of fall practice, however, the death of Rupp's farm manager caused him to rethink his decision to go to Durham. He had already struggled with his quick decision to take on a new job in another state, far from his Kentucky home. Suddenly, he had a ready excuse. The farm would need even more of his personal attention. Duke gave Rupp a week to tell them what he would do. He informed them that he felt they should "go ahead and hire someone else."[25] This would be the last time that Rupp seriously considered another college coaching position.

In 1976, Rupp delighted in the dedication ceremony for the new 23,000-seat arena named after him. Rupp remembered that during the ceremony he received "one of the greatest ovations anyone ever received in Lexington." Suffering from cancer, sick and tired from long years of competition and struggle, Rupp reveled in the memory of that night. "The people stood and hollered and clapped, I imagine about three and a half minutes," he later remembered. "Well, there was something wonderful in that," he recalled, "because none of the students in the audience that night were in school when I quit coaching." "But every game that I've been there this year, or every time that I've been in the building, the thousands of students get up and they say, 'Hello, Adolph!' And I stand up and wave back at them and the crowd stands up and waves back." During this March 1977 interview, Rupp paused, according to the reporter, "his eyes fixed on a faraway object." "You know," he said slowly, "it sure is a satisfying feeling."[26]

Rupp was admitted to the University of Kentucky Medical Center on

November 9, 1977, for treatment of the spine. He died there a month and a day later on December 10, at the age of 76. The funeral service took place at Lexington's Central Christian Church at 1:30 p.m., Tuesday, December 13. The simple, tasteful, traditional service included an organ prelude, made up of three Bach pieces: "Sonatina—from Funeral Cantata No. 106" (God's Time is Best); "Alle Menschen müssen Sterben" (All Men Shall Die); and "Gravement" from Fantasia in C major. A ringing of the carillon was followed by Luther's powerful "A Mighty Fortress Is Our God," and then scripture readings, an invocation, a pastoral prayer, and a "meditation" by Pastor M. Glynn Burke. A benediction, the recessional "God of Our Fathers," and the organ postlude, Bach's "Fantasia in A Minor," concluded the service.[27]

As Rupp had instructed, the pallbearers, including old friends A. B. "Happy" Chandler and Lyman Ginger, took a bottle of bourbon with them to the gravesite at Lexington, Kentucky.

Epilogue

I n December 1977, my senior year in college, I recorded in my diary, "Adolph Rupp—dead of cancer 3 days ago. He meant so much to so many people. At the South Carolina game [at Rupp Arena] his big seat was left empty." In some ways, my feelings about Adolph Rupp have not changed since I wrote those words as a twenty-two-year-old history major, the cocaptain of my Belmont College (now Belmont University) basketball team all those years ago.

I still believe he meant so much to so many people and that he continues to do so. And I still believe that his chair on the sidelines of the home court of the University of Kentucky has been difficult to fill. It has, after all, taken four head coaches—Joe B. Hall (1978), Rick Pitino (1996), Tubby Smith (1998), and John Calipari (2012)—to equal the four NCAA championships that Rupp won alone.

So, who was the real Adolph Rupp, the coach and the man? What is his legacy? What should it have been? How much was he a product of his times? How much did he do? How much more could he have done? How much did he leave undone? Like so much surrounding the Baron of the Bluegrass, the reality often lies obscured beneath many layers of legend. Certainly, Rupp's attitudes and actions—or inactions—on the issue of race are significant, if we are to understand the role that sports played in America in the twentieth century. Race is not the issue that defines Rupp's role, however. This complex man contributed significantly in the pretelevision years—perhaps more than anyone else—to the rise of college sports as a big business in the twentieth century.

While he did not invent the fast break, he perfected its use during and after the World War II years. Despite that, when compared to the sky hooks of UCLA's Lew Alcindor, or the fall-away corner jumpers of Purdue's Rick "the Rocket" Mount, or the sparkling behind-the-back and through-the-legs maneuvers of LSU's Pistol Pete Maravich, his last teams seemed almost plodding on my small, living room television screen. The game had passed him by. Rupp also missed out on the magnificent play for his own teams of Alcindor, Sidney Wicks, Austin Carr, Westley Unseld, Butch Beard, and other African American athletes because of his lackluster recruiting efforts. After the 1970–1971 season, when Tom Payne, Rupp's lone African American recruit, played very well on a 16–9 team, Rupp's very last team, in 1971–1972, was again lily white. Clearly, the game passed him by.

One of the reasons it has taken this book so long to be written is that a new Rupp story came to light so often, sometimes on a weekly basis. Rupp stories seemingly never end. Jim Host, the creator of Host Communications and a student radio broadcaster in the late 1950s and early 1960s, literally has a host of Rupp stories to tell—all delightful.

There was the 1959 trip to California, for example, when Kentucky beat a good UCLA team, 68–66, starring Walt Hazzard and coached by a young John Wooden. After the game in Los Angeles, the team loaded onto the bus, with Coach Rupp characteristically taking the seat directly behind the bus driver. Twenty-one-year-old Host took the seat opposite Rupp behind the barrier by the door. According to Host, when Rupp took his seat, he never looked back to see if everyone was in place—that was expected—he just said to the driver, "Kick her, Doc," and off they went.[1]

They were to play University of Southern California (USC) the next night, so they headed for the hotel for a late meal, but a car ran through an intersection and the bus broadsided the vehicle. The collision threw Host over the barrier and into the well by the door. Bleeding profusely, Host had suffered a head wound and concussion, but he remembered Rupp jumping down into the well and shouting, "My gawd, is he dead?"[2]

Host did not die, although four car passengers perished in the crash. Rupp followed the young student to the hospital, where he was bandaged up well enough to call the next evening's USC game for the radio, a game UK lost 87–73.

After games, Rupp held court in his hotel room wearing red silk pajamas. According to Host, he always had student managers provide sacks of White Castle hamburgers and bottles of Lowenbrau beer. For the Baron, only bourbon whiskey would do. Members of the press would all sit on the floor and Rupp would sit in a big chair. "My gawd, help yourselves. There's beer and there's White Castles."[3]

Rupp himself would fill his glass with bourbon, "exactly half full," and go into the bathroom to the sink and "whisk" just a spritz of water in the glass. He would come back in and take a big swallow and you could see the tears come into his eyes, and he was ready to begin the post-game "press conference."[4]

And with Rupp there were always stories to tell, usually about how brilliant the opposing coach's defensive strategies had been, strategies that Rupp had just dominated by 20 or 30 points. Rupp wanted to be sure that an inferior coach would be around next year to beat again.

No doubt about it. Adolph Rupp made the most of his opportunities to change college basketball in America. Even though his predecessor John Mauer largely had put the fast-break system into place, Rupp perfected it and showcased it to the nation by taking his teams to play in Chicago and New York and to the Sugar Bowl in New Orleans. Although Rupp refused to recruit African American athletes until he was forced to do so by an adamant University of Kentucky administration late in his career, unlike other schools in the Southeastern Conference he never refused to play schools with African American players. Rupp played all comers anywhere, including Memorial Coliseum in Lexington.

For Kentucky, Rupp and the success of the Kentucky Wildcats united the commonwealth. The cliché became true: Kentuckians from Pikeville to Paducah rooted for the Wildcats victory after victory, championship after championship. High school coaches attended Rupp's clinics and tried to emulate Rupp's success. Negatively, basketball success superseded academic success in the commonwealth both in higher education and on the secondary level. A winning basketball team held so much more importance than high test scores or winning debate or speech teams.

Rupp retired as the winningest basketball coach in the history of the college game, with a record of 876–190. His wins total has been bested again and again, and the issue of race increasingly has defined Rupp's legacy in the twenty-first century, indicating the lingering importance of the racial divide in the postmodern world.

Rupp's journey took him and the game of basketball a long, long way. The story of a successful basketball coach at first glance seems simple. What can be more straightforward than the rise of the son of immigrant parents from humble, rural roots in the plains of Kansas to the pinnacle of his chosen profession? But, then comes a central question: How did a boy reared in the small German farming community of Halstead, Kansas, within the confines of the pacifist precepts of the strict Mennonite sect of his parents and neighbors, become the colorful, cursing Baron of the Bluegrass? From Halstead, Rupp's journey took him to Lawrence and Burr Oak, Kansas, to Marshalltown, Iowa, where he served as a high school wrestling coach, to Freeport, Illinois, to Lexington, Kentucky, to London, England, and other cities in Europe and Asia and the Middle East, to hamlets in the rolling hills of western Kentucky and the mountain hollows of eastern Kentucky, to college towns around the Deep South, to the Sugar Bowl in New Orleans and to Madison Square Garden in the Big Apple, and eventually to the National Basketball Hall of Fame in Springfield, Massachusetts, where basketball began in 1891, invented by James A. Naismith, one of Rupp's professors at the University of Kansas.

Acknowledgments

This book would have never come to pass without the generosity of Dr. Humbert S. Nelli, my professor and mentor at the University of Kentucky. Dr. Nelli had researched Rupp for some fifteen years before he retired from UK's department of history. He had already written the best critical study of University of Kentucky basketball, *The Winning Tradition: A History of Kentucky Wildcat Basketball*. Upon his retirement, Dr. Nelli gave me a large body of research material on Adolph Rupp. It had been Dr. Nelli's plan to write his definitive biography. Only Russell Rice, a former sports information director at the university, has produced a Rupp biography, and his short book, *Adolph Rupp: Kentucky's Basketball Baron*, was written from the perspective of a friend, admirer, and fan. Although he was an "insider," Mr. Rice did not have access to the large body of materials and interviews that Dr. Nelli collected and to which I added in the years hence. He did not treat the subject with the depth required and also did not place Rupp in the context of national developments in sports or in American society and culture.

When Dr. Nelli retired from the university, and after some fifteen years of researching Rupp and conducting interviews with those who knew him, he decided not to write his book. So, Dr. Nelli turned his extensive materials over to me, and I agreed to write the biography.

When he gave me the materials, I was stunned. The volume of material has been daunting. Copies of primary documents—court records, notes, game summaries, correspondence, photographs, and business records—are included in the collection. In addition, Dr. Nelli tape-recorded interviews with at least one member of every one of Rupp's teams from 1930 to 1972. Dr. Nelli also interviewed University of Kentucky presidents, politicians, Rupp's assistant coaches, and Rupp's sister in Kansas, Elizabeth Rupp Lawson. The oral history collection is composed of 96 one-and-a-half-hour tapes with more than 120 separate interviews. I want to thank Dr. Nelli for his faith in entrusting me with this project. I only hope I have not let him down.

In other taped interviews, Rupp tells his own story. These are the Russell Rice interviews, deposited at the Louie B. Nunn Center for Oral History at the University of Kentucky. I am grateful for two Committee on Institutional Studies and Research (CISR) Grants from Murray State University to complete transcriptions of the tapes. I hired a professional transcriptionist who completed transcriptions of most of the interviews. They reveal the significance of a national figure in collegiate sports.

I want to thank Murray State University for a number of other awards that aided in research for this book. Murray State granted me two sabbaticals, in 2004 and 2010, and two Presidential Research Fellowships, in 2003 and 2016. In 2008, the university awarded me the Distinguished Researcher Award, the highest award given by the university for research. Without these, completion of this project would not have been possible.

A team of perceptive readers aided this project to the end. I want to thank my copyeditor at the University Press of Kentucky, Elizabeth Van Allen, for her expert care of the manuscript, along with Natalie O'Neal, Ila McEntire, and especially Anne Dean Dotson, who ushered the book through its various stages from proposal to manuscript to book.

Earlier readers at various stages proved invaluable to improving the manuscript. These included Dr. Charlotte Beahan, Dr. William H. Mulligan Jr., Dr. James W. Hammack Jr., and Dr. Kenneth Wolf of the Murray State University Department of History, and Dr. Richard O. Davies, Distinguished Professor of History, Emeritus, at the University of Nevada, Reno.

A special thanks goes to Dave Roos, longtime copyeditor at the *Louisville Courier-Journal* who kick-started this project when it had been moribund for several years; and to a trio of friends and mentors, who read everything I write: Dr. Thomas H. Appleton Jr., Dr. Kenneth M. Startup, and Gary Garth. Thank you for your friendship and for your belief in me. Shannon Ragland lent books and Rupp research unselfishly, and I appreciate the sacrifice.

Student assistants at Murray State have helped with the project through the years, beginning with Jarrett Nantz and Nancy Carstens, who made copies of the original taped interviews. Other valuable student assistants have been Anna Barnett, Jon Dunning, Nick Lambing, and Andrew Landreth. I am also indebted to classes of undergraduate sports history students at Williams Baptist University and Murray State University, whose discussion made me think about Rupp in new ways.

Other friends have lived patiently with the Adolph Rupp project for years, encouraging all the while. These include Dr. C. Pat Taylor, Professor Jerry Gibbens, Dr. Brian Clardy, Dr. James Humpheys, Janice McLain Durham, Bob and Sheree Mantooth, and my pastors Dr. Bill and Jill Shoulta, Rev. Sally Ensley, Dr. Terry Ellis, Rev. Terry Garvin, Rev. Keith Inman, and Father Matthew Bradley.

I want to thank my old basketball teammates and friends, Phil Gibson, Steve Duncan, Paul Austin, Brent Shelton, Alan Vaughan, Duane Clark, and Tom Major at Webster County High School, and Mitch Keebler, Greg Oglesby, Bernard Childress, Corky Cross, Tommy Sidwell, Danny Duvall, Harrison Crabtree, Jay Stapp, and Randy Salyers, at Belmont University. Thanks go as well to my wonderful coaches at Webster County High School in Kentucky, Paul Watts, Maurice Forker, Gene Pendleton, and Harlan Peden. I am especially indebted to Coach Eddie Ford for everything he has done for me through the years. I want to thank Coach Dick Campbell for taking a chance on me at Belmont University.

I wish to thank my mother-in-law and father-in-law, Marlin and Jossie Seaton, both huge UK and Adolph Rupp fans. I want to thank my mother and father, James Wesley and Cammie Mann Bolin, for providing a bookish childhood for me and for loving me unconditionally. I want to thank my brother Steve and his family, and Evelyn's sisters—Rebecca, Marilyn, and June—and their families for believing in me.

Finally, Evelyn and Wesley and Cammie Jo never doubted that this book would come to be. The book, in fact, would not have been completed without their faith in me. Because of that the book is dedicated to them and to Dr. Humbert S. Nelli.

Notes

Prologue

1. The author heard Ralph Beard tell the "silver belt buckle" story on three different occasions, the first in the class that Dr. Humbert S. Nelli taught about the history of Wildcat basketball at the University of Kentucky. Interestingly, in Dr. Nelli's class, Beard made all of the women leave the classroom and stand in the hall. I suppose he thought Rupp's use of the "n" word would not be appropriate for female ears. In one interview I had with Beard I made the mistake of asking Rupp's star guard to tell the story at the very beginning of the interview. After he told the story, he asked, "When are you going to start the recorder?" I said, "Mr. Beard, I have been recording from the very beginning." At that point, Beard became very agitated and threatened to end the interview, and indeed, the interview might have ended there, but I took the tape out of the recorder and gave it to him. Assured of my goodwill, we continued to talk for another hour with me taking notes. He enjoyed talking about the 1948 Olympics more than anything else.

2. This rendition of this oft-quoted anecdote is recorded in Dale Barnstable to Russell Rice, n.d., included in Russell Rice, *Kentucky Basketball's Big Blue Machine* (Huntsville, AL: Strode Publishers, 1976), 201.

3. *Lexington Herald-Leader*, September 2, 2001.

4. Ibid., December 19, 1991; Robert Kaiser, "Loyal to the Legend, Coach Adolph Rupp's Family Strives to Return Luster to His Reputation," *Lexington Herald-Leader*, March 14, 1993.

5. Randy Roberts and James Olson, *Winning Is the Only Thing: Sports in America since 1945* (Baltimore: Johns Hopkins University Press, 1989), 45.

6. James Duane Bolin interview with Marie Jackson, Paducah, KY, September 10, 2010.

7. Ibid.

8. Ibid.

9. Ibid.

10. Ibid.

11. Ibid.

12. Ibid.

13. Adolph Rupp, "Defeat and Failure to Me Are Enemies," *Sports Illustrated*, December 8, 1958, 101.

14. For an excellent overview of the role of sports in American life see Richard O. Davies, *Sports in American Life: A History*, 2nd edition (Malden, MA: Wiley-Blackwell, 2012). Davies's short section on Rupp and the significance of University of Kentucky basketball is balanced and on target. See especially pages 183–84. Steven A. Riess discussed the connection of the rise of sport with industrialism in *Sport in Industrial America, 1850–1920*, and Randy Roberts and James Olson documented the more recent history of sports in *Winning Is the Only Thing: Sports in America since 1945*. Ronald A. Smith concentrated on the development of college sports in *Sports and Freedom: The Rise of Big-Time College Athletics*. John R. Thelin devoted a section on a "Campus Profile of the University of Kentucky" as he discussed scandal and reform in intercollegiate athletics. In *Beer and Circus*, Murray Sperber, Bobby Knight's nemesis at Indiana University, argued that big-time sports changed the culture of campus life for students in America's universities. See Steven A. Riess, *Sport in Industrial America, 1850–1920* (Wheeling, IL: Harlan Davidson, Inc., 1995; Roberts and Olson, *Winning Is the Only Thing: Sports in America since 1945*; Ronald A. Smith, *Sports and Freedom: The Rise of Big-Time College Athletics* (New York: Oxford University Press, 1988); John R. Thelin, *Games Colleges Play: Scandal and Reform in Intercollegiate Athletics* (Baltimore and London: Johns Hopkins University Press, 1994); Murray Sperber, *Beer and Circus: How Big-Time College Sports Is Crippling Undergraduate Education* (New York: Henry Holt and Company, Inc., 2000).

Introduction

1. Peter Cary, "From Mystery Woman to Piano Tuner, They All Remember Adolph Rupp," *Lexington Herald*, December 13, 1977.

2. Rupp yearned for positive attention from the press. Indeed, he demanded it. At the same time, stag parties—as Dr. V. A. Jackson, Kentucky's team physician, called them—usually held in Rupp's or Jackson's hotel room the evening before a road game, gave Rupp and his assistants a chance to relax away from the glare of the media. See V. A. Jackson, *Beyond the Baron: A Personal Glimpse of Coach Adolph Rupp* (Kuttawa, KY: McClanahan Publishing House, Inc., 1998), 10.

3. See Rupp, "Defeat and Failure to Me Are Enemies."

4. Ibid.

5. Dave Kindred, "Rupp: A Top 5 Ornery Charmer," http//iubballjunkie.com/othercoaches.html.

6. Rupp, "Defeat and Failure to Me Are Enemies," 106.

7. Bill Surface and Jimmy Breslin, "Basketball's Bumptious Baron," *True: The Man's Magazine*, March 1960, 58.

8. Kindred, "Rupp: A Top 5 Ornery Charmer."

9. Cary, "From Mystery Woman to Piano Tuner."

10. *Louisville Courier-Journal*, December 12, 1977.

11. Humbert S. Nelli interview with Alex Groza, November 16, 1983, San Diego, CA.

12. James Duane Bolin interview with Stan Key, Murray, KY, August 17, 2002.

13. See Billy Reed, "Eulogy for a Bookie: Ed Curd, Inventor of the Point Spread Dies," *Backstretch: A Magazine for the Thoroughbred Industry* (July/August 2002).

14. The survey was conducted by *Governing Magazine's State and Local Source Book 2005*. See *Murray (KY) Ledger & Times*, August 13, 2005.

15. Rupp, "Defeat and Failure to Me Are Enemies," 106.

16. Dave Kindred, "Rupp: A Top 5 Ornery Charmer."

17. Curry Kirkpatrick, "The Night They Drove Old Dixie Down," *Sports Illustrated*, April 1, 1991.

18. *Lexington Herald-Leader*, December 19, 1991.

19. Ibid., December 22, 1991. It must be noted that Kindred quoted Rupp as using the word "Negro," not "nigger." See Dave Kindred, *Basketball: The Dream Game in Kentucky* (Louisville, KY: Data Courier, Inc., 1976), 86.

20. Ibid.

21. Ibid.

22. See Robert Kaiser, "Loyal to the Legend, Coach Adolph Rupp's Family Strives to Return Luster to His Reputation," *Lexington Herald-Leader*, March 14, 1993.

23. *Lexington Herald*, April 21, 1987.

24. Earl Cox, *Earl Cox: Calling It Like I See It: True Stories and Tall Tales about Kentucky Sports* (Louisville, KY: Butler Books, 2002), 37.

25. Kaiser, "Loyal to the Legend"; see James Duane Bolin, *Bossism and Reform in a Southern City: Lexington, Kentucky, 1880–1940* (Lexington: University Press of Kentucky, 2000); Herbert A. Thomas Jr., "Victims of Circumstance: Negroes in a Southern Town, 1865–1880," *Register of the Kentucky Historical Society* 71, no. 3 (July 1973): 253–71; John D. Wright Jr., *Lexington: Heart of the Bluegrass* (Lexington, KY: Lexington-Fayette County Historic Commission, 1982), 98, 139.

26. Rupp, "Defeat and Failure to Me Are Enemies."

27. Bolin interview with Stan Key, August 17, 2002.

28. Bert Nelli and Steve Nelli, *The Winning Tradition: A History of Kentucky Wildcat Basketball*, 2nd edition (Lexington: University Press of Kentucky, 1998), 76, 95. This source is especially important regarding the Kentucky Wildcats' pre-Rupp years. Hereafter, it will be identified as Nelli, *The Winning Tradition*.

29. Chip Alexander, "Remembering Rupp," http://www.sportserver.com/newsroom/sports/PressBox/special/acc/arupp.html.

30. Ibid.

31. Ibid.

32. David Lowenthal, *The Past Is a Foreign Country* (Cambridge: Cambridge University Press, 1985), xvi.

33. See the Kentucky Humanities Council website for a listing of all Chautauqua performers. www.kyhumanities.org.

34. *Lexington Herald-Leader*, August 26, 2001.

35. Surface and Breslin, "Basketball's Bumptious Baron," 59.

36. The author served as the Humanities adviser for the Rupp character; see also *Lexington Herald-Leader*, August 26, 2001.

37. *Lexington Herald-Leader*, August 26, 2001; Ed Smith to Duane Bolin, e-mail message, September 4, 2002.

1. The Halstead Years, 1901–1919

1. The University of Kentucky Athletics: Adolph Rupp Oral History Project comprises 19 interviews that Russell Rice conducted with Rupp between 1931 and 1972. They are held in the Louie B. Nunn Center for Oral History, Special Collections, at the University of Kentucky. They have been transcribed. See Adolph Rupp Oral History Project, 960H21, A/F 536, 537, 538, 539, 540, 541, 542, 543, 544, 545, 546, 547, 548, 549, 550, 551, 552, 553, 554, Special Collections, University of Kentucky, Lexington, KY. Hereafter Rupp Tapes.

2. Russell Rice, *Adolph Rupp: Kentucky's Basketball Baron* (Champaign, IL: Sagamore Publishing, 1994), 2.

3. Census statistics provided by the Kansas State Historical Society. See http://www.kshs.org.

4. For information on Halstead see the Halstead city website at http://www.halsteadks.com.

5. Rice, *Adolph Rupp*, 3; Rupp Tapes, 536.

6. Rupp Tapes, 536; Humbert S. Nelli interview with Elizabeth Lawson, September 3, 1987.

7. Larry Feese, "Legendary 'Baron' Adolph Rupp Was Born and Reared in Nearby Halstead," *Hutchinson (KS) News*, March 14, 1983.

8. Rupp Tapes, 536; *Evansville (IN) Press*, December 12, 1977.

9. Humbert S. Nelli interview with Elizabeth Lawson, September 3, 1987; Rupp Tapes, 536.

10. Ibid.

11. Ibid.

12. Ibid.

13. See, for example, the *Halstead (KS) Independent*, August 26, 1915. The German language columns disappeared when America entered the war in 1917.

14. *Halstead (KS) Independent*, November 4, 1915.

15. See *Halstead (KS) Independent*, September 12, 1918; September 19, 1918; November 7, 1918; July 3, 1919; April 10, 1919; May 8, 1919.

16. Rupp Tapes, 536.

17. *Halstead (KS) Independent*, November 7, 1918.

18. In a 1915 *Halstead (KS) Independent* article, a writer proclaimed, "The farmer of today is taking his place in the world as a business man." See *Halstead (KS) Independent*, November 18, 1915.

19. Rupp Tapes, 536.

20. Rupp Tapes, 536.

21. For background on the origins of basketball, James A. Naismith, and the Young Men's Christian Association (YMCA) see William J. Baker's introduction in James Naismith, *Basketball: Its Origin and Development* (Lincoln: University of Nebraska Press, 1996), ix.

22. Born in Ontario in 1861, and orphaned at eight, Naismith left home in 1883 to study theology at McGill University in Montreal. After completing a BA degree in philosophy from McGill in 1887, he then pursued his interest in theology at Presbyterian College, a seminary associated with McGill, graduating with an additional degree in religion in 1890. Naismith was eventually ordained as a Presbyterian minister. While in Montreal he decided to pursue a career with the YMCA, an organization founded in London "as an evangelical body of young men primarily fearful of the *moral* dangers of city life." The YMCA came to the United States in the 1850s, and in America the organization concentrated on the "physical and moral needs" of young men in America's burgeoning cities.

Leaving Canada, Naismith entered the YMCA Training School in Springfield, Massachusetts in 1890. After Naismith's one year as a student, the school hired him as a physical education instructor. While still a student in Luther Gulick's summer physical education seminar, however, the thirty-year-old Naismith developed a new recreational game as a class assignment. Under the guidance of Gulick, Naismith worked out the details of the new game. He remembered from his childhood in Canada games such as "duck on the rock" and more informal competitions to throw balls into empty boxes or baskets. He decided to elevate two peach baskets for goals, and, using a soccer ball, he combined elements of lacrosse, rugby football, "duck on the rock," and soccer in his new game of "basket ball." Frank Mahan, the captain of Naismith's first team, suggested "Naismith ball" as the name of the game. Naismith explained his reaction to the name in his account of the invention of the game, *Basketball: Its Origin and Development*: "I told him that I had not thought of the matter but was interested only in getting it started. Frank insisted that it must have a name and suggested the name of Naismith ball. I laughed and told him that I thought that name would kill the game." When Mahan offered "basket ball" as a second choice, Naismith agreed. "We have a basket and a ball, and it seems to me that would be a good name for it," he replied. "It was in this way that basketball was named."

Two teams of nine players each attempted the first game of basketball on December 21, 1891. Players wore uniforms of long gray trousers, short-sleeved jerseys, and gym shoes. Step ladders were placed beside the baskets that had been attached to the balcony rail at each end of the college gymnasium; the bottoms of the baskets had not been cut away. Naismith outlined thirteen rules of the new game, and although the rules have been altered through the years, the "essence" of the game, "throwing a ball into an elevated goal," has not changed. Naismith decided on 13 basic rules of the game:

1. The ball may be thrown in any direction with one or both hands.

2. The ball may be batted in any direction with one or both hands, but never with the fist.

3. A player cannot run with the ball. The player must throw it from the spot on which he catches it, allowance to be made for a man running at good speed.

4. The ball must be held in or between the hands. The arms or body must not be used for holding it.

5. No shouldering, holding, pushing, striking or tripping in any way of an opponent. The first infringement of this rule by any person shall count as a foul; the second shall disqualify him until the next goal is made or, if there was evident intent to injure the person, for the whole of the game. No substitution shall be allowed.

6. A foul is striking at the ball with the fist, violations of Rules 3 and 4 and such as described in Rule 5.

7. If either side make three consecutive fouls it shall count as a goal for the opponents (consecutive means without the opponents in the meantime making a foul).

8. A goal shall be made when the ball is thrown or batted from the ground into the basket and stays there, providing those defending the goal do not touch or disturb the goal. If the ball rests on the edge and the opponents move the basket, it shall count as a goal.

9. When the ball goes out of bounds, it shall be thrown into the field and played by the first person touching it. In case of dispute the umpire shall throw it straight into the field. The thrower-in is allowed five seconds. If he holds it longer, it shall go to the opponent. If any side persists in delaying the game, the umpire shall call a foul on them.

10. The umpire shall be judge of the men and shall note the fouls and notify the referee when three consecutive fouls have been made. He shall have the power to disqualify men according to Rule 5.

11. The referee shall be the judge of the ball and decide when it is in play in bounds, to which side it belongs, and shall keep the time. He shall decide when a goal has been made and keep account of the goals with any other duties that are usually performed by a referee.

12. The time shall be two 15-minute halves with five minutes' rest between.

13. The side making the most goals in that time shall be declared the winners.

When *The Triangle*, the YMCA training-school paper distributed to YMCAs throughout the United States, published the thirteen rules along with Naismith's instructions on January 15, 1892, information about the game spread across the nation. By the time of Adolph Rupp's birth in 1901, only a decade after the game's invention, basketball was known and played in Halstead and other communities in rural Kansas. News of the game came west from New England along with its founder, James A. Naismith. See "Birth of a Game," http://www.kansasheritage.org/people/naismith.html; Naismith, *Basketball: Its Origin and Development*, 59–60; "Naismith Untold," http://web.archive.org/web/20071102090506/http://www.hoophall.com/history/naismith-untold-story.html.

23. Humbert S. Nelli interview with Elizabeth Lawson, September 6, 1987.

24. Russell Rice, *Kentucky Basketball's Big Blue Machine*, 76.

25. *Wichita (KS) Eagle*, December 13, 1977.

26. Rupp Tapes, 536; *Halstead (KS) Independent*, November 11, 1915; September 16, 1915; August 22, 1918; Humbert S. Nelli interview with Elizabeth Lawson, September 3, 1987; Rice, *Adolph Rupp*, 6.

27. *Halstead (KS) Independent*, September 9, 1915; September 12, 1918; October 28, 1915.

28. *Halstead (KS) Independent,* November 18, 1915.

29. Charles Kingsley, an English cleric and novelist, applied the concept on a personal level as he "bullishly walked and rowed great distances for his health." Kingsley's friend, the novelist Thomas Hughes, connected the idea to competitive games in his *Tom Brown's Schooldays* in 1857. One American proponent insisted that "Muscular Christianity is Christianity applied to the treatment and use of our bodies. It is an enforcement of the laws of health by the solemn sanctions of the New Testament." In America, Unitarian minister Thomas Wentworth Higginson promoted the idea of Muscular Christianity in nine essays published in the *Atlantic Monthly* from 1852 to 1862. By the time James Naismith sought out his life calling in the 1880s, the idea had forged a tidy alliance between health, athletics, and Christianity.

In *Basketball: Its Origin and Development*, published in 1941, Naismith included a chapter titled "The Values of Basketball," in which he asserted that "the main purpose of the game is recreation and the development of certain attributes that are peculiar to the game." "Basketball was intended," he continued, "primarily for young men who had acquired their physical development but who were in need of exercise that would stress the skills and agile movements that were lacking in manual labor." Naismith realized the game's limitations: "Games have been called the laboratory for the development of moral attributes; but they will not, of themselves, accomplish this purpose. They must be properly conducted by competent individuals." Naismith went on to list and discuss twelve specific attributes developed by basketball: initiative, agility, accuracy, alertness, cooperation, skill, reflex judgment, speed, self-confidence, self-sacrifice, self-control, and sportsmanship.

It was in his discussion of sportsmanship that Naismith most clearly delineated the ideas and ideals of "Muscular Christianity." He defined sportsmanship as "the player's insistence on his own rights and his observance of the rights of others," a sort of golden rule for basketball. Sportsmanship means "playing the game vigorously," he wrote, "observing the rules definitely, accepting defeat gracefully, and winning courteously." According to Naismith, basketball "is peculiarly adapted to the development of this trait because the players, officials, coaches, and spectators are in such close proximity that an action of one is observed by the others." Naismith's ideas, many of them previously published in *The Triangle*, a YMCA journal, in 1892, and the *American Physical Education Review* (May 1914), had been echoed by President Theodore Roosevelt in his advocacy of "the strenuous life." It was Naismith's hope that the game of basketball would be "played for fun, exercise, and the building of character." See Naismith, *Basketball: Its Origin and Development*, ix, x, 185, 186–87, vii, viii, xvi.

30. Rupp Tapes, 537.
31. Rupp Tapes, 537.
32. Rice, *Kentucky Basketball's Big Blue Machine*, 76.
33. *Halstead (KS) Independent*, December 23, 1915; January 13, 1916.
34. Ibid., February 3, 1916; January 13, 1916.
35. Ibid., February 17, 1916; February 24, 1916; Rice, *Adolph Rupp*, 5.
36. Rice, *Adolph Rupp*, 5, 77; Humbert S. Nelli interview with Elizabeth Lawson, September 3, 1987; *Halstead (KS) Independent*, December 14, 1916; December 21, 1916; February 1, 1917; February 8, 1917; February 15, 1917; March 6, 1917; March 22, 1917.
37. Rice, *Kentucky Basketball's Big Blue Machine*, 77; Bill MacKay, "Rupp's 1st Court Was Hard-Packed Dirt in Halstead," *Wichita (KS) Eagle*, December 13, 1977; *Halstead (KS) Independent*, December 15, 1977; January 6, 1916; February 8, 1917; Rupp Tapes, 536, 537.
38. Rupp Tapes, 536, 537; MacKay, "Rupp's 1st Court Was Hard-Packed Dirt in Halstead."
39. *Halstead (KS) Independent*, November 16, 1916; November 30, 1916; Rice, *Kentucky Basketball's Big Blue Machine*, 77.
40. Rice, *Kentucky Basketball's Big Blue Machine*, 77; MacKay, "Rupp's 1st Court Was Hard-Packed Dirt in Halstead"; *Wichita (KS) Eagle*, December 13, 1977.
41. Naismith, *Basketball: Its Origin and Development*, xvi, xvii.
42. *Halstead (KS) Independent*, February 14, 1918; March 14, 1918; March 21, 1918.
43. Ibid., January 16, 1919.
44. Ibid., February 27, 1919.
45. Ibid., January 23, 1919; January 30, 1919; February 6, 1919; Naismith, *Basketball: Its Origin and Development*, 71.
46. Rice, *Kentucky Basketball's Big Blue Machine*, 77.
47. Rice, *Adolph Rupp*, 5.
48. Rupp Tapes, 536.

2. The University of Kansas and the Jayhawk Café, 1919–1923

1. Rupp Tapes, 536.
2. Ibid.
3. Ibid.
4. Ibid.
5. Rupp tapes, 537; Humbert S. Nelli interview with Elizabeth Lawson, September 3, 1987; Rupp Tapes, 536.
6. Rupp Tapes, 536.
7. Ibid.
8. Ibid.
9. Ibid.; Humbert S. Nelli interview with Elizabeth Lawson, September 3, 1987.
10. Rupp Tapes, 536.
11. Ibid.

12. Ibid.

13. Ibid.

14. Rupp Tapes, 537.

15. *Lawrence (KS) Journal*, December 2, 1896, as quoted in the University of Kansas Athletics website, http://www.kuathletics.com/mensbasketbal/history/century_stories_naismith.html.

16. *Kansas Weekly* as quoted in the University of Kansas Athletics website, http://www.kuathletics.com/mensbasketbal/history/century_stories_naismith.html.

17. Ibid., http://www.rockchalk.com/seasons/coaches.sht.

18. Theodore M. O'Leary, "Dr. Forrest C. Allen—Basketball Wizard," *Jayhawker Magazine and Yearbook*, Mid-Winter Number, 1922, 170.

19. Ibid., 171.

20. At Warrensburg Teachers College (what would become Central Missouri State University), Allen, always successful, posted a record of 107–7. At Baker his teams went 46–2 and at Haskell Institute, 27–5, so his non–University of Kansas record was a phenomenal 180–14. For Allen's record see the Allen biography at the Naismith Basketball Hall of Fame website at http://www.hoopball.com/halloffamers/Allen.htm.

21. Rupp Tapes, 538.

22. Ibid.

23. Ibid.

24. Ibid.

25. Michael Beschloss, "Naismith's Choices on Race, from Basketball's Beginnings," *The Upshot*, May 2, 2014, http://www.nytimes.com/2014/05/03/upshot/choices-on-race-even-from-basketballs-beginnings.html?_r=1.

26. Ibid.

27. Kansas officials planned to display the Naismith document in the new sports complex once completed. See ibid.

28. Rupp Tapes, 538.

29. Rupp Tapes, 540.

30. Rupp came to respect the coach and expressed his respect in no uncertain terms, stating simply, "He was a great man." See ibid.

31. Rupp Tapes, 536.

32. Rupp Tapes, 540.

33. Rupp pronounced "unknown" characteristically in three syllables. See ibid.

34. Rupp Tapes, 540.

35. Ibid.

36. *Jayhawker Yearbook*, 1921, 60.

37. Ibid., 1922, 144.

38. Ibid., 1923, 127.

39. Rupp Tapes, 537.

40. Ibid.

41. Ibid., 540.

42. Ibid., 537.

43. Ibid., 537.

44. Ibid., 551; Rice, *Adolph Rupp*, 10.

45. Rupp Tapes, 551, 540.

46. Ibid., 551, 540.

47. Ibid., 540, 551.

48. Ibid., 540.

49. The various renditions of the story are found in Forrest C. Allen, *My Basketball Bible* (Kansas City: Smith-Greaves Co., 1924), 433; Forrest C. Allen, *Better Basketball: Technique, Tactics and Tales* (New York: Whittlesey House, McGraw-Hill Book Company, Inc., 1937), 465.

50. Rupp Tapes, 540.

51. Allen, *My Basketball Bible*, 433, 434.

52. Ibid., 435.

53. Ibid., 536.

54. Ibid., 438.

55. The team celebrated the victory and the season at a Greek restaurant. Always concerned about food, Rupp remembered the menu: "We had pork chops, green beans, and mashed potatoes." "Well, I could have had that at the Jayhawk just as well, but it was a nice way to celebrate an undefeated season," Rupp concluded. It was "far different than we do things today, but nevertheless we enjoyed it, we lived through it, we all had a lot of fun, we had a lot of respect for Phog because Phog was a strict disciplinarian, we had to do things his way, and I think if we had more men like Phog Allen living today in many places of responsibilities, this would be a far better world." See Rupp Tapes, 540.

56. *Jayhawker Yearbook*, 1921, 1922, and 1923.

57. Ibid., 1923.

58. The Phog Allen quotation and the Paul Endacott quotation are both included in the University of Kansas Athletics website at http://www.kuathletics.com/mensbasketball/history/century_stories_allen_2.html.

59. See *Jayhawker Yearbook*, 1923.

60. Rupp Tapes, 538.

3. Before Big Blue, 1923–1930

1. See Larry Boeck, "Coach Adolph 'Baron Midas' Rupp Is an Alger Hero with Trimmings," *Louisville Courier-Journal*, February 22, 1953; *Louisville Courier-Journal*, September 2, 1970; Rupp Tapes, 538; Rice, *Kentucky Basketball's Big Blue Machine*, 81; *Marshalltimes*, February 1995, 16.

2. Rupp Tapes, 538.

3. Ibid.

4. Ibid.

5. The quotation from Allen's letter of recommendation, published in the *Burr Oak (KS) Herald* in 1924, also appeared in the *Jewell County Record* (Mankato, KS), January 5, 1978.

6. Rupp Tapes, 538; *Salina (KS) Journal*, March 4, 2002.

7. Ibid.

8. Ibid.

9. *Salina (KS) Journal*, March 4, 2002.

10. The *Burr Oak (KS) Herald* is quoted in the *Jewell County Record* (Mankato, KS), January 5, 1978.

11. *Marshalltimes*, 18.

12. Rupp Tapes, 538; *Marshalltimes*, February 1995, 20.

13. Ibid.

14. Rupp Tapes, 538; *Marshalltimes*, February 1995, 21; Rupp himself claimed that he "bought a book on wrestling." See Rice, *Kentucky Basketball's Big Blue Machine*, 81, and Rupp Tapes, 538.

15. Rupp Tapes, 538.

16. *Marshalltimes*, February 1995, 21, 22; Rupp Tapes, 538.

17. Ibid.

18. Rupp Tapes, 538; *Marshalltimes*, February 1995, 22.

19. Ibid.

20. Ibid.

21. Ibid.

22. *Marshalltimes*, February 1995, 26.

23. Rupp Tapes, 538; *Marshalltimes*, February 1995, 22.

24. *Marshalltimes*, February 1995, 22.

25. Ibid., 26.

26. Rupp Tapes, 538.

27. Ibid.

28. Ibid.

29. Rupp Tapes, 538; *Freeport (IL) Journal-Standard*, September 10, 1927; *Marshalltimes*, February 1995, 23.

30. Ibid.

31. Rice, *Adolph Rupp*, 16; Rupp Tapes, 538.

32. Ibid.

33. Rupp Tapes, 538; *Freeport (IL) Journal-Standard*, February 23, 1926.

34. *Freeport (IL) Journal-Standard*, December 5, 1925, December 9, 1925.

35. Ibid., March 22, 1926.

36. Andrew Logue, "Distant Moon, Emotional Strobridge Made Huge Impact," *Des Moines Register*, August 18, 2002.

37. Ibid.

38. Rupp Tapes, 538; *Freeport (IL) Journal-Standard*, May 24, 1926.

39. Ibid.

40. *Marshalltimes*, February 1995, 23.

41. Rupp Tapes, 538; *Freeport (IL) Journal-Standard*, October 6, 1926.

42. *Freeport (IL) Journal-Standard*, December 6, 1926, December 13, 1926; Rupp Tapes, 538.

43. *Freeport (IL) Journal-Standard*, December 31, 1926, January 5, 1927.
44. Ibid., January 10, 1927.
45. Quoted in Rice, *Adolph Rupp*, 15–16.
46. Rice, *Adolph Rupp*, 16.
47. *Freeport (IL) Journal-Standard*, January 12, 14, 15, 17, 23, 24, 26, 1927.
48. Ibid.
49. Ibid., February 7, 8, 9, 10, 1927.
50. Ibid., February 12, 1927.
51. Ibid., February 19, 21, 23, 1927.
52. Ibid., February 26, 1927.
53. Rupp Tapes, 538.
54. Ibid.
55. *Freeport (IL) Journal-Standard*, May 11, 1927.
56. Excerpts from Lipscomb's valedictory address may be found in the *Freeport (IL) Journal-Standard*, March 3, 2003.
57. *Freeport (IL) Journal-Standard*, June 9, 1927.
58. Ibid., October 5, 7, 14, 1927.
59. Ibid., November 2, 1927.
60. Ibid., November 5, 1927.
61. Ibid., November 2, 1927.
62. Ibid., November 5, 1927.
63. Ibid., December 3, 7, 1927.
64. Ibid., December 17, 19, 20, 1927.
65. Ibid., January 24, 25, 26, 28, 1928.
66. Ibid., February 4, 1928.
67. Rice, *Kentucky Basketball's Big Blue Machine*, 83.
68. *Freeport (IL) Journal-Standard*, February 20, 21, 25, 1928.
69. Ibid., February 25, 1928.
70. Ibid., April 2, May 12, June 2, 9, 1928.
71. Ibid., September 8, November 21, 1928; Rice, *Adolph Rupp*, 15.
72. *Freeport (IL) Journal-Standard*, October 6, 1928.
73. Ibid.
74. *Freeport (IL) Journal-Standard*, November 9, 2003.
75. Ibid., November 21, 2003.
76. Ibid., January 5, 1929.
77. Ibid., March 11, 1929.
78. Ibid., March 11, 16, 18, 1929.
79. Ibid., March 22, 23, 1929.
80. Ibid.
81. Ibid., March 23, 25, 1929.
82. Ibid.
83. Ibid., January 22, 23, 1930.

84. Russell Rice listed Rupp's Freeport record as 59–21, but Rice confused Freeport's 1928–1929 and 1929–1930 totals. See Rice, *Adolph Rupp*, 16.

85. Rice, *Adolph Rupp*, 17; Rupp Tapes, 538.

86. Rice, *Kentucky Basketball's Big Blue Machine*, 82–83.

4. Building a Tradition, 1930–1941

1. Nelli, *The Winning Tradition*, 14, 15.

2. Ibid., 15.

3. Ibid. For information on Stanley A. "Daddy" Boles, see his obituary in the *Lexington Herald*, December 5, 1961, and Carl B. Cone, *The University of Kentucky: A Pictorial History* (Lexington: University Press of Kentucky, 1989), 138.

4. The Kentucky high school tournament did not become the Sweet Sixteen until 1955.

5. Nelli, *The Winning Tradition*, 15; Cone, *The University of Kentucky*, 138.

6. Nelli, *The Winning Tradition*, 15, 16.

7. Ibid., 18–20.

8. Ibid., 21–24; Humbert S. Nelli interview with Paul McBrayer, March 24, 1980.

9. For a thorough discussion of the Mauer system see Nelli, *The Winning Tradition*, 24–30. See Humbert S. Nelli interview with Cary Spicer, January 15, 1983, and Humbert S. Nelli interview with Paul McBrayer, March 24, 1980.

10. Ibid.

11. Humbert S. Nelli interview with Paul McBrayer, March 24, 1980.

12. Ibid.

13. Nelli, *The Winning Tradition*, 24; Humbert S. Nelli interview with Paul McBrayer, March 24, 1980.

14. Humbert S. Nelli interview with Carey Spicer.

15. Humbert S. Nelli interview with Paul McBrayer, March 24, 1980; Humbert S. Nelli interview with Carey Spicer.

16. Nelli, *The Winning Tradition*, 30; Humbert S. Nelli interview with Carey Spicer.

17. Nelli, *The Winning Tradition*, 30; Humbert S. Nelli interview with Paul McBrayer, September 6, 1984.

18. Ibid.

19. Bolin, *Bossism and Reform in a Southern City*, 37.

20. Humbert S. Nelli interview with Paul McBrayer, September 6, 1984.

21. Humbert S. Nelli interview with Louis McGinnis, August 6, 1987; Humbert S. Nelli interview with Paul McBrayer, September 6, 1984.

22. Humbert S. Nelli interview with Carey Spicer.

23. *Lexington Herald-Leader*, December 22, 1991. Again in Dave Kindred, *Basketball: The Dream Game in Kentucky* (Louisville, KY: Data Courier, Inc., 1976), 86, Kindred has Rupp use "Negro" rather than the earlier quoted n-word.

24. Ibid.

25. Rupp Tapes, 539; Tev Laudeman, *The Rupp Years: The University of Kentucky's Golden Era of Basketball* (Louisville, KY: *Louisville Courier-Journal* and *Louisville Times*, 1972).

26. Rupp Tapes, 539; Laudeman, *The Rupp Years*; *Kentucky Kernel*, May 23, 1930.

27. Ibid.

28. Rupp Tapes, 539.

29. Ibid.

30. Ibid.

31. Ibid.

32. Rice, *Adolph Rupp*, 18. Accounts of Rupp's hiring at UK can be found in the *Kentucky Kernel*, May 23, 1930; *Lexington Herald*, May 22, 1930; *Louisville Courier-Journal*, May 22, 1930.

33. For information on McVey see Terry Birdwhistell, "Frank LeRond McVey," *The Kentucky Encyclopedia* (Lexington: University Press of Kentucky, 1992), 600–601; Carl Cone, *The University of Kentucky*, 73–111, 114; William E. Ellis, "Frank LeRond McVey: His Defense of Academic Freedom," *Register of the Kentucky Historical Society* 67 (January 1969): 37–54.

34. Frank McVey to George H. Denny, October 8, 1925, Frank L. McVey Papers, Special Collections, University of Kentucky, Lexington, KY, Box 25. Hereafter McVey Papers.

35. Frank McVey Diary, December 21, 1932, McVey Papers, Box VI, C.

36. Board Minutes, "Cost of Buildings Constructed, 1917–1928," December 11, 1928, McVey Papers, Box VI, E.

37. Rupp Tapes, 547.

38. Ibid.

39. Nelli, *The Winning Tradition*, 37.

40. Rupp Tapes, 539.

41. Ibid.

42. Ibid.

43. Ibid.

44. Rupp Tapes, 547.

45. James Duane Bolin interview with Lyman Ginger, August 18, 1998.

46. Ibid.

47. *Kentucky Kernel*, October 3, 1930.

48. See Humbert S. Nelli interviews with Louis McGinnis and Carey Spicer. Nelli has argued convincingly that Mauer had initiated the same system used by Rupp during his early years at UK. See Nelli, *The Winning Tradition*, 34–35.

49. Rupp Tapes, 539.

50. Nelli, *The Winning Tradition*, 35.

51. Rupp Tapes, 539.

52. *Kentucky Kernel*, October 17, 1930, November 14, 1930.

53. Rupp Tapes, 539; *Kentucky Kernel*, November 14, 1930.

54. Ibid.

55. Rupp Tapes, 539.

56. Ibid.

57. *Kentucky Kernel*, December 19, 1930.

58. Rupp Tapes, 539.

59. Ibid.

60. Ibid.

61. Ibid.

62. Ibid.

63. Humbert S. Nelli interview with Carey Spicer.

64. Rupp Tapes, 539; *Atlanta Constitution*, March 4, 1931.

65. *Atlanta Constitution*, March 4, 1931.

66. Rupp Tapes, 539; *Atlanta Constitution*, March 4, 1931; *Kentuckian, 1931.*

67. Rupp Tapes, 539.

68. *Louisville Courier-Journal*, March 5, 1931.

69. Rupp Tapes, 539.

70. Rice, *Kentucky Basketball's Big Blue Machine*, 91.

71. *Louisville Courier-Journal*, March 5, 1931.

72. Rupp Tapes, 539.

73. Rice, *Kentucky Basketball's Big Blue Machine*, 99, 100.

74. Rice, *Adolph Rupp*, 33; James Duane Bolin interview with Stella Gilb, August 18, 1998.

75. Rice, *Adolph Rupp*, 33–34.

76. Humbert S. Nelli interview with Dick Robinson, July 7, 1987.

77. Rupp Tapes, 539; James Duane Bolin interview with Lyman Ginger, August 18, 1998.

78. Dunn is quoted in Rice, *Adolph Rupp*, 21.

79. Humbert S. Nelli interview with Elmer "Baldy" and Stella Gilb, August 10, 1987.

80. Ibid.

81. Ibid.

82. Rupp Tapes, 539.

83. Humbert S. Nelli and James Duane Bolin interview with Paul McBrayer, September 6, 1984.

84. Ibid.

85. Nelli, *The Winning Tradition*, 49.

86. Rupp Tapes, 539.

87. Rice, *Kentucky Basketball's Big Blue Machine*, 90.

88. Ibid.

89. Humbert S. Nelli and Bolin interview with Paul McBrayer, September 6, 1984.

90. Rice, *Kentucky Basketball's Big Blue Machine*, 90; Rupp Tapes, 539.

91. Rupp Tapes, 539.

92. A listing of charter members of the SEC can be found in Rice, *Kentucky Basketball's Big Blue Machine*, 101; Bert and Steve Nelli made the point about the advantages of the new conference for Kentucky in Nelli, *The Winning Tradition*, 45.

93. James Duane Bolin interview with Jim Host, Lexington, KY, July 23, 2014.

94. Ibid.

95. Rice, *Kentucky Basketball's Big Blue Machine*, 101; Rupp Tapes, 539.

96. Laudeman, *The Rupp Years*, "About the Book."

97. Rice, *Kentucky Basketball's Big Blue Machine*, 93.

98. Ibid., 93, 92.

99. Ibid., 93.

100. Humbert S. Nelli interview with Forest "Aggie" Sale, December 15, 1982; *Anderson (County, KY) News*, November 25, 1982.

101. *The Anderson (County, KY) News*, November 25, 1982.

102. Rice, *Kentucky Basketball's Big Blue Machine*, 93.

103. James Duane Bolin interview with Albert Benjamin Chandler III, Lexington, KY, November 17, 2014.

104. Rice, *Kentucky Basketball's Big Blue Machine*, 94.

105. Ibid., 94, 95.

106. Laudeman, *The Rupp Years*, "1937–38."

107. Ibid.

108. Rice, *Kentucky Basketball's Big Blue Machine*, 95.

109. Humbert S. Nelli interview with Bernie Opper, April 19, 1980.

110. Ibid.; Jimmy Jones, "He's Rupp and Ready," *Esquire*, February 1943, 16.

111. Humbert S. Nelli interview with Bernie Opper, April 19, 1980; Zander Hollander, ed., *The Modern Encyclopedia of Basketball* (New York: Four Winds Press, 1973), 16.

112. Ibid., 13.

113. Ibid.

114. Laudeman, *The Rupp Years*, "1934–35"; *New York Times*, January 6, 1935.

115. Ibid.

116. Ibid.

117. *New York Times*, January 6, 1935.

118. Jones, "He's Rupp and Ready."

119. The Rupp quotation and the *New York Post* quotation are both found in Laudeman, *The Rupp Years*, "1934–35."

120. Ibid.

121. Ibid. This quotation is taken from the website http://www.biochem.purdue.edu/~johnson/rupp.htm.

122. *Lexington Herald*, January 6, 1935.

123. See Laudeman, *The Rupp Years*, "1934–35."

124. Nelli, *The Winning Tradition*, 53, 54.

125. Ibid., 54.

126. Ibid.

127. Jones, "He's Rupp and Ready," 53, 136.

128. Ibid., 136.

129. Ibid.

130. Ibid.

131. Ibid., 53.

132. Ibid.

133. Ibid.

134. Ibid.

135. Ibid., 136.

136. Ibid., 137.

137. Rice, *Adolph Rupp*, 69.

138. Ibid., 69–70.

139. Laudeman quoted in Nelli, *The Winning Tradition*, 52.

5. World War II and the Games March On, 1941–1945

1. *Louisville Courier-Journal*, June 7, 1984.

2. Ibid.

3. Nelli, *The Winning Tradition*, 59.

4. "Kentucky Wildcat Basketball, 1943–1944." Basketball File in possession of author.

5. *Lexington Sunday Herald-Leader*, November 9, 1980.

6. *Lexington Leader*, April 2, 1946.

7. Ibid.

8. Ibid.

9. Ibid.

10. Rice, *Adolph Rupp*, 78, 79.

11. H. L. Donovan to Coach Adolph Rupp, January 12, 1944, Herman L. Donovan Papers, Special Collections, University of Kentucky, Lexington, KY. Hereafter Donovan Papers.

12. A. F. Rupp to Dr. Herman Lee Donovan, January 17, 1944, Donovan Papers.

13. Rupp Tapes, 547.

14. Ibid.

15. Carl B. Cone, *The University of Kentucky*, 113.

16. Rupp Tapes, 547.

17. Ibid.

18. McVey Diary, February 2, 1945, McVey Papers, XS; Cone, *The University of Kentucky*, 121; McVey Diary, November 21, 1947, McVey Papers, XIIF.

19. McVey Diary, October 13, 1945, November 3, 1945, McVey Papers, XIIC.

20. McVey Diary, November 25, 1945, McVey Papers, XII (6).

21. McVey Diary, December 6, 1945, in ibid.

22. McVey Diary, October 5, 1946, in ibid.

23. McVey Diary, October 19, 1946, in ibid.

24. Cone, *The University of Kentucky*, 79–81, 118; historical marker at Roy Stewart Stadium on the campus of Murray State University; the 1925 *Murray State Shield* yearbook is dedicated to Graves.

25. Cone, *The University of Kentucky*, 79–81, 118.

26. Rice, *Adolph Rupp*, 99.

27. Rupp Tapes, 547.

28. Humbert S. Nelli interview with Harry Lancaster, May 21, 1980.

29. Rice, *Adolph Rupp*, 81.

30. H. L. Donovan to Coach Adolph Rupp, March 8, 1944, Donovan Papers; A. F. Rupp to Dr. H. L. Donovan, March 10, 1944, in ibid.

31. Rice, *Adolph Rupp*, 88.

32. Harry Lancaster "as told to Cawood Ledford," *Adolph Rupp as I Knew Him* (Lexington, KY: Lexington Productions Inc., 1979), 16.

33. Rice, *Adolph Rupp*, 89–90.

34. Harry Lancaster "as told to Cawood Ledford," 17; Nelli, *The Winning Tradition*, 55; Rice, *Adolph Rupp*, 74.

35. Harry Lancaster "as told to Cawood Ledford," 17; Rice, *Adolph Rupp*, 89.

36. Nelli, *The Winning Tradition*, 56, 64.

37. Ibid., 54, 55.

38. Ibid., 55.

39. Rice, *Adolph Rupp*, 74.

40. Harry Lancaster "as told to Cawood Ledford," 17.

41. Harry Lancaster "as told to Cawood Ledford," 17.

42. Nelli, *The Winning Tradition*, 64; Harry Lancaster "as told to Cawood Ledford," 16, 17; Rice, *Adolph Rupp*, 89.

43. Rice, *Adolph Rupp*, 92.

44. Ibid.

45. Ibid., 78, 79.

46. Rupp Tapes, 547.

47. Ibid.

48. Ibid.

49. Bernie A. Shively to Dr. H. L. Donovan, February 10, 1944, Donovan Papers.

50. Walter H. Ryle to President H. L. Donovan, July 31, 1945, Donovan Papers.

51. Ibid.

52. H. L. Donovan to President Walter H. Ryle, August 3, 1945, Donovan Papers.

53. Rupp Tapes, 547.

54. Ibid.

55. Ibid.

56. Ibid.

57. Ibid.

58. Ibid.

59. Nelli, *The Winning Tradition*, 43, 38, 252.

60. Humbert S. Nelli interview with Harry Lancaster.

61. Ibid.

62. Russell Rice, *Adolph Rupp*, 75.

63. Harry Lancaster "as told to Cawood Ledford," 19.

6. The Fabulous Five

1. McVey Diary, November 22, 1947, McVey Papers, XIIC (6).

2. McVey Diary, December 29, 1948, McVey Papers, XIIC; Rice, *Adolph Rupp*, 99.

3. Harry Lancaster "as told to Cawood Ledford," 19.

4. Humbert S. Nelli interview with Alex Groza, November 16, 1983.

5. Ibid.

6. Tev Laudeman, "His Greatest Team," *Louisville Courier-Journal*, December 12, 1977.

7. Humbert S. Nelli interview with Kenny Rollins, December 5, 1983.

8. Humbert S. Nelli interview with Cliff Barker, November 16, 1983.

9. Ibid.

10. Ibid.

11. Ibid.

12. Ibid.

13. Humbert S. Nelli interview with Kenny Rollins.

14. Ibid.

15. Ibid.

16. Ibid.

17. Ibid.

18. Ibid.

19. Ibid.

20. Ibid.

21. Ibid.

22. Rice, *Adolph Rupp*, 82.

23. Ibid., 82–83.

24. Humbert S. Nelli interview with Alex Groza.

25. Rice, *Adolph Rupp*, 83, 84.

26. Humbert S. Nelli interview with Alex Groza.

27. Rice, *Adolph Rupp*, 83, 84.

28. Laudeman, "His Greatest Team."

29. Humbert S. Nelli interview with Kenny Rollins.

30. McVey Diary, March 21, 1947, March 24, 1947, McVey Papers, XIIC (6).

31. McVey Diary, April 1, 1948, in ibid.

32. Laudeman, "His Greatest Team."

33. Ibid.

34. Humbert S. Nelli interview with Harry Lancaster.

35. Ibid.

36. Humbert S. Nelli interview with Alex Groza.

37. Ibid.

38. Ibid.

39. Harry Lancaster "as told to Cawood Ledford," 23, 25.

7. The Golden Era, 1946–1951

1. Humbert S. Nelli interview with Kenny Rollins.

2. Dave Roos interview with Joe B. Hall, October 3, 2012.

3. Ibid.

4. Ibid.

5. Humbert S. Nelli interview with Kenny Rollins.

6. Ibid.

7. Ibid.

8. Harry Lancaster "as told to Cawood Ledford," 25.

9. Ibid.

10. Rice, *Adolph Rupp*, 105; Harry Lancaster "as told to Cawood Ledford," 25, 27.

11. Humbert S. Nelli interview with Kenny Rollins.

12. Rice, *Adolph Rupp*, 105.

13. See Jon P. Scott, "Adolph Rupp, Fact and Fiction," http://www.bigbluehistory. net/bb/rupp.html#olympics.

14. Ibid.

15. Ibid.

16. Rice, *Adolph Rupp*, 106; Humbert S. Nelli interview with Ralph Beard, April 24, 1987.

17. Rice, *Adolph Rupp*, 106.

18. Ibid.

19. Rice, *Adolph Rupp*, 106, 107; Harry Lancaster "as told to Cawood Ledford," 27.

20. Larry Boeck, "Oilers behind 10 Points, Rally to Tip UK 56–50," *Louisville Courier-Journal*, July 10, 1948.

21. Jon Scott, "Adolph Rupp, Fact and Fiction."

22. Ron Thomas, *They Cleared the Lane* (Lincoln: University of Nebraska Press, 2002), 123, quoted in Jon Scott, "Adolph Rupp, Fact and Fiction."

23. Humbert S. Nelli interview with Ralph Beard.

24. Rice, *Adolph Rupp*, 107.

25. Humbert S. Nelli interview with Ralph Beard.

26. Rice, *Adolph Rupp*, 107–8.

27. Ron Thomas, *They Cleared the Lane*, 123, quoted in Jon Scott, "Adolph Rupp, Fact and Fiction."

28. Murray Olderman, "Between You'n'Me: Barksdale: A Perspective on '48 Olympic Games," *Playground Daily News*, October 17, 1968.

29. Charles Bricker, "Eventually He Made It to the NBA," *Philadelphia Enquirer*, January 15, 1984.

30. Olderman, "Between You'n'Me: Barksdale"; see Scott, "Adolph Rupp, Fact and Fiction."

31. Rice, *Adolph Rupp*, 108.

32. Humbert S. Nelli interview with Ralph Beard.

33. Ibid.

34. Harry Lancaster "as told to Cawood Ledford," 29.

35. Rice, *Adolph Rupp*, 110; Harry Lancaster "as told to Cawood Ledford," 31.

36. Roos interview with Joe B. Hall.

37. Ibid.

38. Ibid.

39. Harry Lancaster "as told to Cawood Ledford," 31.

40. Ibid., 32.

41. Ibid., 32, 33.

42. Ibid., 33.

43. Rice, *Adolph Rupp*, 110.

44. Harry Lancaster "as told to Cawood Ledford," 34.

45. Ibid., 34, 35.

46. Rice, *Adolph Rupp*, 114.

47. Ibid.

48. Humbert S. Nelli interview with Kenny Rollins.

49. Harry Lancaster "as told to Cawood Ledford," 37.

50. Humbert S. Nelli interview with Kenny Rollins.

51. Harry Lancaster "as told to Cawood Ledford," 37.

52. Rice, *Adolph Rupp*, 119.

53. Harry Lancaster "as told to Cawood Ledford," 7, 39.

54. Ibid., 39.

55. Ibid., 119, 120.

56. Ibid., 120.

57. Humbert S. Nelli interview with Harry Lancaster.

58. Rice, *Adolph Rupp,* 120.

59. *HBO Original,* "City Dump, the Story of the 1951 CCNY Basketball Scandal" (Black Canyon Productions, 1998); Ed Bark, "HBO Shoots, Scores with Documentaries on College Hoops," *Wichita (KS) Eagle*, March 24, 1998, quoted in Jon P. Scott, "Adolph Rupp, Fact and Fiction."

60. Ibid., 121.

61. Larry Boeck, "The Mellowing of Adolph Rupp," *Louisville Courier-Journal Magazine,* January 19, 1964.

62. Cone, *The University of Kentucky*, 116, 118, 119.

63. Harry Lancaster "as told to Cawood Ledford," 41.

64. Ibid.

65. Ibid.

66. Rice, *Adolph Rupp*, 123.

67. Ibid.; Harry Lancaster "as told to Cawood Ledford," 42.

68. Harry Lancaster "as told to Cawood Ledford," 42, 44.

69. Rice, *Adolph Rupp*, 124.

70. Ibid.

71. Humbert S. Nelli interview with Alex Groza.

8. Scandal

1. *New York Times*, April 30, 1952.

2. See Rice, *Adolph Rupp*, 125.

3. This information is taken from Humbert S. Nelli, "Adolph Rupp, the Kentucky Wildcats, and the Basketball Scandal of 1951," *Register of the Kentucky Historical Society* 84 (Winter 1986): 51–75. See also Rice, *Adolph Rupp*, 124; and Charley Rosen, *Scandals of '51: How the Gamblers Almost Killed College Basketball* (New York: Seven Stories Press, 1978, 1999).

4. *Lexington Herald*, October 20, 1951.

5. Ibid., October 22, 1951.

6. Ibid.

7. Ibid., October 21, 1951.

8. Rice, *Adolph Rupp*, 125.

9. Ibid., 125, 126; *Lexington Herald*, October 22, 1951.

10. Donovan Papers. Copies of statement and letter, Herman L. Donovan to Adolph Rupp, May 6, 1952, in possession of author.

11. *Lexington Leader*, December 8, 1951; sentencing transcript, a copy of which is in the possession of the author.

12. Sentencing transcript.

13. Ibid.

14. Ibid.

15. Ibid.

16. Ibid.

17. Ibid.

18. Ibid.

19. Ibid.

20. Ibid., 42, 43.

21. Ibid., 51.

22. Ibid., 52.

23. Ibid., 43.

24. Ibid., 44–48.

25. Walter Byers, *Unsportsmanlike Conduct: Exploiting College Athletes* (Ann Arbor: University of Michigan Press, 1977), 56.

26. Reed, "Eulogy for a Bookie: Ed Curd, Inventor of the Point Spread, Dies," *The Backstretch: A Magazine for the Thoroughbred Industry* (July/August 2002) at http://www.thebackstretch.com/ju102/REED702.html.

27. Sentencing transcript, 48–49.

28. Ibid., 52.

29. Ibid., 12, 13.

30. Ibid., 58–60.

31. Ibid., 60–61.

32. Ibid., 61–62.

33. Ibid., 62–63.

34. Ibid., 54–56.

35. Ibid., 56.

36. Ibid., 56–58.

37. "Preliminary Statement of the Joint Meeting of the Executive Committee of the Board of Trustees, the Board of Directors of the Athletics Association, and the Executive Committee of the Alumni Association of the University of Kentucky, 5 May 1952"; copy in possession of author.

38. "Preliminary Statement," 1.

39. Ibid., 1.

40. Ibid., 2.

41. Ibid., 2.

42. Ibid., 3.

43. Ibid., 3, 4.

44. Ibid., 5.

45. Ibid., 5.

46. *New York Times*, November 20, 1951.

47. Ibid.

48. Ibid.

49. A summation of the reactions of various state newspapers was made in the *Lexington Herald*, May 3, 1952.

50. Ibid.

51. Ibid.

52. *Louisville Courier-Journal*, May 1, 1952.

53. Ibid.

9. The Businessman at Home

1. Marla Ridenour, "For Rupp's Secretary, the Work Day Was Never Dreaded," *Lexington Herald*, December 12, 1977.

2. Ibid.

3. Rice, *Adolph Rupp*, 33.

4. Ibid., 34.

5. Mary Phyllis Riedley, "Mrs. Rupp Not a Cage Authority But She Gets the Best Coaching," *Louisville Courier-Journal*, December 12, 1948; David V. Hawpe, "Rupp Thinks His Wife Has Worst Life in the World," *Lexington Leader*, March 9, 1966.

6. Riedley, "Mrs. Rupp Not a Cage Authority"; Riedley, "Adolph Rupp, Family Man," *Louisville Courier-Journal*, March 8, 1959.

7. Riedley, "Adolph Rupp, Family Man."

8. Ibid.

9. Ibid.

10. *Louisville Courier-Journal*, September 2, 1970.

11. Senate of the General Assembly of the Commonwealth of Kentucky, 98 RS BR 2795, 1998 Regular Session.

12. Rice, *Adolph Rupp*, 37; Jennifer Hewlett, "Esther Rupp, UK Coach's Widow Dies," *Lexington Herald-Leader*, March 31, 1998.

13. Ibid.

14. James Duane Bolin interview with Lyman Ginger, Lexington, KY, August 18, 1998.

15. Ibid.

16. "Butts Heads Lions District: Group Hears Coach Rupp," *Lexington Leader*, June 6, 1960.

17. "America Needs 'Squares,' Rupp Says," newspaper clipping found in "Faculty/Staff Biographical File: Adolph Rupp," Special Collections, University of Kentucky, Lexington, KY.

18. Ibid.

19. Ibid.

20. Ibid.

21. Bolin interview with Lyman Ginger; Rice, *Adolph Rupp*, 39.

22. Riedley, "Adolph Rupp, Family Man"; Hewlett, "Esther Rupp, UK Coach's Widow, Dies."

23. Billy Thompson, "Rupp Looks Forward to Coaching Son Herky," *Lexington Herald*, August 14, 1958.

24. Ibid.

25. Ibid.; Humbert S. Nelli interview with Mary Boeck, Louisville, KY, October 28, 1988.

26. Humbert S. Nelli interview with Mary Boeck.

27. D. G. FitzMaurice, "Herky Rupp: Dad More Than Great Coach," *Lexington Herald*, April 21, 1982.

28. Buck P. Patton, "Rupp Takes Time to Write a Player," *Memphis Press-Scimitar*, April 1966.

29. FitzMaurice, "Herky Rupp."

30. Adolph F. Rupp to family, January 3, 1967; this letter can be found in Rupp Papers, Special Collections, University of Kentucky, Lexington, KY.

31. Ibid.

32. Ibid.

33. Adolph Rupp to Mrs. Paul B. Lawson, May 21, 1952, Rupp Papers, Special Collections, University of Kentucky, Lexington, KY.

34. Adolph Rupp to Mr. and Mrs. Paul B. Lawson, April 17, 1953, Rupp Papers.

35. Billy Reed, "Friends and Family," *Louisville Courier-Journal*, December 12, 1977.

36. Rice, *Adolph Rupp*, 35.

37. Reed, "Friends and Family."

38. See Edmund Morris, *The Rise of Theodore Roosevelt*; Bolin interview with Lyman Ginger; Humbert S. Nelli interview with Elmer "Baldy" and Stella Gilb, Lexington, KY, August 10, 1987.

39. James Duane Bolin interview with Stella Gilb, Lexington, KY, August 18, 1998; Humbert S. Nelli interview with Elmer "Baldy" and Stella Gilb.

40. Rice, *Adolph Rupp*, 36.

41. Ibid.

42. Ibid., 40.

43. Ibid.

44. Ibid.

45. Despite this advertisement, stories circulated about Rupp's drinking. For years Rupp tried to maintain the façade of clean living and good health, but even in his early years in Lexington, Rupp enjoyed smoking an occasional cigar. Once when he chastised a player for his mediocre play in practice, Rupp sent the unproductive player on an errand away from the court. "You simply aren't getting a thing done this afternoon," he told the chastened player. "Make yourself useful. Here's a dollar. I'm out of cigars. Run down to the corner and get me some." Although Rupp eventually gave up cigars, his penchant for another Kentucky-made product grew over time. See *Louisville Courier-Journal*, January 10, 1960; "A Message from Adolph Rupp," Kentucky WCTU clipping in author's notes.

46. Bolin interview with Lyman Ginger.

47. Earl Cox, "Adolph Rupp, The Man," *Louisville Courier-Journal*, December 12, 1977.

48. Rice, *Adolph Rupp*, 37. Rupp still liked to go on fishing trips from time to time, even if the fishing itself sometimes failed to satisfy. In 1946, Rupp took Esther and Herky on a fishing vacation. They took off the morning after Lexington's Junior Chamber of Commerce sponsored a "testimonial dinner" to honor his "most successful season in his 16 years" as the Wildcat coach. The festivities, held at the Lafayette Hotel, had been topped off with the presentation of a new Oldsmobile sedan to the successful coach. The Rupps planned to be away for a couple of weeks, "the first real relaxation for the Wildcat chieftain after an extremely strenuous schedule." Even before the season, Rupp had gone to Europe, "to assist in setting up an athletic and recreation program for American troops." Now, it was finally time to relax with his family on a leisurely fishing trip. Rupp had prepared for the trip by shuffling through "a closetful of fishing tackle." He expected "to get in a little quiet fishing somewhere" as part of his long overdue rest. See "Rupp Tonight Receives Applause, Auto: He's Off on the Morrow for Fishing Fun," *Lexington Leader*, April 9, 1946.

49. Rice, *Adolph Rupp*, 35.

50. Tim Cohane, "Rupp! Rupp! How Many Baskets Up?" *Look*, March 15, 1951, 65.

51. Reed, "Friends and Family."

52. Larry Boeck, "The Mellowing of Adolph Rupp," *Louisville Courier-Journal*, January 19, 1964.

53. Jimmy Breslin, "UK's Basketball Baron More Than Genius Coach," *Lexington Leader*, February 3, 1959.

54. *Lexington Herald-Leader*, February 16, 2003; May 30, 1991; September 20, 1986; September 5, 1991.

55. "Rupp Named Adviser," *Lexington Leader*, October 8, 1937.

56. Richard Wilson, "His Academic Role," *Louisville Courier-Journal*, December 12, 1977; James Duane Bolin interview with Thomas D. Clark, Lexington, KY, July 10, 1998.

57. Wilson, "His Academic Role."

58. Ibid.

59. Thomas D. Clark to Harry Caudill, October 22, 1951, Clark Papers (B245, F8),

Special Collections, University of Kentucky, Lexington, KY, quoted in *Register of the Kentucky Historical Society* 103, nos. 1/2 (Winter/Spring 2005): 450; Thomas D. Clark to A. B. "Bud" Guthrie Jr., December 4, 1976 (B249, F26), Special Collections, University of Kentucky, Lexington, KY, quoted in *Register of the Kentucky Historical Society* 103, nos. 1/2 (Winter/Spring 2005): 457.

60. Humbert S. Nelli interview with Thomas D. Clark, Lexington, KY, December 22, 1982.

61. Ibid.

62. Thomas D. Clark to Otis A. Singletary, February 5, 1972 (B258, F18), Clark Papers, Special Collections, University of Kentucky, Lexington, KY, quoted in *Register of the Kentucky Historical Society* 103, nos. 1/2 (Winter/Spring 2005): 449; Humbert S. Nelli interview with Thomas D. Clark, Lexington, KY, December 22, 1982.

63. Kelso Sturgeon, "'Hurt' Rupp Says Raises Bypass Him at U. of K.," *Louisville Courier-Journal*, November 28, 1962.

64. Ibid.

65. "No Raise—Rupp Erupts," *Louisville Times*, November 29, 1962.

66. Ibid.

67. *Lexington Leader*, December 4, 1962.

68. Ibid.

69. Ibid., December 8, 1962.

70. Ibid.

71. Ibid., December 11, 1962.

72. Ibid., December 8, 1962.

73. Larry Boeck, "Rupp Isn't Exactly Speedy with a Buck," *Louisville Courier-Journal*, February 22, 1953.

74. Ibid.

75. Ibid.

76. Ibid.

77. Ibid.

78. Ibid.

79. Red Auerbach and John Feinstein, *Let Me Tell You a Story: A Lifetime in the Game* (New York: Little, Brown and Company, 2004), 84, 83.

80. Rice, *Adolph Rupp*, 34.

81. Ibid.

82. "U. of K. Coach Initiated into Oleika Temple," *Louisville Courier-Journal*, November 25, 1937.

83. Chris Lee, "Beneath Shriner's Fez Lies 'An Unseen Joy' in Helping Other People," *Lexington Herald-Leader*, August 13, 1988.

84. Rice, *Adolph Rupp*, 38; Larry Boeck, "Rupp Leans Heavily upon His Idea of Free Enterprise—and Has Made It Pay Very Well," *Louisville Courier-Journal*, February 22, 1953.

85. "Oleika Temple Nominates Rupp for High Post in Imperial Shrine," *Lexington*

Leader, May 8, 1959; Rice, *Adolph Rupp*, 39; Boeck, "Rupp Leans Heavily upon His Idea of Free Enterprise."

86. Peter Cary, "The Baron Was a Winner off the Court, Too," *Louisville Courier-Journal*, December 13, 1977.

87. "Adolph Rupp Wins Optimists' 'Outstanding Citizen' Award," *Lexington Leader*, February 25, 1949; "Mrs. Chandler, UK's Rupp, Three Others Win Governor's Medallion," *Lexington Leader*, June 1, 1959.

88. Ibid.

89. "New Post to be Offered Coach Rupp by Louisville Professional Cage Team," *Lexington Herald*, February 5, 1947.

90. Ibid.

91. Billy Thompson, "Adolph Rupp May Leave UK for Pro Coaching Post," *Lexington Herald*, January 15, 1959.

92. "'Cincinnati Is Ripe for Good Professional Promotion,' Rupp Asserts in Surprise Statement," *Lexington Herald*, January 15, 1959.

93. Thompson, "Adolph Rupp May Leave UK for Pro Coaching Post."

94. Ibid., "Pressbox Pickups," *Lexington Herald*, January 16, 1959.

95. Ibid.

96. Ibid.

97. Larry Boeck, "The Mellowing of Adolph Rupp," *Louisville Courier-Journal*, January 19, 1964; Tom Wallace, *So You Think You're a Kentucky Wildcats Basketball Fan? Stars, Stats, Records* (New York: Sports Publishing, 2016), 21.

98. *Lexington Herald*, November 14, 1959; "Joe Creason's Kentucky," *Louisville Courier-Journal*, April 8, 1966.

99. "Joe Creason's Kentucky."

100. "Coach Rupp to Speak at Madison Banquet," *Lexington Leader*, December 19, 1933; "Rupp Will Hold Coaching School at Morehead," *Louisville Courier-Journal*, April 8, 1933; "U. K. Varsity Mentor to Talk at Morehead," *Lexington Leader*, June 4, 1933.

101. "Adolph Rupp to Fly to Massachusetts Today," *Lexington Herald*, June 26, 1946; "Rupp to Be Speaker at Marshall Dinner," *Lexington Herald*, March 22, 1947; "Rupp to Speak at Cumberland Cage Banquet," *Louisville Courier-Journal*, May 1, 1947; "Woodward to Honor Rupp," *Lexington Leader*, April 11, 1947.

102. "Rupp among Coaches at Big Texas School," *Lexington Herald*, August 1, 1949; "Rupp and Faurot Guest Lecturers at Mississippi," *Louisville Courier-Journal*, June 6, 1949.

103. "Coaches' Clinic Hears Rupp," *Lexington Herald*, July 27, 1961.

104. "Rupp and Hobson Leave by Plane for Europe," *Louisville Courier-Journal*, September 20, 1951; "Rupp to Conduct Clinic in Germany," *Lexington Herald*, August 18, 1961; Billy Thompson, "Rupp Leaves for Japanese Cage Clinic," *Lexington Herald*, September 3, 1959.

105. Murray Sperber, *Onward to Victory: The Crisis That Shaped College Sports* (New York: Henry Holt, 1998), 333.

106. Cohane, "Rupp! Rupp! How Many Baskets Up?"

107. Andrew Eckdahl, "Rupp Reported Considering Race for Lieutenant Governor," *Lexington Herald*, March 26, 1953.

108. Boeck, "Rupp Leans Heavily upon His Idea of Free Enterprise."

109. Ibid.

110. "When the Basketball Season is Over Rupp Sheds His Jitters on the Farm," *Lexington Herald*, April 14, 1951; Boeck, "Rupp Seeks New Title—With Cattle," *Louisville Courier-Journal*, January 11, 1953.

111. "When the Basketball Season is Over Rupp Sheds His Jitters on the Farm," *Lexington Herald*, April 14, 1951; Kyle Vance, "Rupp Hopes His Cattle Will Emulate His Cats," *Lexington Herald-Leader*, April 22, 1951.

112. Cohane, "Rupp! Rupp! How Many Baskets Up?"

113. *Kentucky Hereford*, January 1951, 39; "H. P. Baca Larry Costs Rupp $3000," *Lexington Leader*, November 28, 1951; see also E. W. Kieckhefer, "Rupp Buys $3,000 Bull at Chicago," *Louisville Courier-Journal*, November 29, 1951.

114. Boeck, "Rupp Seeks New Title—With Cattle."

115. *Kentucky Hereford*, February 1948, 13.

116. "Rupp to Head Hereford Body," *Lexington Leader*, November 11, 1953.

117. Cary, "The Baron Was a Winner off the Court, Too," *Lexington Herald-Leader*, December 13, 1977.

118. *Kentucky Hereford*, January 1951, 14.

119. *Kentucky Hereford*, June 1951, 8; *Kentucky Kernel*, November 13, 1953.

120. F. R. Carpenter to Adolph Rupp, August 16, 1947, Rupp Papers, Special Collections, University of Kentucky, Lexington, KY; R. E. Leone to Adolph F. Rupp, September 2, 1950, Rupp Papers, Special Collections, University of Kentucky, Lexington, KY; see "Another Interesting 'Coach Rupp Trip,'" *Kentucky Hereford*, August 1950, 10–11.

121. "Another Interesting 'Coach Rupp Trip.'"

122. Boeck, "Rupp Seeks New Title—With Cattle."

123. Ibid.

124. James R. Russell, "Adolph Rupp: The Farmer," *Louisville Courier-Journal*, December 12, 1977.

125. Cary, "The Baron Was a Winner off the Court, Too," *Lexington Herald-Leader*, December 13, 1977.

126. James R. Russell, "Adolph Rupp: The Farmer."

127. Ibid.

128. John Jenks, "Rupp Says Cash Buys 4-H, FFA Top Prizes," *Lexington Herald*, October 20, 1959.

129. Ibid.; Joe Bride, "Rupp's Criticism of Cattle Shows Draws Fire from Farm Leaders," *Louisville Courier-Journal*, October 21, 1959; "Former Cattle Judge Answers Coach Rupp," *Lexington Herald*, October 26, 1959.

130. "Bell Farm Bought by Rupp and Son for $410 an Acre," *Lexington Leader*, February 5, 1953.

131. Larry Boeck, "Coach Adolph 'Baron Midas' Rupp is an Alger Hero with Trimmings," *Louisville Courier-Journal*, February 22, 1953.

132. Ibid.; Boeck, "Rupp Seeks New Title—With Cattle"; Boeck, "Rupp Leans Heavily upon His Idea of Free Enterprise."

133. Boeck, "Coach Adolph 'Baron Midas' Rupp is an Alger Hero with Trimmings."

134. Boeck, "Rupps Leans Heavily upon His Idea of Free Enterprise."

135. Humbert S. Nelli interview with Dick Robinson, September 5, 1984.

136. Ibid.

137. Humbert S. Nelli interview with Thomas D. Clark, Lexington, KY, February 4, 1988; Boeck, "Rupp Leans Heavily upon His Idea of Free Enterprise."

138. Boeck, "The Mellowing of Adolph Rupp"; "Ed Curd, 98, Known for Bookmaking, Developed Point-Spread Betting," *Associated Press*, May 16, 2002; Reed, "Eulogy for a Bookie: Ed Curd, Inventor of the Point Spread, Dies," *The Backstretch: A Magazine for the Thoroughbred Industry* (July/August 2002) at http://www.thebackstretch.com/ju102/REED702.html.

139. Reed, "Eulogy for a Bookie: Ed Curd."

140. Ibid.

141. "Whiskey Warehouse Receipts Used by New Get-Rich-Quick Promoters," *Craig Empire Courier*, August 12, 1936.

142. "Rupp, Roger Layne Form Oil Company," *Lexington Leader*, July 31, 1959.

143. "Rupp Heads Firm to Operate Cable Television System," *Lexington Herald*, December 17, 1964.

144. Sol Schulman, "Rupp and Leslie Combs Help Form New Insurance Firm Offering Million $5 Shares," *Louisville Courier-Journal*, August 7, 1960.

145. Bolin interview with Lyman V. Ginger.

146. Boeck, "The Mellowing of Adolph Rupp."

10. From a Canceled Season to the Fiddlin' Five, 1952–1958

1. Nelli, *The Winning Tradition*, 71; C. Ray Hall, "It's 50 Years since the Season That Never Was," *Louisville Courier-Journal*, December 26, 2002.

2. C. Ray Hall, "It's 50 Years since the Season That Never Was."

3. Ibid.

4. Nelli, *The Winning Tradition*, 71, 72.

5. Ibid., 72.

6. Paul W. Bryant and John Underwood, *Bear: The Hard Life and Good Times of Alabama's Coach Bryant* (New York: Bantam Books, 1974), 118.

7. Ibid., 120.

8. Ibid., 120–21.

9. Ibid., 121.

10. Ibid.

11. Ibid.

12. Ibid., 122.

13. Rice, *Adolph Rupp*, 130.

14. Bryant and Underwood, *Bear*, 122.

15. Ibid., 122–23.

16. Rice, *Adolph Rupp*, 131.

17. Ibid., 132.

18. Ibid.

19. Ibid.; Bryant and Underwood, *Bear*, 123.

20. Michael Smith, "Realignment a Way of Life for Former UK Hoopster," *Louisville Courier-Journal*, July 7, 2003.

21. Hall, "It's 50 Years since the Season That Never Was."

22. Ibid.

23. Ibid.

24. Ibid.

25. Ibid.

26. Rice, *Adolph Rupp*, 133. See also Harry Lancaster "as told to Cawood Ledford," 51.

27. Hall, "It's 50 Years since the Season That Never Was."

28. Ibid.

29. Ibid.

30. Ibid.

31. Ibid.

32. Ibid.

33. Auerbach and Feinstein, *Let Me Tell You a Story: A Lifetime in the Game* (New York: Little, Brown and Company, 2004), 83, 84, 70.

34. Ibid.

35. Dan Chandler and Vernon Hatton, *Rupp from Both Ends of the Bench*, 56.

36. Ibid., 56–57.

37. Ibid., 18.

38. Hall, "It's 50 Years since the Season That Never Was"; Bill Mayer, "Mayer: Back in 1953–54, Rupp Just Said No to NCAAs," *Lawrence Journal-World*, March 16, 2003.

39. Chandler and Hatton, *Rupp from Both Ends of the Bench*, 8.

40. *Lexington Leader*, November 13, 1952.

41. *Lexington Herald*, May 10, 1952.

42. *Lexington Leader*, May 11, 1954; May 13, 1954; January 26, 1959.

43. Ed Ashford, "Georgia Tech Stuns Top Rated Wildcats, 59–58," *Lexington Leader*, January 9, 1955.

44. "'Wow' Describes Coach's Feeling after Tech Halted Kentucky Five," *New York Times*, January 19, 1955; *Lexington Herald-Leader*, February 16, 2003.

45. *Lexington Herald-Leader*, February 16, 2003; Russell Rice, *Adolph Rupp*, 137.

46. *Lexington Herald-Leader*, February 16, 2003.

47. Ibid.

48. Surface and Breslin, "Basketball's Bumptious Baron," *Time*, March 1960, 59–60.

49. Nelli, *The Winning Tradition*, 78.

50. Ibid.

51. According to Bert and Steve Nelli, in Puckett's remembrance, "Rupp announced that he was going to take away their movie passes and $15-a-month laundry allowance for a specified length of time. Puckett had been asked to serve as the players' spokesman because he had never been afraid to express his views. After Rupp's announcement, Puckett immediately responded, 'If you need mine for that long you can keep them for the rest of the year. That kind of shocked him,' Puckett noted, 'and he went on down the row and every one of them said the same thing. They all agreed that if Rupp was going to do what he said, we would quit. So we did quit. We went outside the Coliseum. Everybody but Bill Evans.' Evans, the team captain, was married and had not been involved in any of the plans." After going back inside, Rupp went to his office and Harry Lancaster and Evans spoke with the team, telling them that it would be a mistake to quit. All of the players agreed to go into practice, except Puckett. "Old hardheaded me went the other way," Puckett recalled. The *Louisville Courier-Journal*'s account and Puckett's remembrances differ slightly on the particulars of the incident. See *Louisville Courier-Journal*, February 10, 1955, and Nelli, *The Winning Tradition*, 78–79.

52. *Louisville Courier-Journal*, February 10, 1955.

53. Chandler and Hatton, *Rupp from Both Ends of the Bench*, 6.

54. *Louisville Courier-Journal*, January 16, 1955; *Lexington Leader*, February 7, 1955.

55. *Lexington Leader*, February 7, 1955.

56. Ibid.

57. George Koper, "Rupp Is Surprised with Blue Cadillac," *Kentucky Kernel*, March 11, 1955.

58. See Nelli, *The Winning Tradition*, 79.

59. Chandler and Hatton, *Rupp from Both Ends of the Bench*, 11.

60. Nelli, *The Winning Tradition*, 82.

61. Ibid.

62. Surface and Breslin, "Basketball's Bumptious Baron," 60.

63. Ibid.

64. Ibid.

65. Ibid.

66. See Laudeman, *The Rupp Years*, "1957–58"; and Nelli, *The Winning Tradition*, 82.

67. Josh Underwood, "Crigler Reflects on Fiddlin' 5," *Georgetown (KY) News-Graphic*, December 16, 2001.

68. Ibid.

69. Surface and Breslin, "Basketball's Bumptious Baron," 58.

70. Underwood, "Crigler Reflects on Fiddlin' 5"; Surface and Breslin, "Basketball's Bumptious Baron," 60.

71. Chandler and Hatton, *Rupp from Both Ends of the Bench*, 7–8.

72. See Adolph F. Rupp, *Rupp's Championship Basketball: For Player Coach and Fan* (New York: Prentice-Hall, Inc., 1948) and Adolph F. Rupp, *Rupp's Championship Basketball: For Player Coach and Fan,* second edition (Englewood Cliffs, NJ: Prentice-Hall, Inc., 1957), vii.

73. Ibid.

74. Adolph Rupp, "Defeat and Failure to Me Are Enemies," *Sports Illustrated*, December 8, 1958, 100.

75. Ibid.

76. Ibid., 103, 104.

77. Ibid., 104.

78. Ibid., 105.

79. Ibid., 100.

80. Quoted in ibid., 100.

81. Ibid., 101.

82. Ibid., 101, 102, 103.

11. Rupp and Race

1. *New York Times*, April 21, 1963, quoted in Charles H. Martin, "Jim Crow in the Gymnasium: The Integration of College Basketball in the American South," in Patrick B. Miller and David K. Wiggins, *Sport and the Color Line: Black Athletes and Race Relations in Twentieth-Century America* (New York: Routledge, 2004), 240. See also Martin, *Benching Jim Crow: The Rise and Fall of the Color Line in Southern College Sports, 1890–1980* (Urbana: University of Illinois Press, 2010).

2. Martin, "Jim Crow in the Gymnasium," 241, 242.

3. Will Aubrey et al., *The Banner Years: Murray State Basketball, 1925–2013* (Morley, MO: Acclaim Press, 2013), 106–109.

4. Martin, "Jim Crow in the Gymnasium," 243–45; For Perry Wallace at Vanderbilt see Andrew Maraniss, *Strong Inside: Perry Wallace and the Collision of Race and Sports in the South* (Nashville, TN: Vanderbilt University Press, 2014).

5. Earl Cox, *Earl Cox: Calling It Like I See It*, 62.

6. Ibid., 62, 130, 146.

7. Dave Kindred, "Rupp: A Top 5 Ornery Charmer," http://www.sportingnews.com/archives/sports2000/numbers/162698.html; *Lexington Herald-Leader*, December 19, 1991.

8. Billy Reed, "Tainted Glory," *Leo*, January 17, 2006, found at http://www.goerie.com/apps/pbcs.dll/article?AID+/20060111/LE005/60110034/-1/LEO.

9. Ibid.

10. Ibid.

11. Ibid.

12. Ibid.

13. Ibid.

14. Kindred, "Rupp: A Top 5 Ornery Charmer."

15. Carlyle Farren Rupp, "Wrong about Rupp," *Lexington Herald-Leader*, January 23, 1992.

16. Ibid.

17. Merlene Davis, "Herky Rupp Is Still Attracted to the Game His Father Loved," *Lexington Herald-Leader*, March 29, 1985.

18. Auerbach and Feinstein, *Let Me Tell You a Story*: *A Lifetime in the Game* (New York: Little, Brown and Company, 2004), 83.

19. Ibid., 83.

20. Dick Gabriel, "Adolph Rupp: Myth, Legend and Fact," http://www.wkyt.com/global/story.asp?s=4287657&ClientType=Printable.

21. Ibid.

22. Ibid.

23. Ralph D. Russo, "Lifetime of Memories: Alcorn State Coach Whitney Ready to Add 500th Career Victory to Long List of Adventures," *Jackson Sun*, December 19, 1999.

24. See Alexander Wolff, *Raw Recruits* (New York: Pocket Books, 1991), 102–3.

25. Harry Lancaster "as told to Cawood Ledford," 88.

26. Ibid., 88, 89.

27. James Duane Bolin interview with Frank Dickey, Lexington, KY, April 24, 2003.

28. Terry L. Birdwhistell interviews with John W. Oswald, August 10, 11, 12, 1987; transcripts of these interviews may be found in Special Collections, University of Kentucky, Lexington, KY.

29. Ibid.

30. Ibid.

31. See Billy Reed, *Transition Game*: *The Story of S. T. Roach* (Lexington, KY: Host Communications, Inc., 2001), 55; Birdwhistell interviews with John W. Oswald.

32. Jerry Tipton, "Spurned by UK in '60s, Wes Unseld to Coach in House That Rupp Built," *Lexington Herald-Leader*, October 10, 1992.

33. Ibid.

34. Reed, *Transition Game*, 55, 56.

35. Reed, *Transition Game*, 57.

36. Tipton, "Spurned by UK in '60s, Wes Unseld to Coach in House That Rupp Built."

37. Judith Egerton, "'Glory Road' Movie Portrays 1966 UK Basketball Game as Turning Point for Race in College Sports," *Louisville Courier-Journal*, January 6, 2006.

38. Tipton, "Spurned by UK in '60s, Wes Unseld to Coach in House That Rupp Built."

39. Quoted in Betty Boles Ellison, *Kentucky's Domain of Power, Greed and Corruption* (San Jose, CA: Writers Club Press, 2001), 63, 64.

40. Ibid., 64.

41. Birdwhistell interviews with John W. Oswald.

42. Don R. Mills, "Integrating UK Basketball," *Louisville Courier-Journal*, January 13, 2006.

43. Harvey Araton, "Before NBA Link, UK Connected Riley, Butch Beard," *Lexington Herald-Leader*, December 22, 1994.

44. Ibid.

45. Ibid.

46. Egerton, "'Glory Road' Movie Portrays 1966 UK Basketball Game as Turning Point for Race in College Sports."

47. Reed, *Transition Game*, 57; Araton, "Before NBA Link, UK Connected Riley, Butch Beard."

48. Reed, *Transition Game*, 57, 58.

49. Araton, "Before NBA Link, UK Connected Riley, Butch Beard."

50. Birdwhistell interviews with John W. Oswald.

51. Ibid.

52. Ibid.

53. Ibid.

54. Ibid.

55. Ibid.

56. Ibid.

57. Ibid.

58. Ibid.

59. Bernie Shively to John W. Oswald, July 14, 1967, John W. Oswald Papers, Box 7, Folder 247, Athletics (General) 1967–1968, Special Collections, University of Kentucky, Lexington, KY. Henceforth Oswald Papers.

60. Birdwhistell interviews with John W. Oswald.

61. Ibid.

62. Ibid.

63. Rice, *Adolph Rupp*, 204.

64. Terry Pluto, *Loose Balls* (New York: Simon and Schuster, 1990), 241, quoted in Jon Scott.

65. See Chandler's own account of this incident in Albert B. Chandler and Vance Trimble, *Heroes, Plain Folks, and Skunks: The Life and Times of Happy Chandler* (Chicago: Bonus Books, Inc., 1989), 291–98.

66. "Baseball," written and directed by Ken Burns (1994; Arlington, VA: PBS, 2010), DVD.

67. Reed, *Transition Game*, 128.

68. Chandler and Trimble, *Heroes, Plain Folks, and Skunks*, 122.

12. Rupp's Runts and Runners-Up

1. James H. Dickenson, "Rupp's 64 and in Love With His UK Team," *Louisville Times*, February 1, 1966.

2. Ibid.

3. Curry Kirkpatrick, "The Night They Drove Old Dixie Down," *Sports Illustrated*, April 1, 1991, 73.

4. George Bugbee, "Coliseum Boosts Rebel Cage Fortunes," *Memphis Press-Scimitar*, February 22, 1966.

5. Jack Williams, "Rupp Recalls Boos, Cheers, and a Big Night in Athens," *(Raleigh, NC) News and Observer*, February 13, 1966.

6. James Dickenson, "How the Baron of Basketball Makes 'em Gasp," *National Observer*, January 24, 1966.

7. Williams, "Rupp Recalls Boos, Cheers, and a Big Night in Athens."

8. Ibid.

9. Ibid.

10. Ibid.

11. William F. Reed, "The House That Roared," *Sports Illustrated*, February 5, 1990.

12. Williams, "Rupp Recalls Boos, Cheers, and a Big Night in Athens."

13. Barton Gellman and Dale Russakoff, "The Life of Bill Bradley," *Washington Post*, December 12, 1999.

14. *Louisville Courier-Journal*, February 4, 1966.

15. Ibid.

16. Ibid.

17. *Memphis Commercial Appeal*, March 2, 1966.

18. Pat Harmon, "Slickest Passing Team I Ever Saw," *Cincinnati Post*, March 8, 1966.

19. Ibid.

20. Linda B. Blackford, "History Has Put Game in Perspective," *Lexington Herald-Leader*, January 8, 2006.

21. Billy Reed, "Tainted Glory," *Leo*, January 17, 2006, found at http://www.goerie.com/apps/pbcs.dll/article?AID+/20060111/LE005/60110034/-1/LEO.

22. Kirkpatrick, "The Night They Drove Old Dixie Down," 72.

23. Ibid., 73.

24. Ibid.

25. Jerry Tipton, "Rupp Hard to Portray 'Accurately,'" *Lexington Herald-Leader*, October 2, 2005.

26. Ibid.

27. Ibid.

28. Jerry Tipton, "Runts Won as One," *Lexington Herald-Leader*, January 15, 2006.

29. Rich Copley, "Playing Fair with Rupp," *Lexington Herald-Leader Weekender*, January 13, 2006.

30. Jan O'Connor, "'Glory Road' Trek Isn't Finished," *USA Today*, January 3, 2006.

31. Ibid.

32. Kirkpatrick, "The Night They Drove Old Dixie Down," 74.

33. Ibid., 78.

34. Ibid., 74.

35. Kirkpatrick, "The Night They Drove Old Dixie Down," quoted in Jon Scott. This quote and much of the following information comes from a meticulously kept website by Jon Scott at http://www.ukfans.net/jps/uk/rupp.htm (hereafter Jon Scott).

36. Jo-Ann Barnes, "They Changed the Game: Texas Western," *Detroit Free Press*, March 29, 1996.

37. Pat Forde, "Legacy of Rupp Slow to Recede Repercussions of 1966 Title Game Still Echo in Many Ears," *USA Today*, April 2, 1996, quoted in Jon Scott.

38. B. J. Schecter, "Catching Up with . . . Harry Flourney, Texas Western Forward," *Sports Illustrated*, April 1, 1998, quoted in Jon Scott.

39. Mark Bradley, "'Doc' Jackson's Home Is Where His Heart Is," *Lexington Sunday Herald-Leader*, February 8, 1981.

40. Tipton, "Runts Won as One."

41. Ibid.

42. Bill Knight, "At 44, Ex-Miner Lattin Helps Run Houston Business," *El Paso Times*, April 28, 1988.

43. Blackford, "History Has Put Game in Perspective."

44. Knight, "At 44, Ex-Miner Lattin Helps Run Houston Business."

45. *Lexington Herald-Leader*, December 15, 2002.

46. Jon Scott, "Adolph Rupp, Fact and Fiction."

47. Rick Morrissey, "New Face Leads Kentucky These Days," *Chicago Tribune*, November 30, 1997, quoted in Jon Scott.

48. Michael MacCambridge, *The Franchise* (New York: Hyperion, 1997), 146.

49. Frank Deford, "Bravo for the Baron," *Sports Illustrated*, March 7, 1966; *Lexington Leader*, March 3, 1966.

50. Deford, "Bravo for the Baron."

51. *Lexington Leader*, March 3, 1966.

52. Ibid.

53. Ibid.

54. Frank Deford, "Go-Go with Bobby Joe," *Sports Illustrated*, March 28, 1966.

55. John Clay, "The Runts: Still Special after All These Years," *Lexington Herald-Leader*, February 9, 1991, quoted in Jon Scott.

56. Quoted in Frank Fitzpatrick, *And the Walls Came Tumbling Down: Kentucky, Texas Western and the Game That Changed American Sports* (New York: Simon & Schuster, 1999), 33.

57. Dave Kindred, "Calling Rupp a Racist Just Doesn't Ring True," *Lexington Herald-Leader*, December 22, 1991.

58. James Michener, *Sports in America* (New York: Random House, 1976), 145.

59. Ibid., 147.

60. Quoted in Fitzpatrick, *And the Walls Came Tumbling Down*, 33.

61. Michener, *Sports in America*, 147.

62. Birdwhistell interviews with John W. Oswald.

63. Ibid.

64. Ibid.

65. Brad Wolverton, "Glory Road: Epilogue," *Chronicle of Higher Education*, January 13, 2006, A6.

66. Ibid.

67. Kirkpatrick, "The Night They Drove Old Dixie Down," 81.

68. Rice, *Adolph Rupp*, 200.

69. Egerton, "'Glory Road' Movie Portrays 1966 UK Basketball Game as Turning Point for Race in College Sports."

13. Transitional Times, 1966–1972

1. Mark Whicker, "R U Confused by It All? Then This 1 Is for U," *Lexington Herald-Leader*, March 15, 1984.

2. Laudeman, *The Rupp Years*. See the section on the 1966–1967 season, "Lack of Leadership, Riley's Aching Back Put UK on the Skids." Phil Straw, "Riley and Rupp," *Lexington Herald-Leader*, March 15, 1984.

3. Straw, "Riley and Rupp."

4. Ibid.

5. Laudeman, *The Rupp Years*. See the section on the 1966–1967 season, "Lack of Leadership, Riley's Aching Back Put UK on the Skids."

6. Adolph F. Rupp to family, January 3, 1967; this letter can be found in Rupp Papers, Special Collections, University of Kentucky, Lexington, KY.

7. Laudeman, *The Rupp Years*. See the section on the 1966–1967 season, "Lack of Leadership, Riley's Aching Back Put UK on the Skids."

8. Ibid.

9. Straw, "Riley and Rupp."

10. Ibid.

11. Ibid.

12. Laudeman, *The Rupp Years*. See the section on the 1966–1967 season, "Lack of Leadership, Riley's Aching Back Put UK on the Skids." Straw, "Riley and Rupp."

13. Laudeman, *The Rupp Years*. See the section on the 1966–1967 season, "Lack of Leadership, Riley's Aching Back Put UK on the Skids." Straw, "Riley and Rupp."

14. Laudeman, *The Rupp Years*. See the section on the 1966–1967 season, "Lack of Leadership, Riley's Aching Back Put UK on the Skids."

15. Thomas D. Clark to A. D. Kirwan, February 14, 1967 (B252, F23), Clark Papers, Special Collections, University of Kentucky, Lexington, KY, quoted in *Register of the Kentucky Historical Society* 103, nos. 1/2 (Winter/Spring 2005): 449.

16. Laudeman, *The Rupp Years*. See the section on the 1966–1967 season, "Lack of Leadership, Riley's Aching Back Put UK on the Skids."

17. Straw, "Riley and Rupp."

18. James Duane Bolin interview with Stan Key, Murray, KY, August 17, 2002.

19. Of course, Lew Alcindor later became Kareem Abdul-Jabbar.

20. Perry Wallace went on to play for the Vanderbilt Commodores as the first African American basketball player in the Southeastern Conference. His story is told in Andrew Maraniss, *Strong Inside*.

21. Charles H. Martin, "Jim Crow in the Gymnasium," 243–45.

22. Robert L. Johnson to Bernie Shively, Memorandum, March 29, 1966, Oswald Papers, 1963–1968, Box 16, Folder 437.

23. Billy Reed and other prominent sportswriters have long contended that the issue of race was manufactured by revisionist writers and critics of Rupp long after the 1966 national championship game. But correspondence in the John W. Oswald Papers indicates clearly that this issue was very much on the minds of UK administrators and coaches immediately after the game.

24. Joe B. Hall to Adolph F. Rupp, Memorandum, April 7, 1966, Oswald Papers, 1963–1968, Box 7, Folder 242. Coleman went on to become one of the first three African American basketball players at Eastern Kentucky University in 1966 and was later drafted

by the San Diego Rockets in the 10th round of the 1970 NBA draft. See http://nkaa.uky
.edu/record.php?note_id=184.

25. Maraniss, *Strong Inside*, 88.

26. Ibid., 90.

27. Ibid.

28. Ibid., 91.

29. Ibid., 91, 94.

30. Brian Bennett, "Tom Payne: Happy Ending a Long Way Off," *Louisville Couri-er-Journal*, April 4, 2001.

31. Bennett, "Tom Payne."

32. Bennett, "Tom Payne."

33. Stan Key to Duane Bolin, February 9, 2003, in author's possession.

14. Forced Retirement and Post-UK Years

1. "Rupp to Retire on July 1—It Says So in the Rules," *Louisville Courier-Journal*, January 15, 1972.

2. Ibid.

3. Ibid.

4. Ibid.

5. Bob Cooper, "Public, Legislators Divided on Rupp Retirement," *Lexington Lead-er*, January 28, 1972.

6. Ibid.

7. "Rupp to Retire on July 1—It Says So in the Rules."

8. Birdwhistell interviews with John W. Oswald.

9. Ibid.

10. Thomas D. Clark to Otis A. Singletary, February 5, 1972 (B258, F18), Thomas D. Clark Papers.

11. "Rupp to Retire on July 1—It Says So in the Rules."

12. Dick Beardsley, "Colonels Issel, Dampier, Pratt Plug for Rupp," *Louisville Couri-er-Journal*, February 4, 1972.

13. Ibid.

14. Rice, *Adolph Rupp*, 198, 199.

15. Ibid, 199.

16. Tom Wallace, "All-American Trio Fondly Remember Rupp," *Cawood on Ken-tucky*, August 1, 1987, 6.

17. Dave Kindred, "The Right Mixture of Love, Hate Kept Rupp on Top," *Washing-ton Post*, December 13, 1977.

18. Ibid.

19. Rice, *Adolph Rupp*, 199.

20. Ibid., 200.

21. Ibid., 199.

22. Ibid., 201.

23. Ibid., 203, 204.

24. Ibid., 203.

25. Ibid., 202.

26. Ken Rappaport, "'The Fiddlin' Five' Was Probably Rupp's Best Team," *Henderson (KY) Gleaner,* March 13, 1977.

27. Rupp funeral service program.

Epilogue

1. James Duane Bolin interview with Jim Host, Lexington, KY, July 23, 2015.

2. Ibid.

3. Ibid.

4. Ibid.

Index